Praise for *Belongi*

"[Geoffrey L.] Cohen alternates between t successful social psychological interventions ... iocusing on modern interventions that are being used to astounding effect. . . . If we want more people to have the chance to maximize their abilities and their contributions to society, reading *Belonging* is the right place to start."

—Matthew Lieberman, *Science*

"No one before Geoffrey L. Cohen has pulled together all the research relevant to diversity and inclusion in a single volume, helping us to understand belonging through a social psychological lens. The book is masterful, showcasing highly effective interventions. An inspiration!"

—Peter Salovey, president of Yale University

"*Belonging* combines rich science, compelling stories, and beautiful prose to illuminate the social psychological principles behind the need to belong and how to foster belonging and connection in a fractured world. Reading this book will yield insights into your own motivation and behavior and will help you understand the source of many pressing problems of our time."

—Sonja Lyubomirsky, author of *The How of Happiness*

"This is perhaps the richest book on belonging you'll ever read. It's absolutely fresh, bringing together sometimes unexpected evidence and ideas to yield a transformative understanding of human belonging. . . . The inspiration one draws from every page of this book is an enhanced sense of what is possible. It revives the very thing we need most in these times: hope."

—Claude M. Steele, author of *Whistling Vivaldi*

"This book shines piercing illumination on one of today's most timely topics—the causes and consequences of belonging to modern social groups. Importantly, it maps scientifically grounded routes to minimizing the harmful consequences while optimizing the positive ones. The world needs this book."

—Robert B. Cialdini, PhD, author of *Influence* and *Pre-Suasion*

"An exhilarating book, filled with actionable insights about making the world better around you."

—Dacher Keltner, author of *The Power Paradox*

"[*Belonging* is] a serious scholarly tome that addresses a major societal problem: our sense of belonging, which affects behavior in ways that can cause war or create peace. . . . Academic collections that serve programs in psychology/sociology and management and large public libraries will find this appropriate."　　　　　　　—*Booklist*

"An intriguing investigation of our need to belong and how to make that process easier for the bashful among us. . . . A well-written, inviting treatise to be a better person."　　　　　—*Kirkus Reviews*

"In *Belonging*, Stanford University professor Geoffrey L. Cohen considers today's fractured society and, citing years of research, offers suggestions for bridging cultural divides and creating a more empathetic world."　　　　　　　　　　　—*Library Journal*

Belonging

Belonging

*The Science of Creating Connection
and Bridging Divides*

Geoffrey L. Cohen

W. W. NORTON & COMPANY
Celebrating a Century of Independent Publishing

Copyright © 2022 by Geoffrey L. Cohen

All rights reserved
Printed in the United States of America
First published as a Norton paperback 2023

For information about permission to reproduce selections from this book, write to
Permissions, W. W. Norton & Company, Inc., 500 Fifth Avenue, New York, NY 10110

For information about special discounts for bulk purchases, please contact
W. W. Norton Special Sales at specialsales@wwnorton.com or 800-233-4830

Manufacturing by Lakeside Book Company
Book design by Lovedog Studio
Production manager: Julia Druskin

Library of Congress Cataloging-in-Publication Data

Names: Cohen, Geoffrey, L., author.
Title: Belonging : the science of creating connection and
bridging divides / Geoffrey L. Cohen.
Description: First Edition. | New York : W. W. Norton & Company, [2022] |
Includes bibliographical references and index.
Identifiers: LCCN 2021061609 | ISBN 9781324006183 (hardcover) |
ISBN 9781324006190 (epub)
Subjects: LCSH: Belonging (Social psychology)
Classification: LCC HM1111 .C637 2022 | DDC 302.5/45—dc23/eng/20220215
LC record available at https://lccn.loc.gov/2021061609

ISBN 978-1-324-06594-4 pbk.

W. W. Norton & Company, Inc., 500 Fifth Avenue, New York, N.Y. 10110
www.wwnorton.com

W. W. Norton & Company Ltd., 15 Carlisle Street, London W1D 3BS

1 0 9 8 7 6 5 4 3

For Mom, Benie, and Emrey

Contents

A Crisis of Belonging and What We Can Do About It

THROUGHOUT MY YEARS AS A SOCIAL PSYCHOLOGIST, I HAVE learned how important a sense of belonging can be. Today, many people who once took that feeling for granted seem unmoored and adrift. In the turbulent election season of 2016, my colleagues and I conducted a survey of law school students at a selective university to determine who felt most alienated on campus. The two groups who felt least like they belonged were black women and politically conservative white men. These two groups seem to fall at the farthest poles of our political discourse. Yet they shared a feeling: They felt like outsiders. The defining feature of our era seems to be that few groups feel confident in their sense of belonging.

Belonging may seem like a comfortable but inessential luxury. However, it has potent, wide-ranging effects. We all know the sting of feeling as though we're unwelcome at work or school, at a party or a bar, or even in brief encounters in a checkout line or with a rude waiter in a restaurant. Feeling excluded is experienced in much the way physical pain is, with both activating many of the same neural networks in the brain. Psychologists call it "social pain," saying people are as motivated to alleviate it as they are to slake thirst and find shelter.

Research shows that when our sense of belonging is threatened even momentarily, we're more likely to feel worse about ourselves, perform below our potential, behave impulsively, see others as hostile, and lash out defensively when provoked. On the other hand, even fleeting experiences of belonging, such as glimpsing pictures of people who care about us, can have far-reaching benefits. They raise our sense of well-being and self-worth, improve our performance, lessen our defensiveness and hostility, increase our tolerance of outsiders, and make us more compassionate. We become more humane.

This book will show how a sense of belonging isn't just a by-product of success but a condition for it—in school, work, homes, health care settings, negotiations, politics, community policing, and virtually every domain in which humans deal with other humans. The book will also show that there are a number of small, specific steps, backed up by social science, that we can take to nurture a sense of belonging in ourselves and others.

Finding ways to foster belonging has become an urgent social mission. The feeling of being different, a stranger in a strange land, and even a stranger in your own land, seems so common now that presidential hopeful Pete Buttigieg proclaimed a "crisis of belonging."

About one in five Americans suffers from chronic loneliness, with a 2020 survey revealing that young adults suffer the most. As the Police implied in their song "Message in a Bottle," it seems we're not alone in being alone. Loneliness is "one of the most toxic environmental risk factors that we're aware of in terms of all-cause mortality," says genomics researcher Steve Cole, defining it as "the extent to which people feel disconnected from the rest of humanity." Most of us understand the risk of exposure to radiation, cigarette smoke, and other physical toxins, but we find it harder to appreciate the power of social-psychological toxins. Chronic loneliness is as destructive to our bodies and health as smoking a pack of cigarettes a day.

As Americans have become disconnected from their community and society, they have suffered what Angus Deaton and Anne Case call "diseases of despair." The researchers discovered that in 2017, 158,000 Americans died either through a slow process of addiction to alcohol, painkillers, or other drugs or through suicide by gunshot or overdose.

That's "the equivalent of three full 737 MAXs falling out of the sky every day, with no survivors," they write. The number of these deaths has been rising over the past two decades, and Deaton and Case argue that the increase is due in large measure to the social pain of feeling disconnected.

Social pain is also felt by refugees around the world, whose numbers have swelled so much since 2015 that they now make up 1 percent of the global population. When the Somali novelist Nuruddin Farah learned he was exiled and could no longer return to the place where he had grown up, it was as if his very sense of self had been shattered. "In that instant, I felt at once displaced and incredulous, as though a mirror had broken. Eventually I would ask myself if on account of what had taken place, I became *an*other."

The crisis of belonging is aggravated by mistrust. Some Americans believe that members of the opposing political party are out to destroy the nation. In 2016, my colleagues and I found that 15 percent of each political party saw the other side as a terrorist threat. According to political scientists Nathan Kalmoe and Lilliana Mason, about the same percentage in each party said "violence would be justified" if the opposing party were to win the 2020 election. Forty percent said supporters of the other side were "downright evil."

The joy and sense of meaning that people find in social bonds are exploited by hate groups, whose activities are on the rise. Hate crimes reached a ten-year high in the United States in 2019, and their number remained just as high in 2021 (the last year for which data are available).

Many forces fuel division and undermine belonging: racism, sexism, and other institutionalized biases; a media that monetizes fear; a social media that has made much of social life performative and voyeuristic rather than authentic; a rise in individualism; economic policies that exacerbate inequality and poverty; unemployment, low wages, and job insecurity; homelessness and eviction; violent neighborhoods; lack of educational opportunity; weakened ties to churches, families, and other social institutions; political polarization; and so on.

These powerful societal factors can leave us feeling hopeless, but science suggests that each of us can combat them. How? The answer is surprisingly simple: by changing the situation we are in, sometimes even in the smallest ways. Our ability to do so is like a superpower.

In spite of the toxicity of our politics, the betrayals and traumas of our past, and the hostilities and injustices in the wider world, many of us have experienced how a single relationship and even a single encounter can be a powerful and healing source of belonging. While I was studying social psychology, I worked in group homes and tutoring programs for disadvantaged teens and adults. An experience I had mentoring a man named Mike taught me to appreciate the power of even a brief encounter as a source of belonging.

Mike lived in a group home and was trying to piece his life back together after a suicide attempt. He had tried to hang himself but was cut free before he died, though not before his brain had been starved of oxygen, causing damage to his hippocampus, the seat of memory. After that trauma, he had trouble forming new memories. He would often forget we had a scheduled outing, but he'd always happily come along nonetheless. He appreciated that these little excursions provided him the opportunity to integrate himself into the wider world. One of our outings made a lasting impression on me. Mike wanted to go shopping for audio equipment, and though I knew he didn't have the money, I drove him to a store. Once inside, Mike asked to speak to a salesperson, and I watched the scene unfold with trepidation. I knew it would be clear to any salesperson that Mike was somehow "off." He asked the same questions over and over, and he had trouble forming coherent sentences, let alone carrying on a conversation. But that day Mike was lucky enough to be paired up with a young salesman who exemplified openness, patience, and respect.

I watched as he gave Mike a tour of the store's offerings and answered all his questions, some repeatedly, all the while smiling amicably and nodding, listening thoughtfully to Mike. I had never seen Mike as happy as he was after that encounter; it was like glimpsing a possibility of what could be. The encounter had made him feel like someone who mattered, and it called to mind work in psychology I'd studied showing that slight adjustments in the way we interact with people in our daily lives can do much to nurture belonging.

This book turns the most important insight of the social and behavioral sciences into a strategy for self-help and social change: the power of the situation. Research shows that the situation, right here and right now, shapes us far more than we think. What we do, think, and feel isn't just driven by far-off, impersonal forces—or by our inherent personality, ability, and character—but also by what happens around us in the classroom or boardroom, at the dinner table or the bar. What happens in the blink of an eye, including the blink of an eye, can make a big difference. Yes, history and culture matter, but we as individuals are, to a degree more than we think, gatekeepers for how much such forces matter at any given moment.

A metaphor is useful. The current weather of a place is uncontrollable and influenced by many forces, such as barometric pressure, the moisture in the atmosphere, and latitude and longitude, as well as historical forces, such as drought and deforestation. But in spite of these forces outside of our immediate control, human beings have managed to populate virtually all regions of the globe by creating shelters out of the raw materials available, such as igloos and huts, and also by designing increasingly innovative dwellings and accoutrements, including umbrellas, scarves, coats, even high-tech survival gear for extreme temperatures. I see interventions that foster belonging as akin to psychological shelters and protective gear that we design to shield people from the harsh gusts of history and the stinging rain of our social world.

For almost thirty years, my research has laid the groundwork for what have become known as "wise interventions"—interventions that nurture people's belonging and self-worth, an influential and rapidly growing area of social psychology that has been hotly debated in major media and taught in universities, on stages, and in boardrooms around the world. The interventions are simple and often counterintuitive solutions with powerful and even life-changing effects.

The term "wise" was first brought into the academic canon by one of my all-time favorite sociologists, Erving Goffman, whose insights pervade this book. He observed that the gay subculture of the 1950s had picked up on the term to refer to straight people who were "in the know," meaning they could be trusted to see the full humanity of gay people in spite of their rejection by the rest of society. My mentor, the social psychologist Claude Steele, borrowed the term to describe successful educational approaches for students of color, and Greg Walton has used it more generally to describe social interventions that are mindful of people's psychology. Key to our being "wise" is a desire and readiness to see a situation from the perspective of others we're sharing it with and to take note of how aspects of the situation may be affecting them. A situation in which we are comfortable might feel threatening to others, which we might not appreciate unless we're mindful.

The research on wise interventions is anchored in many large-scale and rigorous lab and field experiments that would not have been possible without multiple collaborators and generous funding. The word "experiment" is important because most of the studies randomly assign people to the intervention and compare outcomes with people in a control group not given the intervention. That is the best way to determine any intervention's causal impact.

Yet the overall message of this extensive body of expert research is hearteningly simple. Subtle, brief, psychologically "wise" interventions at the level of the encounter can make a world of difference in people's ability to make the most out of life's possibilities, unlocking our hidden potentials.

Wise interventions are not off-the-shelf solutions that can be applied willy-nilly, wherever or whenever. When they're used in that way, they tend to fail or backfire. Making interventions wise depends on thoughtful empathy for those we are trying to support. When we make our interventions wise in this way, we cultivate the confidence and resilience that a sense of belonging builds, and we create the conditions for success at school, at work, in our politics, and in our communities.

In Part One of the book, I'll introduce you to a lost art that emerged out of the social sciences during World War II, which I call situation-crafting. Fellow researchers and I have built upon this craft to discover simple means of creating situations that foster belonging and bring out our individual and collective best. It is the craft of knowing when, where, and for whom to use wise interventions. In Part Two, I'll explore the psychological and social forces that threaten belonging, such as Us-vs.-Them antagonism and stereotyping, and how situation-crafting through wise interventions combats them. In Part Three, I'll discuss particular challenges, along with their solutions, in strengthening belonging in school, work, health care, our communities, and our politics. In the final chapter, I'll sum up the key takeaways from our journey.

The research that grounds this book has yielded simple and successful strategies in classrooms, disadvantaged neighborhoods, college campuses, iconic Silicon Valley companies, and rapidly diversifying communities here and abroad. Tens of thousands of students, teachers, employees, patients, and doctors have benefited from wise interventions. Each chapter will feature inspiring stories of how people and organizations have used these strategies to boost achievement, retain talent, and foster open-mindedness, health, and happiness.

Encounters that involve people who are unlike each other in meaningful ways define our diverse and unsettled world. The stakes of these encounters are high. They have the potential to increase both understanding and misunderstanding—to unite or divide us. This book strives to remind readers that our differences and unease can be a common bond. Andrew Solomon, in his brilliant book about the varieties of human experience, *Far from the Tree,* remarks that "difference unites us." Likewise, the very psychological processes that drive us apart are ones that we share and that, together, we can overcome.

While we have limited ability to alleviate the societal tensions and afflictions that inflame the current crisis of belonging, the insights and tools in this book will empower you to strengthen your own sense of belonging and to foster it in your loved ones and those you teach, coach, manage, or argue with. They will help you make any given encounter an opportunity to enhance your sense of belonging and help others feel more included. I wrote this book out of my hope and belief that the ideas and discoveries of social science can help all of us turn everyday encounters—even those that can otherwise become hostile or deflating—into occasions for understanding, connection, and growth.

Part One

The Science and Art of Situation-Crafting

Chapter 1

The Potential of the Situation

How Situations Shape Us and How We Can Shape Situations

A FRIEND WHO GREW UP IN A LOW-INCOME AREA OF CALI-fornia told me that many kids in his high school were loud and disruptive in class. But one teacher was renowned for his ability to get all his teen students to sit, listen, and learn, even the ones who acted out in other classes. My friend thought the teacher's success was due in part to a ritual he engaged in with every one of his students. He always referred to them not by first name but with honorifics, for example, calling them Mr. Garcia or Ms. Castro. This, my friend believed, sent a message of respect.

The teacher's ritual is an example of situation-crafting: shaping a situation, even in seemingly minor ways, in order to foster belonging. Just a small gesture or a thoughtful comment can often alter a situation, or people's perceptions of it, in ways that relieve tensions and make them feel appreciated and included.

In the middle of the twentieth century, psychologists began to make stunning discoveries about how much people's behavior—and their feelings and thoughts—can be changed when social situations are altered. These revelations flew in the face of a vast body of work in psychology up to that time. The overwhelming emphasis in the field had been placed on personality, with the notion that once our personality is formed, due to nature, nurture, or a combination of both, it is largely fixed for the rest of our life. From that point of view, an individual's behavior emanates from internal dynamics.

The field shifted when psychologists discovered the powerful effect of situations on behavior: For instance, the same person might act shy in the classroom but outgoing at a sports event. Yes, personality matters, according to the field that became social psychology, but the situation matters more than we think. Rather than explain behavior in terms of individuals and their proclivities—good or evil, smart or stupid—we can see situations as drawing out behavior that is good, evil, smart, or stupid. As research on the power of situations blossomed in the mid-twentieth century, social psychologists learned that even people's deep-seated prejudices and attitudes about large social issues could be transformed by situations—not only in the moment but sometimes to lasting effect.

Consider the story of a man who underwent one such transformation.

All my life, I had work, never a day without work, worked all the overtime I could get and still could not survive financially. I began to say there's somethin' wrong with this country. I worked my butt off and just never seemed to break even.

I had some real great ideas about this great nation. (Laughs.) They say to abide by the law, go to church, do right and live for the Lord, and everything'll work out. But it didn't work out. It just kept gettin' worse and worse.

I really began to get bitter. I didn't know who to blame. I tried to find somebody. I began to blame it on black people. I had to hate somebody.

The natural person for me to hate would be black people, because my father before me was a member of the Klan. As far as he was concerned, it was the savior of the white people. It was the only organization in the world that would take care of the white people.

Is this a disgruntled coal worker out of a job? A disaffected Trump supporter who believes the United States is under siege by illegal immigrants stealing citizens' jobs? No. These are the words of Claiborne P. Ellis, who went by C. P., speaking to oral historian Studs Terkel, as recorded in Terkel's book *American Dreams: Lost and Found*. Many Americans have been feeling they've been left behind and looked down on for decades. But what is fascinating about C. P. Ellis is not just that he spoke those words so long ago. It's that he underwent a remarkable turnaround in 1971 due to a situation that showed him a new path forward.

Before that happened, C. P. had joined the Ku Klux Klan as his father had. He rose to become the Exalted Cyclops, or chief officer, of the KKK in Durham, North Carolina. Speaking with Terkel, he offered an emotionally raw account of his motives for joining. Coming from a poverty-stricken family, he left school in the eighth grade because his father had died and he had to support the family. He had never felt as if he mattered and he explained that his feeling of disempowerment drove him to the Klan. "I can understand why people join extreme right-wing or left-wing groups," he reflected. "They're in the same boat I was. Shut out. Deep down inside, we want to be part of this great society. Nobody listens, so we join these groups."

Then he took a job at a service station. Every Monday night a group of men came to buy a Coca-Cola and talk to him. Soon they invited him to a Klan meeting. "Boy, that was an opportunity I really looked forward to! To be part of something," he recalled. He was inducted.

During the Klan initiation ceremony, as he heard the applause of the hundreds of Klansmen gathered while he knelt before a cross, he felt he was somebody "big." "For this one little ol' person," he told Terkel, "it was a thrilling moment."

The Klan understood the powerful pull of offering people a sense of belonging. Belonging is the feeling that we're part of a larger group that values, respects, and cares for us—and to which we feel we have something to contribute. The word "belong" literally means "to go with," and our species has evolved to journey through life with each other. Infants are born unable to care for themselves; alone in the wild, adults are vulnerable to predation. It's by working together that we survive and thrive. Our desire to be part of a group is "among the most powerful forces to be found," wrote the eminent social psychologist Solomon Asch. If our lives are bereft of a feeling of connection, we can become vulnerable, as C. P. did, to appeals by groups that make the belonging they provide contingent on acceptance of views and behavior that don't reflect our true values. Experimental research finds that after being excluded, people conform more to the judgments of peers who offer new sources of belonging, even when their judgments are patently wrong. Excluded people are also more prone to believing in conspiracy theories that ascribe complex social problems to malevolent actors working in secret. Fortunately for C. P. and his community, while he initially felt the Klan brought him status and fellowship, he began to perceive otherwise, and he left the Klan and repudiated his racism. It happened in a series of steps.

First, he started to realize that he was being manipulated, that his sense of belonging did not have an authentic base. He suspected that the Durham City Council members were using him and his fellow Klansmen. For instance, he would get a phone call and a voice would say, "The blacks are comin' up tonight and makin' outrageous demands." He'd be asked to bring some members to the meeting to cause a ruckus and deflect the discussion. The politicians—and most of their constituents—didn't want integration, but the city council couldn't oppose it openly. Instead they used the Klan members as covert operatives to do their dirty work.

One day, C. P. walked down a street in town and saw a councilman, who, upon noticing him, darted across the street. That action planted a seed of distrust, and C. P. started to see other signs that the council was taking advantage of the community's racism to advance its own agenda. C. P. told Terkel, "As long as they kept low-income whites and low-income blacks fightin', they're gonna maintain control." But when he shared this insight with his fellow Klan members, they brushed it off, showing no respect for his concern. C. P. began to grow disillusioned with the Klan.

Then C. P. was given an extraordinary opportunity to find the sense of belonging he wanted by joining a very different type of group. He was invited to join the Durham Human Relations Council, a group of citizens, black and white, from all walks of life who were brought together to discuss social issues. The council was fashioned as a "charette," the term used for a group that brings representatives of all stakeholders together for a specific project, such as community policing reform, to find a solution. We sorely need such groups today. The word comes from the historical practice in France of sending a cart—the *charrette*—to town to pick up the final projects of art students who were working furiously at home to finish them on time. A current-day charette provides a method of quickly resolving a problem that has long defied solution. In Durham, the problem was whether to integrate the local schools because the one that black students had attended had caught fire and was in disrepair.

To invite a chief officer of the KKK into such a group was a stroke of situation-crafting genius—and a big gamble. C. P. had been targeted by the charette organizer, Bill Riddick, because C. P. was known to be an outspoken opponent of school integration and because his voice in the community was influential. He was what the social psychologist Kurt Lewin, whom we'll meet again later in this chapter, called a "gatekeeper," a person with control over the flow of information and influence into a group.

Why did C. P. accept the invitation? He may have seen it as an opportunity to prevent integration. Perhaps he saw the invitation as an honor. Maybe he was on a renewed search for belonging, given what he was observing in the Klan and among the politicians. Or he may have simply figured "why not?" and opened the door when a serendipitous opportunity knocked.

It started badly. At the first meeting, C. P. sat in angry silence as he listened to black people complain about prejudice and segregation in schools and at work. He took the floor and made this highly offensive comment: "No, sir, the problem is black racism. If we didn't have niggers in the school, we wouldn't have the problems we had today."

Then something happened that stunned C. P. One of the group members, Howard Clements, who was black, stood up and said, "I'm certainly glad C. P. Ellis came because he's the most honest man here tonight." For his part, C. P. was disarmed. He felt heard. He told Terkel, "I felt a little more easy because I got some things off my chest."

At the next meeting, Clements nominated C. P. to be one of two chairpersons of the school committee, another honor. He was elected. Now C. P. was presented with an opportunity for exploration and discovery that he would never have chosen on his own. His co-chair was a prominent black activist, Ann Atwater, whom C. P. had, in his words, "hated with a purple passion." He didn't know if he could work with her. "A Klansman and a militant black woman, co-chairmen of the school committee. It was impossible. How could I work with her?" he recounted. His disaffection from the Klan hadn't yet changed his views about black people. He told Terkel he "still didn't like blacks" and "didn't want to associate with 'em." But what he did want, he said, was to be respected by his new group because it gave him "another sense of belongin', a sense of pride" and "helped this inferiority feelin'" that had haunted him. I imagine that the belonging he sensed in the charette felt more authentic than what he had received from the Klan, less conditional on his subscribing to a certain set of beliefs. Perhaps he felt more accepted for who he was in the charette. Regardless, C. P. was intent on making the committee a success.

The charette was drawing on a powerful tool of situation-crafting—providing people in opposition a goal, a mission that cannot be achieved unless people work together. C. P. recalled that he told Ann Atwater, "You and I have a lot of differences and we got 'em now. But there's something laid out here before us, and if it's gonna be a success, you and I are gonna have to make it one."

Ellis and Atwater chaired a series of public discussions for ten days about problems in the schools. Their respectful collaboration fostered understanding and trust between them. One day after the meeting, Ann said to C. P., "My daughter came home cryin' every day," because her teacher was making fun of her in front of the class. C. P. said, "Boy, the same thing happened to my kid." His boy was being made fun of by his "white liberal teacher" for having a father in the Klan. At that moment, C. P. recalled thinking, "Here we are, two people from far ends of the fence, havin' identical problems." They had both felt the sting of shame and ostracism. The situation had opened the door to honest, even painful, sharing, and research shows that sharing vulnerabilities is another powerful way to bridge divides.

In a stunning turn of events, C. P. voted in favor of integration, tearing up his KKK membership card in front of the community audience. C. P. went on to become a staunch advocate of desegregation, and when he later became a union leader, he won the majority of votes from black union members. He and Ann became close friends, and when C. P. died in 2005, Ann delivered the eulogy.

C. P. Ellis's change of heart wasn't all due to the charette experience, of course. He might never have had the experience if he hadn't already been ambivalent about his membership in the Klan. Like many turning points, this one seemed due to a felicitous confluence of events. C. P. might seem exceptional, the rare extremist willing to be critical minded about an allied group. But as we'll explore later, C. P.'s disaffection from the Klan is a quite common phenomenon among members of hate groups. Unfortunately, many of those poised to disavow the groups aren't afforded or don't pursue opportunities to make their way out, as happened for C. P. What catalyzes change is that the right situation presents itself to the right person at the right place and time.

In a way, C. P.'s story begins even earlier, in a history of which he was probably unaware. In adopting the rules of their charette, Bill Riddick and the members of the Durham Human Relations Council were drawing on a tradition of work in social psychology pioneered by the man considered the father of the field, Kurt Lewin.

THESE DAYS, MANY BOOKS refer to the new science of X or Y. I'm going to take a different tack. This book is about an old and largely forgotten science—and, I think, art. I'm rebranding it as situation-crafting, but it's grounded in a rich tradition of research that flowered in another vexing era, the years before and after World War II. A number of fellow social scientists and I have drawn heavily on it in developing our research. We have added new tools and insights. But back then, before we arrived on the scene, it was called the science of experimental sociology, later folded into the canon of social psychology. Rather than just describing and analyzing society as it was, the goal was to use science to create a new and better world—by creating artful situations that unlocked our potential for good, even when society seemed at its worst. Whereas other social sciences were the science of *what is*, this was the science of *what could be*—a science not of human nature but of human potential.

This science was born out of the rise of fascism that culminated in World War II and a mass genocide that stunned the world, a crime of horrific scale perpetrated by a country renowned for its high culture. How could this have happened?

The pioneer of the new science, Kurt Lewin, was a German Jew. Lewin emigrated with his wife, Gertrud, to the United States in 1933, shortly after Hitler took power. They made the move despite Gertrud's being in the midst of a difficult pregnancy. Lewin understood the urgency. As a professor at the University of Berlin, he had monitored the rising tide of fascism and anti-Semitism enveloping the culture. Lewin was more prescient than many about how readily the German military and citizenry might be induced to perpetrate horrors. He urged many reluctant fellow professors and friends to leave the country as soon as possible too, and many did. But tragically, despite furious efforts, he was unable to obtain travel visas for his mother and sister. They were both killed in concentration camps.

Lewin's witness of the Nazis' horrors injected an urgency into his work. He wasn't content to describe, interpret, and explain people and their behavior. He was determined to find ways to catalyze positive social change. His focus was on fostering more robust democracy, which he saw both as the social system with the greatest potential to allow people to flourish and as a bulwark against totalitarian abuses. His perspective differed from that of his contemporaries, German psychologists Erich Fromm and Theodor Adorno, who gained acclaim for promoting a theory of the "authoritarian personality." They argued that people's character is fixed from an early age and that the Nazi rise was due to many Germans having been parented in ways that taught obedience to authority, suspicion of "others," and lust for power.

Lewin, by contrast, credited the Nazi rise to the group's elaborate manipulations of the public through potent propaganda and massive public rallies, youth groups, and a parallel system of brutal intimidation. The Nazis had deviously recrafted the everyday situations that Germans experienced. In Lewin's view, the authoritarian system that the Nazis set up, not an intrinsic authoritarian national character, caught the German people in its grip.

While the theory of the authoritarian personality became clouded in conflicting data and its strongest form was rejected by social scientists, Lewin's research has stood the test of time. He developed a bold experimental approach to evaluating the role of situational changes in shaping people's behavior, which led to many of the field's most important findings. Of course, Lewin knew, situations don't have monolithic effects. There is always an interplay with the people involved, who read different meanings into each situation and respond accordingly. To understand behavior, we need to understand the dance between the person and the situation.

Much of Lewin's research was directed at helping people feel included, listened to, and appreciated. To my read, he was trying not to control people but to create the conditions that supported their flourishing together. True to that mission, Lewin conducted his teaching and research in an open, collaborative style. He mentored many female students at a time when they were subjected to a great deal of sexism. He was also much less formal with his students than most professors of the day. He joked with them as with friends and invited them to call him by his first name. So unconventional was his style that one day in class he reclined on a table as he continued to guide discussion. He held soirees at his home with colleagues and students. One acolyte who attended some of these get-togethers, the anthropologist Margaret Mead, wrote that Lewin "was like the fire around which other people gathered for warmth and for light by which to read their own thoughts more clearly." His work became so influential in part because he had mentored so many protégés. He invited them to assist in his own studies. They then advanced the field in their own creative ways.

Lewin liked to say, "If you want truly to understand something, try to change it," which is my lab's motto. In contrast to the tame ambitions of much social science today, Lewin launched one of his papers with no less a goal than to understand what explains a group's tendency to engage in "persecution of a scapegoat, apathetic submissiveness to authoritarian domination," and "attack upon an outgroup"—and, conversely, what explains when people in a group rise up and rebel.

Lewin wanted to know what made some cultures receptive to authoritarian politics and others not. Rather than simply observing cultures, which was how everyone else studied the topic, Lewin had the brazen idea that he could create cultures.

A series of studies on what he called "experimentally created social climates," which he and his students conducted in 1938 at the University of Iowa, showed that the behavior of groups of ten-year-old boys in a local boys' club could be dramatically altered depending on the leadership style of the adult in charge of them. Groups of five boys engaged in fun activities of the era: soap carving, mask making, mural painting, and making model airplanes. They met once a week for about three months.

In some cases, the man in charge of them took a strict authoritarian approach, telling the kids exactly what task to do, whom they should do it with, and how they should do it. He kept the boys in the dark about what they would do next, making the situation unpredictable for them, a tactic of many an authoritarian regime. He remained mostly aloof from the boys, only occasionally offering one or another a word of praise or criticism that, per Lewin's script, focused less on their work and more on the personal qualities of the kid. I imagine the use of subtly coercive comments like "You're such a respectful boy, Johnny," rather than task-focused comments like "That's a beautiful soap carving!"

With other groups, the leader used a democratic style. He suggested the children come up with their own ideas for activities. While he encouraged them to work together, he left the choice of whom, if anyone, to work with up to them. He didn't stifle conflict but helped them cope with it. If the kids ran into issues with projects, such as how they should share a limited supply of paints, the leader would suggest two or three solutions and let the group choose. He made space for children to dissent yet still feel they belonged. He helped them work out disagreements so that each child could get a chance to do the activities he most enjoyed. The leader helped to make the democratic spirit "out of many, one" a reality in the situation. He also joined in with the boys' work and offered them constructive criticism and praise on aspects of their work rather than their personal qualities. In this way, he showed he was engaged in their endeavor and helping them to grow it. The intervention was not a strong-armed attempt to get the kids to act a certain way but rather a set of practices to enable them to identify, integrate, and act on their own wills. Each individual was a creative and participating force in the direction of the group.

In all his interventions, Lewin took aim not at an outcome but at a process. Here it was the process by which decisions were made. What decisions the children actually made were up to them.

As these carefully crafted situations played out, Lewin and his students watched from peepholes in a burlap wall divider. This was, to my knowledge, the first time that researchers observed people's behavior in a theater of their own creation.

The leader's style transformed the climate of the club and the behavior of the boys. The boys in the democratic groups were friendly with one another and eagerly engaged in the projects, having lots of fun. Conflicts that arose were minimal and resolved easily. Those in the authoritarian groups acted in one of two ways. In some of these groups, the kids grew openly hostile toward one another. Lewin was an extensive and meticulous data collector, which followed from his desire to capture the whole "climate" rather than just one variable. In the groups that became hostile, he calculated that a boy cursed, hit, pushed, or screamed at someone almost once every ninety seconds, almost twice as frequently as in the democratic group. The boys mimicked the aggressive domination of their leader. In other authoritarian groups, the boys became docile and apathetic, quietly doing what they were told but with little enthusiasm. But when the leader left the room, the boys would often begin lashing out at one another. Lewin wrote that they had felt "bottled-up tension," which was held in check by the authoritarian leadership style but "burst out unmistakably" once they believed they were unobserved.

The boys' work also suffered under the authoritarian leader. They didn't have as much a sense of ownership over it. They would more often abandon their work as soon as the leader left the room and engage in quarreling. Authoritarian leadership might generate good behavior in the short term, but it didn't lead to much true affection for other group members or commitment to the work. Based on his observations, Lewin's team noted that the group spirit and feelings of belonging in these authoritarian groups seemed to diminish over time. The kids overseen by the democratic leaders, meanwhile, kept on happily working together when their leader ducked out. They also produced work that was judged as more creative, and there was a continued group spirit that energized the boys. Tension, that bane of group life, was minimal because the kids felt they all belonged and had a voice.

Another contrast between the groups was that the attention of the boys in the democratic groups was directed almost entirely toward their collaborative work. Their talk was all about what they should do, such as how to fix a problem with a mural or asking someone to lend a hand. But the talk among the boys in the authoritarian groups was what Lewin called "ego involved." They were preoccupied with trying to get the leader's attention or with asserting they had done a better job than another. Often they engaged in nasty putdowns of one another. They had "gone Darwin."

This little experimental drama was Shakespearean in its ability to cast light on the sources of so many human foibles and follies that arise once a situation is laid down. Most striking was the ability of the authoritarian leader to unleash the boys' tendency to treat each other as enemies and threats rather than sources of pleasure and affirmation. While most aggression took place within these groups, sometimes intergroup war broke out. It usually began with a provocation. Some stray boys from a neighboring club would wander in. "Why don't you learn to talk, you sissies?" the boys would snarl at the intruders. "Let's have a war!"

Scapegoating was also more likely under authoritarian rule. Lewin would orchestrate little frustrations, like the arrival of a "hostile stranger" who would step into the room, criticize the boys' work, and then leave. Then tension in the group would boil over. Sometimes, the group concentrated its angst on a scapegoat, a single person in the group whom they would bully so much that the victim left. For at least a little while after he left, the rest of the group would engage in friendly cooperation; the ousting of the scapegoat seemed to have eased their tension.

Lewin was careful to contrast the democratic leaders with a group of "hands-off" leaders who produced disappointing results. These leaders thought they were being democratic but were really, as Lewin described them, "laissez-faire." From the perspective of the boys, they were physically present but "psychologically unimportant." Bedlam often broke out in these groups.

You can see the results yourself on video. Lewin's findings inspired later research on interventions that bring democratic procedures into the workplace, schools, and even the criminal justice system, as we will see later in this book. Lewin's insights resonate today given many Americans' proclivity for conflict and scapegoating of fellow citizens.

Hearing about Lewin's results may provoke criticism that he was manipulating the boys. Indeed, social psychologists have wrestled with ethical issues for decades. Controversial studies went too far in their manipulation. But as Lewin's analysis of the Nazification of German culture suggests, we are being manipulated all the time by forces we do not see. Governments, businesses, institutions, cultures, and other people in our lives craft our everyday situations in ways that are intended to produce a response they want. Lewin showed that in spite of these larger forces, a leader, or even an ordinary individual with some acuity and influence, can counter unhealthy social currents with positive ones.

Lewin himself was the first to apply these insights out in "the wild" of actual offices as a consultant to companies. In one famous study, he was hired by the Harwood Pajama Factory, in the town of Marion, Virginia, to address the problem of low levels of engagement among its seamstresses. Morale was so low and resentment of the management so high that some employees had even sabotaged the equipment, expressed hostility against their supervisor, or quit altogether. Tension ran high, with an "Us-vs.-Them" mentality setting in among the workers and management. Managers complained that any little change, like reducing the number of buttons to be sewn on the pajama shirts to lower production costs, would provoke outrage. They shared sexist theories with Lewin about why the seamstresses weren't more committed and productive, which Lewin dismissed. The managers had often used a dictatorial top-down approach with the women, but Lewin thought that a more democratic style of management would bring better results.

To start, he showed the women respect by asking them to share their views of the problem. Speaking with a German accent, Lewin might have been seen as an outsider. But he also made his own efforts to belong, by talking the women's talk. Lewin's biographer writes that "after his first baffled attempts to understand their southern drawl" amused the seamstresses, he adopted some of their expressions, such as telling them "That's snake oil" when he thought the justifications they offered for the problems were bogus. Based on what he had learned from them and the lessons he had gleaned from his past research on group dynamics, he suggested a number of ways to boost performance. One was to bring in a number of high-performing workers from other factories so that the Harwood women could see how productive these others were, expanding the frontiers of expectation. Sure enough, productivity began to increase.

Even more successful was Lewin's suggestion that the management give the women some latitude in setting their own production goals. A group of employees were brought together in small, intimate groups to discuss ways to improve the working procedures and set their own daily production target per worker. They were given the title "special operator" to recognize their distinctive role. Management didn't lecture the employees. Instead, they sought to make them aware of the problems that the company was contending with, helping them discover for themselves that it was necessary to cut costs to remain competitive. Management offered some plans of their own but also agreed to many of the workers' suggestions. The seamstresses in a "business-as-usual" control group displayed a 20 percent drop in productivity over the next few weeks after management had introduced new changes, and 9 percent quit. But the work of those who participated in the wise intervention not only rebounded from a short-lived drop in productivity, but ultimately surpassed the level of output before the change. No one quit.

Lewin was like a wizard of situation-crafting. He was even able to inspire a change in Americans' eating habits, a devilishly difficult challenge. In another real-world assignment, this time for the U.S. federal government during World War II, Lewin teamed up with his admirer-become-friend, the famous anthropologist Margaret Mead. They were called to chair a new organization, the Committee on Food Habits, to solve a vexing problem. Choice cuts of meat were being strictly rationed so that as much high-quality protein as possible could be fed to the troops overseas. Government officials were worried that Americans on the home front wouldn't be getting enough protein themselves, so they wanted the committee to find a way to convince Americans to serve their families organ meats—liver, kidney, tongue, brain, and intestines—which were distinctly unpopular but rich in nutrients. Lewin targeted his influence efforts at the gatekeeper—in that place and time, the homemaker. Many home-front war efforts used a declamatory "do this" message or a patriotic "it's good for the war effort" pitch. With Lewin's guidance, the Committee on Food Habits took an empowering "it's up to you" approach. The group suggested, "Just try it for variety," which led to the christening of the dreaded cuts as "variety meats."

Lewin and his research team also brought homemakers together into small groups, away from the sway of their husbands and children, to talk about the barriers that stood in the way of serving these meats to their families. The homemakers were asked if they saw any ways to overcome these barriers. At the end, when the women were asked to indicate by show of hands how many intended to try the meats at least once, everyone raised a hand. A group norm was thereby established, and many of the women followed through on their commitment. Among the women who participated, the serving of the meats increased tenfold relative to a control group given a lecture about the importance of trying the new foods. This result was in striking contrast to an earlier effort to increase the eating of vegetables, in which Margaret Mead gave a lecture as a "prestige expert" to "express publicly my high approval of turnips—which had no effect at all."

Lewin's discoveries about the power of such participatory group processes to create change lie at the heart of today's widespread group intervention practices, such as Alcoholics Anonymous meetings. Participatory management practices in business, which are unfortunately not as widespread, also arose from Lewin's work. Lewin's pioneering strategies are starkly different from the command-and-control approach of persuasion, propaganda, and the mind-control techniques of cults. His participatory process sometimes even gave rise to creative collective solutions to problems that no single individual or authority had imagined. Lewin's approach didn't control. It catalyzed.

So did the charette that helped open C. P. Ellis's mind.

We can seldom simply will ourselves or another person to change. Instead, changes in situations, lived experiences, lead people to change. Situation-crafting is the science and art of creating those transformative experiences. There are five vital resources for doing this.

1. *Time:* C. P. changed his views because he attended the charette at a moment when he was disillusioned with the quality of his relationships and therefore open to change. Timing our influence attempts to periods in which people may be feeling particularly acute doubt about their belonging can be especially powerful, such as when they've joined a new school, are trying out for a sports team, or are start-

ing a new job. We may be able to craft those situations in simple ways that send powerful messages that people are welcome and appreciated. And by intervening early, we make time an ally. Early success often compounds into later and still greater success.

2. ***Participatory processes:*** In Kurt Lewin's interventions, change was not coerced in an authoritarian way. Likewise, C. P. was a full participant in the process of his own change, and the leadership style of the charette was democratic.

3. ***Reference groups:*** C. P. didn't change alone. He changed with the help of a new reference group, a group of people with whom he came to identify and refer. The word "refer" carries a lot of meaning here. Scientific studies emphasize the idea of referring to the group for information on what to think, feel, and do. As C. P.'s story shows, the choice of our reference group is a fundamental one: It's about whose hearts and minds are in our heart and in our mind. C. P. came to care about Ann Atwater and, through her, other members of the community he had been closed off from. He started to see this community from their perspective, appreciating more of what they saw, feeling more of what they felt. Lewin thought the reference group was the single most important driver of change. A group, Lewin thought, is like the river a person swims in. It was near futile, he said, to try to convince an individual to go in a direction opposite to the norms of the group. There was no use trying to persuade C. P. to go against the norms of the KKK or the pajama seamstresses to go against the norms of production, Lewin would say. That was like swimming upstream. Instead, Lewin advised putting people in a new river. Take them out of their existing reference group, for a

time at least—away from their family, say—and place them
in a new group with new norms, new currents.

4. *Self-affirmations:* C. P. wasn't barraged by the coun-
    cil with all the ways he was ignorant, stupid, and wrong.
    Instead, the opposite happened. He was affirmed. First, his
    offensive comment had been transformed by Clements into
    a symbol of virtue and the basis of inclusion. Here was an
    admirable citizen who could speak his mind, Clements's
    comment conveyed—just what the group needed. Clements
    had affirmed C. P.'s value not only as a man but as a con-
    tributor to the group's mission. Second, in stark contrast
    to the Klan, C. P.'s acceptance was not conditional on his
    adherence to a certain set of beliefs. Third, he was elected to
    an honorific position. Likewise, Lewin's democratic leaders
    created situations that permitted each member to feel that
    his or her perspective mattered. These are all examples of
    what social psychologists call self-affirmations, experiences
    that make the self "firm."

    The term self-affirmation, introduced into the psycho-
    logical canon by Claude Steele, differs from the daily affir-
    mations once hilariously parodied by Al Franken as Stuart
    Smalley on *Saturday Night Live*. Self-affirmations are not
    hollow praise or self-flattery but situational opportunities
    we create for people to express who they are and to be val-
    ued for it. To make the self truly firm requires that the affir-
    mation be credible and meaningful. You'll see examples of
    the power of affirmations throughout this book. In general,
    self-affirmations allay the defensiveness and self-absorption
    that take hold when people feel under threat.

    While it is often vital to speak out against prejudice when
    it occurs—one can only imagine the hurt caused by C. P.'s
    offensive comment—we'll explore later that the manner in
    which we do so makes a world of difference. The charette was

designed as a forum to allow all views to be freely expressed, without condemnation, out of the understanding that only by being respectful to those with opposing views will we be able to engage them in productive discussion. Had C. P. been condemned, no matter how justified, he might never have returned to the group or come to the further set of realizations about his racism that changed his life.

5. ***New roles:*** C. P. played new roles first as a community leader, then as a friend to Ann Atwater. He didn't embrace these roles all at once. But when he started to inhabit these roles, they became identities. The word "identity" derives from a word for "sameness" or "oneness," and it is when a person and a role become one that the role has become an identity.

Time, participatory processes, reference groups, self-affirmations, and roles are not material resources in the way that, say, money and jobs are. They are psychologically experienced resources, and as such they depend for their power on perception. Even time is experienced relative to one's perspective. What counts as the "right time" in social life is largely dependent on a person's psychological readiness. While that can be difficult to perceive, if we listen and look carefully, we can often sense when we have an opportunity to make a wise intervention. There's a wide range for creativity and personal expression within the constraints of what I refer to as the three Ts of situation-crafting. The right psychological message (tailoring) occurs for the right person (targeting) at the right time (timeliness). What would have otherwise been an inconsequential experience becomes a turning point.

Throughout this book, we will see that there is often more potential for change in a situation than we imagine. To intervene wisely and tap into the potential of the situation requires us to be aware of something that's often difficult for us to fathom: that the situation as others see it may be different from the way we ourselves see it. Every situation is a complex brew that each participant contributes to and has a perspective on. One person may feel a strong sense of belonging in a situation while others don't, but that same person may experience intense doubt about belonging in a different situation in which others feel confident. Because situations are always experienced from a human point of view, what seems to be one situation is actually as many situations as the number of people in it.

This makes it much harder to answer the question at the heart of ethical behavior: How would I want to be treated if I were in that situation? Much of my research aims to illuminate when and for whom situations threaten the belonging of the people in them, why our sense of belonging can be so fragile, and what we can do to support belonging in situations where people feel like outsiders. That's where we will turn in the next chapter.

Chapter 2

Belonging Uncertainty

Belonging Can Be Fragile, but It Can Also Be Fostered

H AVE YOU EVER GONE HOME AFTER SOME TIME AWAY BUT not *felt* at home? Maybe you returned from college to your parents' home, like the hero in the movie *The Graduate*, Benjamin, whose parents and their social circle now seem like creatures from another planet to him. It's the same house where you grew up, the same people, the same physical reality by and large. But it doesn't *feel* like home. This experience, which I imagine we've all encountered in some form, highlights the fact that home is a psychological experience—not just a place, but how the place makes us feel. The same is true for almost any social situation. Time and again, research has shown that it's our subjective experience of situations, not just their physical reality, that explains much of their power over us. You can have many friends around you yet still feel lonely. Conversely, you can be physically far from those you love yet still feel connected.

So when crafting situations to nurture belonging, we need to pay attention not just to the physical features of the situation but to the way the situation is being perceived, felt, and experienced. We often have trouble appreciating how differently a situation is being experienced by others, even by people we feel close to.

Research shows that people bring aspects of their lives from outside a situation with them, shaping how they see new situations and how they behave in them. Those life experiences are often unknown to others, like invisible forces warping situations. Students from a harsh family background may bring experiences from home into the classroom. Members of minority groups may bring memories of racial insults with them, leading them to see the same classroom differently. A college student relayed the story of seeing a racial slur written in the bathroom stall right before a geology class. While the professor lectured about rock formation and sedimentation, her mind was under siege with thoughts and emotions about what she had seen. Who had written the slur? Why? Was the perpetrator sitting next to her? She couldn't focus enough to learn.

There are many other examples of ways in which we bring the past with us, our memories and expectations shaping the way we interpret new situations. Divorced people carry sensitivity from the pain of their experience, perhaps an expectation of betrayal that haunts their new relationships. People who have been humiliated for being overweight in childhood may carry a burden of shame into adulthood. We all have conditioning from life experiences that molds the way we see situations, which can make even ordinary situations different for the different people in them. Indeed, it can be jarring to realize that some encounter we had was experienced altogether differently by another person.

A PIONEER OF PSYCHOLOGY, Abraham Maslow, placed the need to belong midway up his famous hierarchy, or "pyramid," of needs. At the base, he put physiological needs, such as food and shelter, ascending to the need for safety, then for love and belonging, then for self-esteem, and finally for self-actualization. But Maslow didn't conduct formal scientific research into the need to belong.

One of the first to do so was Englishman John Bowlby in the middle of the twentieth century. He was concerned about the effects on children of being separated from their parents during World War II. Two million young children had been sent away from their homes in cities to the countryside to protect them from bombings. Many were taken in by families, while others were placed in institutional care. Bowlby's focus was on how our early life experiences, particularly how we were parented, either imprinted us with a strong sense of belonging to carry throughout life—or failed to do so. In a powerful report for the World Health Organization in 1952 entitled *Maternal Care and Mental Health,* he changed the way parents and institutions treat children by arguing that the absence of an early bond harmed the healthy development of children, including their physical, emotional, and cognitive maturity, with costs that could persist for a lifetime. Later research qualified this bold statement. Some children respond worse than others, and individuals can recover by developing a strong bond to another caregiver or even by finding an accepting relationship later in life. But his fundamental insight has endured: Healthy development depends on connection. Child-rearing practices that we take for granted today, like letting a mom hold her newborn immediately after birth, stem from his research.

Bowlby's colleague Mary Ainsworth followed up on his work by conducting a study that's like a parable for the vital role of belonging in people's ability to thrive. She had a mother and her infant enter a room, then asked the mother to sit down on a chair to one side of the room and put her infant on the floor at her feet. Across the room was a wide assortment of alluring toys. Ainsworth dubbed the setup the "strange situation." It was meant to illuminate which children might be adventurous enough to go play with the toys.

Some of the infants stayed close to their mothers, while others ventured over to the toys to explore. Ainsworth also noted that the children who went to play showed a great enthusiasm for and curiosity about the toys and that they were quick to share their wonder with the mothers. The infants pointed at the toys while looking over at their mothers so as to share the experience. She described these children as feeling "delight in exploring the wonders of the world." They seemed to *see* the room not as strange at all but as full of tantalizing possibility. They lifted, dropped, and turned the toys, playful acts in which

Ainsworth's contemporary, Solomon Asch, saw the "germs of the highest forms of human endeavor."

By contrast, many of the infants who stayed close to their moms seemed uninterested in the toys, not even looking at them. When Ainsworth introduced a stressor in later studies—a stranger entered the room and the mother left—the venturesome infants recovered faster, pulling themselves together and resuming play when their mom returned, while many of the clingy kids didn't.

While it might seem that infants that cling to parents are the more bonded, Ainsworth concluded the opposite: The children who seemed most independent were in fact the most confidently connected. A powerful parent-child bond allows children to feel nurtured whether they're physically close to a parent or not. They seemed to display a faith that, should trouble arise, their parent would be available to support them. Ainsworth described children who demonstrated that bond as having a "secure base" from which to tackle life's challenges, a perch from which new situations seem less threatening.

But even such a secure base can be pulled out from under us, as psychologists have found in the decades since Ainsworth's and Bowlby's enduring insights. Belonging is less like a keystone belief and more like a perception that's continually being re-created anew in every situation. I became interested in researching belonging partly due to my own intense experience of feeling my own sense of belonging unexpectedly vanishing. When I took up my first assistant professorship, I was sure I would be outed as an idiot. One day when the chair of my department slapped me on the shoulder and asked, "How's your course going?" I suspected he'd heard some gossip about how bad my class was. After I agreed to let a student journalist take a picture of me for an article about teachers in the campus newspaper, I started to think he was planning to pillory me on the front page, envisioning a headline about the worst professor on campus. I asked him to delete the picture. I hadn't expected to feel so unsure of myself, but I found the environment of the campus disorienting and intimidating. I thought I had developed a firm belief in my abilities and a sense of belonging in my profession, but as much research has shown, even those of us who have developed a strong sense of belonging may suddenly find it forsaking us in new circumstances.

We all feel like outsiders sometimes. Whether a minority or first-generation student on a college campus, a member of the traditional working class in a high-tech society, a foreigner, a queer person, a young person in the company of older people, an older person in the company of younger people, even a well-off member of a majority group amid those who are even better off, we all know the sting of feeling we don't belong.

If and when we find our niche, our lives can sometimes feel filled with potential threats to our sense of belonging. Schools can be hotbeds of bullying and elaborate, often brutal cultures of social shaming and ostracism, even in the earliest grades. Middle school can be especially fraught, as children grapple with the new challenges of adolescence. For those of us who move on to college, the environment can feel alienating; finding our social footing can prove to be a prolonged and painful search. Many students of color feel the pain of bias, as do women studying in science and math. What's more, with a shift over the past several decades to a more liberal culture prevailing on campuses, many conservatives and centrists feel shunned. Even being a graduate student or an assistant professor doesn't guarantee a sense of belonging to an academic community, and in my own experience it can torment you with fears of inadequacy.

Workplaces can be rife with discrimination, harassment, and authoritarian managers. However, threats to belonging need not be overt. The little sins of omission—the missed "thank you," the lack of acknowledgment for your contribution—can add up to a vague feeling of "I don't belong here." Management professor Mary Rowe had an experience almost fifty years ago as a university ombudsman that she has thought about ever since. A black woman employed at the university told Rowe she was going to resign, and when Rowe asked why, the woman said, "It's just . . . *cold*. I don't belong here." Rowe convinced her to postpone resigning for a few weeks and to keep a log of what people said and did to her at the office so that they could address the problem.

A month later, the woman silently handed over the log, and Rowe saw to her surprise that next to each carefully marked date was . . . nothing. When Rowe asked the woman to explain, she responded, as Rowe writes, that "No one had spoken to her about her work, or the holiday, a recent public success in that lab, or even the weather." The problem lay in what wasn't said, that is, in the lack of basic collegiality.

Out in our communities, nasty encounters with people who see us as "other" can sneak up on us—on a walk in the park, being greeted at a restaurant, or in the grocery store line. In our circles of friends and family, we can doubt how secure our acceptance is and feel slighted by a long-unreturned phone call or a friend's lack of empathy about a hardship we're going through. LGBTQ children are often shamed and outright shunned by their families. Even those of us who usually feel a strong sense of belonging, with robust family bonds, strong support from friends and colleagues, and good ties to community groups, can find ourselves feeling isolated and unsure of how we fit in when we start a new job, move to a new town, or simply go to a party.

Media and social media are devastating to our day-to-day secure base, research suggests. How many of us have been calm, feeling good about ourselves and the world, perhaps all set for bed, only to have our heart rate accelerate when we peek at our Twitter account or our Facebook news feed? At their best, these forms of media provide benefits of information, entertainment, and connection. At their worst, they are the tools of a reign of social terror. Thanks in part to research in psychology, the media moguls know that stories that spark fear, disgust, and outrage capture people's attention more than those that trigger positive emotion or neutral processing. They have slanted their coverage and content to profit from these emotional appetites. This bias is one reason that annual surveys of Americans in the first eighteen years since the turn of the century show that most people believed that the frequency of violent and property crimes in their country was increasing when in fact it was decreasing. Trusting your fellow citizens is difficult when you feel they're increasingly made up of people looking to do you harm.

Meanwhile, the algorithms that determine people's news feeds online are optimized not to inform them but to grab their attention with controversial and alarming stories that make them feel unsafe. Media outlets have also become increasingly siloed into partisan platforms, opening a divide in the information and viewpoints that the public consumes.

Though social media can be a tool to connect us, it's full of misinformation and provides an easy channel for spreading hate and ostracism. It's made the world feel increasingly like a high school cafeteria. Many people also feel the added pressure of having many eyes on them from an early age, which makes it harder to establish a strong, authentic self. Psychologist Jean Twenge has linked the disturbing increase in teen mental illness to the rise of social media. One randomized experiment involving thousands of Facebook users found that participants who were prompted to shut down their Facebook accounts for a month spent more time hanging out with family and friends, compared with participants who were not prompted to leave Facebook. Members of the group who left Facebook were also more balanced in their news consumption, were less extreme in their political attitudes, and experienced fewer day-to-day events that made them angry at those expressing views different from theirs. Overall they felt better about their lives and less depressed. Remarkably, the researchers compared the effect of their "subtractive intervention" with the standard benefit found for many "proactive" psychological interventions such as therapy. Leaving Facebook had about a third of the positive effect of many of these proactive interventions. Indeed, 80 percent of the volunteers reported that deactivation of their account was good for them, so much so that many said they planned to stay off the site. As one volunteer commented, "I was more focused on my own life. . . . I felt more content."

In another experiment, with adults who had yet to open a Facebook account, those who then joined the site became less involved in civic and political activity than members of a group who didn't join. Joining Facebook meant less time participating in volunteer and political action groups, hobby clubs, and charities—the very kind of communal work that, research finds, promotes trust, belonging, and health. Likewise, a great way to people to get more pleasure out of their face-to-face interactions—a key contributor to their happiness and health—is to put their smartphones away.

This is not to say social media platforms are invariably bad for us. Their impact on us depends on our relationship to them, as is the case for any media we consume. And just limiting our use of social media to twenty minutes a day helps to minimize its costs and maximize its benefits. But many of us, especially the young, don't know how to avoid the pitfalls.

We can all become vulnerable to doubts about our belonging at any given moment, depending on the situations we find ourselves in and how we interpret them. Greg Walton and I coined the term "belonging uncertainty" to refer to the state of mind in which one suffers from doubts about whether one is fully accepted in a particular environment or ever could be. We can experience it in the workplace, at school, at a snooty restaurant, or even in a brief social encounter. Belonging uncertainty has adverse effects. When we perceive threats to our sense of belonging, our horizon of possibility shrinks. We tend to interpret ourselves, other people, and the situation in a defensive and self-protective way. We more readily infer that we are incapable or that we aren't meant to be there, that we will not understand or be understood. We're less likely to express our views, especially if they differ from those of others. We're more sensitive to perceived criticism. We're less inclined to accept challenges that pose a risk of failure.

Some may wonder if belonging uncertainty can rise to the level of paranoia or even neurosis. Can't we be oversensitive to slights? Those portraying college students who complain about bias on campuses as delicate "snowflakes" have suggested this. But those of us who have not been encumbered by a prolonged experience of rejection, prejudice, or abuse may be unable to see the situation as others do, and we should make allowance for this gap in our awareness. Slights can be subtle yet accumulate into a devastating message. As one black high school student put it,

Once, a classmate suggested that I was only elected as a student leader for diversity's sake, not because I was actually deserving. Or, another time, a teacher assumed I was studying for general chemistry, when in fact, I was enrolled in AP. It's hard to pinpoint what exactly is wrong in these moments—taken on their own. But when you add them up—and they happen all the time—it builds to this sense that I don't belong.

ALTHOUGH MASLOW PUT the need to belong midway up his hierarchy of needs, research over the past several decades suggests that belonging should be located closer to the base of the pyramid, as a need nearly as vital as food and shelter. What's more, that's true not just in infancy but *throughout* our lives.

Two researchers, Roy Baumeister and Mark Leary, synthesized a large body of work to make this point in one of the most well-cited papers in social psychology, published in 1995. They highlight that we have evolved as a fundamentally social species and have an instinct to seek social connection. Evolutionary biologists argue that being members of a group was essential to our survival and that our species developed a fear of being isolated. This fear brings on a keen physiological reaction. I recall how threatened I felt by one of my first experiences of social rejection and the physical effects the incident had on me. In an all-too-common ritual of the era, the instructor of my first-grade gym class had two kids each pick teams from our class. I was the last one picked. It's the first personal experience of humiliation I can remember. My reaction was physical as well as psychological: My stomach clenched, my face reddened, and my palms became sweaty. The experience also became part of my emotional memory, seated in the old brain structure of the amygdala, so that whenever I simply knew there would be a team sport in gym class, I had a similar physical reaction.

In one of the simplest yet most profound psychological studies of our era, a team led by Kip Williams revealed how a related form of rejection, but one that was seemingly trivial, affected adults. The participants played a four-minute video game of catch with what seemed to be two strangers, who were ostensibly playing from another terminal somewhere else in the world. The players were represented by avatars, and unbeknownst to the participants, the other avatars were actually preprogrammed by the researchers to stop passing the ball to the participants at a certain point in the game.

What was the effect observed over many studies? In a word, as Williams puts it, "pain." Compared with participants who played the same toss game but were not excluded, the players who were excluded expressed feeling less of a sense of belonging, self-esteem, control, and meaning in their lives. They also displayed greater activation of the brain regions associated with the experience of pain. Although some people are more sensitive to rejection than others, the psychological effects of this experience of ostracism hold up for men and women, the anxious and not so anxious, extraverts and introverts. The effects occur even when the other players are described as people the participants might find repugnant, such as members of the Ku Klux Klan. Other research shows that such brief experiences of rejection can put people on the alert for more, leading them to be overly sensitive to new slights, such as when a friend says she'll call over the weekend and fails to do so.

If the threats we perceive to our belonging become chronic, the physical effects can add up. Studies have revealed the cumulative medical damage arising from continual threats to belonging, such as being subjected to prolonged discrimination. The genes that stimulate bodily inflammation are activated, a biological response to adversity that, when chronic, is like "fertilizer for early death," Steve Cole, a pioneer of research linking social environments to gene expression, told me. Our central nervous system activates a threat response when it "perceives" ourselves to be alone, a survival mechanism that ratchets up heart rate, blood pressure, and the release of stress hormones. The chronic activation of the threat response helps explain the higher rates of cardiovascular illness, cancer, and other diseases among people who feel shunned or rejected for a variety of reasons. Though the origin of their despair is different, damage is done through the same psychological and biological pathways.

The effects of belonging have been measured using a set of simple but powerful methods. For those interested in getting a good assessment of their own or others' degree of belonging, I provide a number of the best surveys at my website (geoffreylcohen.com). One method is simply asking people how much they agree or disagree with statements like the following:

> *When something bad happens, I feel that maybe I don't belong*
> *at [school or workplace name].*
> *I fit in well at [school or workplace name].*

Sometimes researchers ask people to respond to a question like the one below by rating how frequently they've felt this way:

> *When you think about [school or workplace name], how often, if*
> *ever, do you wonder, "Maybe I don't belong here"?*

Simple as these measures may seem, they have been able to predict a host of life outcomes in addition to the health issues described above, ranging from later college enrollment to the likelihood of dropping out of college, from whether female college students persist in getting a degree in fields related to science, technology, engineering, and math (STEM) to how employees perform at work.

All of this research suggests that we have good reason to be on the alert for threats to our belonging. Yet while we're sensitive to what endangers our *own* belonging, we tend to be much less aware of the threats that *others* experience. Many incidents on college campuses have demonstrated how suffused they can be with threats to belonging— and how the extent to which college feels like a home depends on your point of view. One glaring incident unfolded at Yale University in 2015. In light of a number of revelations of college students dressing up in blackface, both decades ago and in more recent years, Yale's diversity office sent out a message to students recommending that they exercise sensitivity in choosing Halloween costumes. A faculty member, Erika Christakis, wrote an email in response, arguing that students should be able to dress any way they choose, as a matter of free speech. "American universities were once a safe space not only for maturation but also for a certain regressive, or even transgressive, experience," she wrote. "Increasingly, it seems, they have become places of censure and prohibition. . . . If you don't like a costume someone is wearing, look away, or tell them you are offended."

Many students responded harshly, one declaring, "You should step down. You're disgusting. You shouldn't sleep at night."

In a videotaped confrontation, which went viral, Erika's husband, Nicholas Christakis, was challenged by a group of students to apologize for his wife's message and to show understanding of why it was hurtful to them. In a long and increasingly heated back-and-forth exchange, one African American student tells him, "You . . . have not said 'I hear you.' I hear that you are hurting, and I am sorry that I have caused you to feel pain." He responds, "I apologize for causing pain, but I am not sorry for the statement. . . . I stand behind free speech. I defend the right for people to speak their minds." The confrontation only escalated from there, with one student breaking down in tears.

It's difficult to watch so much emotion boiling over and to see so little mutual understanding achieved. Then, at the end of the confrontation, one student exclaims, "It is not about creating an intellectual space! It is about creating a home!"

I can imagine no other statement that captures so well the clash in perspectives. For white members of the Yale community, it's comparatively easy to see the campus as a big dinner table of equals, all sitting together, all respected, and all enjoying each other's company and talking freely about whatever comes up as if they were at home. Meanwhile, for many minority students, the dinner party is a tense affair. They don't know if they are welcome at the table. A situation that some see as idyllic can seem infused with danger to others.

IN HIS NOVEL *OLD SCHOOL*, author Tobias Wolff describes how a campus that seems like "home" to many can present subtle but potent threats to belonging for others. The novel's narrator is a student who has just arrived at an elite and mostly Catholic preparatory school in 1960. As he climbs the stairs to his dormitory one day, he whistles a tune that he had overheard the summer before while working for a German chef. Unbeknownst to the student, the song is a Nazi military march. What's worse, the student is overheard in the stairwell by a Jewish handyman who survived the Holocaust. The student is whisked away to the dean's office. Desperate to win sympathy, he agonizes over whether to tell the dean that his own father was Jewish. But he decides against it:

> *There was no obvious reason for being cagey. In my short time at the school, I'd seen no bullying or manifest contempt of that kind, and never did. Yet it seemed to me that the Jewish boys, even the popular ones, even the athletes, had a subtly charged field around them, an air of apartness. And somehow the feeling must have settled in me that this apartness did not emanate from the boys themselves, from any quality or wish of their own, but from the school—as if some guardian spirit, indifferent to their personal worth, had risen from the fields and walkways and weathered stone to breathe that apartness upon them.*

Is it all in his mind? He sees no overt bullying or expressions of anti-Semitism. The Jews are even integrated as athletes and popular kids. Perhaps there are hints of anti-Semitism that the narrator perceives. He might also feel some distancing, some perception of him as "other" that is a figment of his own imagination. But as Wolff captures, a sense of not belonging can be almost entirely atmospheric: a vague "air of apartness" that we feel, the source of which we can't put our finger on. The narrator is aware of the long, painful reality of anti-Semitism and is therefore alert to its possibility. The campus doesn't *feel* like home in the way it does for the Catholic boys.

Extensive research finds that students experience plenty of prejudice and insensitivity on college campuses today, and not only students of color. A female friend of mine had been interested in studying organic chemistry in college, so she went to talk to the chair of the department about majoring in it. His first question for her was, "Why is a pretty girl like you thinking about majoring in organic chemistry?" The chair might have thought he was being complimentary. But as a result of that single encounter, my friend never stepped into the chemistry department again, even though she had loved the subject.

Although situations are "out there" in front of our eyes, they are experienced behind our eyes. Much of their impact depends on the meaning we make of them. With my friend, it wasn't simply the objective comment from the professor that did damage but the meaning she ascribed to it. She told me that she had wondered if the comment was like the proverbial smoke from a hidden fire, an early sign of the sexism she could expect if she undertook studies in chemistry. She was well aware of the problem of bias against women in STEM. Indeed, research shows that such awareness is sufficient to erode women's confidence and enthusiasm about pursuing work in these fields.

It's all too easy to see such responses as overreactions. But the meaning of a situation isn't something that each of us alone gets to choose. When two people see the same situation differently, it's often because they are literally in different situations in light of their knowledge and past experiences. Take the case of a restaurant in a predominantly white neighborhood in the pre–Civil Rights era. Many white diners would enter without a second thought, but for a black couple, the same restaurant would be a place of threat.

Even today, far too many social settings are understandably threatening to minorities in ways that white people can find hard to perceive. In a 2021 study, black and white Americans were shown a picture of an Antebellum-era plantation house in which they were told slaves had once served. Unsurprisingly, black participants reported that they would not feel at home or comfortable at the house. Most of them mentioned slavery when asked for their thoughts. But white participants anticipated feeling much more at home and comfortable at the house. Few even mentioned slavery, instead making such comments as "I loved the columns and the white paint." Although the two groups saw the same physical house, psychologically it was an altogether different experience for them.

As we will see, in spite of the formidable forces of history and culture that shape people's perceptions right here and right now, we still have some latitude to define the meaning of situations for ourselves and others.

ACCORDING TO SOCIAL PSYCHOLOGISTS, most behavior is an adaptation to the situation. Making situations truly more equitable is a key mission of situation-crafting. The material and human resources of schools in disadvantaged neighborhoods ought to be brought to the higher standards of those in wealthier communities. Workplaces can be made more diverse, with management teams that reflect the demographics of our society.

But as we try to make situations better in these large-scale ways, we must also attend to the meanings that people make of their situations. Even the most well-intended and well-resourced efforts to support people will be disappointing if they convey—or fail to refute—harmful messages about belonging. The Moving to Opportunity program provided a random group of poor families the opportunity to move to a less impoverished neighborhood, allowing their children to attend better-financed schools. This program had many positive effects years later, with some students more likely to attend college and earn higher salaries. But the early hoped-for effects on children's academic test scores didn't materialize, and boys who moved were more likely than a control group to engage in nonviolent criminal activity. Although we do not know for sure what caused these effects, one reason may be that many of these students felt uncertain of their belonging in their new neighborhoods and schools. Indeed, a measure of belonging in their new community— the number of friends they made with higher-income youth—proved a powerful predictor of their upward mobility.

Even though belonging may be easily derailed, it can also be easily affirmed. When I was a self-doubting assistant professor, I found that a brief stimulating conversation with a student or an email about how much someone was enjoying my class could put my mind at ease. These small moments of connection can have big effects. In one creative study by Kent Harber and his colleagues, volunteers were told to wear a heavy backpack and asked to judge the steepness of a hill before them. They saw the hill as less steep when they were with a friend rather than by themselves. And if they were alone, they saw the hill as less steep when they were simply asked to think about a good friend. In a series of experiments headed by Greg Walton, fleeting and even seemingly meaningless experiences conferred a sense of belonging. When college students were led to believe that they happened to share a birthday with a math major, they felt a stronger sense that they could belong in math and even worked harder on a math puzzle than did students who thought they had a different birthday.

I've been struck by the parallels between ways we can create a welcoming environment and ways to host a social gathering. We all know what it's like to go to an event and feel like an outsider. As a good host appreciates, no matter how lovely the party or wonderful the guests, if you feel ill at ease, you might as well have stayed home. Maybe you have just moved to the area or started a new job. The get-together is a great opportunity to mingle with new neighbors or colleagues, but you might worry about the impression you'll make. That worry might be provoked by bad experiences you've had at parties in the past. You might feel uncertain about whether you belong because the invitation arrived late and you wonder if you're truly wanted there, or perhaps because you failed to bring a dish for what you discover is a potluck, or even simply because you trip on the doorstep as you enter the home. (I've experienced each of these situations.) A good host can make all the difference in the experience you have, greeting you with a big smile and a warm pat on the back, even if you've come tumbling into the entryway. The host might introduce you to guests and point out common interests to help kick-start conversation. Now the party feels more welcoming, and the other guests seem less intimidating. You initiate conversation with them more comfortably, and you enjoy getting to know them. If you perceive a slight by one of the guests, it doesn't loom as large as it would if you felt ill at ease. In schools, workplaces, and all other social spaces, each of us can do our part to act as good hosts.

Greg Walton and I crafted a wise intervention to address people's feelings about whether they belong when they enter a new situation. The intervention produces such good results that it is used in many colleges, middle schools, and high schools throughout the country, as well as in graduate school and workplaces.

We wanted to see if we could help combat the effects of belonging uncertainty by helping students of color to see the everyday slights and adversities that almost all of us experience in a different light. The problem of discrimination, we knew, must be combated head-on, vigorously, by the government, the school system, and in each of our homes. But by helping students shore up their sense of belonging, despite the threats to it, we thought we could help them make their way through the treacherous terrain with more confidence.

To get a feel for what campus life was like for first-year college students, we asked a wide range of individuals from all sorts of backgrounds to keep daily diaries for a week in which they entered the major experiences of their day, many of which might threaten their sense of belonging. Here is a sample of entries from different participants:

> *My teacher returned my paper covered in red ink.*
> *Everyone is going out without me, and they didn't consider me when making their plans.*
> *My teacher canceled her meeting with me.*
> *A peer didn't email me back.*
> *I haven't gone on any dates.*
> *I wasn't recognized at awards dinner.*
> *Dumped by girlfriend.*
> *My boyfriend didn't call.*

Of course, not all the adversities were social:

*I'm working on a paper that is due tomorrow and I have writer's
  block.*
Found a dead mouse under a pile of my clothes.

At the end of each day, students were sent an email that asked them
to record a number from 1 to 10 indicating how bad their day was.
They also filled out a short survey about the extent to which they felt
they fit in and belonged on campus.

We analyzed the entries and discovered a pattern. While there was
no difference in the number of dispiriting incidents reported overall by
different ethnic groups, these incidents seemed to have a more damaging effect on black students, undermining their sense of belonging.
Their sense of belonging would bounce back when they had a good day,
but it would fall again with the next bad one. It was as if black students'
belonging were continually on trial, making their campus experience
feel more perilous and exhausting. For white students, there was no correlation between daily adversity and their feelings of belonging.

Walton and I decided to look for ways to help black students not
associate experiences of adversity with feeling like an outsider. We
drew on research showing that one powerful part of our situation is
the stories we hear. Stories tell us what to expect, what's "normal,"
and what's possible. They give us hope, especially when we are feeling down and isolated, afflicted with the feeling that we alone are
in pain.

The first consideration was timing. We recruited a group of college
students who were near the end of their first and often stressful year
on campus; our sample included both black and white students. We
figured we had much more leverage early in the transition to college
than later. If you have a few good encounters early on, you're set up
for a positive experience. But if you get the cold shoulder, you're more
likely to start wondering if you belong. The first year of college is like
a launching pad for the remainder of your time there—the friends you
make, the professors you meet, the classes you take.

We asked the students to come to the psychology department for a one-hour study about "attitudes and experiences" at their school. We told them we wanted their help in interpreting some results from a student survey and in creating materials to help future students prepare for the college experience. This affirmed them and put them in an empowered role.

In the first part of the study, we handed out a set of stories for them to read based on ones written by juniors and seniors at their school. Here's one example:

Initially my transition here was pretty easy. Going out on Old Campus was easy and fun, and I met a lot of people early on. After Winter Break, things got harder because I realized that all my really good friends were at home and I didn't have friends like that at school. However, I decided that instead of searching for friends, I should pursue my interests and let things fall into place. I got involved in extra-curriculars, and I met people who had common interests and unique perspectives. I also got to know people in class as study partners who became close friends. I found a comfort zone by exploring my interests and taking the leap into an active life here. But this took time and before I found my niche there were times when I felt quite lonely. (Participant #77, white female)

Because these were college students, we thought that the lessons of the stories would be strengthened with scientific data. We shared the results of a survey we had conducted, which revealed that most juniors and seniors had wondered during their first year as college students whether they really belonged. Most had felt intimidated, like an impostor; many had wondered, at one time or another, whether their admission had been a mistake. Participants read these results as part of a survey summary. Here's an example:

73%–86% of upperclassmen reported that, during their freshman year, they:

- ◆ "sometimes" or "frequently" worried whether other students would accept them in the context of classes and coursework.
- ◆ "sometimes" or "frequently" worried that other students at [school name] viewed their abilities negatively.
- ◆ "sometimes" or "frequently" felt intimidated by professors.

Students who had these doubts could now see that such doubts were more common than not among those starting college. For the black students, a particular benefit was seeing that white students also felt these doubts. We had found in our research that black students tend to interpret their belonging uncertainty as stemming from being a minority on campus. The material showed them that doubting one's belonging in college is a feeling shared by almost everyone, not just members of particular groups.

We also used statistics to reinforce another message that had been embedded in our stories: With time and effort, most students come to feel they belong. For instance,

82%–97% of upperclassmen reported that, since their freshman year:

- ◆ their comfort in the academic environment at [school name] has improved "some" or "a lot."
- ◆ they are "confident" or "certain" that most other students accept them in the context of classes and coursework.
- ◆ they are "confident" or "certain" that other students at [school name] view their abilities positively.
- ◆ they are "confident" or "certain" that professors at [school name] accept them.

All in all, participants got to see the hidden perspectives of a reference group: their fellow students. The stories and assurances didn't come from professors or administrators, people outside their reference group. By learning these new perspectives, students might look at their adversities on campus a little differently, as a normal part of adjusting to college. Like encouragement we might get from a close friend at a time when we feel adrift, the message in our study sought to make people feel less like a ship lost at sea and more like cotravelers taking the first steps on a journey full of possibility. The stories turned uncertainty about belonging into a basis of connection rather than shame.

Then, as a final part of the study, we took another page from Lewin's work, asking the students to participate. We asked them how the information they read echoed their own college life. We asked them to share the experiences they'd had over the course of their first year on campus. We told them that they could write an essay and, if they so chose, they could read it on video for future students to see. Almost all of them elected to do so. Walton and I included these participatory elements in the procedure in order to encourage students to make the insights from the study their own. Indeed, research shows that while receiving motivational advice about how to do better in school has little effect, *giving* advice works wonders; students get better grades when they give academic advice to another.

So that we could measure the impact of this wise intervention on the students, we had a control group of students read and respond to reflections by older students about how college students' political views may change over time, with no comments related to belonging. Relative to this control group, our wise intervention increased the sense of belonging in college reported by the black students, whereas it did not have an effect on white students' reported sense of belonging. Our interpretation of these results was that for black students, their belonging uncertainty stemmed, in large part, from their experience being a minority on campus and from contending with a racial stereotype that insinuated "People like me don't belong here." The intervention provided students with an alternative understanding of their belonging uncertainty: Most people (not just black people) feel it to some extent.

Compared with black students in the control group, those who received our wise intervention were also more open to taking intellectual risk. After reviewing a catalog of courses at their school, accompanied with student comments, more of them expressed greater interest in taking demanding courses that would challenge them but also expand and enrich them, as opposed to "gut" courses that guaranteed a good grade but had otherwise little to offer.

But the big benefits of the intervention happened after it ended and participants integrated it into their lives. The participants continued to keep diaries of daily adversities, and when we analyzed these later entries, we found that black students' sense of belonging was less tethered to their day-to-day adversity. They still experienced the same dispiriting events but, it seems, saw them through a different lens.

The intervention also served as an on-ramp to opportunity, driving still more lasting effects. More of the black students in the intervention group began reaching out to advisers and professors for assistance with their schoolwork and more began to find mentors. They seemed to be psychologically more ready to embrace the opportunities in school. Research has shown that an enduring mentoring relationship with an adult on campus is one of the most powerful determinants of success in college and beyond. That may help explain why, three years later, we found, to our surprise, that black students receiving our intervention earned higher final cumulative GPAs in college relative to their black peers in the control group, halving the gap between their grades and those of their white peers.

What's more, research led by Shannon Brady tracked these students for over a decade and found that many of the black students in the intervention group kept in touch with their mentors long after they had graduated. One student told a moving story of how her college adviser had flown all the way to Poland to see a poster she presented at a conference summarizing her graduate research. In addition, while the students in the intervention group didn't end up in more lucrative or prestigious careers—perhaps because virtually all of our sample, coming from a select college, ended up with good careers—they did report finding their careers more satisfying, less stressful, and more meaningful. And they were more involved in their communities and happier with their lives.

This wise intervention, which Walton and I named the "social-belonging intervention," does not boost students' skills or grit; it assumes the students have those already. The intervention isn't the *cause* of students' success; it's a catalyst for it.

I liken the effects of wise interventions to the kinds of small interventions that have whopping effects in science fiction stories like Ray Bradbury's "A Sound of Thunder." A time traveler goes back to prehistoric times and accidentally steps on a butterfly. Though just an "exquisite thing, a small thing," the butterfly's death changes the course of civilization. As Bradbury writes, it's just that small thing that can "upset balances and knock down a line of small dominoes and then big dominoes and then gigantic dominoes, all down the years across Time." Wise interventions are ideally the right small thing, just what is psychologically needed for a specific person in a specific time and place to set them on a better path.

When Walton and I published these results, they caused a stir, with some researchers doubting our findings. But under the lead of Walton and two other social psychologists, David Yeager and Shannon Brady, this intervention has since been administered to students at roughly forty colleges and universities nationwide, with the results strongly replicated. These collective interventions have resulted in a 13-percentage-point increase in full-time college enrollment among poor urban youth admitted to college and a 35 percent decrease in the achievement gap between students from disadvantaged and advantaged backgrounds. The benefits cut across various sources of disadvantage, not just race but also social class. According to a 2020 report, overweight students, who can struggle with the stigma of obesity, also benefit, not only in terms of higher grades but, because of the link between stress and being overweight, a lower body mass index. Striking benefits have also been seen with women and ethnic minorities in college science courses when they share their stories with one another, closing achievement gaps in both course grades and persistence in the science track.

The intervention is not aimed at helping only people from disadvantaged and minority groups. It's a general-purpose intervention for anyone struggling with uncertainty about whether they belong.

Take, for example, that life stage that is defined by belonging uncertainty: adolescence. Too many kids take a bad turn at this age, seeking esteem and belonging by engaging in reckless behavior with peers. When we gave the intervention to middle school students, using a fresh batch of stories that we collected from older, seasoned teenagers, it had comparable positive effects. Even more impressive results were found by Geoffrey Borman and his team, who tested the social-belonging intervention in an entire school district, not once but twice, in two experiments at two different districts with over a thousand students each across seven to eleven separate schools. The intervention increased sixth and seventh graders' GPA and reduced disciplinary incidents and absences; and this was true for students from all ethnic groups. Compared to a control group, students who had completed the intervention felt a stronger sense of belonging in school, trusted their teachers more, and wanted to succeed in school more, effects that persisted through the full academic calendar. On the whole, literally hundreds of absences and disciplinary infractions were prevented because of the intervention (the researchers estimate 545 and 507, respectively). A similar intervention improved the academic persistence of Middle Eastern refugees living in Europe.

The social-belonging intervention can also help employees as they take on a new job. A few years ago, Walton and I were approached by Google and asked to consult with them in creating a similar intervention addressing belonging uncertainty for women at the company. We did. Although we didn't get to review the data ourselves, Google informed us that while the company's internal research showed new female employees tended to lose job morale over their first nine months at Google and new male employees did not, instituting the intervention erased the morale decline among female employees.

Wise interventions are only tools for situation-crafting. They are far from cure-alls. None of them is a one-off solution that can protect an individual from a hailstorm of harsh treatment, bias, and discrimination. But in an environment with genuine opportunity, they tend to have cumulative effects because they help people to see the situations they encounter as offering them more opportunity to exercise their talents, to build positive relationships, and to receive support and respect than they had expected before. These interventions can set in motion a virtuous cycle of positive reinforcement, helping people to progressively strengthen and protect their sense of belonging long after the intervention has ended. In fact, we see this virtuous cycle in many studies of wise interventions, especially when they meet the requirements of the three Ts of situation-crafting: The right psychological message (tailoring) is given to the right person or persons (targeting) at the right time (timeliness). Under these conditions, a wise intervention will be more likely to make an authentic connection with people's lives.

The metaphor of protecting individuals against inclement weather remains useful. We can do much to shield people from the adverse situations they face right here, right now. A female director of a major Silicon Valley firm told me about her early days as she rose in the ranks of a large technology firm. Having read some of my articles, she commented, "Your research is the story of my life." She described one experience that she believed had made a big difference in the direction of her career. She was about to give a presentation to shareholders. It felt like a make-or-break moment in her career. She was well aware of the fact that she was one of only a few rising female leaders in the industry at the time, which amplified her stress and doubts about belonging. As she awaited her introduction, the CEO walked up to her, looked her in the eyes, and said, "You are changing this company." Though only five words, they were powerful, she said.

The CEO's comment, the charette for C. P. Ellis, Lewin's small groups for kids and homemakers, the social-belonging intervention for students and employees—all of them shaped situations, just a little bit but in a powerful way, to make them less threatening and more inclusive, allowing people from varied walks of life to feel they were more appreciated, respected, and able to contribute. These and other wise interventions help people to realize the potential already present in themselves and their environment. Sometimes you can change aspects of the physical context to foster belonging, sometimes not. But as we'll continue to explore, you can almost always help people to apply a new mental lens to their situation so that it is less threatening to their sense of belonging.

Part Two

Causes
and Cures

Chapter 3

The Pernicious Power of Us vs. Them

Why We Seek Belonging by Excluding Others

PAIGE WAS ONE OF A SMALL HANDFUL OF JEWISH STUDENTS in her class. She was excited to have been admitted to a select magnet school in the ninth grade. But soon after she had joined in 2016, two male classmates perpetrated an anti-Semitic stunt. One took a photo of the other lying on a beach with the words "I h8 Jews" written in the sand in front of him. They texted the photo to a group of classmates, including Paige. When Paige saw the photo, she tossed her phone down in disgust. After her parents looked to see what had upset her, they reported the photo to the school's principal.

Paige had seen other signs of anti-Semitism at the school. Swastikas were drawn on some classmates' notebooks. She had overheard students calling a teacher an "obnoxious Jew." One group of classmates had made a display of reading Hitler's *Mein Kampf* in the cafeteria at lunchtime. Some had told derogatory jokes about Jews with Paige present. In response to the "I h8 Jews" photo, one student had commented that it would make a great cover photo for the yearbook. Anti-Semitism seemed to be not a matter of an aura emanating subtly around the school, as Tobias Wolff described in *Old School*, but something of a fad.

The principal took some disciplinary action against the two boys, but, as the *New York Times* reported, other types of efforts that might have addressed the larger issue of anti-Semitism in the student culture weren't undertaken. No schoolwide convocation was held, and none of the proven interventions to reduce bullying and prejudice, which we'll discuss, was tried. Before the incident, the school leadership seems to have taken the laissez-faire approach that Lewin showed can lead to havoc, and the situation became increasingly distressing for Paige. The leadership may have seen the problem as one of a few miscreants—subscribing to the "bad apple" theory—rather than one of social climate. Paige's friends reportedly disowned her, and other classmates shunned her, saying they were offended that she'd taken offense. It was just a joke, they said, and she had overreacted. She had also broken a social code held by the students: You don't "snitch" to adults. They closed ranks to exclude her.

As with many conflicts, this one escalated—at first slowly as Paige's parents sought a response from the school, but then heating up as the school did little and her parents decided to sue. The state attorney general's office conducted an investigation. As press coverage went national, the college admissions of the two boys were rescinded. As for Paige, she said of her school, "I knew I didn't belong there." She moved to a new school the next year. Parties on both sides were left with regret and confusion about how things had become so inflamed.

As I read about this incident, I thought about how the students' callous display of anti-Semitism highlights a paradox in us. We are given to excluding in order to feel included—or, as Peter Gabriel put it in his song "Not One of Us," "How can we be in, if there is no outside?" It seems that expressing anti-Semitism had become "cool" at this school, a means of earning social currency and belonging. If the students who objected to Paige's response are to be taken at their word that they didn't harbor anti-Semitic beliefs, then they seem to have been motivated by a desire to conform to the norms of belonging that were prevalent among their peers. That desire, a large body of research in social psychology shows, is at the root of a great deal of the Us-vs.-Them behavior that causes much harm.

+ + + +

GIVEN THE WARS, GENOCIDES, and other violent flare-ups that blemish so much of human history, it's easy to think people are innately driven to break up the world into an Us and a Them and to demean, attack, and kill those they see as one of Them. Thomas Hobbes likened social life to a "war of all against all." Sigmund Freud argued that beneath the tip of the iceberg of human consciousness lies a roiling id in the unconscious mind. Subscribing to these notions, the hero of the science fiction film classic *Forbidden Planet* beseeches his nemesis, an overzealous scientist with an outsized faith in the powers of reason, "All men are monsters in their subconscious minds, Dr. Morbius." The main role of social norms and laws from this perspective is to curb our harmful innate impulses.

More recently, evolutionary biologists have argued that we've been bred by natural selection to form ourselves into groups and to instinctively see those we perceive to be outside our group as threatening. Biologist Robert Sapolsky links aggression to the amygdala, a deep brain structure that is involved in the processing of threat. "From massive, breathtaking barbarity to countless pinpricks of microaggression," he writes in his fascinating book *Behave*, "Us versus Them has produced oceans of pain. Yet our generic goal is not to 'cure' us of Us/Them dichotomizing. It can't be done, unless your amygdala is destroyed, in which case everyone seems like a Them." He goes on to describe how our "brains form Us/Them dichotomies . . . with stunning speed." Even a "fifty-milliseconds exposure to the face of someone of another race activates the amygdala."

One of the often-cited sources of evidence to support the contention of a basic impulse to create Us-vs.-Them dichotomies is a 1971 study by the Polish psychologist Henri Tajfel, a Jew who had fought in World War II as a French army soldier and had been taken prisoner by the Nazis. He wanted to understand how people could be capable of such abhorrent fidelity to a group as the Nazi persecutors had displayed.

To look for answers, he devised a rarefied petri dish of a situation in which study participants would be under no compelling social pressure to align into groups. The purpose was to see if the impulse to ally with a group was so strong that it would arise even when the groups were based on arbitrary and meaningless distinctions: In the situation Tajfel created, there was no history of conflict between the groups, no interaction within or between the groups, and no self-interest or other objective reason to favor one's group over the other.

Tajfel brought fourteen- and fifteen-year-old boys from a suburban public high school in Bristol, England, to his laboratory. They were told that the experimenter running the study was investigating the humdrum topic of how people form judgments. In one of a series of supposed judgment tasks given in different studies, grids of dots flashed up on a screen and then disappeared. The boys were asked to guess the number of dots, writing their answers down confidentially. After that, they were broken into two groups, and they were told they were being divided according to the answers they had given. An assessment of their answers, they were told, had supposedly shown that some of them consistently underestimated the number of dots, while others consistently overestimated them. The boys were also told that this was the basis of their division into the two groups: underestimators and overestimators. After being escorted to a private cubicle, each boy was told to which group he belonged. Vital to the design of the study was that the boys were also told that neither group was more accurate overall. Tajfel wanted them to think that there was no objective basis to take pride in their group. Unbeknownst to the boys, they were assigned to the two groups on a random basis.

Yet when the boys were then asked to privately allocate monetary rewards and punishments to the others—on an entirely anonymous basis, knowing only the other boys' group membership—the boys tended to award more money to those in their own group. For some participants, the favoritism bordered on the perverse. When given the option for both groups to get substantially more money overall, but for their own group to get a little less than the other group, they preferred a second option: for both groups to get less money overall but for their group to get more than the other. The boys were willing to sacrifice extra money just so the artificially constructed "others" wouldn't get more.

Many subsequent studies have replicated the results, with variations in the situational setup. Inspired by this research, I once asked my five-year-old daughter if she'd prefer to get $5 for her and $10 for her brother, or $1 for her and 50 cents for her brother. Without pause, she chose the second. (Many years later, having studied biology, she said that her frontal cortex had been insufficiently developed to suppress her amygdaloid instincts.)

Tajfel referred to such arbitrary groupings as "minimal groups" because they're based on only a sliver of rationale for allegiance, if that. A more recent study in this area, conducted in 2011 by Yarrow Dunham and his colleagues, showed favoritism toward one's minimal group even among children as young as five years old. In addition to showing bias in the allocation of the prizes, the children reported that they liked the members of the group they were assigned to more than the children in the other group. Research with adults showed that participants scored those in their group higher on a number of virtuous qualities, including being understanding and responsible.

A key finding from this research is that people assigned to minimal groups not only favor their own group but deem those in their group as being like themselves in a wide range of characteristics. Their ratings of other group members on a number of characteristics—those that have nothing to do with the rationale that the participants are given for dividing the groups—correlate relatively highly with their ratings of themselves. It's as if people think to some extent, "My group is an extension of me."

Our willingness to seize on even arbitrary Us-vs.-Them distinctions seems like a psychological reflex. It makes us vulnerable to manipulation by those who would profit from dividing the world into arbitrary groups. Regardless of whether the reflex is learned or innate, the research seems to paint a pessimistic picture of our ability to act with grace and compassion across group divides. But if that's true, how do we explain stories like this one?

In 2007, Wesley Autrey, an African American construction worker in New York City, was standing on a subway station platform with his two young daughters when a white man nearby convulsed in a seizure and fell onto the tracks. The headlights of an incoming train were fast approaching. Autrey immediately dove onto the tracks to help the stranger, landing next to him. As the profile of Autrey in *Time*'s annual list of "100 Most Influential People" reported, "He realized there might be a chance of survival if he could keep the man still until the train passed. It passed over them with inches to spare, so close that there was grease on Autrey's cap from the train. . . . It was an astonishing act of bravery and selflessness." Autrey was dubbed the "Subway Superhero."

That a man would snap into action so swiftly to risk his life for a stranger, and one from a racial group with members who have historically oppressed his own, demonstrates that far from being simply "programmed" to vilify "the other," we are also capable of seeing one another's humanity and impulsively helping strangers, even ones the culture has encouraged us to see as other.

Many heroes who helped other people at great peril to themselves say they leapt into action without thought, according to research by cognitive scientist David Rand. The impulse was so strong that many say they had no choice. Elizabeth Midlarsky of Teacher's College at Columbia University and her colleagues reported on one moving example from an interview with a Polish woman named Maria. She hid thirty Jews in her home as the Nazis slaughtered millions of them in Polish towns. When asked why she did it, Maria said, "Helping to give shelter was the natural thing to do, the human thing. When I looked into those eyes, how could I not care. Of course, I was afraid— always afraid—but there was no choice but to do the only decent thing." The poet and Nobel laureate Czesław Miłosz wrote in *The Captive Mind* that the people who stood up against tyranny and violence in mid-century Europe did so out of a "revolt of the stomach." In our more everyday social decisions, research suggests that cooperation comes to us faster and more spontaneously than does greedy competition.

This impulse to help others seems as much like a psychological reflex as any urge to vilify the "other." We may never know the extent to which this prosocial impulse is learned or ingrained in our genetic makeup. The question may not ultimately matter, because our "nature" is developed through learning that starts from the beginning of life. A series of studies published in 2020 by the psychologists Rodolfo Cortes Barragan, Rechele Brooks, and Andrew Meltzoff found that even infants as young as eighteen months will spontaneously help a stranger seemingly at the expense of their own self-interest.

In one of these studies, infants and their parent are brought to a lab room, one pair at a time. An adult whom the infant has never met sits at a table nearby. The stranger "accidentally" drops a glimmering, aromatic strawberry that falls within reach of the infant. The drama unfolds as scripted: The stranger tries to pick up the strawberry but can't reach it. The infant, watching, knows the adult wants the fruit and now has a choice of whether to give it to the stranger. But a strawberry is a highly tempting treat for an infant; the parents in this study reported it as one of their children's favorite foods. The infants are free to grab and gobble up the fruit, or they can even bring the fruit to their parent. But about 60 percent of the infants do neither: They pick up the strawberry and almost immediately, as if without thought, hand it over to the stranger.

As Barragan explained to me when I pressed him, the experimenters did all they could to set up the situation so that the infants felt they could do as they pleased. In a warm-up session, they had allowed the infants to play with the toys in the room however they wished, with the adult present. Some scholars suggest that this kind of spontaneous, voluntary sharing of immediately edible, highly valued, delectable foods with non-kin is uniquely human. We don't know if it's learned or innate. Regardless, the takeaway is how readily and how early in life giving behavior arises.

Perhaps we are by nature no more Hobbesian brute than caring altruist. As Erving Goffman once quipped, "Universal human nature is not a very human thing." I propose this variation: *Uniform* human nature is not a very human thing. Our nature is different in different situations. What *is* universal is our vast potential to behave in such diverse ways. As the anthropologist Clifford Geertz wrote, "One of the most significant facts about us may finally be that we all begin with the natural equipment to live a thousand kinds of life, but end in the end having lived only one." The key question is not "What is our nature?" but "What are the elements of situations that draw out the better angels of our nature?"

+ + + +

THE GROUP WE BELONG TO or aspire to belong to, our reference group, is one of the most powerful situational influences on us. When we identify with a group, it's as though we're driving with an insistent backseat driver, urging us what to do, where to turn, what to look out for, and how to handle other drivers. Because we want to belong to our group, we have a strong tendency to follow these directives, which are often unspoken, taking the form of norms that we learn the group endorses. Eventually, we may come to internalize and anticipate the strictures of our copilot. A great deal of work in social psychology demonstrates that members of a group feel a strong compunction to conform to the group's expectations. That's especially true when the group has at its disposal means of norm enforcement, and virtually all groups have at least informal methods of keeping group members in line.

Much of what we see as Us-vs.-Them behavior is motivated by our desire to conform to a group—to fit in with and belong to our group. Indeed, while most ordinary individuals are loath to perpetrate violent behavior, many will do so on behalf of a group to which they belong. That doesn't make the behavior less problematic, but, as we will see, it points to some powerful means of changing that behavior, even when the perpetrators seem vicious at heart.

When I read about Paige's experience at her school, I thought of a famous study of conformity, widely known as the Stanford Prison Experiment. It was conducted by my colleague Philip Zimbardo, and I've been fortunate to have access to his original documentation through Stanford University. Although the study has come under criticism in recent years because of the methods he used, I have examined the criticisms and have collected follow-up data from the original participants. I believe that the study, properly understood and viewed in conjunction with other research that we'll examine later, offers useful insights into understanding when and why people conform to a group's expectations of harmful behavior.

The study design was elaborate and is now considered unethical in many respects. It was conducted before the widespread use of institutional review boards, which now review all research for adherence to ethical standards. Reading about the details of the situation-crafting Zimbardo did, I was struck that some of them are generally overlooked in accounts of the study, even those in leading textbooks.

The year was 1971, and Zimbardo had recently joined the Stanford psychology department. He created a mock prison in the basement of the department building and placed an ad in a local newspaper asking for volunteers for a "psychological study of prison life." Subsequent research has suggested that those who would respond to such a request might possess higher levels of aggressiveness, narcissism, and authoritarianism. That does not negate the importance of the findings, I believe, but does indicate that a more truly random group of people might have behaved differently from the way the volunteers in Zimbardo's study did. Twenty-four adult men who responded were then randomly assigned to play the role of either a prisoner or a guard.

The study began with the actual local sheriff going through the motions of arresting the men chosen to be prisoners, in plain sight of their neighbors, family, or friends. They were handcuffed, read their rights, and driven to the police station, where they were fingerprinted and booked. Next they were blindfolded and taken to the department prison. There the prisoners were told to follow a list of rules, which included remaining silent during rest periods, using the lavatory for only five minutes, standing whenever the warden or prison superintendent was present, and obeying "all orders issued by guards at all times." The prisoners wore hospital gowns and were assigned identity numbers; the guards were to refer to each by number, as "Prisoner 416," for example, instead of using names. These were all forms of debasement, meant to deprive the men of what Goffman saw as the situational supports that sustain our sense of self.

As for the guards, they were told that they should maintain "law and order" and "command the respect of the prisoners." They were also instructed to imagine that the prisoners were real threats and that they should be alert about "the possible dangers" posed by them. Zimbardo had done groundbreaking research on deindividuation—the process by which people shed their individual identities and give themselves over to the will of the group—and the experiment was intended in part to reveal the degree to which those who were designated guards would deindividuate in these circumstances. Zimbardo had the guards wear khaki uniforms and sunglasses and carry nightsticks. Meanwhile, he and his research assistants played the role of wardens and other administrative staff. They were authoritarian in style and instructed the guards to perform additional debasement rituals on the prisoners, strip-searching them, delousing them with a spray, and bolting onto their right ankle a heavy chain to be worn at all times. Guards who resisted were subjected to pressure by the wardens. One guard was told "to be a tough guard. . . . You have to be firm and you have to take action." The authoritarian nature of the context in which the guards were operating is often overlooked in much coverage of the study. Authoritarian leadership can turn a situation into a breeding ground for conformity.

Some of the guards went well beyond being tough, acting with outright cruelty. Zimbardo's report notes that after the prisoners rebelled on the second day, the guards "got a fire extinguisher which shot a stream of skin-chilling carbon dioxide and forced the prisoners away from the doors; they broke into each cell, stripped the prisoners naked, took the beds out, forced some of the prisoners who were then the ringleaders into solitary confinement, and generally began to harass and intimidate the prisoners." They had prisoners urinate and defecate in buckets in their cells. One guard became particularly obnoxious, strutting through the barracks and barking orders. He carried out what he later referred to as "little experiments" to "see just what kind of verbal abuse people can take before they start objecting." For example, he said to one prisoner, "Go tell that man [a prisoner] in the face he's the scum of the earth." The guards nicknamed the most brutal of themselves "John Wayne." Some guards instructed the prisoners to engage in degrading, homoerotic rituals, which is why the Stanford Prison Experiment was later referred to in many press articles written about the shameful behavior of American military prison guards at Abu Ghraib during the Iraq War. Zimbardo also testified as an expert witness at the trials of some of these military prison guards.

As for the prisoners, some of them suffered intense distress. One of them was described as experiencing "acute emotional disturbance," which included "disorganized thinking, uncontrollable crying, and rage." Another later said in an interview for a documentary, "I began to feel I was losing my identity. . . . I was 416, I was a number." Several prisoners who suffered severe psychological reactions were "released" early.

In some popular coverage of the study, the guards' behavior is taken to reflect violent, even evil, instincts that were brought out by the situation. Given an opportunity to behave sadistically, some popular interpretations argue, the men who played guards freely and spontaneously chose to do so, thereby revealing the innate horrors of human nature. In other coverage, the participants' behavior is said to show how people spontaneously conform to the social roles they're assigned. However, neither of these views is accurate. The guards' behavior was far from natural or spontaneous. The prison was designed to be what Goffman called a total institution—characterized by authoritarian leadership, social isolation, debasement rituals, dehumanizing social norms, and the absence of clear channels for dissent. When one or all of these elements have not been included in variations on this experiment, outcomes have been different. In one toned-down replication, for example, the prisoners revolted and ascended to dominance. Zimbardo's prison was a precisely crafted "evil" situation.

Critics have also pointed out that the prisoners thought they could not leave, and the ones who were permitted to leave experienced—or pretended to experience, the critics say—emotional or medical crisis. Zimbardo says the prisoners could have left if they had asked. But regardless, what's not in dispute is something equally if not more troubling: Not one of the guards left, even though several later expressed regret for their actions. The most they would have lost for quitting was the $15 daily payment in the study. They saw "following instructions" as a requirement of "the job." Yet they could have quit or rebelled; they weren't under guard themselves. The door to the barracks was unlocked. In a sense, the prison was their own minds.

After the study ended, some of the guards said they had been cruel because they were playacting. Zimbardo disputes their assertions, and we can't know for sure what was going on in their minds. This ambiguity happens as well, of course, in life outside of such crafted situations. Were Paige's schoolmates only joking? Again, we can't know. But what we do know is that whether or not they were only playacting, they, like the guards in the study, caused real harm. "It harms me," one of the former prisoners said to a guard in a post-study interview, clarifying that he meant it in the "present tense." The guard, dubious, asks why. The former prisoner responds, because "I know what you can turn into."

In our lives, the roles we either freely choose to play—or are pressured to play—take on a reality. We to a large degree become our roles—at least in the eyes of those subjected to our behavior.

Whether the students who tormented Paige meant to cause harm or not, whether they freely conformed with the anti-Semitism norm or felt coerced to, they caused harm. The story of Paige's experience and the Stanford Prison Experiment are cautionary tales about the powerful desire we humans have to conform to what's expected of us, especially in settings and institutions that entangle us in a web of social pressures. We may, eventually, even lose our sense of who we "really are" when we conform to roles that are not in keeping with our ideals and desires.

Christopher Browning, a historian and an esteemed specialist on the Holocaust, in his analysis of a German police battalion that killed thousands of Jews on behalf of the Nazis, describes them as "ordinary men" leading middle-class lives: tailors, gardeners, and salesmen in their twenties and thirties, many with wives and children. When these soldiers were informed about the plans for the first mass shooting, the older men were told that any of them "could step out" if they "did not feel up to the task." Of the five hundred officers, only twelve left. Why? Along with the confusion and ambiguity of the situation, Browning writes that their participation was due to "the pressure for conformity—the basic identification of men in uniform with their comrades and the strong urge not to separate themselves from the group by stepping out." In an altogether different context, the writer James Baldwin described the racism that Americans passively watched inflicted on their fellow citizens of color: "A civilization is not destroyed by wicked people," for "it is not necessary that people be wicked but only that they be spineless."

A takeaway is that we should all be aware of how the groups we align ourselves with may be exercising influence over us. Kurt Vonnegut captured this lesson in his introduction to *Mother Night*, a novel about an American spy who survives in Germany by posing as a Nazi propagandist but who plays his role with zeal and creativity. In the end, as he awaits sentencing in an Israeli court, he concludes that his crimes against humanity were more fundamentally "crimes against himself." Vonnegut writes that the moral of the story is, "We are what we pretend to be, so we must be very careful what we pretend to be."

I was reminded of Vonnegut's passage in 2018, twenty-seven years after the original Stanford Prison Experiment. My team had sent a follow-up survey to all the former participants we could track down. Asked what he had learned about himself, one former guard wrote, "I had done what was expected of me, instead of staying true to myself."

This is not to say that it's inevitable that everyone in a coercive situation will "lose themselves." It's a testament to the human spirit that some of us can retain our sense of self even in situations that deprive us of all supports. Even Jews in concentration camps, stripped of all material possessions and in the most fearsome of circumstances, made little mezuzahs and other tiny religious ornaments out of odds and ends. Such small acts in which we reconnect with our values and our sense of self actually do more good than we often realize, helping us to resist harmful social norms and stereotypes.

Who we are—whether monster or do-gooder—depends to a surprising degree on *where* we are: the *situation* we're in, which has often been crafted for us before we arrive. As Paige's experience illustrates, too often the forums in which we spend so much of our time—our schools, offices, playing fields, clubs, and even our homes—exert pressure to conform to harmful behavior, as though a force field invisibly permeates the air around us, encouraging us to put up barriers between an "us" and a "them." To understand the nature of this force better, I've conducted research to zero in on the kinds of social influence that impel people to commit harmful behavior, even without any coercive pressure.

I EXPECT ALMOST EVERY parent of a teenager is aware of the often subtle but powerful social pressures on their child. I've certainly seen the wear and tear on my own children. In my research, I've studied how the pressure to conform contributes to harmful behavior toward others in order to discover ways to help children, parents, teachers, managers—all of us—resist it. One study, which I conducted with my colleague Mitch Prinstein, shined light on how teens are susceptible to "going along" in order to belong, as well as on which teens are at greater risk.

We conducted the study in the early 2000s. At the time, Prinstein was often likened by his students to the actor Matthew Broderick, who played Ferris Bueller in the famous John Hughes movie. Prinstein had the same carefree spirit, which made him among the most popular teachers at Yale. His experience in high school, I suspect, was much different from mine. Growing up as a quiet kid in New Jersey in the 1980s, I got bullied and belittled, and, as is often the case, I'm ashamed to say, I learned to do the same thing to other kids. Once, I got in a fight with another kid in high school. As I pushed him, I failed to see the pencil sharpener jutting out of the wall behind him. It stabbed his back, and I watched in horror as he keeled over. Then I heard applause, and I turned to discover a large group of my classmates clapping and howling with approval. That was to be the height of my popularity in high school. I felt simultaneously pleased and disgusted with myself, having learned a visceral lesson in how violence could be a means to belong.

Prinstein, I suspect, was one of the "likable" kids he has spent his career studying—the kind of kids who manage to be both cool and kind and bring out the best in their peers. Prinstein and I struck up a few late-night conversations. His interest in teen popularity, which led to his book titled *Popular*, and my interest in belonging combined in a decade-long collaboration. We were both interested in the power of the situation to drive ordinary people to inflict harm. Rather than crafting an extreme "total" situation, we wanted to explore the dynamics of conformity in the daily experiences of teens. We did so through a forum that has since become a major part of their lives—social media.

We focused on high school students and designed our study according to strict ethical standards. All of the students involved, and their guardians, were told that their participation was voluntary and they could quit at any time. Their guardians, informed of the nature of the study, signed permission slips for their participation. We also assured the participants that any distress they experienced would be no more intense than is typical of the emotions the students go through in their regular lives. Prinstein and I watched carefully for any signs of more extreme distress and were ready to intervene should any occur. We also had to withhold the purpose of the study from the students so that we could observe how they naturally responded. Once people know that you're studying conformity, they take care not to conform. But after the study was done, we explained our rationale for the research to the students. We then asked them to write down their thoughts about the experience. Not one student complained. Virtually all expressed enthusiasm about the study, with many students also saying they had learned something valuable from their participation. Participants left the study not only "whole," I think, but wiser.

Here is how our study went. We recruited a group of eleventh-grade boys at a suburban school who were broadly representative of the entire male student body. At the beginning of the year, we made three assessments. First, the kids self-assessed how antisocial or "deviant" they were. You might call this a measure of "Hobbesian" personality. The kids rated, confidentially, how much they got into fights, damaged property, carried weapons, stole, did drugs, and drank alcohol. Second, to supplement this measure, we also assessed each boy's reputation among his peers, using what is called a peer-nomination procedure, a well-validated, albeit labor-intensive, way to glean students' reputations at their schools. For example, how often were the students described as someone "who says mean things, threatens, or physically hurts others"? We also assessed how much each teen felt uncertain about his belonging, using a measure of social anxiety that asks kids to rate how nervous they get about being rejected by other kids and how much they worry about what other kids think of them.

We wanted to create a situation in which the kids cared about how they were being seen and experienced the social pressures as real. Prinstein and I spent a year crafting a faux online chat room. To my knowledge, ours was the first experiment to investigate what fifteen years later would become a national pandemic: online bullying.

We asked several different groups composed of roughly ten boys to come to the school's computer lab. Each boy sat at his own computer. We told them that several chat rooms were under way at the same time involving other boys in other rooms throughout the school, and that they would each participate in one of these chat rooms without knowing the true identity of the kids taking part. The purpose of the study, we said, was to understand how kids communicate online.

For each of the students, it appeared that four boys logged into the chat room, showing up as anonymous students identified as Participant A, B, C, or D on-screen. In fact, the only participant in the chat room who was real was the student himself, who, in every case, was Participant D. Unbeknownst to the actual participant, the three others were programmed by us with predetermined scripts.

We had crafted information about these three faux participants to make them appear either as all "cool" kids for half the participants in our study or as all unpopular kids for the other half. How? The chat-room instructions requested that, right after logging in, each participant type in his favorite activities, such as "listening to music" or "watching sports," and provide the first names and last initial of their three best friends at the school. Their answers were displayed on-screen. For the first group of participants, the activities and best friends listed in each of the three faux participants' response boxes suggested they were "cool." For the second group, the answers suggested these three faux participants were less popular, some being "geeks." We based the answers about their favorite activities on ones stereotypically considered cool, such as "playing sports," "going to parties," and "listening to hip hop," or ones stereotypically uncool, such as "working with computers" and "reading." We reinforced the impression that the faux participants were either cool or uncool by giving their friends first names and initials that corresponded to members of the "cool" or "uncool" cliques at the school.

Prinstein and I had programmed a series of questions for the participants in the chat room to answer, with all the participants' answers displayed publicly on-screen. The questions were crafted to measure how strongly the actual student, Participant D, would endorse harmful, even violent, responses to various social situations. For instance, one social situation presented in the chat room was being out with friends when one of them starts to vandalize a building. What, the chat room prompt asked, would the participants do? We provided a range of responses that the four chat-room members were asked to choose from, such as, for that particular situation, "tell your friend to stop" or "join in." Another situation was that a student who is "kind of a loser" says hi as you pass him in the hall, with answers ranging from "say hi back" to "push the kid and knock his books over."

The faux participants gave their responses first, one at a time, and, again, with their answers publicly displayed ostensibly for all to see. We programmed Participant A to select the most antisocial answer, Participant B to give the same answer, and Participant C to select a slightly less antisocial option.

As we had hypothesized, the boys who thought they were in the company of the cool students gave more antisocial responses than those who thought they were in the company of uncool students. These results reinforced the theory in social psychology that groups with higher social status—ones we are more likely to see as a reference group—exercise more conformity pressure than lower-status groups do. In fact, the perceived high status of the participants in the chat room mattered three times more in how students answered than anything in the profiles of the boys' behavioral history or reputation we had compiled. The "bad apple" theory of human behavior suggests that it would be the "bad" or "Hobbesian" kids who would give the most antisocial answers. While the students who had a history of antisocial behavior did give more antisocial responses, the social pressure to conform to high-status peers mattered much more than that. From a potential victim's perspective, it would be far better to be in the company of a "nasty" kid under weak social pressure to bully than a nice kid under strong social pressure to bully.

Of course, how students answered the questions might not reflect how they would actually behave. So Prinstein and I included a last exercise to test how they would act, choosing to see whether they would opt to exclude one of the participants from the chat room. We knew that feeling excluded is one of the most painful experiences in teens' lives, often at the root of depression and even suicide. In this last round of soliciting answers from participants, we started with having Participant A answer another question about personal interests and had him give some uncool responses, such as "spending time with my parents." The chat-room instructions then stated that participants could vote someone out of the chat room but that three of the four of them had to agree on whom. The instructions emphasized they didn't have to vote anyone out if they didn't want to. Participant A was programmed to vote to exclude no one, but both Participants B and C voted to exclude A. The actual participant cast the deciding vote. Of the students with the uncool faux participants, 52 percent voted to exclude A, while of the students with the cool faux participants, 86 percent voted to exclude him. The impulse to conform to antisocial answers was matched by an impulse to conform to antisocial actions.

Finally, Prinstein and I measured whether the students would now truly subscribe to the views they had conformed to. In other words, were they merely playacting, or had they internalized high-status peers' answers as their own? To assess this, we asked the students to log off of the chat room and then give responses to the same social situations we had presented earlier—but this time in private, as a chance "to rethink your answers in case you weren't sure the first time." No one, we assured them, would ever see their individual responses to these new questions. They were instructed to "feel free to give a different response" from the ones they had given earlier. Still, most of them didn't change their answers. For those with the cool faux participants, what "*they* believe" seemed to have become what "*I* believe." This was a striking testament to how powerfully our views can be shaped by the views of a group we want to conform to and ideally belong in. We often rationalize our conformity by changing our own attitudes to bring them in line with our public behavior. We may even adopt harmful beliefs to justify ourselves. (As I mentioned, Prinstein and I thoroughly debriefed participants at the end of the study, and re-surveying them later revealed that we had erased these effects on expressed attitudes.)

Who was most vulnerable to this exclusionary conformity? It wasn't the kids with a history of bullying and bad behavior at their school. It was the kids who at baseline expressed the greatest uncertainty about whether they belonged and the biggest fear of being rejected by classmates.

We don't usually think that a vulnerability to feeling excluded is a risk factor for harmful behavior. Imagine being a teacher or parent confronted with a teen who has harmed or bullied other kids.

We might diagnose the teen as lacking sensitivity, ethics, or compassion, leading us to prescribe a remedy to repair the deficit, perhaps through punishment or moral persuasion. However, these solutions would be unlikely to remedy what may be the real cause of the harmful behavior—belonging uncertainty and the conformity it provokes. The solutions might even aggravate the problem.

Many years after Prinstein and I ran this study, I had an experience as a father that reminded me of the predicament we had placed our participants in and the power of situations to lead us to stray from our principles. My thirteen-year-old son had just done something regrettable with some other boys. Nothing outlandish, but something that he and I both knew deviated from his own principles. I asked him why he did it. He didn't even like the other boys much. One of the best parts of being a parent is when your child tells you something straight from the heart. Looking at the floor, he said, "Sometimes I care more about my ego than about myself." As we talked more about why he had taken part, it was clear he'd been motivated by wanting to belong.

Comparing the bullying of high school kids to the behavior of abusive prison guards and Nazi police may seem extreme, but it's important to understand that there is an underlying connection to the desire to belong. Just how strong a role the need to belong plays in hurtful Us-vs.-Them behavior, and in strategies to remedy it, has been demonstrated with some of the most extreme practitioners—hate groups.

THE REASONS PEOPLE JOIN violent extremist groups are complex, and their paths into the groups vary widely. Some are indoctrinated into their hateful beliefs early in life by their parents. Others drift into the groups of their own volition, often through participation in a vast online propaganda and recruitment network. Still others are targeted by recruiters who befriend them. No predominant personality type has been identified as most likely to join, and few who join suffer from mental illness. Multiple childhood traumas and a lack of educational attainment or economic opportunity can contribute, but these factors are far from determinative. As one of the leading researchers of supremacist groups, Peter Simi, who spent seven years living among them, says, "The folks attracted to these types of groups are a much broader cross-section than we'd often like to admit." He added, "What we see from the data is a lot of different kinds of folks get involved in these groups. The most educated person can be susceptible." One commonality, however, is that many are seeking to bolster their sense of belonging to a community, and they don't truly subscribe, at least at first, to the group's extremist beliefs. Arie Kruglanski, a pioneer of research into the psychology of extremists and the author of two books on the topic, writes that "extremist groups supply individuals with a strong sense of in-group belongingness."

Kruglanski interviewed a former member of a neo-Nazi group, Christian Picciolini. Picciolini went on to form an antiextremism organization, the Free Radicals Project, focused on why people join hate groups and helping them to leave. Picciolini's story echoes much of the psychological research. He said in a talk that former extremists "will all tell you the same thing": They became extremists "not because of dogma or ideology" but "because they wanted to belong." James Baldwin likewise expressed the desperate allure of attaining a sense of security by conforming with racism. Some people have been "raised to believe" that "no matter how terrible their lives may be," there's one bit of knowledge that consoles them like "a heavenly revelation: At least, they are not black."

Picciolini conformed to white supremacist dogma out of feelings of rejection. He recounts that he felt socially isolated as a kid and neglected by his parents. They were Italian immigrants who ran their own small business in Chicago and were hardly ever at home. They also moved the family out of a community of Italian immigrants when he was young to one in which he felt like an outsider. An introvert who found making friends difficult, Picciolini was frequently bullied at school. When he was fourteen, he was recruited by the founder of Chicago Area Skinheads, Clark Martel, who lured him in by first boosting his pride in his heritage. As Picciolini recalls, Martel told him, "You're

Italian, you should be proud of that." He also told him that by joining he would "go from this lonely person who didn't have any friends
to somebody who would have to be respected and revered." Picciolini
recounts, "He had offered me a lifeline." He says "belonging and respect
from peers were very important to me," so much so that he went along
with the hateful propaganda Martel fed him about Jews and black people, even though he says that he "questioned the ideology every day,"
but "internally, of course, because in that environment I couldn't ver-
balize it. . . . You didn't want to seem vulnerable." His thoughts about
the allure of the group match those of many other former members, as
shown in Kruglanski's research.

According to Kruglanski, joining an extremist group is often motivated by a loss, or a threat of loss, to belonging. Members often report
experiences of humiliation before joining, such as being arbitrarily
stopped at checkpoints, which strips them of their social worth. They
might have had high hopes for a career but then perceived few paths
open for achieving success, feeling marginalized and cut off from the
opportunities they believe they're entitled to. What is also relatively
common is that recruits have been abandoned by their family or at
least feel they have been. Many also believe that they and people like
them are losing their power and rightful position in their society. Both
real and perceived indignities like these are interpreted as unfairness,
which makes people feel excluded.

When people feel excluded, they tend to become more aggressive
toward—or supportive of violence against—those they feel excluded
by. They also become emotionally numbed to the hurt caused by the
violence they perpetrate or support. Kruglanski has given surveys to
people living in tumultuous geopolitical contexts throughout the world
and consistently finds that those who feel that they or their group has
been subjected to prolonged exclusion or humiliation express more
support for violence. Experiments led by my colleague Peter Belmi
recruited Americans from a wide range of social groups and asked
them to imagine or recall an experience in which they felt devalued
because of their membership in a group. They expressed more sup-

port for stealing, vandalizing, and other antisocial behaviors directed at workplaces, schools, and other mainstream institutions compared with participants in a control group. When they were asked to take a test and report their score, they cheated more.

Critically, the threat to social belonging need not be experienced personally. It can also be felt on behalf of others in one's group. Many Islamic terrorists come from wealthy families, and a disproportionate number are well educated. But they see their fellow Muslims losing power in an increasingly secular world and being subjected to persecution, with limited opportunities for education and employment and a lack of access to political power.

A relationship between feeling that one's social worth or that of one's group is being demeaned on the one hand, and antagonism against other social groups on the other, was also suggested in a study conducted by the political scientists J. Eric Oliver and Tali Mendelberg. They wanted to identify the predictors of hateful beliefs in the United States. They discovered that racism, anti-Semitism, and authoritarian beliefs about the need to preserve power hierarchies were clustered by zip code. The researchers further found that the number of those professing these beliefs was highest in zip codes with the highest percentage of residents without a college degree. Whether an individual was liberal or conservative, their degree of political knowledge, and their level of income were all lesser factors. While more research is required to provide a definitive explanation of why prejudice takes root in such areas, converging evidence suggests that many of those lacking a college degree in the United States feel disrespected and left behind in the modern economy. The lack of a college degree is, in fact, among the strongest predictors of feelings of alienation and despair in our country. (Of course, plenty of prejudice is also found among the educated and well-off.)

What's more, for any given individual surveyed in this study, educational attainment was not as strong a predictor of hateful beliefs as was the percentage of those in the zip code without a college degree. This result points to a troubling aspect of prejudice. It seems to be a form of social contagion. The more people in the area we live in who endorse prejudice, the more likely we are to adopt it as well, which may be another result of a defeated need to belong: It leads people to conform to hateful beliefs. Love may or may not be a social disease, as Bon Jovi sang. But hate is.

Violent extremist groups have learned the power of luring people to join or support them by providing them with a sense of belonging and bolstering their feelings of personal significance. Leaders in these groups also understand that they can enhance their allure by intensifying people's grievances with cognitive poison: hateful ideologies that explain "our" suffering in terms of "their" actions. These ideologies often frame the struggle as a historic battle of "good versus evil," a potent strategy for mobilizing violence. Research suggests that when we think our side is the side of virtue and reason and the other side is that of evil and irrationality, we favor militant action against "them" rather than communication and negotiation.

Further exploiting vulnerable people's desire to belong, extremist groups often portray committing acts of terror as a path to virtue, as well as an opportunity to do something meaningful, even historic, for the cause. Kruglanski told me this aspect of the ideology gives extremists a mental "permission slip" to be angry and violent. And once members have perpetrated violence, they tend to justify their actions by subscribing more strongly to the beliefs of the group, which in turn makes it easier to hurt or kill again. Eventually they may internalize the ideology as part of their identity. The "psyche-logic" behind terrorism explains why presenting group members with logical arguments and evidence is largely ineffective in getting them to abandon these groups and often fuels deeper commitment. It's not about logic.

The importance of hate groups offering a sense of belonging is also showcased by research into how white supremacist group members react when another member reveals that his own DNA doesn't meet the supremacist standard for "whiteness." Researchers Aaron Panofsky and Joan Donovan pored through postings from 2004 to 2016 on one hate site, Stormfront, which describes itself as "the voice of the new, embattled white minority." They identified 639 cases of people reporting the results of genetic ancestry tests they'd taken, many of which indicated the poster's genetic mix was far from the ideal they had in mind.

Why would people post results that would seem to exclude them from the group? Most were looking for reassurance that they still belonged. For example, one posted, "I received my results today, and I am 58% European, 29% Native American and 13% Middle Eastern. I am pretty sure Middle Eastern is Caucasian too, as well as European, so it means I am 71% Caucasian?" In response, fewer than 5 percent of the more than two thousand comments shamed or excluded the poster or assaulted him for not being truly white. Over a thousand of the comments directly or indirectly reassured the poster of his whiteness. Some commentators made scientific criticisms of the tests. Others offered comforting rationalizations. They argued that the testing companies can't be trusted because they're run by liberals and Jews. Still others just provided support with no rationale. "I wouldn't worry about it," one wrote. "When you look in the mirror, do you see a Jew? If not, you're good." Much of the intent of the responses in the 639 cases they examined, the researchers report, was to offer "permission to remain white."

The way to reach members of hate groups, Christian Picciolini suggests, is to offer them an alternative source of belonging. Research suggests that violent extremist groups have an Achilles' heel in this regard. The groups are often based on authoritarian leadership and a "you're either with us or against us" mentality. They're filled with back-stabbing and infighting. The belonging that these organizations provide is not authentic but conditional on people's conformity. Picciolini recounts that he decided to renounce white supremacy not because of any scientific or logical arguments but because in his work as a music store clerk, he had regular positive interactions with minority customers, and he preferred their acceptance of him to the ugliness of his Skinhead experience.

Many of the successful deradicalization programs, as reviewed by Kruglanski, incorporate the power of providing a new source of belonging. They change terrorists' views by fostering their attachments to family, community, and meaningful work. Many offer vocational programs and involve the detainees' families and community leaders. The United States devised just such a program late in the Second Gulf War, with only a small fraction of tens of thousands of detainees ever being rearrested.

Terrorism expert Bruce Hoffman, whose book *Inside Terrorism* is widely used in courses and trainings about combating terrorism, tells the story of how a tactic deradicalized members of the vicious Black September terrorist group, which was on a rampage in the early 1970s. They had assassinated Jordan's prime minister in 1971, with one of the killers lapping up his blood as it oozed from his body. Then they murdered twelve Israeli athletes in the 1972 Olympics. But only two years later, the group had been silently dismantled, without incident. Not one of the assassins had been imprisoned or killed. How did this happen? The Palestinian Liberation Organization (PLO), wanting to be taken seriously as a political force rather than be associated with terrorism, crafted a secret mission to peacefully resolve the situation, one that illustrates the power of providing extremists with an alternative source of belonging.

First, their agents scoured the Middle East for beautiful single women. Then they held a "PLO version of a college mixer" for the hundred or so men from Black September. The men were then told that if they married, they would get $3,000, equivalent to roughly $15,000 today; a steady job; and an apartment in Beirut with a gas stove, a refrigerator, and a color TV. If they had a baby within a year, they would get a $5,000 bonus.

Without exception, each of the men married, settled down, and became a law-abiding citizen. When invited to travel to another country by the PLO, which would entail the risk of imprisonment, none accepted. The men had new roles, as husbands and fathers; a new reference group, their family and work colleagues; new sources of self-affirmation as providers; and new lives with new opportunities.

Obviously, to suggest that terrorism and violence in the Middle East will be solved by a series of mixers would be grossly naive. The beliefs and resentments inciting the conflict are many and run deep. What's more, sometimes punitive measures may be needed, if not as part of the solution, as a means to restore justice for the victims and their families who have been caused so much pain. Another caveat is that we don't know how the women in this story experienced the situation and how much say they had. But, as Hoffman writes, the lesson of the story isn't about any specific intervention but about how "clever, creative thinking can sometimes achieve unimaginable ends." The research and the story of the PLO's success in this instance lead Hoffman to this contention: Rather than focus on killing terrorists and destroying their organizations, which is the prevailing approach to counterterrorism, "we should perhaps focus at least some of our attention on weaning individuals from violence. It could hardly be any less effective than many of the countermeasures that have long been applied to terrorism—with ephemeral, if not nugatory, results."

One way we can all help in our everyday lives to nurture belonging in those subscribing to hateful beliefs is by suspending our judgment of them and engaging in open-minded, curious conversation with them. The psychologist Marshall Rosenberg pioneered the art of engaging in difficult conversations with people seen as racist, sexist, anti-Semitic, and xenophobic. Illustrating the potential for productive interaction, he recounts that one day, on a cab ride to the airport, his driver murmured, "These kikes get up early in the morning so they can screw everybody out of their money." Rosenberg, who is Jewish, was livid, but he took a few deep breaths and asked his driver why he felt so frustrated. The man, Rosenberg writes, unloaded stories of his sadness and pain. After ten minutes of being heard, the cab driver abruptly stopped. He felt listened to. It was only then that Rosenberg gave his point of view, including his feelings about the harm and anger that the driver's words had caused him. As Rosenberg talked, he made clear that he was not trying to cast blame, which would just put the driver on the defensive, but was only trying to help him understand the situation as Rosenberg experienced it.

Rosenberg sums up the wisdom he has picked up over years of hard conversations: "When my consciousness is focused on another human being's feelings and needs, I see the universality of our experience. I had a major conflict with what went on in his head, but I've learned that I enjoy human beings more if I don't hear what they think. Especially with folks who have his kind of thoughts. I've learned to savor life much more by only hearing what's going on in their hearts and not getting caught up with the stuff in their heads."

Christian Picciolini also attests to the power of such thoughtful listening. He says he changes extremists' views "not by arguing with them, not by debating them, not by even telling them they're wrong." Instead, he patiently asks questions and listens. His willingness to extend kindness and empathy reassures them that he regards them as individuals worthy of his attention and even care. This gives extremists a secure base from which to question their ideology and consider alternatives. He connects them to a new reference group, his staff—many of whom are former extremists themselves—who introduce them to new norms, ideas, and resources for living their lives. The approaches used by Picciolini and Rosenberg also resonate with psychological experiments showing that brief experiences of connection, such as imagining a loved one, reduce intergroup hostility.

+ + + +

TAKING A PUNITIVE APPROACH toward those who profess hateful beliefs or who do harm, though sometimes necessary, can have unintended costs when it is used as the only tool to address the problem—like the anti-Semitism that Paige experienced. It can stoke further division and exacerbate the uncertainty about belonging that may be motivating the behavior.

I was moved by a newspaper article written by a black high school student, Rainier Harris, that spoke to this problem. He described the "casual racism" he experienced attending a selective private school. Though he entered the school with high hopes, he wrote, "even in this high-achieving environment, among peers who are 'supposed to know better,' I have felt constantly diminished." One white student posted a birthday message on social media for a black friend, but in what he thought was an innocent joke, he posted a picture of a different black friend—as if to say in jest, "all black people look alike." That student had also used the N-word with his white classmates. As these and other incidents were reported to the school administration, the offenders were expelled during Harris's sophomore year. Harris told me he thought that was unfortunate. He didn't want other kids kicked out. He wanted them to understand the impact of their behavior and to change. "What I really saw as core," Harris told me, "was trying to reach an understanding of each other and where things had gone wrong." He also knew how devastating expulsion can be to students and their families.

Harris would have preferred that the school take the restorative justice approach to addressing the problem, which Harris had learned about in an after-school program, Youth Justice Board. The organization brings teens together in Lewin-like discussion groups to consider barriers to social justice and strategies to overcome them. At the heart of the approach, says Sean Darling-Hammond, an expert in this area, is the goal to encourage better behavior—not through exclusion but through improved relations. At schools, that means building better relations both among students and between students and staff. The process involves exercises in community-building and in social-emotional skill-building. There are also conversations between offenders and victims, which are led by trusted facilitators who assuage defensiveness and keep the conversation from going off the rails. These efforts have a direct effect on improved relationships between victim and offender. They also have an indirect one, allowing troubled students to increase their potential to form new and deeper connections. Much research suggests that restorative practices, when properly implemented as a schoolwide norm rather than a one-off or occasional special event, have dramatic benefits for students' belonging and behavior and for the culture of the school.

Harris believes the approach would have allowed him to communicate his experience of the painful treatment to broaden his fellow students' awareness of the effects of what they saw as harmless fun. He told me he believed they didn't intend malice. Like Paige's persecutors, they just thought they were being funny.

Underscoring that we can all find ways, individually, to do our own situation-crafting, Harris decided to reach out to one of the expelled students, who had been a friend. He sent a message saying he regretted that things had escalated. In response, the former friend wrote to him, "I'm sorry, Rainier. I didn't realize why what I said was wrong. I didn't know it was racist." The two exchanged more messages, sending each other funny memes and sharing plans about the courses they'd take in their senior year. Later that year, when George Floyd was killed at the hands of police, this friend sent Harris another apology.

Restorative justice is one of a number of approaches that have proved effective in bridging Us-vs.-Them divides, including long-standing ones such as the conflict between Palestinians and Israelis. Some approaches have even eased hostility and mistrust in the aftermath of genocide. My colleagues and I have also developed wise interventions that have shown positive results in bridge-building. We'll explore these solutions in the next chapter, with a focus on a key discovery of social psychology: One of the most effective means of fostering understanding and uniting people who have been in opposition is to rally them around the pursuit of a common purpose.

Chapter 4

Turning Them
into Us

Crafting Situations to
Bridge Group Divides

A COLONY OF RHESUS MACAQUE MONKEYS ON THE TINY island of Cayo Santiago, off the coast of Puerto Rico, grew more closely knit after Hurricane Maria devastated their habitat in 2017. Slamming into Puerto Rico and the surroundings with savage fury, Maria obliterated over half of the island's green vegetation, which provides the monkeys shelter. Thirty-six monkeys were killed. Fortunately, the remaining population of nearly two thousand had plenty of food despite the damage, because the island has for over eighty years been a primate research haven. The monkeys are not native. Four hundred of them were brought from India to the island in 1938 by primatologist Clarence Carpenter so that their social behavior could be studied. After the hurricane, they were well-provisioned with food and water, but they had experienced a great trauma. A group of researchers decided to study how their relations with one another might be affected by the destruction.

Extensive observations had been made through the years of the monkeys' interactions with one another, and the researchers had detailed mappings of the social relations among them. They knew which individuals were related to one another, which were the most sociable with the most connections, and which of them tended to keep more to themselves. In the wake of the hurricane, the monkeys engaged in more social contact with one another, increasing their grooming of one another, a leading form of bonding among many primate species. The monkeys also congregated more closely, sitting nearer one another. Females initiated more contact with males. Monkeys who had the fewest social connections before, and who had kept largely to themselves, changed their behavior the most, forming many more bonds. A particularly fascinating aspect of the findings is that the monkeys focused on building more bonds outside of their kin groups and closest social networks. They focused on expanding their networks rather than intensifying their bonds with those to whom they were already close. As the researchers put it, these monkeys sought "to benefit from broader social integration, rather than focusing on reinforcing relationships" they already had. They did not, in other words, partition themselves off into groups of us and them. They became more unified. What's more, biological anthropologist Michael Platt, who has studied the colony, has found that some of the bonding rituals the monkeys engaged in are strong predictors of health and longevity. In the face of a horrifying threat, they instinctively "knew" that being more closely knit was good for their well-being.

This charming story of social bonding among distant cousins of humans speaks to our primate inclination to come together when facing adversity. We understand, deep in our psyches it seems, that we are all better off when we are more unified. One of the most influential and intriguing social psychology experiments ever conducted drew on this understanding to explore how situation-crafting can either elicit this bonding or drive us apart.

+ + + +

ON A SUNNY MIDSUMMER DAY IN 1954, a bus pulls into a Boy Scout campground in the midst of the densely wooded and mountainous Robbers Cave State Park in eastern Oklahoma. Eleven boys, ranging in age from ten to eleven, file out and are whisked to a cabin they'll be sharing. They unpack and start to get to know one another, and then begin exploring the grounds together. The park is a kid's paradise, with a lake for boating, a creek with a swimming hole, and famous caves to explore, in which Jesse James and his gang had hidden out, giving the park its name. The next day, another bus pulls into the park. Eleven more boys of the same age unload and are directed to a different cabin that's on the other side of a thick forest. Each group has no idea the other group is in the park.

All the boys are from white, Protestant, middle-class families in the Oklahoma City area. None of them has met before. Each group quickly coheres into a well-bonded unit, with some boys given endearing nicknames, such as the ironic "Baby Face" for one of the bigger boys. The two groups express an esprit de corps by naming themselves, one selecting "Rattlers" and the other "Eagles."

Within two weeks, some of them will be crying at night and telling their counselors they want to go home. As is sometimes said of the experience they went through, their lovely summer getaway had become more like the brutal Us-vs.-Them war in William Golding's *Lord of the Flies*.

The experiment was conceived and led by social psychologist Muzafer Sherif. His goal was to correct the prevailing psychological views at the time of the sources of prejudice, which ascribed it variously to early childhood trauma, a Freudian death instinct, displaced aggression, and plain ignorance. No, Sherif thought, the seeds of prejudice lie not in *us* but in the *situation*.

In order to test that contention, Sherif first had to find a way to make these two groups of strangers hostile toward one another. He masterminded a precisely crafted situation. After segregating the two groups, he encouraged bonding within each group with all sorts of activities, such as building campfires, cooking, going on hikes, swimming, and canoeing. Only after the boys had developed a strong sense of camaraderie did they learn that another group of boys was in the park. Almost immediately, the members of both groups began making derogatory comments about the other group, even though they had not yet met.

Next Sherif introduced competition over scarce resources. The two cabins were pitted against one another in a tournament involving a series of contests, including tug-of-war, touch football, baseball games, and a treasure hunt, and the boys were told that only the team that won the most would receive a set of prizes, including a monetary reward. The two groups quickly became hostile toward one another, even labeling the other with nasty, dehumanizing names, like "Dumb Stinkers," "Sneaks," and "Cheats" (harsh for the era). Fights broke out in the mess hall. A norm that group members should engage in this behavior took hold, and a kid's ability to hurl clever insults and plan devious mischief became a badge of honor and source of belonging within his group. The children morphed into what Sherif described as "disturbed, vicious . . . wicked youngsters."

The Rattlers won the tournament and were awarded the prizes, including cash. The Eagles, in anger over their loss, raided the Rattlers' cabin, turning over the beds and shoving mattresses into the rafters. The groups grew so hostile that the boys would opt to skip a movie or a fun outing if they knew the other group would be there. Through all the nastiness, the counselors, who were really assistants to Sherif, per Sherif's instruction, failed to discipline the boys. He wanted the counselors to play a role like that of Kurt Lewin's laissez-faire leaders.

Next, Sherif wanted to test the hypothesis that even such hostile groups would become friendly if the situation were changed to unite them around a common purpose. But first he showed that the usual approaches to fostering understanding between hostile groups were ineffectual, such as a sermon on brotherly love that a pastor gave. The boys applauded the sermon but resumed hostilities. Instead Sherif believed in the power of what he called *superordinate* goals to bring people together. These are tasks that are of high value to both groups and that can't be achieved by either group on its own.

In the last week of the study, Sherif orchestrated a series of faux emergencies for the boys to help with, which they were told required all hands. The boys quickly began getting along. One day they learned that there was a problem with the water pipe that carried their water from a nearby reservoir to the camp's tank, and they needed to fan out to search for what had happened. Another day, when the kids were hungry after a long day, the food delivery truck ran into a ditch, and the only way to pull it out was for all the kids to band together. This they did ironically with the same rope they'd yanked back and forth in tug-of-war. By week's end, all the name-calling and bullying had ended. The groups became so friendly that when the bus taking them back home stopped for refreshments, the Rattlers used their tournament prize money to buy everyone malted milkshakes.

The Robbers Cave study was so elaborately crafted that we might question how accurate a reflection of actual human interrelations it is. But we often find ourselves in situations in our daily lives that pit us against one another in competition over limited resources—with the resources limited, sometimes artificially, because of the policies of those in power. Schools send mixed messages to students, typically preaching the gospel of cooperation and tolerance but then implementing class rankings and honor rolls that implicitly set students against one another. In workplaces, employees are often either expressly or implicitly judged by comparison to one another. Bonus systems and performance appraisals often require managers to assess their team members relative to one another, with employees well aware that they're doing so. In sales teams, people's progress toward goals may even be posted for all to see, with large financial rewards at stake. Scientists compete for publication space in scientific journals, even though much more research could now be published online. American politicians compete in winner-take-all elections, which encourages them to demonize their opponents. At the larger social scale, some working-class white Americans have been encouraged by politicians and media coverage to see immigrants as being in competition with them for a scarce supply of jobs and economic rewards. Some white people see these minorities as gaining political clout and social status at their expense and the jobless getting social welfare, while white people like them are left to fend for themselves. The media and social media stoke these resentments.

Geographic separation also contributes to animosity between groups—be they Trump supporters and opponents, LGBTQ rights advocates and evangelicals who oppose those rights, or pro-choice and pro-life activists—creating what James Baldwin called a "poverty of empathy." A 2021 study found that political segregation has so permeated America that within zip codes, and even within neighborhoods in those zip codes, political microclusters form. So separated are Democrats and Republicans that for the average American voter, fewer than a third of their everyday encounters are with someone who supports the other party. For about twenty-five million voters living in the more urban and rural areas of the United States, only one in ten of their encounters are across party lines. Fewer encounters across lines of difference offer less opportunity to discover the humanity of the other.

Further reinforcing the impact of geographic distance, Xuechunzi Bai and colleagues analyzed the degree to which various locales—countries, states in the United States, universities—stereotyped ethnic groups as inferior. In each case, greater levels of ethnic stereotyping were associated with greater levels of ethnic segregation.

So it seems that one solution to the "poverty of empathy" is to increase social contact, ideally in contexts that foster cooperation. Indeed, one 2020 study of Israeli and Palestinian campers found that social affiliation with one another over three weeks—measured in terms of whether they had been assigned to share a bunk bed, sit at the same dinner table, or participate in the same dialogue groups—virtually wiped out the tendency to form friendships only within their group. Cross-group friendships made at camp, moreover, predict enduring reductions in outgroup prejudice and an interest in peace even a year later.

In our everyday lives, we are free to socialize across boundaries and to share perspectives and information. But the prospect of doing so has come to seem so inconvenient, unpleasant, and threatening that far too few take the trouble to engage in such dialogue. Many of us choose to watch and read almost exclusively the sources of information that support our beliefs and positions, widening the chasms between "Us" and "Them." Our ability to silo ourselves has vastly expanded in the modern era, with online social networks, private schools, and gated communities. In America's individualistic society, extended families are no longer the force they once were, when custom required frequent close contact even when members maintained different lives and viewpoints. It's as though many of us have imposed on ourselves an almost complete social isolation from those we see as outgroups.

But as Sherif inspired bonding by providing the boys with shared goals, we can craft situations to bring people together to work toward common goals. One of the most powerful ways of doing this is by establishing new social norms for group life.

Norms are like the rules of the game of social life. Our lives are saturated with such rules, explicit and implicit, for how to behave toward each other in order to "succeed at the game." Do we believe it's "every man and woman for themselves" or "you can't go it alone"? Goffman analyzed interpersonal encounters in this light. In conversations, for example, you're permitted a range of moves. You take turns, and if you say something useful or funny or clever according to shared norms, you score points. We don't tend to think of our social encounters so explicitly as opportunities for gamesmanship. But we do often act according to what we think the rules—the norms—of a situation are. Even Tajfel's minimal group study—heralded as evidence of our innate proclivity for Us-vs.-Them thinking, as we saw in the last chapter—suggests the power of implied norms: The most ingroup favoritism occurred when the experimental instructions *required* participants to allocate more money to one group than another, thus defining the situation as a zero-sum game.

The dramatic degree to which our behavior can be modified by norms to encourage cooperative behavior was demonstrated in a study by Varda Liberman, Steve Samuels, and Lee Ross. They had people actually play a game, one that's famous in the study of human behavior: the Prisoner's Dilemma. The classic "version" pits two people playing the role of prisoners against one another. They're in separate rooms and can't communicate. Both prisoners are told that if they squeal on the other and the other does not squeal on them, they will go free while the other will remain in prison. But if both of them squeal, neither will be set free. In the study Liberman and colleagues created, two players of a game compete over a pot of money. They have only two options for a given "move," and they are told they'll both make their move at the same time. They can either choose to be selfish and try to grab the whole pot of money, or they can choose to share the pot. If they both go for the grab, they both get nothing. If one goes for the grab and the other opts to share, the grabber gets the whole pot and the sharer ends up with nothing. But if they both opt to share, they each get half the pot. The game gives people incentives to be greedy but reveals that greed is not so good for collective outcomes, as is often the case in social situations and society generally.

With one group of college students, the experimenter offhandedly refers to the contest as the "Wall Street Game" and with another group calls it the "Community Game." In the first group, 71 percent of players went for the grab. In the other group, 67 percent chose to share.

Most people think the name will make only a slight difference in the players' choices. They think the outcome is much better predicted by people's niceness or greediness, as the researchers here also showed. But in fact, the players' reputations among their peers as nice or greedy didn't predict players' choices at all. Few appreciate the powerful way in which the name of the game changes the norms in play and, through this, the way players define the situation. The name sets the norm for what makes you a "good player." In the Wall Street Game, sharing makes you a "sucker" because the rules of Wall Street condone being a lone wolf, and if you don't think the same way, you'll be the one exploited. To go for the grab in the Community Game makes you a "parasite" because the rules of community-building dictate that we look out for each other. People play the game not so much based on strategic self-interest, as commonly thought, but based on the norms for what it means to be a good person in this situation. The study also offers a lesson in empathy: People who behave selfishly may be doing so not because they have a selfish personality but because they have come to define the "game" of social life—perhaps because of coaching, perhaps because of a betrayal that left them feeling burned—as the Wall Street Game.

The takeaway is that situations can be crafted as games with norms that pit players against one another, or as games with norms that lead people to derive pleasure and identity from acting in cooperative ways, including toward those they might regard as one of "Them." One of the best examples is work by Elliot Aronson on what he called the Jigsaw Classroom.

ARONSON IS AMONG THE most ingenious situation-crafters in the history of social psychology. Reading his book *Social Animal* when I was a college student led me into social psychology. Aronson was a great storyteller, and I was fortunate to attend a few talks he gave. He would entrance his audiences with the stories of his studies, and no wonder, given his results. His original Jigsaw Classroom study produced such strong results that variants of his intervention have been widely adopted by schools.

Aronson was inspired to conduct the research through his experience of residential racial segregation in his home city of Austin, Texas, where a superhighway divided the neighborhood mostly populated by poor blacks and Mexican Americans from one mostly inhabited by well-off whites. In 1971, Austin was attempting to integrate its schools for the first time, in spite of the fact that the Supreme Court had struck down state-sponsored segregation way back in 1954 and ordered states to integrate "with all deliberate speed." At first, integration did not go well. Racial animosity heated up, and minority students' grades and self-esteem took a hit, a pattern echoed throughout the nation.

Aronson wanted to recraft the classroom situation so that integration stood a better chance of success. His first step was to take a look at what the classroom was like.

Aronson and six of his graduate students visited elementary school classrooms and did nothing but observe. He told his students to list characteristics they noticed by order of prevalence. When they compared notes, they were surprised to discover they had all put the same thing at the top of their list: The classroom norms were really competitive. The teacher would ask a question, and then six or seven hands would dart up, with the kids practically leaping out of their chairs, competing for the scarce resources of the teacher's attention and approval. Then, when the teacher called on one of the kids, a groan would go out from the other kids who had their hands up. "Meanwhile," Aronson told me, "there are another 20 kids"—black and brown kids—"who are looking down at the floor who don't know the answer. And that happens over and over again." Aronson added, "It very quickly dawned on all of us that the . . . black and brown kids were almost guaranteed to lose" in the game of classroom competition "because they had come from substandard schools."

He knew that whatever changes he introduced, the children had to participate in the process of change themselves. Lecturing kids to be nice and cooperative wouldn't work. You had to change the nature of the game kids thought they were playing. He considered how to do so. A story about Ben Franklin had stuck in Aronson's mind. While Franklin had served as a Pennsylvania state legislator, he wanted to get an older, crotchety legislator to like him. He thought about giving him a gift but then decided to flip the script. Get him to give a gift to me, Franklin thought. Get him to pretend to like me, and his heart and mind will follow. So he asked the legislator if he could borrow a rare book from him, which Franklin later returned with gratitude. The legislator soon became fond of Franklin. And the very fact that the legislator had initially disliked Franklin increased his need to justify his doing him a favor. Later, two of Aronson's colleagues, John Jerker and David Landy, demonstrated experimentally that freely choosing to do someone a favor increases liking for that person. So Aronson thought that whatever the situation he crafted, it should be one where the kids are giving things to each other.

As he considered how to change the rules of the classroom game, Aronson was inspired by sports, an arena where people from diverse backgrounds learn to band together as brothers and sisters. He was thinking of something "like a basketball team, with five or six members." This led him to the idea of having kids work together in small teams. He also drew on the work of Muzafer Sherif and incorporated a superordinate goal.

In Aronson's original version of the intervention, in five classrooms, all of the kids first individually studied a single "jigsaw" piece of a larger lesson. If the lesson concerned Native American cultures, one piece might pertain to the Cherokee, and four others to the Navaho, Sioux, Apache, and Iroquois. This way each student became an "expert" on one piece. Next the kids got together in five-person "learning groups," which the teacher needed to ensure were racially mixed and made up of one expert on each lesson piece. The teacher told the kids they would be tested at the end of class on the full lesson. To learn it, the kids had to work together.

Each student had a gift to give, and each had two roles to play. In one, as a teacher, they conveyed knowledge to the other kids in the group, a self-affirming role of empowerment. In another role, they had to be good students, learning what the four others knew. The superordinate goal was for all of them to learn the whole lesson, which could be achieved only by transcending racial division to work together.

Aronson created a situation in which students had to learn to be emotionally intelligent and socially skilled to succeed. If a kid was slow to communicate content, heckling didn't help. They gradually realized that it was in their self-interest to be good cooperators rather than competitors. They had to learn to ask good questions of each other and to listen carefully and respectfully to one another. In the process, they learned to lift each other up and to avoid harmful stereotypes. A key element, Aronson said, is that "students have to unlearn competitiveness."

Aronson evaluated the impact of the method after six weeks, comparing the five classrooms that had done Jigsaw learning with similar classrooms studying the same material in the traditional way. The children who went through the Jigsaw process showed marked reductions in prejudice and made more friends across racial lines, relative to children in the traditional classrooms. They also showed gains in self-esteem and school performance. The positive effects on the students were visible. When Aronson conducted some workshops to display his method, teachers visiting to observe would ask, "What are you doing in this classroom?"

Aronson points out a number of important features in the method, which take advantage of the resources for situation-crafting laid out in

Chapter 1. First there is *timing*. By instituting Jigsaw when kids are at a formative age, in fifth and sixth grade, he says, you open their hearts, and by the time they get into tenth and eleventh grade, "They're a little more open to differences of all kinds." Kids also enter a new reference group with new norms and new roles that supply new ways to relate. Also important is that self-affirmation is built into the situation. Kids all feel they matter and belong. Finally, the participatory nature of the process further fosters the sense of belonging.

The original study inspired hundreds of follow-ups and classroom innovations. How often teachers have kids do Jigsaw exercises can vary widely, from once a day to perhaps once or twice a week. Researchers have played with the incentive structure and objectives of the game to great effect. One winning strategy is to have the learning teams compete—with the prize going to the group not with the highest average test score but the highest average improvement. Kids start to take pride in each other's growth. Another's success becomes their own. Jigsaw has been used successfully not only with elementary school students but with high school and college students as well.

In 1982, Aronson received a touching letter from a student about how important the Jigsaw Classroom was to him:

> I am a senior at U.T. [University of Texas]. Today I got a letter admitting me to the Harvard Law School. This may not seem odd to you, but let me tell you something. I am the 6th of 7 children my parents had—and I am the only one who ever went to college, let alone to graduate, or go to law school.
>
> By now, you are probably wondering why this stranger is writing to you and bragging to you about his achievements. Actually, I'm not a stranger although we never met. You see, last year I was taking a course in social psychology and we were using a book you wrote, The Social Animal, and when I read about prejudice and Jigsaw it all sounded very familiar—and then, I realized that I was in that very first class you ever did jigsaw in— when I was in the 5th grade. And as I read on, it dawned on me

that I was the boy that you called Carlos. And then I remembered
you when you first came to our classroom and how I was scared
and how I hated school and how I was so stupid and didn't know
anything. And you came in—it all came back to me when I read
your book—you were very tall—about 6½ feet—and you had a
big black beard and you were funny and made us all laugh.

And, most important, when we started to do work in jigsaw
groups, I began to realize that I wasn't really that stupid. And the
kids I thought were cruel and hostile became my friends and the
teacher acted friendly and nice to me and I actually began to love
school, and I began to love to learn things and now I'm about to
go to Harvard Law School.

You must get a lot of letters like this but I decided to write
anyway because let me tell you something. My mother tells me
that when I was born I almost died. I was born at home and the
cord was wrapped around my neck and the midwife gave me
mouth to mouth and saved my life. If she was still alive, I would
write to her too, to tell her that I grew up smart and good and
I'm going to law school. But she died a few years ago. I'm writing
to you because, no less than her, you saved my life too.

Sincerely, Carlos

ANOTHER SUCCESS STORY in building bonds with norms and
superordinate goals is Outward Bound, an outdoor survival program
that brings kids from all kinds of backgrounds together to go on grueling wilderness adventures in which they have to work together to
survive for one to two weeks. "The wilderness," write the political scientists Donald Green and Janelle Wong, who conducted an important
study of the program's effects, "functions as a leveler, pushing all of the
participants to their physical limits." Moreover, the kids are isolated
from their family and friend groups, "unfreezing" them, as Kurt Lewin
would say, to be shaped by a new group and new norms. The experi-

ence is also replete with opportunities for self-affirmation. The kids overcome adversities, and they keep diaries to reflect on the values by which they want to live their lives. Studies have shown that participating in Outward Bound builds self-esteem.

For their study, Green and Wong asked the Outward Bound administrators to randomly split participants ranging in age from fourteen to seventeen into groups of ten at their base camp. In some groups, everyone was white, including the adult instructor. In others, three of the ten kids were black or Latino.

Three weeks after the kids completed the program, the researchers got in touch with the white participants and assessed their racial tolerance with a survey that asked them whether they agreed or disagreed with such statements as, "If a person of a different race were put in charge of me, I would not mind taking advice and direction from him or her," and going beyond race, "I would never want to be around a teenager who was gay." Even though the program was no more than two weeks long, the effect was huge. A full 58 percent of the participants in the diverse groups gave the most tolerant response to all five questions compared with 32 percent in the all-white groups. The diverse groups' experience seemed to teach them a deep lesson about our common humanity, as they expressed more positive attitudes toward ethnic minorities and gay people as well.

It's easy to overlook what is missing in both Jigsaw and Outward Bound that is normally present when we try to create inclusive spaces. There are no lectures. No mention is made of tolerance or equality. Attempts to combat prejudice through such instructional means have proven largely ineffectual. The power of these carefully crafted situations is that they make children full participants in the process of their own change.

+ + + +

ONE OF THE LEADING scholars of prejudice, social psychologist Elizabeth Paluck, conducted remarkable studies demonstrating other ways situations can be crafted to awaken new norms and combat hostility between groups. Paluck's work is particularly courageous for testing approaches out in the field, among groups in conflict, in contrast to much social psychology research today, which is conducted within the confines of laboratories and universities or with online samples. In 2000, while Paluck was a doctoral student in my department, she made the brazen decision to go to Rwanda to conduct a test of an intervention that she hoped might help heal the deep social wounds from the horrific massacre of Tutsis by their fellow citizens, the Hutus, who were often neighbors.

The divide-and-conquer tactics of German and then Belgium occupiers in the first half of the twentieth century had fostered division in Rwanda, turning a subtle distinction between these two ethnic groups into a fault line by granting favors and positions to one group over the other. The resulting resentments were inflamed by the Rwandan government. In one hundred days of slaughter in 1994, an estimated 800,000 Tutsis were killed, mostly with machetes and firearms that had been distributed by the government. That is 8,000 murders per day. As in earlier massacres such as the Holocaust, ordinary citizens proved all too willing to do the dirty work. Most of the massacre took place where people had grown up and lived most of their lives, and much of it occurred at the hands of neighbors. Even priests and nuns were reported to have killed Tutsis who had sought refuge in their churches. Others stood by and did little to stop the horror.

The memory of the genocide was still raw when Paluck arrived. Many villagers lived with grief and psychological pain. Fear of a new outbreak of violence was palpable. The villagers were contending with what Paluck described as "a monumental crisis of trust." How could they ever live in peace and goodwill with such deep wounds? The barriers seemed overwhelming.

But what better way to build hope and open people's eyes to new possibilities for relating than a love story? Stories can transcend divides by uniting people around a shared hope for what could be. To paraphrase the author Philip Pullman, information and arguments might reach the head but "it takes 'once upon a time' to reach the heart." Paluck teamed up with the creators of a new radio soap opera called *Musekew-eya* (New Dawn). Radio had been used as a tool to spread hate during the genocide. Could radio help reverse the damage?

The reconciliation soap opera was created by Rwandan officials and the Dutch nongovernmental organization Radio La Benevolencija, with the guidance of Ervin Staub, a professor of psychiatry and a Holo-caust survivor who has written extensively about the roots of violent behavior. The story of *Musekeweya* is akin to Shakespeare's *Romeo and Juliet*, about lovers from two rival villages. Talking about ethnicity was banned after the genocide so the writers had to use fictional villages to stand in for Hutus and Tutsis. Just as in the real conflict, in the soap opera, tensions boil over due to scarcity of land, government favoritism of one group, and warmongering by demagogues. One village attacks the other. Death, trauma, and pain follow.

The passionate affair of the two star-crossed lovers acts as a light-ning rod for the conflict between the two villages. But unlike in Shake-speare's tragedy, the couple prevail, and they become a beacon for new norms. They defy fate and the social pressures of their communities by organizing the youth into a protest group. Like any hopeful story that rings true, *Musekeweya* doesn't avoid tough issues. Many of the charac-ters deal with trauma. There are harrowing scenes of grief. Characters cry, give up, change for the worse. But hope also sprouts, as when the villagers support one another, care for the sick, and deal with problems together. They banter, sing, laugh, and drink banana beer together, rit-uals that remind them of the beauty of life during peacetime.

To test the impact of the reconciliation soap opera on bridging the social divide in the country, Paluck identified twelve villages represen-tative of Rwanda. She organized a team of research assistants, many of them Rwandan, to bring a stereo and cassette tapes to the com-munity space in those villages once a month for a year. In six ran-domly selected villages, the assistants played tapes of the soap opera focused on reconciliation, and in the other six, they played tapes of a soap opera focused on AIDS education; these latter villages served as a control group. Villagers freely chose whether to come and listen.

Beyond the content of the show, a key element of the situation Paluck and her collaborators created was that villagers listened *together*. They sat around the radio in community spaces. When the lovers were thwarted, the villagers would cry out in distress. When the characters frustrated them, they shouted advice. When the village fool in the soap opera mocked the demagogue, the villagers laughed together. When the lovers reunited, they cheered. When a wise elder in the story commented, they sometimes expressed their agreement. For instance, after one elder spoke of the importance of tolerance and respect, villagers cheered, "We should repeat those words!" After the show ended for the night, villagers often mingled and talked about the story.

When interviewed at the end of the year, 95 percent of Paluck's participants said the characters reminded them of people in their village. Some even nicknamed fellow villagers after the characters, which may have helped them relate the story to their own lives and relationships. The story seemed to have humanized fellow villagers they had reason to fear or hate.

What other kinds of change could be expected from such an experience in a place with such a painful recent past? It's naive to think it would cause these listeners to abandon mistrust, hate, or fear. But it might inspire them to think that they could and should adopt some new social norms, especially given that they listened to the story with other villagers who seemed to feel the same way. That's what Paluck found.

The villagers who had listened to the reconciliation soap opera were more likely to approve of intermarriage between Hutus and Tutsis. Those villagers, more so than the ones who had listened to the other soap opera focused on AIDS education, disagreed with the statement, "I advise my children (or the ones I will have in the future) that they should only marry people from the same regional, religious, or ethnic group as our own."

The reconciliation soap opera also encouraged villagers to be more open to trusting one another. Those who listened to it agreed less with the statement "It is naive to trust" than did the control group. These villagers also disagreed more strenuously with the prevailing norm that people "should keep quiet" when they "disagree with something that someone is doing or saying." The program seemed to have empowered them to take a nonviolent stand, a key finding given that the massacre had spread in part because bystanders had failed to intervene. The soap opera also opened villagers up to positive strategies to find identity and belonging through social support rather than scapegoating. They disagreed more with the norm that they "should never talk about the experiences that have caused me great pain and suffering."

Finally, as a measure of empathy, the research team asked villagers if they ever "imagine the thoughts and feelings" of four groups: prisoners, genocide survivors, the poor, and political leaders. More of those who had heard the reconciliation soap opera said "yes" regarding each of these groups than did those who had heard the health soap opera.

It's not that people who heard the soap opera about reconciliation embraced and forgave one another. They did not wipe the slate clean. But they softened. They took what, according to much other research, is often the first step toward change—an expanded perception of what could and should be, a shift in felt norms.

One effect of these changes is that villagers should feel more open to expressing dissent and more hopeful that differences can be resolved without violence. Recall from Lewin's research that healthy groups deliberate in a democratic manner. The reconciliation program seemed to promote just this. As a prize for their participants, each village was awarded a stereo and six cassette tapes. There was only one stereo and many people who wanted to use it. How did the villagers deal with this dilemma? Their conversation was covertly recorded and later analyzed by research assistants.

In the villages exposed to the health soap opera, the deliberations were typically swift, with one person recommending the use of the stereo be overseen by the village elder, followed by silence and acquiescence. But for the villages exposed to the reconciliation soap opera, the deliberations were "livelier and more contested." After the first recommendation, oftentimes a second villager would dissent and recommend a different solution. Debate ensued. But these villagers also expressed hope alongside dissent, a hallmark of a healthy democratic process in which belonging is protected in spite of disagreement. What's more, the villagers made more positive comments about their ability to find a solution. As one of them said, "We've been coming together to listen all this time; why can't we come together to listen to this stereo, just as we did before?"

WHEN NEW JERSEY PASSED antibullying legislation for its schools, it turned to Elizabeth Paluck to provide another approach for establishing new norms to reduce group conflict. In middle schools scattered throughout the state, she recruited about twenty-five seventh and eighth graders to form a "seed group" at each school—not unlike the eclectic group of kids in the movie *The Breakfast Club,* I imagine, but with more racial diversity. The seed groups in Paluck's program are breakfast clubs that don't end after the afternoon together. They press on and turn their revelations of a common humanity into a new norm.

Here's how her intervention went. Across the 28 schools in which she intervened, she recruited 728 kids total, of whom 500 actually went ahead and participated. These kids made up the seed group at each school. The groups were truly a seed, as altogether they comprised fewer than 3 percent of the 11,938 students attending these schools. At an average school of 450 students, about 15 participated in the seed group. These 15 kids were representative of the school population. They met in small groups ten times over the course of the year, each time for about an hour, and with an adult who took Lewin's democratic leadership approach to working with them. Another 28 schools formed a control group, where there was no intervention beyond the schools' standard programs and policies to deal with bullying.

The adult leader almost never lectured, never pressured the kids with the kind of strong-armed salesmanship common in persuasion and educational campaigns. Instead the leader specified the purpose, the end goal, and left the means for achieving that goal squarely with the kids, a signature of good democratic leadership. The program, the kids were told, was about "making your school a place where all students feel accepted." Students agreed that it would be great to cut down on how much students "get into conflicts or drama" with each other and "get into situations where one person is embarrassed, excluded, or feeling badly about themselves."

The kids in the seed groups were affirmed and put in empowering roles as "change makers" and "influencers." They were told by the leader that research shows a single person's actions can spread through an entire social network, and because they are the foremost experts in life at their school, they know best what the problems are and how to fix them. We don't have the answers, the adult leader admitted. You do. We do. Working together, we'll create them. The group meeting, the kids were promised, will be a safe space where they can talk openly and honestly. "It's OK to say something negative about the school, and it's OK to disagree with each other as long as we all show respect."

Taking a page from Sherif, Paluck had the kids engage in fun, cooperative games to increase the belonging students felt within the group, and she introduced numerous channels for kids to participate more fully in the group process, another key of situation-crafting. For instance, students could submit ideas anonymously in a "Make Change Box." When students left the group, they could still stay in touch online and share their ideas through a website that the researchers had created.

Throughout the year, the adult leader guided the kids to become situation-crafters at their school, asking questions like: What are the triggers for threats to students' sense that they belong and are accepted? When there's drama, fighting, mean jokes, rumors, and gossip, what can people do to improve the situation? How can we make these improvements real? The leader tried to encourage publicly visible actions because these create new social norms. Kids launched solutions such as "pay-it-forward" campaigns, in which they set a norm to practice random acts of kindness, which are then paid forward by the beneficiary; a grassroots anti-"drama" advertising campaign; hashtags to deter conflict, which the kids posted on social media and emblazoned on white boards throughout the school; and a "bank of behaviors" that listed concrete ways kids can help one another to feel included and respected in trigger situations. One popular activity was for the kids in the seed groups to give out orange wristbands labeled "Respect" or "Make Change" to students they saw as exemplifying the new norms. They distributed over 2,500 of them, creating another visible indicator of the new norm.

At the end of the year, official records revealed that relative to the control schools, the schools that had implemented Paluck's intervention showed a 25 percent reduction in disciplinary incidents among all students. That translates into almost seven hundred fewer disciplinary incidents.

One element turbocharged the intervention. Just by chance, some of the seed groups had more "social referents," a concept Paluck borrowed from Sherif, reminiscent of the notion of a gatekeeper. These are the well-liked kids who students look up to and seek to spend time with, like the high-status kids whose powerful influence Prinstein and I had demonstrated in our chatroom study. Paluck identified the number of kids in each seed group who had scored in the top 10 percent of nominations of kids that other students had said they liked to hang out with—a kind of popularity index.

The number of the more popular kids, the social referents, in each seed group made a big difference. At schools where, by chance, only about one kid in the seed group was a social referent, the intervention was ineffective. But add just two more, and the full impact kicks in. Add two more again, and the effectiveness doubles, more than halving the rate of disciplinary incidents schoolwide. A tiny number of student leaders can seed a transformative norm throughout the school.

All the schools in this study, including the control schools, subsequently adopted the program for themselves, with training from Paluck and her team. Australia has launched a major trial of the program. Paluck's full curriculum, based in scientific research and wonderfully laid out in a series of illustrative modules, is publicly available at her website (http://www.betsylevypaluck.com/roots-curriculum).

+ + + +

WHEN WE SEE GROUP divides as arising from situational forces rather than just bad actors, our eyes are opened to ways of altering situations to bridge even deeply entrenched Us-vs.-Them divides. A 2020 study by the political scientist Salma Mousa tested the power of one other means of using superordinate goals and norms to do so: sports. She wanted to find ways of healing the divide between Christian and Muslim citizens of an Iraq ripped open by war and genocide. Beginning in 2014 with ISIS's capture of the city of Mosul, 19,000 Iraqi civilians had been killed, with Christians and other religious and ethnic minorities, such as the Yezidas and Shi'a, singled out. Those who weren't killed were made slaves or fled. The result was a mass displacement of three million Iraqis. Cities that had been home to Christians for centuries were emptied of them. After the violence mostly ended, psychological aftereffects endured. Relations between Christians and Muslims remained tense, scarred by distrust.

Mousa had been thinking about South Africa's 1996 Rugby World Cup win. After South Africa's apartheid regime had fallen, the country's new president, Nelson Mandela, orchestrated the creation of the first integrated rugby team, with both black and white players. Mandela believed that sports could help unite a country that was bitterly divided after fifty years of racial hegemony. Defying the odds, the team won the cup. In one moving ceremony, the black and white players stood together, arms across one another's shoulders, and sang the anthems of both the old South Africa and the black resistance movement.

Working with a local organization in cities throughout northern Iraq shaken by the violence, Mousa created an adult soccer league, with teams competing in an eight-week tournament. On a random basis, she created two groups of teams. For one group, all of the players were Christian, which, because the region is predominantly Christian, represented business as usual. For the other group, three of the players on each team were Muslim. To help build rapport between the Muslims and Christians, Mousa asked the coaches to hold icebreakers at the beginning of the season. She also requested that they ensure all players had roughly equal time on the field. Mousa explained to me that the coaches also came up with one "on-the-fly" act of situation-crafting: instructing the players to speak only in Arabic. Whereas Christians in the country are generally able to speak Arabic, most Muslims didn't know the Christians' native language, Eastern Aramaic. When the Christian players spoke to one another in Aramaic in early games, their Muslim teammates felt alienated. This small improvisation by the coaches marked a "turning point in integrating Muslim players," Mousa said.

Unfortunately, there were too few Muslim players to rigorously analyze any changes they experienced. But for Christians on the integrated teams, as the players got to know each other, they engaged in many moving instances of camaraderie across religious-ethnic lines. When the Muslims on one team said they couldn't afford taxis to the games, their Christian teammates chipped in to pay for the rides. When some Christians wanted to invite their Muslim team members to go to a café at which Muslims were unwelcome, the Christians negotiated with the owners to admit them. When no Muslim players showed up at a dinner event for the teams, several Christians called their Muslim teammates to persuade them to come. By the end of the season, many of the Christians described in various words having bonded with their Muslim teammates. "When the game is over," one said, "we hug, kiss, congratulate each other even when we lose." Players even invited teammates across the religious divide to their homes.

Mousa more formally measured the effects of the integration of teams as well. She asked them in a survey, for example, to what degree they believed that the division of the country into Muslims and Christians was "arbitrary." Those on the integrated teams agreed more strongly that the division was arbitrary than did those on the nonintegrated teams. Mousa also created a number of opportunities for Christian players to act in supportive ways toward Muslim players. They could nominate a player from another team for a good sportsmanship award, for example, and she recorded how many nominated a Muslim. She also evaluated how many Christian players signed up for a mixed team the next season and how many trained with Muslims in the off-season. In all instances, Christian players from the integrated teams showed markedly more tolerance. For example, while only 14 percent of Christian players from the nonintegrated teams trained with Muslims regularly in the off-season, 63 percent of those on the integrated teams did.

Mousa also measured the effects on players' "off-the-field" behaviors. These included whether four months after the season, Christian players attended a gala dinner-and-dance event for both Muslims and Christians; whether Christians redeemed a coupon for a restaurant in the Muslim city of Mosul; and whether they donated money to a general humanitarian organization or to one that exclusively served Christians. She found no effect on these outcomes when she compared integrated with nonintegrated teams overall. On the other hand, there was evidence that simply being in the integrated *league* Mousa had created—regardless of whether players were on an integrated team—increased tolerance in these areas. Further, when Mousa looked at the subset of teams that had made it to the league finals, not only did the integrated teams show greater levels of off-the-field tolerance, but if they won, they demonstrated the greatest levels of tolerance of all. This finding points to other ideas for situation-crafting that could be explored in the future. Perhaps if players were led to define team success in terms of cooperation, effort, and growth rather than league victory, the benefits could be more widely spread.

The damage to the social fabric of Iraq due to so much violence is profound, and many years and larger-scale efforts will be required to mend it. But Mousa's study underscores the value of creating opportunities for groups that have been in conflict to work together toward common goals—and, in so doing, to establish new norms for relating. Racially and ethnically integrated sporting competitions; community improvement projects, such as litter cleanup days; interreligious events; fundraisers to help the needy; bipartisan public initiatives; and many other such activities can achieve sometimes remarkable progress in building bridges.

+ + + +

PRESSURES TO CONFORM TO group norms in order to feel accepted can be forces for great evil but also forces for good. As we'll explore in Part Three, we can find many ways in our everyday lives, our schools, our workplaces, and our communities to help change perceptions of the correct ways to behave toward those who are seen as other.

We have not evolved to vilify and demean others but to respond adaptively to situations as we perceive them—or as we have been led to perceive them. If we perceive others as threats, we'll likely be more inclined to distance ourselves or be aggressive toward them; if we don't perceive them as threats, we'll be more receptive. Some people throughout the ages have bucked conformist pressures and spoken out for the oppressed and vilified. But far too many of us far too often fail to do so. Social psychology suggests that our failures to speak up arise in good part from norms, groups, and fear of ostracism, all of which can be addressed through situation-crafting.

However, many threats to belonging arise from some unfortunate aspects of human psychology that are bred into us through culture or evolution. These lead us to misread situations and the people we encounter. If we're to combat the crisis of belonging, we must understand how these features of our psychology can cause us to demean and exclude people.

Chapter 5

Blaming the Person, Ignoring the Situation

How to See and Respond to What Is Really Going On

E LLIOT ARONSON ONCE SAID, "SOCIAL PSYCHOLOGY IS A story of sin and redemption." That is because social psychologists study the least savory human behaviors, such as ostracism, aggression, prejudice, and genocide. But we also offer hope for bringing out the better angels of our nature.

One of the most widespread and least appreciated "psychological sins," which wreaks havoc on belonging, is called the Fundamental Attribution Error, and the following story illustrates how catastrophic its consequences can be.

AT ABOUT 10:00 P.M. on July 23, 2015, Robert Doyle and his wife were driving home to Beverly Hills, Florida. As they passed through nearby Citrus Hills, Doyle called 911 and reported, "I have some maniac trying to follow me, trying to run me off the road."

At the same time, in the car behind the Doyles, Cathy Gonzalez, the wife of the driver Candelerio, whom Doyle had called a maniac, was on the phone with another 911 operator. She was reporting that *Doyle* had endangered *them* by driving aggressively. "We're driving a full-size truck and a trailer. You can't just drive like an idiot," she said, referring to Doyle. "Somebody needs to smack the crap out of this idiot."

Meanwhile, Doyle grew heated, telling the 911 operator, "My gun is already out. I'm locked and loaded."

The Gonzalez couple had their eight-year-old daughter and seven-year-old grandson in the back seat, who are heard on the tape of Gonzalez's 911 call yelling, "He's got a gun!" Still, Candelerio followed the Doyles to their home, even as his wife pleaded with him not to. He said he wanted to report Doyle's address to the police. Both men and their wives believed the other driver was the aggressor, and both apparently saw their own behavior as totally justified by the situation.

After Doyle pulled into his driveway, Gonzalez parked his truck on the road in front of the house. He got out and approached Doyle, who wielded his gun. Doyle's wife pleaded with her husband not to shoot. But he did—five times, hitting Gonzalez with four bullets and killing him. The fifth bullet hit the wall of the house across the street. Doyle held Cathy and the two children at gunpoint until the police arrived. They arrested Doyle. A year later, a judge dropped the charges against him because he determined Doyle had acted in self-defense, within his rights as stipulated by Florida's Stand Your Ground law.

Who was the real aggressor? Who started it? Why did this conflict escalate to such a violent end? "What idiots!" flashed through my mind as I read a news account. Then I realized that I was engaging in the same bias that probably gave rise to this road-rage tragedy. It's the bias that snaps into play like a mental reflex. While no single explanation can account for the aspersions we cast on other drivers, one factor certainly at play is the Fundamental Attribution Error. It's an impulsive cognitive bias that leads us to see the behavior of others as emanating from some underlying essence—who the person is—rather than from the situation they are in. Instead of considering the possibility that someone who cut into our lane was distracted by worries about a problem at work or perhaps was avoiding a hazard in their lane, we tend to make their behavior personal, both by attributing it to some flaw in their nature and by taking it personally. We often do this despite knowing virtually nothing about the other person or people. We decide they are rude, selfish, prejudiced, sexist, stupid, and so on, belittling them with sometimes wild oversimplification. We commit this error most when somebody else does something that we think we ourselves would never have done—when they seem to be *different*. The Fundamental Attribution Error is the cognitive mill that turns the grist of our social lives into gossip, judgment, and rage.

We commit the bias with people we don't know, such as strangers in the street and celebrities we read about in the news. Look at the comment feed in virtually any Twitter or other social media post about someone doing or saying something different, disagreeable, or regrettable, and you'll find the poisonous products of the Fundamental Attribution Error. But we also often commit this bias with people we know well and care about.

A poignant example of misreading someone's behavior, even after having gotten to know them, was shared by the actor Clarke Peters. Peters worked with Chadwick Boseman on the set of a movie after Boseman had risen to acclaim for his role in *Black Panther*. When they were working together on a movie about a militia group, in roles that were extremely physically demanding, Peters resented Boseman. He said that Boseman had become a huge star, was "surrounded by people . . . fawning over him," with a "Chinese practitioner who's massaging his back when he walks off set, a make-up lady who's massaging his feet, his girlfriend . . . holding his hand." Peters concluded that Boseman had become full of himself, demanding excessive pampering. A few months later, he realized his error when Boseman's death from stage 4 colon cancer was announced. Boseman had been in horrible pain. During the shoot, there was more happening in his situation than most there could see.

We often commit the Fundamental Attribution Error in our everyday lives, with coworkers and bosses, friends, and even family and spouses. A girlfriend who has abruptly broken up with you is a callous user. A professor who has been insensitive in discussing the effects of racism is a privileged bigot. A boss who has rudely trounced on a view you've expressed in a meeting is a power-hungry egomaniac. A student or employee who's failing to meet your standards is a slacker. We also cast such categorical aspersions on whole groups of people and whole cultures, races, and ethnicities. Many Greeks think "Albanians are terrible drivers," while many Germans think the "Dutch are the worst drivers." Such generalizations have been at the root of many offensive jokes about racial and ethnic groups.

In our everyday lives, the Fundamental Attribution Error leads us to discredit the power of a slight or, on the flip side, the power of a smile or basic acts of politeness. It leads us to underappreciate the power we have to affect the behavior of others because we are part of their situation. The Fundamental Attribution Error also makes us simplistic in our understanding of others. We think that an action represents some simple, corresponding essence: You argued for X; you must believe X. You performed badly; you must lack ability. You committed a crime; you must lack character. We feel as though we're forever catching people dead to rights in revealing who they really are, when what we should realize is how little we know of their circumstances.

One of my former professors, Kenneth McClane, wrote an essay about growing up in Harlem and his relationship with Lynwood, one the toughest bullies in the neighborhood. This man had gunned down someone in front of McClane's house. Lynwood was said to have "left mayhem and horror trailing in his wake" and was reputed to "kill for kicks" with "no feeling for anyone." Yet McClane wrote that this same man was gentle and inspiring to him. According to McClane, Lynwood took on the role of a father figure for him, checking his report cards and telling him he'd make something of himself and "go to college." The Fundamental Attribution Error leaves little room in our minds to imagine the complexities and contradictions of people.

Learning about this bias can help us to be more mindful day to day in our encounters and to look for situational influences on others' behavior. The story of the error's "discovery" begins with a deceptively simple study conducted more than fifty years ago by Edward Jones and Victor Harris at Princeton University. They asked participants to describe the point of view of a writer of a political essay. Some participants were told that the writer had been instructed to argue a certain position, and others were told the writer was allowed to choose. The surprising result was that even when the writer was said to have no choice, participants reported that they believed the writer subscribed to the position he had argued. In other words, they attributed the writer's viewpoint to the person rather than the situation the writer was in.

This finding inspired much subsequent research that established how pervasive and powerful what later came to be known as the Fundamental Attribution Error, or FAE, is. The linchpin study was conducted by one of my mentors at Stanford, Lee Ross, who gave the bias its name. He noticed that he himself had failed to account for the situation in judging how prepared he was to become a professor. In his dissertation defense as a graduate student, an unexpected question from one of his examiners, which Ross didn't know the answer to, caused him to doubt himself. He recalls that as he assumed a professorship at Stanford, "I ruminated about my lack of readiness." Relative to the grand poobahs at Stanford, he felt he didn't belong. But then he was asked to be an examiner in the dissertation defense of a student at Stanford, and he discovered that he relished the opportunity to show his colleagues he "knew a thing or two about our field." He knew no more than when he was the student defending, but he felt entirely different about himself when in the examiner position.

To explore how the human mind might underplay the role of situations in our evaluations of ourselves and other people, Ross conducted a study that's another one of the most influential in the history of social psychology. It came to be called the Quiz Bowl Study.

Ross had two college students at a time come to his laboratory, and an experimenter told them they would be playing the role of either the quiz show contestant or the questioner. Their role would be determined at random by which of two cards with the hidden labels "Questioner" or "Contestant" they picked. Those who picked the Questioner card were then asked to generate on the spot ten challenging "general knowledge" questions by drawing on their own expertise and interests. Those playing the contestant had thirty seconds to answer each of these questions. On average they answered only four out of ten questions correctly.

All the students were then asked to rate both their own general knowledge and that of the other student they had played the game with. Eighty percent of those who had played the contestant role rated themselves as inferior in knowledge to the questioner. But that's absurd. They knew their roles had been randomly determined, and the game was obviously fixed to allow the questioners to come across as masterful. We all have esoteric stores of knowledge, little bits of trivia that we have accumulated over the years, and whether someone else happens to know the same specialized things says little about their overall knowledge. What's more, when Ross showed clips of the game to students who hadn't participated but who were told about the study setup, they also rated the questioners as more knowledgeable. Meanwhile, questioners rated themselves just a bit above the contestants. They seemed to account for the situational advantage conferred on them. What was so striking was that the other students didn't. A situational advantage became warped in people's minds into a sign of individual merit.

Much additional research on the FAE has shown that we far too often fail to account for how situations in real life have also been crafted, intentionally or not, to confer advantages on some and disadvantages on others. This tendency contributes to beliefs that students from difficult homes are less motivated or less capable because of who they are rather than what their home situation is. It also provokes assessments of employees who are contending with more time-consuming red tape than others, or with other challenges in their work situations, as less competent or less hardworking. The FAE leads to all sorts of harsh judgments of others.

Ross called the bias fundamental because it involves a basic attribution question we ask about people's behavior: Is it fundamentally about them? What is more, unfortunately, the FAE is fundamental in our everyday lives. It is among the most established effects in social psychology. In large-scale attempts at replicating numerous psychological effects, the FAE emerged as the most robust effect, being replicated in 100 percent of the studies testing it.

One qualification is that there are some circumstances in which we tend not to overlook the situational factors. We tend to appreciate the power of financial incentives and the threat of violence to influence behavior. But we are blind to so many other situational influences, especially the subtle and not-so-subtle ones that threaten people's sense of belonging.

IN JULY 2017, Google engineer James Damore posted a ten-page memo on the company's internal mailing list titled "Google's Ideological Echo Chamber." In it he wrote that "I strongly believe in gender and racial diversity, and I think we should strive for more. However, to achieve a more equal gender and race representation, Google has created several discriminatory practices," which, he wrote, included "programs, mentoring and classes only for people with a certain gender or race" and "special treatment for 'diversity' candidates."

A focus of the memo was his objection that "at Google, we're regularly told that implicit (unconscious) and explicit biases are holding women back in tech and leadership." He offered a number of other explanations for the comparatively low number of women in technology jobs, asserting that there are "biological causes" and that women's personalities differ from men's, on average. For example, he claimed that "women generally have a stronger interest in people rather than things" and that they express their extraversion "as gregariousness rather than assertiveness." Under the heading "Neuroticism (higher anxiety, lower stress tolerance)," Damore speculated that this neuroticism "may contribute to the higher levels of anxiety women report on Googlegeist," the name of Google's annual employee survey. Damore also argued, "We always ask why we don't see women in top leadership positions, but we never ask why we see so many men in these jobs," asserting that men hold more of these positions because they have a stronger natural drive for status.

Damore's screed was akin to an observer of Lee Ross's Quiz Bowl Study commenting that "those contestants just don't seem to have the ambition and drive that the questioners do; and they seem awfully nervous and neurotic too!" What is more, the women Damore was writing about were working at one of the most prestigious and competitive companies in the whole technology sector; that fact alone would hardly seem to suggest that they lack drive. Damore seems to have fallen prey to the FAE in attributing differences in women's presence and career advancement at the company as due to the women rather than their circumstances. He was also buying into stereotypes, which, as we'll explore in the next chapter, are among the most pervasive ways we blind ourselves to the situations of others and create the conditions for their exclusion and failure.

The memo stirred up a tempest within Google, and it was sent ripping around the web. Within a week Damore was fired. His is a cautionary tale about how strong the inclination is to blame the person rather than the situation. Zeroing in on a small subset of research findings, Damore ignored a large body of other research showing the role of situational factors in creating gender disparities. As we all do at times, Damore seems to have fallen victim to another cognitive bias, another one of the most pernicious, called the confirmation bias. It leads us to accept information that supports our views and ignore information that contradicts them. As Paul Simon put it in his song "The Boxer," "A man hears what he wants to hear and disregards the rest." When paired with the FAE, the confirmation bias leads us to weave increasingly convincing stories about other people and groups that are more fictions of our minds than reflections of reality.

Damore seems to have been unaware of the harm caused by the long history of gender discrimination. He was also unaware of the harm caused now by putting the onus for inequality on individuals rather than societal conditions. In an interview, he said he was surprised by the furious reaction to the memo. He apparently had not absorbed the lesson that he had been shaping the workplace situation by demeaning women.

The FAE also shapes our understanding of people like Damore who express and act on harmful views. The prevailing assumption is that if people espouse sexist or racist views, they do so because they *are* an inveterate sexist or a racist and are unwilling or unable to change their views. Yet while there are people who embrace bigoted views and will resist any attempts to dissuade them, many people's ideas have been shaped by the bigotry that pervades our social situations. It is systemic—meaning situational at an institutional or societal scale— infusing even our day-to-day encounters. We commit the FAE when we discount these systemic forces and condemn as hopeless the individuals who hold harmful views—individuals who, like C. P. Ellis and Christian Picciolini, might change for the better and even become allies under the right circumstances. By ignoring systemic situational factors, we also let off the hook the people in power who craft our situations. Some of the features of workplaces that either support or undermine belonging are obvious and under some amount of corporate control, such as the visibility of female and minority leaders in a company. The effects of some policies, if leaders chose to implement them, can be impressive. As we'll see in later chapters, parental leave policies, protocols to foster pay equity, and mentoring programs have been shown to have a large effect on women's success.

In any specific case, we don't know the source of harmful views and how changeable they are. But the more important question is how to create a corporate culture that fosters all employees' sense of belonging. Change the situation, and hearts and minds will follow. Being awake to even seemingly subtle aspects of the situation can help. Once, at a visit to another tech company, I had observed how the only Latino and black people in sight were the ones who worked the valet service or front desk. I imagine that many white employees had hardly noticed this, and if they did, it didn't trigger any psychological response. I noticed mainly because I knew the research suggesting that these kinds of situational cues can send a message to minorities about whether they belong in other roles at a firm. It's hard to see the importance of these cues when they're not "charged" for you. It is difficult in my experience to get past the "bad apple" view of corporate problems and get leaders to start asking about the larger situational context and how to change it.

OUR BLINDNESS TO HOW differently the same situation may be experienced by different people makes it all too easy to commit the FAE. A situation that seems to be "out there" in front of our eyes may be experienced altogether differently from behind the eyes of another person. For example, in a school, we may be under the impression that all the students are "in the same place" and, in any given class, they are all getting the same instruction. Any differences among students in how well they learn and how they behave seem to arise from variations in their attitudes, personalities, or abilities. But differences among students may arise from the classroom situation being experienced differently by each of them. A friend of mine who is a teacher told me a story about a boy who came to class one day wearing sunglasses and refused to take them off when she asked him to. She sent him to the principal's office to be disciplined. Later she learned he had a black eye from a fight he'd been in with classmates, and he didn't want to take his glasses off because he was embarrassed about having been roughed up. For him, on that day, the classroom had become a place where he might be shamed, which his teacher couldn't see.

The same classroom may be experienced as threatening by some children and supportive by others. Some colleagues and I conducted research with over six thousand middle schoolers in more than three hundred classrooms in schools throughout the nation to assess how they experienced their classroom. They were asked, for example, whether or not they would rate it as a place where they felt stressed. Also, was it a place where they felt cared for by their teacher? The differences in the assessments students gave *within* the same classroom far exceeded the average differences *between* classrooms and even between schools. The same was true for how much students learned over the year, as roughly measured by improvements in test scores. Parents tend to think that the particular teacher their child has, or which school their child attends, determines most of the child's experience and learning. But these results suggest that's not true. A classroom isn't just a physical place common to all students but a distinctive psychological reality for each student in it. In the study, it was as if some classmates were, in fact, in quite different classrooms.

One key factor that can make a classroom experience different for different students was brought to light in a famous study conducted by Harvard social psychologist Robert Rosenthal and a school principal, Lenore Jacobson, in the 1960s. This study is a classic, an encapsulation of timeless wisdom relevant not just for teachers but for managers, educators, coaches, and parents. It's another cautionary tale about making the mistake of seeing individuals as either simply having abilities or not, rather than being mindful of the situation they're in—particularly how they're being viewed and treated. Avoiding this mistake can make a large difference in how individuals perform on tests in school, on work assignments, or in any endeavor. According to organizational psychologist Dov Eden, the study "is great science that is underapplied." Although the study's findings have been borne out by much subsequent research, the original still stands as the best illustration.

Rosenthal and Jacobson studied how information given to teachers about the intellectual ability of students, which was not based on any actual assessment of the students' abilities, affected the performance of their students. They told teachers that certain of the students entering their class in the new school year had been identified as having superior intellectual potential that hadn't yet shown up in their school performance. They called the students "bloomers." In fact, those students identified as bloomers had been chosen by the researchers randomly.

The study was conducted in the spring of 1964. Rosenthal came to Spruce Elementary School in San Francisco, where Jacobson was the principal (they called it "Oak School" in the write-up of their study). Jacobson announced to the teachers that Rosenthal would be giving the children a special type of IQ test. The teachers received the following memo.

STUDY OF INFLECTED ACQUISITION
(Harvard—National Science Foundation)

All children show hills, plateaus, and valleys in their scholastic progress. The study being conducted at Harvard with the support of the National Science Foundation is interested in those children who show an unusual forward spurt of academic progress. These spurts can and do occur at any level of academic and intellectual functioning. When these spurts occur in children who have not been functioning too well academically, the result is familiarly referred to as "late blooming."

As part of our study we are further validating a test which predicts the likelihood that a child will show an inflection point or "spurt" within the near future. The test which will be administered in your school will allow us to predict which youngsters are most likely to show an academic spurt. The top 20 percent (approximately) of scorers on this test will probably be found at various levels of academic functioning.

The development of the test for predicting inflections or "spurts" is not yet such that every one of the top 20 percent will show the spurt or "blooming" effect. But the top 20 percent of the children will show a more significant inflection or spurt in their learning within the next year or less than will the remaining 80 percent of the children.

The children at your school are tested at the end of the academic year. Over the summer, you will receive a list of the top 20% of students in your class, the "bloomers," ranging from 1 to 9 students, in case you might find it of interest to know which of your children were about to bloom.

The nature of the study was shrouded in mystery. Parents weren't told anything at all about it, nor were their children. And beyond getting the memo, the teachers weren't told anything either. The test of "inflected acquisition" was just a standard IQ test for children, which the teachers administered to their students at the end of the year. At the beginning of the next school year, Jacobson sent each of the thirty-six participating teachers a list of roughly five future "bloomers," or allegedly high-potential students, whom the test had supposedly identified. Unbeknownst to the teachers, these students were actually randomly selected.

Most descriptions of the study leave out the memo, but I've duplicated it here because it was carefully designed by Rosenthal and Jacobson, in a turn of situation-crafting I imagine Kurt Lewin would have admired. The way the study was set up sent a number of implied messages. One was that because some kids are bloomers, it's important to keep looking for signs of their potential, not to prematurely judge their abilities. Also implied was that the bloomers were special, so they deserved particular attention. The memo took further pains to convey that the information about the bloomers could be trusted. The study was being conducted by scientists from Harvard, after all, and the faux technical language used to describe the test—"Study of Inflected Acquisition"—reinforced that they had expertise, tapping into the power of "prestige effects."

Describing this study makes me a bit uncomfortable. The ethics of deception is a topic that social psychologists have grappled with for decades. Today, the study could not be performed in the same way, as it would violate the profession's ethical guidelines. I also find the imperious tone of the memo somewhat off-putting. But I find the mission of the study admirable. Rosenthal and Jacobson wanted to determine if teachers' perceptions of their students' potential would affect students' experience of the classroom and how well they perform. They found a large effect.

Rosenthal and Jacobson readministered the IQ test at the end of the next school year to the same children. Across all grade levels tested, first grade to fifth, the students who had been earmarked as bloomers gained 4 IQ points more than the "non-bloomers"—which, to put in context, is about a third of the gap generally found in IQ test scores between stigmatized minorities and whites. The effect was especially striking in first and second grade, where the average gain was 12 IQ points. In the book Rosenthal and Jacobson wrote about the study, they profile a few of the most remarkable transformations. One student, Mario, gained 69 IQ points, while another, Maria, gained 40. There didn't seem to be any negative impact on the non-bloomers. In fact, they gained more IQ points in the classrooms where the bloomers gained more.

Rosenthal and Jacobson dubbed the phenomenon the "Pygmalion effect," after the sculptor in Greek mythology, who fell so in love with a sculpture he had carved of a woman that the God of Love, Aphrodite, brought the sculpture to life. The researchers were implying that bestowing loving care on students will animate them. The teacher is like a sculptor of human potential, a "Pygmalion in the classroom."

The study received a hailstorm of criticism. Some of the critics asserted that the data were flawed. But Rosenthal worked with the eminent statistician Don Rubin to confirm their robustness, which has been reconfirmed by an independent analysis of the data by the economist Tom Dee. A different objection was that the researchers seemed to be blaming teachers for failing to believe in their students' potential and to be ignoring the effects on school performance of poverty, racism, and social policy. But Rosenthal and Jacobson were not blaming teachers. Teachers are no more to blame than any of us, because all of us can and do fall prey to cognitive biases that blind us to the potential in others.

Nor did Rosenthal and Jacobson overlook the hardships students contend with. They highlighted them. In fact, many of the students at the school were from first-generation Mexican immigrant families who faced economic and social challenges, and one of the important findings of the study was that the students who benefited most from being seen as special were children from these immigrant families. The study underscored that teachers seemed to have absorbed negative cultural stereotypes that these children were innately less capable, and the intervention appeared to open their eyes to the potential of the children.

Rosenthal and Jacobson were also not arguing that only some students deserve special attention because they demonstrate more potential, as some critics asserted. Students were *randomly* identified as bloomers precisely to investigate whether a teacher seeing *any* student as having good potential would have positive effects on learning. The bottom line, backed up by many subsequent studies, is that all students should be viewed as having the capacity for growth. We must not commit the FAE by dubbing them as "gifted" or "middling," or as "bad apples," "bullies," or "dullards." As Carol Dweck has argued in her work on the growth mindset, all students can be coached to adopt a growth perspective, and teachers can be encouraged to apply that perspective to all of their students, avoiding the "fixed mindset" assessment that is so common and so difficult to change once students have been pegged.

Yet another controversy about the study concerns what teachers did differently with the bloomer students versus others. Some researchers have conjectured that a number of aspects of teacher behavior may be at play. Teachers may show more signs of caring, perhaps smiling more at kids they see as special. They may say the same words but with a warmer voice. Paul Ekman, a pioneer in the study of emotions, points to the power of small gestures that speak volumes: "a fixed gaze" and "raised eyebrows" convey "high hopes" compared with a "wandering gaze" and "bored expression."

Teachers might also excuse misbehavior among their "special" students, perhaps being a bit slower to apply a stereotype to a kid they see as promising. Teachers might also look more closely for evidence of growth and be more patient with students as they await improvement. They might be more likely to notice a clever remark a child makes or disregard poor handwriting and instead appreciate the insightful substance of an essay. Rosenthal also told me there is one more "laughably simple" explanation: When teachers believe in their students, they teach more. "You don't teach much if you think the kid is dumb," he said.

All in all, teachers who "expect more, get more," as Rosenthal and

Jacobson put it, which leads them to craft a classroom situation that inspires students and helps them perform better.

While some critics questioned whether the Pygmalion effect could be repeated, many follow-up experiments have confirmed it, not only with students' IQ scores but with the performance of soldiers in the military and workers in factories. It has even been shown to affect the warmth and depth we elicit in our everyday conversations. The latest edition of Rosenthal and Jacobson's book includes a meta-analysis of 345 studies. Subsequent research, however, uncovered an important qualification about when the desired outcomes will be seen. My favorite review of the Pygmalion effect in the classroom, by Stephen Raudenbush, found that after combining all the data from the studies done to date, an overall positive effect of teacher expectations emerged along with a key caveat: The benefits to students of being identified as bloomers occurred only when teachers got their list of "special" students either over the summer (before they had met them) or in the first few weeks of school. But if only two weeks of contact with their students had passed before teachers received the list, the benefits failed to appear. Timeliness matters. It was as if teachers' minds closed after they had formed an initial impression.

Building on the findings of the original study and follow-ups, some researchers have drawn on the lessons of Kurt Lewin to create training workshops for teachers to raise their awareness of how they can craft classroom experiences for their students that bring out their potential for learning. There is no need to deceive teachers. Empower them with knowledge.

Christine Rubie-Davies, a psychologist and educational scholar, for example, conducts workshops in which she discusses the Pygmalion research with teachers and then, acting as a democratic leader, asks them to generate new teaching ideas based on it. She also provides them with ongoing forums for discussing their progress. The educational psychologists Joseph Allen, Robert Pianta, and their colleagues have conducted similar training sessions with middle and high school teachers, focused on helping teachers create positive emotional encounters with their students, adding videotaped classroom sessions so that teachers can monitor with coaches their biases and progress in overcoming them. Look at it as the educational equivalent of grand rounds for physicians. Both training techniques have proved successful. Rubie-Davies found that students taught by a random group of elementary school teachers who attended her workshops achieved 50 percent larger gains in math achievement than the students in classes of teachers in a control group. Joseph Allen and his colleagues found that students taught by a random group of middle and high school teachers who attended his program rose from the 50th to the 59th percentile in their scores on the statewide achievement test. Meanwhile, the students of teachers in a control group didn't improve at all.

Research on the Pygmalion effect is a testament to the importance of shifting our focus away from people's talents and other interior essences—not just in schools, but in offices, in sports coaching, and with parents raising their children—to how the situation in which they're learning, working, or performing can be crafted to bring out their best. We should remember that, like teachers, we are all Pygmalions of other people's situations—often more so than we know.

A student of mine told me a story that illustrates the power and complexity of high expectations and how they can inspire people to change situations for the better. Anderson grew up poor in Brooklyn and got mixed up in the wrong crowd. He was arrested for a property crime and sentenced to ten years in prison. While serving his time, the new Cornell Prison Education Program was introduced. Taught by college professors, it offered a way for inmates to get their college degree. Anderson impressed his teachers, who saw him not as an inmate but as a human being with potential. One of the founders of the program got word of Anderson, and one day, she sat down with him and told him, "If what they say about you is true, I'm going to get you into Harvard." Anderson was taken aback. He would have been happy just to have his sentence reduced. Harvard seemed outrageous. "I thought she was insane," he told me.

But as Anderson's reputation as a young man with potential spread among the prisoners and the guards, they changed his situation in ways that made success possible for him. Even if he didn't believe in himself, they did. "The gangbangers and drug lords started to believe in me too," he said. One prisoner, a former drug lord, took it upon himself to protect Anderson from the other inmates as well as from the guards, who could also be "pretty wicked." This prisoner even got Anderson assigned to a different cell when he heard that some envious prisoners might attack him. "We're going to get you out of here," he told Anderson. "You're going to be the one." Another time, Anderson was about to be sent to a different prison, a common practice to keep prisoners from forming close attachments with one another. Anderson was panic-stricken because he knew that this would put an end to his participation in the education program and his prospect for a better future. But at the last minute, a guard intervened. He talked to the warden and got Anderson an exemption from the relocation policy. For Anderson's part, the word he uses to describe the shift in his mindset is "lifted." "It was no longer about making it through breakfast without getting stabbed." Anderson didn't end up at Harvard but at Stanford, on parole during his time there, and he graduated. Certainly, he has skills and talents, but these were far from enough. It was a belief in his potential and all the imaginative acts of situation-crafting it inspired that changed his fate.

THE DEGREE TO WHICH we so often choose to demean and even demonize individuals rather than attend to the ways a situation might be influencing them is a theme in Cormac McCarthy's novel *All the Pretty Horses*. In one scene, an American cowboy meets a Mexican ranchero, and to the cowboy's surprise, the ranchero tells him that although Anglos tend to think Mexicans are superstitious, Americans are more so. The ranchero then recounts that he once watched, baffled, as an American man took a hammer to his car because it wouldn't start. A Mexican, he explains, would never do this. A car "cannot be tainted, you see," he continues. "Or a man. Even a man. There can be in a man some evil. But we don't think it is his own evil. Where did he get it? How did he come to claim it? No. Evil is a true thing in Mexico. It goes about on its own legs."

The ranchero's key point is that Anglos have a peculiar way of thinking, that the behavior of people and things can be explained by mysterious essences inside them. "The mind of the Anglo is closed in this rare way," he says. "At one time I thought it was only his life of privilege. But it is not that. It is his mind. . . . It is not that he is stupid. It is that his picture of the world is incomplete. In this rare way. He looks only where he wishes to see."

When we see people as simply evil, or as idiots, maniacs, selfish users, irresponsible reprobates, what have you, we are engaging in a form of superstition. We think evil behavior must reflect a correspond-ing evil essence inside of a person, when evil is the product of a storm of variables that descend on a person. The ranchero is also spot on that this way of thinking takes an extreme form among Anglos. Although the FAE is apparent in many if not most cultures, it is especially strong in the United States and other individualistic cultures. In these cul-tures, we tend to attribute life successes or failures to assets *within* individuals, like diligence and intelligence, while ignoring the impor-tance of assets like trust and belonging that take their form as relations *between* individuals.

A result of this peculiar way of thinking is that Americans have created a cult of personality, buying into the notion that people's per-sonalities and potential can be summed up in a set of measurable traits, using tests such as the Myers-Briggs, and that people neatly fall into "types." We should have learned to question that contention long ago.

In 1968, Walter Mischel lobbed a grenade into the edifice of per-sonality research by exposing the poor predictive power of personal-ity tests. Researchers would measure a trait such as honesty and then use people's scores on it to predict their behavior. They investigated whether a child who scores high in honesty actually behaves honestly and whether a child who behaves honestly in one situation behaves honestly in others. To their surprise the correlations were tiny. At best, only 4 percent to 10 percent of the differences among people could be explained by some underlying personality trait.

Five decades after Mischel conducted that research, we still haven't listened to the findings. When I was growing up in the 1980s, my father worked in industry, and he was a big fan of the Myers-Briggs test. First conceived in the 1920s by the mother-daughter team of Katherine Briggs and Isabel Briggs Myers—two devoted homemakers, novelists, and amateur psychoanalysts—the Myers-Briggs test was designed to bring the gospel of psychologist Carl Jung to the masses. The instrument is now used by 80 percent of Fortune 500 companies and thousands of clinical and health centers throughout the world. My father prided himself on being able to instantly classify a person into a Myers-Briggs category, and he did this with gusto for all family members. He would read our fortunes and futures, always with confidence in the objectivity of his prognostications. That's why it was a surprise to me to learn years later that the Myers-Briggs is horrible at predicting people's work and life outcomes. In fact, it's barely more predictive than astrology—which is to say that the Myers-Briggs is, by and large, not predictive at all. Of course, there are more valid measures of personality than the Myers-Briggs, but the overwhelming conclusion across a large body of studies is that personality matters *less* than we *think* while the situation matters *more* than we *think*.

None of this research means that personality does not exist. It just means that our way of conceptualizing it is far from ideal. Even Walter Mischel demonstrated that people have consistent "behavioral signatures" over time, patterns of behavior that stretch, like a personal autograph, over wide-ranging situations. Some kids are honest with grown-ups but not with their peers. Some people are hardworking at work but lazy with household chores. No one else is quite like you in your quirky, idiosyncratic pattern across different situations. If we spent more time getting to know individuals and understanding their nuances and perspectives, we'd be better able to predict them.

It's true that IQ tests can predict some outcomes, but not nearly as much as people think. We might believe the tests measure some underlying essence—one's raw intelligence—that determines people's fates. But most studies show that IQ tests, as well as other personality instruments assessing grit and conscientiousness, explain only about 10 percent to 20 percent of the variability among people in terms of their school performance, work productivity, or career success.

A study published in 2021 consolidated data from almost fifty thousand participants who had completed a standardized test of intellectual ability in high school between two and seven decades ago; their participants included a large and nationally representative sample of Americans. The researchers tracked various outcomes related to the employment, health, and well-being of these former students, all now well into adulthood. The researchers wanted to know, among other things, if test scores predicted better outcomes. But to my mind, the major finding was how little the tests predicted. For physical and mental health, marital status, time with friends and family, participation in leadership roles, civic involvement, employment, income, job satisfaction, and sense of purpose in life, scores on the test accounted for no more than 6 percent of the differences among test takers, and for most of those outcomes, they predicted much less. The two exceptions were how many years of formal education test takers went on to obtain, and the prestige and complexity of their jobs. But even here, the tests left 75 percent to 85 percent of the differences among students' fates unexplained. The results underscore the fact that success is hard to predict, that it is a product of a complex dance between a person and a lifelong series of situations.

By placing too much weight on tests such as these, we do many people damage. Scores on these tests are widely used, for example, to determine students' academic opportunities, such as placement in gifted and talented programs. Remembering the Pygmalion effect, we should ask: Do the tests prophesy the future, or does our misuse of them create the future?

Meanwhile, we develop more and more tests to measure more and more things—emotional intelligence, social intelligence, practical intelligence, musical intelligence, and so on. I'm a fan of the ambition to recognize the diversity of human talents. But these tests risk diverting our attention away from the situation, leading us, as the ranchero put it, to look only where we wish to see.

To take one example, a 2016 study found that whether employees spoke up and expressed their ideas and concerns at work was, consistent with our intuitions, partly predicted by their personalities. But the impact of personality was overridden by whether the employees at the company perceived social *norms* that favored speaking up. If a company were interested in getting people to speak up, they'd be better off putting their energy into cultivating new norms rather than selecting gregarious employees.

Another misconceived set of tests includes the SAT, GRE, and other so-called aptitude assessments. They are privilege-laundering devices. It is as if we've taken the tests that the questioners generated themselves in the Quiz Bowl Study and turned them into assessments of innate aptitude. In other words, these tests take the advantages that people have accrued by dint of their race, gender, or economic prosperity and transform them into an indicator of ability or merit. Research has shown that SAT scores reveal little more about students' likelihood of success than do their high school transcripts. When colleges use SAT scores as a guide to admissions, what we *can* predict is that fewer qualified ethnic minority applicants will be admitted. That is because these tests don't accurately reflect the preparedness of minority applicants, as Greg Walton and Steve Spencer have shown. For instance, the SAT predicts that minorities will earn a lower college GPA than they actually do achieve in a college that takes steps to support their belonging, such as by implementing the social-belonging intervention discussed in Chapter 2. Partly because of the growing recognition of bias in these tests, the University of California system and many other colleges throughout the country no longer require SAT scores as part of their applications.

What if we spent the billions of dollars that we now spend on testing and used it instead to craft better situations in schools, workplaces, and the criminal justice system?

Beyond leading us to blame individuals and ignore situations, our cult of personality gives rise to hubris. We think that once we have someone "pegged" as an "introvert" or a "genius," we can predict how they will behave. We can't, at least not nearly as well as we think. This everyday arrogance has been dubbed the overconfidence effect. When researchers ask people to predict others' behavior, even the behavior of people they know well, they are far less accurate than they think they will be. In one study, undergraduates who thought they could predict with 100 percent accuracy what their roommate would do in various little social situations—such as whether they would comb their hair before posing for a photograph or would agree to participate in a short documentary—were wrong 20 percent of the time. Even professionals are overconfident. As research by Cade Massey and Richard Thaler has shown, National Football League teams pay more for their top picks in the annual draft than almost any analysis of the players' later "market value" would justify. In general, we overestimate how much of a team or an organization's performance, and even the quality of our own relationships, depends on picking the right people rather than creating the right conditions for them to thrive.

We're even overconfident in predicting our own behavior. Ask students to predict their future: Will they get an A in their favorite course? Switch roommates? Go to psychological services? Their predictions are far less accurate than they think they will be.

It's not that the concept of personality is inherently flawed. The point is that the same person may exhibit certain traits or behaviors often described as being part of one's personality in some circumstances and not in others. An officer of an urban youth program with whom I worked told me about a case in point. A low-income child under his care showed great determination in finding shelter and food for his mother and himself every day, exhibiting the trait often called grit. Yet that same child, when faced with poor grades, had stopped trying to succeed in school. What is it about these two situations that could lead to such different responses? One factor is that the immediate effects of poor grades pale in comparison to lacking food or shelter. Over the long term, of course, doing well in school could offer a lasting solution to the problem of feeding and housing oneself and one's loved ones. Yet it's difficult to focus on the future when one's daily life is so precarious. Qualities like grit and self-control do not come from within the individual alone. Whether in the classroom or the neighborhood, such qualities live in the interaction between the person and the situation.

The most undersold discovery in social psychology and, indeed, in social science in general is the sheer complexity of human behavior, which the FAE leads us to simplify. We don't like to admit it, especially we scientists of human behavior, but we don't know why people do what they do most of the time. Every situation is a unique and complex convergence of many forces. Contrary to sci-fi yarns that present a dystopian future where "Big Brother" has every citizen's personality pegged and filed, and where artificial intelligence predicts everyone's behavior so well that we finally have to admit there is no such thing as free will, people are hard to predict. One large-scale study, published in 2020, tested how well artificial intelligence algorithms could predict outcomes like children's high school GPA or whether a family would run into economic hardship, based on extensive data about children and their families from age zero to sixteen. Even the best algorithms left 95 percent of the diversity in outcomes unexplained. That means that lots of children and lots of families did better, and a lot did worse, than the algorithms predicted. "What is" offers a poor guide to "what will be" and, I would add, an even worse guide to "what could be."

What's the practical lesson? The utility of humility in our social lives. One of the greatest scientists of all time, Isaac Newton, had to admit at the end of his life that he felt "only like a boy, playing on the sea-shore, and diverting myself in now and then finding a smoother pebble or a prettier shell than ordinary, whilst the great ocean of truth lay all undiscovered before me." As we have seen, assuming we know more than we do often does more harm than good not just in science but in social life.

+ + + +

ONE THING THAT MY father expounded on was the notion of talent and genius. He was a theoretical physicist, and I think he was steeped in the mythology of great men in his field. He too was partly the product of his circumstances. "Einstein just saw things differently," he told me. "He came up with the special theory of relativity working alone in a patent office." While it certainly was the case that Einstein saw things differently, he also had a lot of help from other people, including his wife, Mileva, who was also a physicist. In spite of collaborating on Einstein's first paper, she removed her name from the publication, it seems, to support her husband's career. This fact does not diminish Einstein's accomplishments. It only highlights that he, like the rest of us, had help from his social situation. And the FAE predicts that we will downplay facts such as these when we tell the history of the luminaries of the past.

The FAE-driven belief that innate talent determines success in a specialized field of endeavor leads to discrimination against women and African Americans in those fields. This was demonstrated in research by Sarah-Jane Leslie, Andrei Cimpian, Meredith Meyer, and Edward Freeland, published in the premier journal *Science*. They surveyed 1,820 faculty members, postdoctoral fellows, and doctoral students from a variety of disciplines at public and private universities throughout the United States, asking them to indicate the degree to which they agreed with various statements signaling the importance of innate talent for success, such as "Being a top scholar in my discipline requires a special aptitude that just can't be taught." They found that the degree to which the people in a given discipline answered in the affirmative predicted the degree of underrepresentation of women and African Americans there. The same effect was seen in both STEM and non-STEM disciplines. Scholars in musical composition, economics, and philosophy all espoused the same belief in the importance of raw talent, and these fields all had as few women as math and most of the hard sciences.

To make a long story short, the effect remained robust when the researchers controlled for the selectivity of the discipline (as measured by the estimated percentage of applicants admitted each year to their department, their average GRE scores, or the number of hours people worked on average per week). In fact, these beliefs in raw talent emerged as *the* strongest predictor of gender and racial gaps.

A related study by the social psychologists Elizabeth Canning, Mary Murphy, and their colleagues zeroed in on a single university and showed a similar pattern in student grades. Among the 150 professors surveyed, the researchers found great variability in how much professors agreed with such statements as "To be honest, students have a certain amount of intelligence, and they really can't do much to change it." Those professors who agreed more with these statements, expressing a strong belief in innate ability, taught courses in which all students earned lower grades, but especially students from African American, Latino, and other underrepresented ethnic minority groups. The racial achievement gap in grades given was nearly twice the size for these instructors than it was for those faculty members who were skeptics of the notion of innate intelligence. These effects held up even when controlling for the age, gender, ethnicity, teaching experience, and tenure status of the professor. In fact, instructor beliefs emerged as the strongest predictor of achievement gaps. To illustrate the implications, consider this finding: Black students with a white teacher who didn't espouse an innate intelligence mindset were better off than black students with a black teacher who did.

Why did teacher beliefs matter so much? The courses taught by professors who believed in raw talent did not appear to be more demanding from the perspective of the students in them. Students in both types of courses reported spending similar amounts of time on their coursework. Where the students diverged, in terms of their own reported experience of the class, was in how much they thought their instructor tried to motivate them to do their best and how much the instructor emphasized learning. Teachers can send subtle and not-so-subtle messages about how much they think learning matters. In one high school I'm familiar with, a science teacher reportedly told his class, "There are fake A and real A students, and I can always tell the difference. Fake A students are the ones who spend countless hours reading the textbook and put in too much work. They lack the common sense to reason easy solutions that real A students grasp."

We indoctrinate our children into the FAE and the cult of genius from an early age. It's part of the situation we and the rest of society craft for our kids. We do this in various ways, often well intentioned—for instance, by praising them for their intelligence rather than for their effort or clever use of strategy. Carol Dweck and her colleagues have shown in several elegant studies that such "ability praise" teaches kids to believe that innate ability rather than effort drives success, which contributes to failure in the long run. Andrei Cimpian has illuminated how much the FAE is part of our culture—and perhaps, he'd argue, part of our cognitive wiring—by demonstrating that young children, ages five to seven, tend to attribute advantage internally. If you ask them, "Why do the Blarks on Planet Teeku happen to have more money than the Orps?" they'll tend to answer, "Because they're smarter." And the degree to which they do so predicts the degree to which they think the powerful group deserves to be on top.

Many parents and educators worry about exposing children to violent and sexual content, as they should, but we should also pay attention to the harm done by media programming that sends toxic messages about who belongs. Consider three findings that suggest that sometimes the message that "geniuses belong" can send the implicit message that certain other groups don't. In several studies conducted as recently as 2017, children as young as six or seven, when asked to pick someone who is "really, really" smart, were more likely to pick someone who is male. Returning to the study that surveyed faculty members in various disciplines, people in fields characterized by a belief in raw talent were more likely to agree with statements like "Even though it's not politically correct to say it, men are more often suited than women to do high-level work in my discipline." In later experimental research, Cimpian and his colleagues presented men and women with an internship opportunity in one of various fields. For some, representatives of the company singled out raw "brilliance" as key to success. You had to be an "intellectual firecracker," with a "sharp, penetrating mind." For others, they emphasized "great focus and determination" or being "passionate about the job." No matter the field, women expressed less interest in the internship and more anxiety about belonging there when the description emphasized brilliance. Men, meanwhile, expressed *more* interest and more confidence.

WHAT CAN WE DO to fight against the FAE? First, we can coach ourselves to consider how the situation that people are in may be affecting them and us. Research shows that liberals tend to make more sympathetic attributions than conservatives when it comes to explaining social problems, but when it comes to explaining the more ordinary outrages of their daily lives, they seem to revert to the FAE. A little activity that I practice with my students and kids can help. Bring up an outrage, maybe something from your personal life or the news, something as simple as "A man cut in front of me at the grocery store." Then ask, why did he do it? Once everyone exhausts the off-the-shelf internal attributions like "He's a selfish SOB," you can raise the possibility of situational attributions and solicit them. Some will be simple: "Maybe he didn't see that there was a line." Others will be quite imaginative: "Maybe he had to rush home to his sick dog." People become eager to offer explanations. I see this as mental calisthenics. We retrain our minds so that explanations beyond the culturally programmed ones come readily. In technical terms, they become more cognitively *accessible* or *available*, more likely to pop into our consciousness at key moments and guide our response. Variants of this approach have even been used to lower the reactivity of children easily provoked to aggression, who often have a bias to see hostility in others' actions. By making these kinds of activities public, such as in classrooms, we can also create a norm of "attributional charity" in our schools, work-places, and homes.

A powerful example of the benefits of such mental calisthenics comes from a wise intervention designed by Daphne Bugental and her colleagues to prevent child abuse. Strange as it may seem, child abuse, like other forms of violence, seems to stem in part from the FAE. Parents sometimes think their baby is crying and grouchy because either they themselves are bad parents or their child is bad and trying to manipulate and control them. They're at special risk of doing this under stress, and Bugental, in her research, first targeted parents at risk of abuse because they either had been abused themselves or were dealing with major life stressors. She intervened at a timely moment, soon after the birth of their child.

Paraprofessionals visited these parents roughly every two to three weeks for a year, on average a total of seventeen times. The first thing they did was to give parents information on how to support their chil-dren's healthy physical, emotional, and intellectual development. But the key part of the intervention was a mental calisthenic activity to help parents "reframe and resolve" caregiving challenges. For this, the paraprofessionals didn't lecture or chasten the parents but posed Soc-ratic questions that involved parents as active participants in the pro-cess of their own cognitive change. Each week, the paraprofessionals would ask the parents for a caregiving challenge they had experienced over the last week, and then they'd tailor the activity around this prob-lem. For instance, many parents complained that their baby sometimes seemed inconsolable. Parents were asked, "Why do you think that hap-pened?" If they responded, "Because my baby hates me" or "Because I'm a terrible mother," the paraprofessional would prompt them again. "Why else might your baby be upset?" Such prompts continued until parents generated a reason that did not blame either themselves or their infants. To nudge parents in this direction, the paraprofessional might add a comment, such as "Sometimes babies get upset because something is making them uncomfortable, like their digestion, their diaper, or their formula. Do you think this is a possibility?"

The next step was to focus parents on strategies to solve the problem based on their new causal analysis. Parents came up with situational solutions, such as using a different amount of formula, trying a new brand of diapers, cuddling with their baby, or singing to them. In every session, they were prompted to think back on the strategies they had tried after the last session and whether those strategies were successful. Parents weren't simply given reasons and strategies but were taught to generate them on their own and monitor their impact.

At the end of the year, Bugental compared the outcomes of the parents going through this wise intervention with a group of parents who had been randomly assigned to receive only the information about healthy child development during similar home visits. Parents in both groups completed questionnaires assessing the frequency with which they engaged in abusive behaviors, such as shaking an infant, which is a common cause of infant trauma and death that many parents tragically aren't even aware constitutes abuse. Only 4 percent of the intervention group abused their child compared with 23 percent in the control group. The children in the intervention group were also judged as healthier by an independent medical assessment. In addition, Bugental and colleagues tracked down nearly two-thirds of the families after the intervention and found that the parents who had received it were less depressed and less avoidant with their children. That is, they were less likely to sulk, walk out on their child, or not talk to their child in response to conflicts, all reactions that threaten belonging and thus do more harm than good. The researchers even found evidence that these parents' children had less physiological stress and behaved less aggressively.

Checking in on our mental state when we find ourselves becoming annoyed or hurt is also important. Feeling busy, burned out, stressed, insecure, or tired exacerbates our tendency to commit the FAE. Giving ourselves what the eminent happiness scholar Sonja Lyubomirsky calls "psychological timeouts" can help. Various activities can open up some mental space for calm and renew our energy so that we can pause to consider a wider range of explanations for another person's behavior and choose our response wisely. Let's look at a few examples of these timeouts.

One study had viewers of a violent assault write about their thoughts and feelings, which was a way of calming their reactions. They were then less likely to assert that the victim of the assault must have done something to deserve it, relative to viewers who didn't write about their thoughts and feelings.

In a study inspired by the work of Ethan Kross, a twenty-minute online intervention prompted married couples to think about their disagreements from the "perspective of a neutral third party who wants the best for all involved, a person who sees things from a neutral point of view." They were then asked to generate strategies to call this perspective to mind when disagreements got heated. Compared with married couples who were not prompted to look at their disagreements in this way, the intervention group felt happier about their marriages over the next year.

One more way of checking ourselves and calming our minds is through a type of self-affirmation known as *values affirmation*: Take a mental step back and remind yourself of the values you stand for. This technique, pioneered by Claude Steele, involves answering two questions—"What are your values?" and "Why are they important to you?"—usually by writing down the reflections provoked. (Typically, a list of sample values is provided to help people in the task, and usually this list excludes any values related to the threatening situation; examples of values-affirmation activities are available at geoffreylcohen.com.) Because values reflect our deepest commitment, when we reflect on them, we bring our sense of who we are, and particularly our awareness of our better nature, into clearer focus, curbing our defensive need to blame others.

In research I collaborated on with Shannon Brady and Camille Griffiths, we found evidence that values affirmation made first-year teachers of minority youth less prone to committing the FAE. After writing about their core values, the teachers rated a hypothetical low-performing student as more likely to turn his performance around in future grades, relative to a control group of teachers who had written about an unimportant value. The values-affirmed teachers also reported having better relationships with their students several months later, relative to the teachers in the control group. At the end of the year, the values-affirmed teachers were judged by outside experts to have offered their students a more rigorous and demanding classroom experience. We interpreted this finding as suggestive that the affirmation lessened teachers' tendency to see their students as having inherently low potential to learn.

We're more likely to beat back the FAE by crafting our own situations and those of others in ways that foster the awareness and perspective we need to overcome our mental reflexes. Of course, we can do this on our own, but homes, schools, and workplaces can also create environments that replenish rather than exhaust our headspace and heartspace.

IN AN EPISODE OF the science fiction TV series *Black Mirror*, a woman loses her husband to a car accident. To replace him, she mail-orders an automaton, which, upon downloading all her late husband's tweets, emails, and online posts, is able to imitate him almost perfectly. And in fact there are perks. He's far better in bed than her late husband (having downloaded a trove of her favorite porn). But, she discovers later, it's not really *him*. The automaton is different in those subtle, small ways that speak volumes. It's common knowledge that her late husband hated disco music. But few knew, as she had once learned when they had fought over a radio station in the car, that he loved the song "How Deep Is Your Love" by the Bee Gees.

What she discovers is that her love for her husband came in part out of his ability to be a reliable surprise to her, just when she thought she had him pegged. What a blessing that is, *Black Mirror*'s episode seems to be saying.

Our typecasting of people—presuming we can sum up who they are and will always be—not only causes exclusion and harm but saps our social lives of so much potential, wonder, and possibility of bonding with others. To use a term in psychology, it "ordinizes" social experience, rendering ordinary that which actually is—and could be still more—extraordinary.

A study conducted by Nick Epley and Juliana Schroeder demonstrated the joy people tend to get from chance encounters with strangers. In a poetically titled paper, "Mistakenly Seeking Solitude," they showed that train riders they interviewed consistently predicted that having a conversation with a stranger would be unpleasant. But when the researchers randomly assigned some of the passengers to do just that, they experienced precisely the opposite. It made them happier. Although we don't know what makes these serendipitous encounters more pleasing than the solitude we often choose instead, I suspect that the answer has something to do with the delightful surprise of connecting with an unfamiliar mind.

Rather than make snap judgments about people and why they're behaving as they are, we can work to be mindful about the harmful effects of the FAE on our relations with others. We can coach ourselves and our children to take a step back to consider the situation rather than leaping to conclusions about a person.

This work can be challenging, especially when our culture has polluted our minds with stereotypes of race, ethnicity, gender, physical disability, economic attainment, and so many more. Stereotypes are a Fundamental Attribution Error applied not only to an individual but to a whole group. In the next chapter, we'll explore just how embedded they are in our minds, how harmful they are, and what we can do to fight back.

Chapter 6

They're All
the Same

Why We Stereotype Others and
How We Can Stop Doing It

IN RALPH ELLISON'S CLASSIC NOVEL ABOUT RACE IN AMERICA, *Invisible Man*, the narrator likens being black to being invisible "because of a peculiar disposition of the eyes of those with whom I come in contact. A matter of the construction of their *inner* eyes, those eyes with which they look through their physical eyes upon reality." Those who fail to see him are gazing through the mental constructions known as stereotypes, the grossly generalizing and mostly negative characterizations of whole social groups. Stereotypes commit the Fundamental Attribution Error on whole categories of people: "poor white trash," "stupid blondes," "sexist pigs." Stereotypes are one of the most ingrained and damaging contaminants in human thinking, and they can be remarkably impervious to refutation. They pervade not only American culture but cultures around the globe, everywhere dividing up societies into an "Us" who belongs and a "Them" who does not.

In an introduction to a later edition of his novel, Ellison comments, "Most of all, I would have to approach racial stereotypes as a given fact of the social process and proceed ... to reveal the human complexity which stereotypes are intended to conceal." In my research, I have grappled with the social fact of stereotypes, with their power to blind us to the distinctive, surprising, complicated individuality of those we encounter. Stereotypes lead us as ordinary people in our everday lives to threaten the belonging of others, even when we don't consciously believe the stereotypes.

Most of us don't choose to be blind in this way. We all, growing up in any society, learn a host of stereotypes. While we may come to consciously reject many of them, they linger in our minds, distorting our views of individuals we encounter and shaping the way we treat them. What's more, our biases do not have to be overt to inflict great harm, and we do not have to feel disgust, disdain, fear, or anger toward others to treat them in biased and harmful ways. Elie Wiesel, who won the Nobel Peace Prize for his writing about the Holocaust, suggests that our failure to care for those we see as different from ourselves—to empathize with them and show them understanding, kindness, and support—by no means requires hatred. "The opposite of love is not hate," he said. "It is indifference." That indifference stems from our failure to see and therefore to feel others' humanity. We're indifferent about who they really are and don't consider them as unique individuals, instead allowing our minds to follow a script about them.

The comedian Dave Chappelle, an African American, addressed this problem in one of his routines. He described his reaction as he drove through rural Ohio, observing many poor whites addicted to heroin and other opioids. "You know what this reminds me of?" he recalls asking himself. "It reminds me of us." The white folks, he says, look exactly like African Americans did during the crack epidemic of the 1980s and 1990s. He goes on to say the experience gave him "insight into how the white community must have felt watching the black community go through the scourge of crack. Because," he zings his audience, "I don't care either." His attitude is, "Hang in there, whites. Just say, No. What's so hard about that?" He's satirizing how insensitive we can all be in the ways we see "others." He's speaking to the indifference Elie Wiesel indicts.

We make a grave error if we believe that prejudice is committed only by people who are bigots and that it is only a matter of overt hate or revulsion. Prejudice is also a matter of everyday indignities, subtle but cutting slights. And it's a matter of the thoughts and feelings we fail to have, the actions we fail to take. The acts of outright hatred grab the spotlight of media attention, but the cumulative toll of less overtly biased behavior, like not offering a job applicant an interview or not appreciating another person's contribution, mounts up. When we fail to understand how stereotypes affect our own ways of perceiving and treating others, we are like one in a colony of ants who each lift a tiny bit of dirt over and over to create an anthill of discrimination. If we are to better foster belonging in our societies, we must correct our vision of others so that we see them as individuals rather than caricatures based on stereotypes.

Ralph Ellison's narrator isn't invisible. He's just not seen. But what do we mean by this? Of course, his physical presence can be easily seen. But that's not the type of seeing Ellison is remarking on. Seeing is not merely a matter of visual perception. To see, as psychologists have shown, is a mental and emotional act. Our minds bring expectations to perceiving the people before us. If we're walking down a city street and spot something scurrying across the sidewalk, we might see it as a rat and be taken aback, only to discover it's a plastic bag blown by the wind. We take in visual cues and build images in our minds based largely on learned expectations. Many painters have explored this nature of our vision, such as the Impressionists and Cubists. They tried to see in a more elemental way, to more fully appreciate the wonder of sight and to honor an older meaning of the word "see" as to "behold in the imagination" and to "recognize the force of" the landscapes and individuals they portrayed.

To begin to appreciate how much stereotypes distort our vision and how we might improve it, imagine that you're watching from the back of a classroom as Hannah, a fourth-grade student, answers questions posed to her by an examiner. She gets some easy problems wrong and some hard problems right. What should you conclude about her ability?

This is the situation that adult participants faced in a 1983 study by John Darley and Paget Gross, except that they didn't sit in a classroom but instead were divided into two groups and told they would first watch a video of Hannah going about her everyday life in her home neighborhood. One group saw her playing in the fenced-in playground of a school that looked like an abandoned warehouse in a neighborhood pocked with rundown houses. This group was told that Hannah's dad was a meat-packer and her mom a part-time seamstress. Another group watched a video of Hannah playing in a lush park amid large, well-maintained homes with expansive green lawns. This group learned that Hannah's dad was an attorney and her mom a writer. Both groups then watched exactly the same video of Hannah answering questions and were asked to evaluate her intellectual ability. The fact that she got some hard questions right and some easy questions wrong was important because had she either excelled or done terribly, the assessments would be less open to interpretation. Ambiguity is fodder for stereotypes. Indeed, the two groups evaluated Hannah's abilities dramatically differently.

When asked to estimate how many questions Hannah got correct in the classroom video, the participants who believed she was from a poor family estimated on average that she was correct 30 percent of the time, while those who thought she was from a wealthy family guessed on average that she was right 67 percent of the time. What's more, those who thought she was poor judged her ability to be halfway between the third- and fourth-grade level, while those who thought she was wealthy judged her as a full grade level ahead, midway between the fourth and fifth grade.

When the participants were asked to offer qualitative assessments of Hannah's thinking abilities, they described two dramatically different girls. "Hannah has difficulty accepting new information" was one comment made about "poor" Hannah. "Rich" Hannah, by contrast, was said to have "the ability to apply what she knows to unfamiliar problems." The two groups even perceived the nature of the test she had taken differently. Even though everyone heard the same questions, those who thought Hannah was poor rated them as easier. "Hannah failed an easy test," poor-Hannah viewers thought, while rich-Hannah viewers concluded, "Hannah did fairly well on a hard test." Like Ellison's invisible man, Hannah was not seen directly but through the filter of a stereotype.

Students from less well-off families are subjected to this kind of unintended bias in classrooms on a daily basis. Whether or not teachers believe a student has good potential to learn can affect the quality of the learning experience that the student will have, as we saw in the Pygmalion study. On top of that, students tend to get "pegged" as high or low potential, and students labeled as low potential are put into remedial programs. Research shows that these programs tend to be pipelines of academic failure and that minority and poor students are assigned to them in disproportionate numbers. One damning study of bias in evaluating students' academic potential showed that relying on the relatively more objective measure of a standardized test to decide on whom to admit into gifted and talented programs—rather than teachers' subjective judgments—would dramatically increase the number of minority students enrolled in these programs. Given that standardized tests can also be biased, this result suggests a surprising degree of bias in some teachers' assessments of student potential.

Being subjected to bias can also lead students to become disengaged and disillusioned with school. A student of mine, who is a first-generation Mexican American and now a professor at a university, told me that her brother experienced such a downward spiral. He was just as smart as she was, she said, but one incident at high school threw him off course. One day he had an epileptic seizure during lunch. When he awoke on the cafeteria floor, with the principal and teachers surrounding him, he was asked, "What did you take?" They thought he must be on drugs, and the accusation—with its implication that he was living out a stereotype of being a poor Latino—stung. He was eventually cleared of any misdoing but not of the belief that his teachers thought poorly of him. He grew indifferent to school. His schoolwork and relationships with teachers deteriorated, and soon he was hanging out with the wrong crowd. Eventually he dropped out.

Research into why students spiral downward in school in this way has shown that the process often begins with a biased disciplinary action. When teachers don't seem to respect students, the students can often tell. They feel it and act out or underachieve, causing teachers to see them more negatively, and so on, in a long chain of mutually reinforcing actions and reactions. The kids may build up a bad reputation, as teachers share their stereotypical judgments with one another. In two multiyear studies by my colleagues and me, minority children in middle school (sixth to eighth grade) reported feeling increasingly distrustful of their teachers. Their trust dropped only a little bit each academic term, but it decreased consistently so that by the end of middle school, there was a wide gap in the trust expressed by minority students and their white peers. This drop in trust predicted a greater likelihood of minority students acting out. The downward trajectory seemed to be triggered by the social fact of discrimination: Soon after starting middle school, minority students really were disproportionately more likely to receive harsher disciplinary sentences than their white peers, especially in ambiguous "judgment call" situations, which led them to question the legitimacy of school and its rules.

The Hannah study is but one of many that have demonstrated that people perceive the same actions in a less flattering light when they're committed by a person who is negatively stereotyped (although one study showed different results). In a striking example from 2010 focused on gender bias in the workplace, social psychologist Victoria Brescoll asked study participants to evaluate a hypothetical police chief. One group was led to believe the chief was male, and the other group was led to believe that the chief was female. For both groups, the chief was said to have a solid record in the police department. When given just this information, there was no significant difference in how the participants evaluated the chief. Two other groups of participants were given the same information, but they were also told that the chief had one bad mark on his or her record, having failed to send in enough officers to quell a protest that turned violent. The participants didn't judge the male police chief any differently for this mistake, but they rated the female chief much lower in status and less deserving of her job. Male and female evaluators showed the same degree of bias, suggesting that it even overpowered the desire to favor an ingroup.

Brescoll has gone on to conduct many more studies revealing biased assessments of women. For instance, when women get angry or simply talk a lot, they tend to be perceived as less competent and lower in status. But when men do the same, they tend to be viewed as more competent and higher in status. Some fascinating research suggests that women tend to adjust their behavior so as not to be pegged by this stereotyping, restraining their expression of anger and the amount they speak in male-dominated situations. On the Senate floor, for example, while male senators with higher status talk more than male senators with lower status, female senators don't talk more as they achieve more status.

Many of the studies of the effects of stereotyping in the United States have explored its impact on African Americans because, as Ellison so viscerally conveyed, they have pervasively suffered from it. One body of work, reported in 2015 by the social psychologists Jason Okonofua and Jennifer Eberhardt, has examined the treatment of black children in schools. Teachers were asked to judge the behavior of a student based on a written record. Some teachers were told the student's name was Jake, which is generally perceived as a white name. Other teachers were told the student's name was Darnell, which is generally perceived as a black name. Both groups of teachers then read about how the student fell asleep in class and how even after his teacher told him to pay attention, he just laid his head on his hands and closed his eyes. Then they rated the student's character and recommended various actions on numerical scales.

With only that information, the teachers rated Jake and Darnell equally in terms of how much of a troublemaker he was and how severely he should be punished. That might be surprising, but, after all, teachers are generally dedicated to nurturing students and treating them fairly. Yet, in a next phase of the study, they were told that on another day, the student strolled around the classroom talking to friends and causing a disruption. Now there was more fodder for the stereotype. Assessments of the two students diverged. The teachers evaluating Jake rated him pretty much the same. But for Darnell, it was an altogether different story. The teachers came down hard on him, rating him as more of a "troublemaker" and perceiving his behavior as part of a larger pattern, recommending he be subjected to more severe disciplinary action, some even advising he be suspended. For the black kid, it was as though teachers applied a "two strikes and you're out" policy.

Stereotypical judgments can ruin lives. Substantial research shows that being suspended can do irreparable damage to a student's sense of belonging and prospects for success. Suspension is a "solution" that makes the problem much worse, undermining children's sense of belonging and putting some on a path to unemployment and incarceration. It's a fate minority children are subjected to disproportionately, with complaints of unfairness too often dismissed.

Questions have been raised about whether laboratory experiments such as these reflect the way stereotyping actually plays out in the real world. To try to assess that, Travis Riddle and Stacey Sinclair evaluated data from over 32 million students attending 96,360 schools throughout the United States. They found that in counties with higher levels of racism, as measured by survey data from another national data source, harsher disciplinary measures were taken against black students relative to white ones. This effect held up even when the researchers statistically controlled for the county's population, proportion of black residents, average educational attainment, crime rate, geographic region, and level of economic mobility. It was, admittedly, a small effect. But when we are dealing with such important outcomes compounded across millions of students, even small effects matter, especially for the affected children and their families.

These findings of bias in the schooling of black students call to mind a remark by Martin Luther King Jr. He said that one thing he feared about school desegregation was that black children would be taught by white teachers who don't love them.

It may seem unrealistic to expect that teachers should love their students, but the more I delve into the research on teaching, the more it seems to converge on the importance of love—not the type between parents and their children, surely, but love in the sense that Martin Luther King Jr., Gandhi, and Nelson Mandela meant it, a faith we choose to have in the inherent worth and dignity of another human being. Stereotypes undermine this faith, constricting our hearts, blinding us to one another's full humanity. As quoted earlier, the writer and concentration-camp survivor Elie Wiesel believed the opposite of love to be not hate but indifference. He also called indifference the "epitome of evil." The many ways in which stereotyping has distorted the views of people from various groups and deprived them of the faith and love they deserve from others have certainly led to evil.

The perceptual distortions caused by stereotypes lead to many forms of heartlessness. For example, it's easier for us to love children than adults, and one way white people fail to love black children is by seeing them as older and less innocent.

In 2014, a white police officer in Cleveland shot and killed Tamir Rice, a twelve-year-old African American boy playing with a toy gun at a city park. Social psychologist Phillip Goff, who was heartbroken over similar cases of black youth victimized by police and the courts, showed that black children are less likely to be seen as children. After age ten, Goff found, black children as a group are rated as needing "less protection" and "less care" than white children. They're also seen as less "cute" and "innocent." Goff also asked various samples of adults, made up mostly of white people and including urban police officers, to try to guess the ages of black and white child lawbreakers based on photographs of them. The black and white offenders were matched for physical attractiveness, which has been shown to affect assessments of people, and the offenders ranged in age from ten to seventeen. People tended to see all of the offenders as older than they were, no doubt because they had already been labeled "criminals." But they overesti-mated the age of the black child offenders by twice the amount they overestimated the age of the white child offenders, judging the black children on average as almost five years older than they actually were.

The damage of stereotyping doesn't stop once children grow up, though. The distorting lens applied to black adults has been laid bare in research on hiring decisions. Despite popular coverage and frequent citations of a study by two economists, Marianne Bertrand and Sendhil Mullainathan, one of the study's findings is rarely reported. The headline result was that faux résumés sent to firms throughout New York City and Chicago were almost twice as likely to receive a callback if the name the researchers put on the résumé was one commonly perceived as white, such as John or Quinton, than if the name was one perceived as black, such as Jamal or LaKeesha. Indeed, a black candidate would have to have eight more years of extra on-the-job experience to receive as many callbacks as a white candidate. But, in addition, those evaluating the black candidates' résumés also revealed a kind of blindness in reading them, failing to appreciate the quality of the applicants' credentials. For each name group, the researchers sent two versions of the résumé, one with stand-out credentials—more on-the-job experience, more skills, fewer gaps in employment—and the other with weak credentials. Better credentials predicted more frequent callbacks for the white applicants but not so for the black applicants. It's as if the credentials for black candidates were invisible.

Another study that pulled back the curtain on systemic discrimination against black people in hiring decisions was conducted by Devah Pager, a sociologist. She had trained black and white actors to apply to entry-level jobs throughout Milwaukee. She carefully crafted the credentials of the two groups of applicants to be equivalent. In total, these actors, all male, interviewed for 350 jobs throughout the city. Who applied to which job was decided by the research team on a random basis. The result? White applicants received a callback 26 percent of the time, and black applicants were called back less than half that, only 10 percent. Pager also probed the effects of an applicant having a criminal record or not, which she also varied for her applicants. Overall, the penalty for having committed a felony was about the same as the penalty for being black, which led to Pager's most striking and disturbing result: A white applicant with a felony record was slightly *more* likely to receive a callback than a black applicant without a felony record (17 percent versus 14 percent).

What's more, if an applicant was black *and* had a felony record, callbacks dropped to 5 percent. Employers' minds seemed to have been mostly shut to the notion that a black applicant with a prison record should be given a chance and seen as having any potential. However, when employers talked with white applicants with a prison record, they might offer a stern warning that if the applicant stole anything or didn't show up, "this relationship is over," but they also often said they believed in giving the applicants the benefit of the doubt. A number of employers made a comment similar to this one from an interview with a white applicant: "I have no problem with your conviction; it doesn't bother me." They saw greater potential in a white applicant who had made a mistake than in a black one who had.

DISCRIMINATION IN OUR SCHOOLS and workplaces is joined by a steady drip of daily indignities that the stereotyped are subjected to. One especially well-crafted study illuminates the distinctly different ways that black and white people tend to be treated during the tension-provoking experience of being stopped for a traffic infraction.

Jennifer Eberhardt has dedicated her career to understanding how race shapes much of social life in America. She is black and the author of a powerful book, *Biased: Uncovering the Hidden Prejudice That Shapes What We See, Think, and Do*. Some of her work has examined the subtle but potent racism that police officers express in seemingly benign interactions with black people.

In the early 2000s, Eberhardt held a conference that brought together social scientists and police officers to discuss the spate of police shootings of black suspects that had occurred at that time. To all the academics' surprise, the police, while admitting that the shootings were a grave problem, said it was not the problem that was most often on their minds. An officer, they said, might fire a gun once in his or her career. What they really needed help with, they said, was dealing with the everyday encounters of the police beat, such as ordinary stops and conversations with members of the black community. Too often these encounters would needlessly escalate, sometimes with catastrophic results. But even when the results weren't catastrophic, they left a lingering distrust among many community members. That undermined the police force's ability to fight crime, they said. Without trust, there was no community cooperation and less information that could help the police keep the peace and protect the people.

Eberhardt teamed up with a doctoral student, Nick Camp, and a linguist, Rob Voigt, in an unusual partnership with the Oakland Police Department to study just these kinds of encounters. They reported their findings in 2017. The Oakland Police Department made the courageous decision to share with the researchers the body-camera videotapes of 981 police traffic stops conducted by 245 different officers, a trove of data that nobody had examined. Eberhardt and her team focused on the mundane encounters that many of us have had, those in which no arrest is made—the vast majority of the stops they had footage for. The conversations in these stops initially seemed unremarkable across the board. But close analysis revealed that powerful psychological messages were being sent to drivers, and the messages were systematically different as a function of the driver's race.

The conversations were transcribed, and then coders, who were unaware of the race of the driver, evaluated the content of a large random subset of police utterances (there were too many to do this with all of them).

Here are excerpts of how the police talk to white drivers:

> "Sorry to stop you. My name's Officer Ryan with the Police Department."
> "There you go, ma'am. Drive safe, please."
> "It just says that you've fixed it. No problem. Thank you very much, sir."

Here are excerpts illustrative of how the police talked to black drivers:

> "All right, my man. Do me a favor. Just keep your hands on the
>   steering wheel real quick."
> "John, can I see that driver's license again? . . . Is that—that's
>   you?"

Notice a difference?

The utterances that officers made to black drivers were judged by the coders to be less friendly and respectful than those made to white drivers. They were also, interestingly, judged to be more "judgmental," with more negative words.

Eberhardt and her colleagues then ran all 36,768 utterances that police made through computational linguistic models, an artificial intelligence technique that is able to measure the frequency of words and phrases that cluster around linguistic themes. This analysis provided a more detailed understanding of the differences in how officers acted with white versus black drivers. First, the officers expressed more *solidarity* with white drivers. They were more likely to make such comments as "drive carefully." Second, they appeared more *comfortable* with white drivers. They didn't trip over their words as much, say "uh" or "um" as much, or interrupt their speech with an awkward pause as often. Research shows that black people may see these signs of discomfort as evidence of racial bias. Finally, the officers were more *polite* with white drivers. They said "please" and "thank you" much more. They apologized more, such as saying, "Sorry to bother you." They used formal titles like "sir" and "ma'am" rather than referring to the driver on a first-name basis or, when the driver was male, as "man" or "bro." With white drivers, they used questions more and commands less, such as asking, "Would you mind putting your hands on the wheel?" rather than "Put your hands on the wheel."

Suggesting how much social stereotypes can infiltrate everyone's minds, the researchers found that black officers showed the same bias as white officers.

To white drivers, the message more often conveyed was "I respect you," "I care about you," or "I see you." For black drivers the message was more often, "Just do as I say—I don't care about you," or "I don't see you." As the authors summarize, "Regardless of the cause, we have found that police officers' interactions with blacks tend to be more fraught," not just in terms of outcomes like arrest, excessive force, and death "but also interpersonally, even when no arrest is made and no use of force occurs." They go on to say, "These disparities could have adverse downstream effects, as experiences of respect or disrespect in personal interactions with police officers play a central role in community members' judgments of how procedurally fair the police are as an institution, as well as the community's willingness to support or cooperate with the police."

The impact of such everyday indignities as Eberhardt and colleagues document can add up to a heavy toll. The newscaster Bryant Gumbel, an African American, referred to it as a "tax," calling it "the added burden that comes with being black in America. And it's routinely paid no matter how much education you have, how much money you make, or how much success you've earned. . . . It's about the many instances of disrespect and incivility your color seems to engender."

The abuse inflicted by stereotyping and stigmatizing has been perpetrated on many other populations of people lumped into social groups. Poor whites, particularly from rural communities, have been stereotyped as "white trash," "rednecks," and "crackers," and belittled as lazy, feeble-minded, dirty, and morally degenerate. The physically disabled have been subjected to stigma throughout history. Subtly or not so subtly, people tend to move away from them or fail to make eye contact with them. The disabled are also condescended to as though they are less intelligent, and they're discriminated against in hiring. Stutterers are stereotyped as being excessively shy, anxious, fearful, and again lacking in intelligence.

Even what might seem to be positive stereotyping can be damaging. Asian Americans are subjected to the "model minority" stereotype, depicted as "a uniformly high-achieving racial minority that has assimilated well into American society through hard work, obedience to social mores and academic achievement." But that stereotype contributes to the fact that little funding is devoted to the study of the needs of Asian immigrants and Americans of Asian descent who are experiencing poverty and educational challenges. Wesley Yang writes poignantly in his book *The Souls of Yellow Folk* that "as the bearer of an Asian face, you paid some incremental penalty, never absolute, but always omnipresent, that meant . . . you were presumptively a nobody, a mute and servile figure, distinguishable above all by your total incapacity to threaten anyone . . . a peculiar burden of non-recognition, of invisibility." This stereotype may also help explain the underrepresentation of Asians in politics, Hollywood, and corporate leadership.

How aware are we of the myriad stereotypes affecting people's lives? Far too little. That's in large part because stereotypes can operate unconsciously, even for people who profess egalitarian values. Research suggests that most Americans value egalitarianism and many consciously disavow stereotypes. But when we have an excuse to exclude, in situations of ambiguity, we often do. Our minds have a way of rationalizing unfair treatment.

Compounding the problem is that when people are called out on stereotyping, they often respond defensively. But when someone reacts as though they've been disrespected by us, we might consider the possibility that we did commit some act of bias, whether by commission *or* omission. Indeed, often the problem is what we *didn't* do. We didn't smile. We didn't say "please," "thank you," or "excuse me." We conveyed that we didn't fully see the person.

HOW CAN WE WORK to lessen the power of stereotypes over our treatment of others? The first step is to acknowledge that we can fall under their sway, as much as we want not to be.

In his essay about pseudoscience, "Cargo Cult Science," the renowned physicist Richard Feynman wrote, "The first principle is that you must not fool yourself—and you are the easiest person to fool." He could have just as easily been commenting on social beliefs as he was scientific ones. Scientists and everyday people alike find it ever so easy to point out the biases that distort their peers' perceptions, but they find it hard to see their own biases. It's a perennial human penchant. Two thousand years ago, Saint Matthew beseeched, "Why do you look at the speck of sawdust in your brother's eye and pay no attention to the plank in your own eye?"

One evening not so long ago, I went to an Indian restaurant for dinner and, being quite hungry, was impatient to be seated. Walking up to a brown-skinned man in a long, white apron, I asked him for a table.

He frowned and said, "I don't work here."

Of course he works here, I thought to myself: He's wearing an apron. Then I looked down and was aghast to discover that what I had seen as an apron was actually a long pair of white shorts. My vision had been fooled by a stereotype: Indian men in an Indian restaurant are restaurant workers. For a moment, my mind went on the defensive. This man was to blame, my churlish mind said: "Why would anyone be wearing shorts that long?"

My rational mind thankfully overcame my reptilian brain, and I apologized. Sitting down at my table, I felt like a driver incredulous at the wreck he had caused. How was it possible that I, someone who had studied biases in perception for decades, committed such an offense? Of course, I knew that stereotypes can act unconsciously. But I'd not really, really believed I could be so vulnerable—that my very perception could give me a false read on reality. The cultural conditioning we're subjected to makes us all vulnerable to such transgressions. After my mind calmed, I thought what good fortune it was to have learned that I had made a mistake. My self-congratulatory mood didn't last too long, though. How many other misjudgments had I made in the past without ever learning of my error? A visual error can be quickly refuted but not so with many errors of social judgment. And most of the time with such errors and the slights they cause, we go on our merry way with no awareness of the harm we've done.

We don't lack motivation to be fair or objective. We're just defensive at the insinuation that we're not. Surveys show that most Americans value equality and fairness in principle. But the common reaction to being told that we have to correct for biases is defensiveness. That's why most proposed solutions to prejudice don't work. Antibias training in schools or workplaces has yielded disappointing results, just as Muzafer Sherif's attempts to teach his camp kids through religious sermons to "love thy neighbor" didn't work. Research by Taylor Phillips and Brian Lowery shows that merely reminding white Americans that black Americans are disadvantaged in academics, housing, health care, and jobs leads them to defensively claim that their own lives are filled with hardship too. The well-off of all races do the same when reminded that the poor are disadvantaged. Of course, everyone's lives may have hardship. But there's no logical reason why hearing about one group's suffering should lead us to, in effect, comparatively downplay the hardships of others. A logical thing to do would be to express empathy.

As we work to find ways to combat the power of stereotypes, it's important that we take our counterproductive defensiveness into account. Asking people to be fair or objective doesn't work well, because people already think they *are* fair and objective. Sociologist Emilio Castilla asked one group of managers to evaluate various employees for promotion, either male or female and all equally qualified, and he told one group that it was very important for them to be fair. Did this intervention decrease bias against women in promotion decisions and raises? No. It increased bias.

Eric Uhlmann and I found similar results. We asked a group of participants to indicate whether or not they agreed with a number of statements that reminded them of how important it was to be objective in making judgments: for example, "In most situations, I try to do what seems reasonable and logical." When we compared their decisions in a hypothetical hiring task with those of people who didn't answer these questions, we found that those reminded of the importance of objectivity responded with greater gender bias. They applied gender stereotypes that simply crossed their minds thanks to a little "prime" that Uhlmann and I introduced earlier, a set of verbal puzzles that contained words like "pink" and "Barbie." It seems that when people are reminded of how much they value objectivity, they think that they *are* objective and therefore feel more free to act on biased thoughts that cross their mind, in effect allowing the stereotype to have more power over them. It's as if people say to themselves, "If I think it, it must be true."

So what can we do? As we work to change our institutions and laws, we can also do much in our day-to-day lives to minimize the damage due to stereotyping.

One strategy is to consider the *situation* we're in—how it might be contributing to our bias, often unconsciously. A powerful illustration of this idea comes from research by Heidi Vuletich and Keith Payne. They analyzed the effects of psychological interventions with students from a number of colleges aimed at overturning implicit bias against black people. While a few of the interventions reduced bias immediately after they were administered, over the long term none had durable impacts. The researchers argue that the nature of the schools that students attended played a role in this fade-out. They measured the average level of bias displayed by students in general on the campuses, and they found that the bias exhibited by the students who had experienced the interventions reverted to the norm on their campuses.

What was it about the campus situation that exerted this pull? In part, perhaps, it was the attitudes expressed, whether overtly or unconsciously, by students and faculty. But one physical feature of some campuses also appeared to play a role: the public display of a Confederate statue. The students on campuses with such a statue had higher levels of implicit racial bias. This finding speaks to the haunting effects of historical expressions of racism. Not only do these statues cause pain for many black students and faculty; they may help to sustain implicit antiblack bias. Another factor that predicted higher campus-wide levels of bias was lower ethnic diversity among faculty. In Part Three, we will see examples of practitioners at schools and workplaces who have taken a hard look at characteristics of their environments and changed them to combat bias and promote belonging for all. At an individual level, we can craft our own situations for the better. We can seek out friends and join reference groups that reinforce the attitudes we want to have, as well as expose ourselves to information that challenges widespread cultural stereotypes—all simple but powerful strategies supported by research.

We can also coach ourselves in ways that encourage *respect*—one word with social currency for both adults and teens. "Respect," my teenaged son says to a friend as he bids him goodbye and they bump fists. As I thought about why the word has garnered such wide cultural recognition, I looked up its etymology and discovered that its original meaning is "to look again" or "to look harder"—to "re-spectate." A small word, it's jam-packed with wisdom. The word has embedded in it a means of combating our stereotypical thinking: *Look again*—and harder. Remind ourselves to look for the individual and to reject the stereotype. It's a partial antidote to the self-deception that Feynman suggested we so easily slip into.

The power of getting people to pause, reflect, and look again was demonstrated in a collaboration between Jennifer Eberhardt and her colleagues with the Oakland Police Department. They asked officers to follow a new protocol before they made a stop: Ask yourself, "Is this stop intelligence–led? Yes or no?" This question gets officers to think before they act and to consider whether they really have due cause to make a stop. The practice introduces "psychological friction" between thought and action. The year the policy was introduced, police stops of African Americans fell by 43 percent, while crime rates continued to decline.

Another way in which we can "look again," and make ourselves aware that stereotypes may be guiding our assessments and treatment of others, is by gathering information that will divulge whether bias is at play in the situation we're in. One of my favorite interventions in this spirit was conducted by the renowned scholar of prejudice John Dovidio and his colleagues in a collaboration with the Department of Defense in the 1990s. The department was concerned about racial disparities in promotions to senior officer, which persisted even though many of the minority candidates were fully qualified, or "in the zone," as the military puts it. It was as if the minority candidates weren't being fully seen.

Dovidio and his colleagues suggested a small intervention to get hiring personnel to look more carefully. Over a three-year window, the researchers asked department employees to monitor any racial imbalances in promotion rates and, if any were found, to explain them. This was more than an instruction to be "objective" or "fair." It was guidance to study what the data showed about the situation. There was also accountability. When people know they have to explain their decisions, they are better able to correct for their biases because they look at their decisions as outsiders would. The intervention helped the department employees appreciate that they were, in fact, making biased decisions that disfavored officers of ethnic minority descent. As a result of this small intervention, the racial disparity in promotion rates disappeared. A similar intervention designed by Emilio Castilla eliminated the tendency for managers at a large service-sector company to give bigger pay raises to their male and white workers than other workers. After the intervention, these gaps disappeared. What's more, pay raises for minority employees became much more aligned with their on-the-job evaluations.

Another way to stave off stereotyping is with psychological timeouts, which, as discussed in Chapter 5, help create the mental space for us to think more deeply and reflectively about our situation. When the mind is restored in this manner, it is less likely to rely on fast mental shortcuts like stereotypes—and more receptive to considering the nuances of the situation and the individuality of the people in it. These timeouts are most important when our situations at work, school, or home make us hurried and stressed. They include values-affirmation activities and various mindfulness practices, such as savoring everyday experiences, focusing attention on breathing and bodily sensations, and even practicing meditation.

To return to the theme of situation-crafting for a moment, let's again reflect on what the interventions we have discussed do *not* do. They don't try to "fix" racist people. That may be a by-product, but it's not where the interventions take aim. They foster people's awareness of the situation, its impact on them, and their contribution to it. All parents, teachers, managers, coaches—all of us—can take some time to reflect on how we may be threatening the belonging of our children, students, employees, and people we encounter out and about in our daily lives because of stereotypes that shape our perceptions of situations and the people we share them with.

In the next chapter, we'll explore the ways that people's awareness that they are in a stereotyped group—and that they must continually deal with the mere possibility of bias—undermines their belonging, through the phenomenon of stereotype threat. Then we will again consider ways we can recraft those situations to create belonging and opportunity for all.

Chapter 7

How Am I Seen?

How We Experience Being Stereotyped, and How Situation-Crafting Can Help Push Back

THE THREAT TO BELONGING INFLICTED BY STEREOTYPES arises not just from discrimination. Even when people in stereotyped groups face no objective bias in a given situation, knowing that their group *could* be seen in demeaning ways is damaging to their psychological and physical well-being. Robin DiAngelo, author of *White Fragility,* has written about the pervasive negative messages that are sent to black people in the United States. She says that messages of "white value" and "black insignificance" are "raining down on us 24/7, and there are no umbrellas." That storm outside can create inner psychological turmoil.

The rapper Eminem portrayed how a "psychological storm" can unsettle even people from historically non-oppressed groups in the movie *8 Mile.* Playing the part of an alter ego of his younger self, a white rapper named Rabbit, he is trying to make it in Detroit's music scene, as Eminem had. We first meet Rabbit in a backstage bathroom as he stares at himself in the mirror, blasting music in his headset. He's trying to calm down because he's about to compete in a rap battle. If he wins, it could be a big break. But winning will be grueling. Rap battles, we are about to see, are bruising competitions, the verbal equivalent of kickboxing. Each player gets forty-five seconds to send a barrage of verbal jabs at his opponent, improvised on the spot. The blows can be devastating, landing not on the body but on the ego, which can be just as painful. To make matters worse, the audiences are unforgiving, gleefully jeering when they smell blood. A rapper who pauses too long, stutters, or flubs a rhyme is toast.

Rabbit knows all this awaits him, and we movie watchers can see that he's feeling stressed. But even so, we're surprised when he rushes to the bathroom to vomit. The situation is so stressful for him for a perfect storm of reasons. Research suggests that the dread of social disapproval can be as stressful as awaiting painful electric shocks. That's in part because as a social species, we fear that in standing in front of a crowd, we're vulnerable to exclusion. In Rabbit's case, his love of rap adds to the stress. He desperately wants to be great. On top of these factors, he's an outsider: a white guy in a game that is believed to be by and for black people. That's still true today, but the sentiment was stronger in the 1990s Detroit of the movie.

Rabbit is well aware that he's seen as not fully belonging. Just to make the point glaringly clear to him, when he tries to enter backstage with the other performers before the contest, a bouncer at the door stops him and says he has to go in through the front door like the regulars—an ironic parallel to the racial segregation that blacks had to deal with in public spaces before civil rights legislation. He gets through to backstage with the help of a black friend, but the bouncer adds a parting dig: "Your boy got an attitude problem."

When Rabbit steps onstage, he's the only white person in the joint, feeling the brunt of what social psychologists call "solo status," the experience of being the only person in your group in a social situation. He's onstage with his competitor. The performer who wins a coin toss decides who will go first. Rabbit wins and chooses to go second. The other guy launches a blistering flurry of insults at Rabbit, many of which, we can see, are hitting their mark. "You're just a white with a mic," his opponent riffs, "faker than a psychic with a caller ID." Save your "bullshit" for "storage," he raps, "'cause this is hip-hop, you don't belong, you're a tourist."

Now it's Rabbit's turn. We know that among his friends he's considered a genius rapper. For Eminem, it's an opinion that would later be shared by millions. So we're anticipating a brilliant counterattack. But Rabbit stares vacantly into the audience. We can only imagine his internal monologue. "They're right, I don't belong here." "They all think I'm a joke." "If I choke, I'll prove them right." The audience starts to chant, "Choke." Rabbit and his competitor stand on the same stage, but behind their eyes they're in a totally different situation. After an excruciating few more seconds, Rabbit walks offstage without rapping a word.

Rabbit has experienced an extreme case of what psychologists call underperformance, when we don't do as well as we're capable of at something we care about. Almost all of us have fallen under its spell at some point, perhaps when playing in a sporting event, when giving a public talk, in a job interview, or on a date. Trying to understand underperformance takes us straight to the power of belonging. Eminem didn't actually experience the exact scene from the movie, but as he writes in his memoir *The Way I Am,* he had plenty of experiences of choking. "It was the *White Men Can't Jump* theory," he explains. "No one thought the white boy could win."

Watching Eminem perform poorly in the early days of his career, as he writes he did at several major competitions, many people likely inferred that he simply didn't have much rapping talent, that he lacked wit or grit or just "didn't have what it takes." But a big factor in his poor performance, it seems, was what psychologists call stereotype threat. Being white, he knew he was stereotyped as not belonging in rap, and he felt intense anxiety that he would live up to the stereotype in the eyes of his audience. That's the underlying fear that leads Rabbit to freeze up.

For those of us who have not been stereotyped, the power of this fear may be impossible to fully appreciate. But almost all of us have experienced a degree of anxiety about how we're being perceived, perhaps when starting a first job, going to a new school, or meeting a romantic partner's family for the first time. We might feel it to some extent in any given social interaction. Psychologists also have a name for this more general fear that we'll be evaluated negatively: social evaluative threat.

I suffered from it with one professor I worked for, Professor Armstrong. Although a kindhearted man, he was renowned for his disdain of bullshit. Among his infamous marginalia on student papers was a drawing of a pile of stinking manure with a shovel stuck in it. Not one to leave anything unclear, he even penciled in little squiggly lines to portray whiffs of noxious effluvium rising from the heap. Meetings with him were fraught. He wouldn't hesitate to challenge or criticize something you said as soon as it came out of your mouth.

Our meetings generally went something like this. I'd come to his office after a week of preparation. But almost unfailingly, when I shared an idea I had for some research or an interpretation of some results, he'd look at me with cool indifference, his eyebrows arched in what I read as bemused skepticism. Then he would ask me a question for which I had no good answer. Not realizing it would be fine to say I was unsure of the answer, I would stumble through an incoherent response, my mind racing with a punishing stream of thoughts: "Does he think I'm dumb? If he thinks I'm dumb, maybe I am dumb." I was aware of the vicious cycle: Because I was worried about looking dumb, I acted dumb, which further ratcheted up my worry about looking dumb. Nonetheless, I couldn't stop the mental loop once it started. Fortunately, Professor Armstrong was so tough because, as he once explained to me, he cared about his students and worried that if he didn't challenge them so rigorously, they wouldn't be prepared to make it out in the "real world." He also wasn't relentlessly critical, and even the smallest praise from him, a little nod of approval or, wonder of wonders, a "that's a nice idea," and I would leave the meeting elated.

When I later began researching stereotype threat, I looked back on my struggles with doubts about how Professor Armstrong viewed me, and I was struck by how situational my fear was. Outside of classes and meetings, he was personable, and he sometimes invited me and the others in the lab to his home for dinner. We'd have stimulating conversation, and I would feel completely comfortable, openly sharing thoughts, with not an "am I being dumb" doubt flitting through my mind.

I also recalled how my whole assessment of my belonging in the profession would flip 180 degrees depending on how a meeting with him had gone. So despondent would I become after a bad meeting that I'd be down for the whole week and start entertaining backup career plans, a favorite being to open a café in a Mexican beach town.

As I reflected on this, I recalled that Erving Goffman wrote that our social self, what he evocatively referred to as our "face," is our most "personal possession," which can give us great "security and pleasure" but which, he warns, we must always remember is not our property but merely "on loan." To some extent, whether we feel a security of self—what we generally call self-esteem—depends on whether we are granted that security by the people with whom we share a situation. Even for the most confident of us, the most privileged, the most obviously talented, certain situations may evoke social evaluative threat.

For people who are negatively stereotyped, no skeptical glance from a Professor Armstrong may be required to trigger the sense of danger. I can only imagine how much more stressful my meetings with him might have been if I were, say, black. For individuals in stereotyped groups, the fact of the pervasive stereotype acts all on its own as the skeptical glance. They live with the awareness that certain situations can contain trip wires that could blow their sense of security to bits. Even such an establishment figure as Katharine Graham recounts that when she took the helm of the *Washington Post* in the 1960s as the first woman to head a major American newspaper, she "felt I was always taking an exam and would fail if I missed a single answer."

In situations where the stereotype predicts inferior performance, as in taking a standardized test, the ensuing social evaluative threat often undermines performance, becoming a self-fulfilling prophecy. The seminal research revealing the workings of stereotype threat was conducted by Claude Steele and his colleagues in the early 1990s. As a black man in America, Steele was acquainted with this threat. In his book *Whistling Vivaldi*, he recounts the shock of discovering, when he was seven years old and prohibited from swimming in a public pool in his town, that he was considered essentially different from white people, that he was "black." As a research psychologist, he decided to study the ways in which people attempt to cope with being stereotyped. One story that stuck with him came from the black writer Brent Staples, who found that if he whistled a piece by Vivaldi as he walked out and about at night, he shielded himself from the harsh gaze of the stereotypes about black men. It was his own bit of situation-crafting that helped to integrate himself into a tense situation. "The tension drained from people's bodies when they heard me. A few even smiled as they passed in the dark." Steele wanted to discover other ways to diminish the threat for people who are stereotyped.

A number of black writers, such as James Baldwin, W. E. B. Du Bois, and Ralph Ellison, had portrayed the psychological experience of being subjected to widely known stereotypes. The black narrator in Ellison's *Invisible Man* describes a moment of liberation from stereotype threat. He decides to eat a sweet buttered yam that he bought from a street vendor out on the street for all to see. It's as if he is escaping from a psychological cage, and as he enjoys the succulent yam, he muses that one of racism's greatest triumphs is to "cause us the greatest humiliation simply by confronting us with something we liked."

Steele and his colleagues scientifically investigated the nature of stereotype threat, its extent and effects, and helped discover ways to combat it. He teamed up with two other scholars, Joshua Aronson and Steve Spencer. While Spencer focused on how stereotype threat undermined the performance of women in math and science, Steele and Aronson decided to focus on whether stereotype threat might be at play in the racial achievement gap in academic performance that seems to begin early in children's schooling and to grow over their time in school.

In an influential 1995 paper entitled "Stereotype Threat and the Intellectual Test Performance of Academically Successful African Americans," Steele and Aronson showed that stereotype threat did indeed undermine test performance, which helped to explain the persistent and widespread academic underperformance of stereotyped minority students. "Underperformance" here has a meaning parallel to the one experienced by Eminem's alter ego. It refers to the phenomenon of students performing worse than their preparation and skills would lead us to expect, as based on statistical models. The findings of the original study have been corroborated in a host of follow-up work by both Steele and Aronson and others. I'm going to focus on their first study, though, because to my eyes it still stands as among the most rigorous and rich.

If you're a product of the American education system, you probably took a standardized test of some kind almost every year from first grade until you graduated high school. If you went to college, you likely took the SAT or ACT. If you went to graduate school, you probably took either the GRE, the LSAT, the MCAT, or the GMAT. America has a standardized test fetish, beholden as the country is to a near-religious fixation on measuring supposedly inherent abilities. For decades, admissions decisions have hinged on student scores, and thousands of students who have otherwise stellar records are cut off from educational opportunity because of low test scores. That continues to be true, even though, as Steele, Aronson, Spencer, and many other researchers have shown, the tests are systematically biased against some groups.

For their study, Steele and Aronson brought Stanford college students to their laboratory. Half of the students were black and half were white. They selected students whom they had determined to be highly motivated to do well in classes, with their sense of self wrapped up in being excellent students. All these students, being Stanford undergraduates, were high achieving.

Each student arrived for a session dedicated to him or her individually and was greeted by a well-dressed white male experimenter. After escorting the student to a table, the experimenter explained that the student would be given some verbal problems to solve. For one group of students, the experimenter explained that the problems would provide a "genuine test of your verbal abilities and limitations." As the experimenter left the room to allow the students to take the test, he asked them to try hard to "help us in our analysis of your verbal ability." For another group, the experimenter said that the problems were designed to help them understand "the psychological factors involved in studying verbal problems." As the experimenter left the room, he asked these students to try hard "even though we're not going to evaluate your ability" in order to "help us in our analysis of the problem-solving process." I'm quoting from the script of the study because, as we've seen, situation-crafting derives much of its power from the specific words chosen. These words were chosen either to summon the stereotype of black students having lower intellectual ability or to shutter it out.

Both groups took the same test, which was difficult, even for these select students, consisting of the hardest problems on the verbal section of the GRE. That was another element of the situation-crafting. If the test wasn't challenging, stereotype threat might not be triggered. What's more, the students had only thirty minutes to complete thirty problems, so every second wasted in a reverie of doubt would be significant, increasing the chances that any mental preoccupation would undermine performance results.

The results were striking. Black students who were told that the test measured ability did much worse than white students told the same. But for the group of students told that the test merely assessed the problem-solving process and had no bearing on their ability, black students did much better, closing much of the gap with their white peers.

To uncover the thought processes that might account for the differences in performance, the researchers had another sample of students go through the same procedure. This time, though, after they had been told the purpose of the test but before they took it, they were given some survey questions to answer and some tasks to complete. One survey asked them to indicate how much they enjoyed various activities, some of which were stereotypical of what black people might enjoy, like Ellison's sweet yams but in this case rap and basketball. Black students who had been told the test they'd be taking would measure their intellectual ability rated these activities as less enjoyable than black students in the group told the test had nothing to do with ability. The researchers concluded those who downplayed their interest were making an effort to buck stereotyping.

That stereotype threat had been triggered was also suggested by how the two groups of black students completed a task that asked them to make full words out of various fragments, like _ _ CE. Black participants in the first group filled in more racial words, like "race," while those in the second group filled in more nonracial words, like "face." Those in the first group also engaged in what is referred to in social psychology as self-handicapping, responding to another survey question by reporting that they had gotten fewer hours of sleep the night before. The interpretation here was that they were preemptively offering explanations for what they expected to be their imminent poor performance. By contrast white students responded similarly regardless of whether they were led to believe the test was going to assess their ability or not. Poignantly, when given the option to indicate their race on the survey, 75 percent of black students expecting to take a test of their ability left the response line blank. For all the other groups, everyone indicated their race. The researchers interpreted this as another indication that stereotyping was on the minds of the black students in the group that thought the test was measuring ability.

The research on stereotype threat has been somewhat controversial. For one thing, the standardized test companies objected to the evidence that test results are systematically skewed to disfavor stereotyped groups. Some criticism has also been made from within the research community. I address the main technical criticism in the Notes. Much has also changed since the studies were run in 1995, including the election of the first black president. Nevertheless, two comprehensive meta-analyses, one as recent as 2019, suggest that stereotype threat has a powerful impact on performance but under key conditions like the ones Rabbit faced: in situations where people care about doing well and are pushed to the frontiers of their ability.

Stereotype threat does not arise because people believe the stereotype might be true of them. As Steele says, stereotype threat at its core is a situational mistrust. In situations where the stereotype applies, you don't know if you'll be seen through what he calls its "diminishing lens." Even people with high self-esteem may worry about being diminished in this way at school or work or in some other arena in which they want to succeed.

You don't even have to be the person who is being evaluated to experience stereotype threat. Because the threat is caused by a concern about how your social group is viewed, it can be activated even when other people in your group—and not you yourself—are in a situation where these other group members might be seen stereotypically. One of my long-time colleagues from Stanford, Julio Garcia, helped me understand this. Although he always did well on standardized tests and performed well academically, as a member of a stereotyped minority group, he still felt stress when other Latinos might do or say something that lent support to the negative stereotypes of them. Stereotypes can hijack group solidarity and weaponize it. Because members of groups feel bonded with one another, stereotypes can make them feel threatened by one another.

Garcia and I devised a set of experiments to explore this effect, which we reported in 2005. We essentially reran the stereotype study Steele and colleagues had conducted, but with a twist: Our black participants didn't take a test. They simply *watched* a black classmate, actually an accomplice of the experimenter, prepare to take a test described to him as measuring "your verbal abilities and limitations." The accomplice then expressed some doubt about his ability to do well, saying "I'm so bad at these standardized tests." We compared this group of black onlookers to a control group that watched the same black classmate prepare to complete some "verbal puzzles" and express no doubt. Later on, these onlookers filled out some surveys that they thought were for another study but that really served to measure whether they felt threatened. Relative to the control group, black participants in the first group reported feeling lower self-esteem, agreeing less with such statements as "I feel smart" and "I feel that others respect and admire me." Some of them, when they returned to the same room as their classmate, put their chair farther away, literally distancing themselves from association with that person. Garcia and I found similar results among female math and engineering students when they watched a female classmate prepare to take a test described as measuring math ability.

Many of us have experienced a version of this sense that we're being threatened by the way *someone else* from a group we identify with, and are seen as part of, is behaving. As Americans, if we travel abroad, we might be conscious of the "ugly American" stereotype of loud, careless, sloppy people and become zealous about trying to avoid giving any scrap of evidence that the stereotype might be true. I did when visiting France once. The stereotype was evoked when I was chastised by a passerby for accidentally dropping a gum wrapper on the sidewalk. Later, I was sitting in a café when an American man in a Hawaiian shirt and loud, multicolored jam shorts from the 1980s sat down at another table with a friend. He called out to the waiters, commanded them about as if they were servants, and spoke to his friend so loudly that all the other customers sitting at other tables could hear him. I felt acutely ashamed, as though all the French people in the room were seeing me—and all Americans—as just like him. This is one of the ways that negative stereotypes can make the same situation different for the people they demean. People feel their sense of self to be at stake even when they themselves are not performing or being directly evaluated. I could return home and be safe from the gaze of the ugly American stereotype. But the impact of being under the scrutiny of a stereotype almost every waking moment of every day at school or at work can be debilitating to people's sense of belonging.

Greg Walton and I wanted to assess the effects of stereotype threat on black students' sense of belonging in a set of studies we conducted in the early 2000s. We thought that being negatively stereotyped would lead black students to be relatively more likely to question their belonging in the face of an experience that for white students seemed minor. We enlisted black and white college students and broke them into three groups. We borrowed a technique from the social psychologist Norbert Schwartz to create a potential threat to students' sense of belonging in an intellectually challenging discipline: computer science. We asked the first group to list two friends they had in computer science and the second group to list eight friends. All those in the first group found it easy to list names. Almost all of those in the second group found naming eight friends hard, sometimes impossible. We thought the effort required to come up with eight friends might lead black students to conclude, "Maybe I don't belong here." As for the third group, it was the "control"—we didn't ask them to list friends. Next, we asked everyone in each group to rate how much they felt they belonged in computer science and to rate their potential to succeed in the discipline relative to their peers.

Black and white students found it equally difficult to list eight friends in computer science. Where they differed was in how they *interpreted* that difficulty. The black students in the list-eight-friends group reported a lower sense of belonging in computer science than did black students in the other two groups. They also assessed themselves to be well below average in their potential to succeed in computer science, at the 30th percentile, while black students in the two other groups rated themselves slightly above the 50th percentile. White students, rating themselves at about the 43rd percentile on average, were unaffected by the friend-listing task.

For black students only, the difficulty of generating friends' names seemed to have provoked the thought, "People of my race don't belong in computer science." Evidence for this interpretation came from the answers that the black students in the list-eight-friends group gave to another question. They were asked whether they would advise each of two classmates, whose profiles we gave them, to pursue a degree in computer science. The photos in the two classmates' profiles showed that one was black and the other white. Black students did not differ in what they recommended to the white classmate. But while 77 percent of black students who had been asked to list two friends or no friends recommended that the black classmate go into computer science, only 30 percent of the black students in the list-eight-friends group did so.

You might think that black students felt demoralized because they listed a lot of white people. But that didn't seem to have been the case. At the end of the study, we asked participants to identify the ethnicity of each of their friends. We found that the number of white people that our black participants had listed didn't correlate with their sense of belonging. What *did* correlate with their sense of belonging was how difficult they rated the friend-listing task. It was as if black students had interpreted their mental effort as evidence that computer science was out of reach for "people like me."

Some have suggested that research on stereotype threat shows how much of the racism and sexism that people perceive can be "in their heads." This view gets it backward. The reality of racism and sexism in our culture teaches people to be wary of stereotyping, even in situations where it has yet to occur or may not occur. This can make rituals that seem normal to the nonstereotyped, like the standardized test, freighted with dire meaning and far from an equal playing field.

No doubt, people can be oversensitive and see slights that aren't really there, as explored by Greg Lukianoff and Jonathan Haidt in their book *The Coddling of the American Mind*. But it's also true that many people, especially those in positions of power and free of the continual threat of stereotyping, may fail to see slights in their environments that are in fact there and are obvious to those who are stereotyped. What's more, after people are "burned" by prejudice, even just once or twice, they can become vigilant to the possibility of being burned again, and rightly so. It's a form of psychological conditioning, the basic mechanism through which we learn the dangers of our environment. In research led by my former student Kody Manke, after a single experience of stereotype threat, women and students of color showed lingering aftereffects weeks later: Women performed worse on a subsequent test, and students of color reported a greater expectation that they would be stereotyped in school, relative to control groups who had not been threatened. The experience of being under the gaze of the stereotype can be so intense that people come to expect and perceive it. And you don't have to be directly burned. It's enough to know you live in a society where bias and exclusion are a real and continual possibility.

What kinds of experiences teach people to be vigilant in this way?

+ + + +

THE MOVIE *THE POST*—in which the longtime publisher of the *Washington Post*, Katharine Graham, is brilliantly played by actress Meryl Streep—and Graham's autobiography, *Personal History*, on which the film drew heavily, speak powerfully about the ways people learn that stereotypes diminish them and others in their group. In the book, Graham recounts that from an early age, she was taught that women had no place in the publishing industry. True to form, Eugene Meyer, her father, left the *Washington Post* not to his daughter but to her husband, Phil Graham. Meyer told her "no man should be in the position of working for his wife." We could ascribe this attitude to Meyer's sexism but that would be to commit the Fundamental Attribution Error on him. In that era, the 1940s, sexism was the norm. My mother, who went to work in the early 1970s after getting married, recalled how her own father, an exemplar of kindness and generosity, was baffled by her decision and said to her, "Why are you taking a job away from a man?" As Graham writes, "I adopted the assumption of many of my generation that women were intellectually inferior to men, that we were not capable of governing, leading, managing anything but our homes and our children." When she nonetheless took the role of publisher after her husband passed away, she writes, "I seemed to be carrying inadequacy as baggage."

The psychological strain of her experience was brought to excruciating life in one particular scene in the movie. Graham has called a board meeting, in which she plans to propose a price at which shares of the *Post* are to be offered to the public. She knows she'll face a good deal of resistance, because board members will deem the price too low. But the solvency of the paper depends on her ability to make the pitch. She had been so nervous about getting it right that she rehearsed the pitch over and over. She knows her stuff. She might even feel a bit confident, thanks to all her preparation. But as she walks down the hall to the boardroom, she glances to her side to see a hallway memorial to the people who founded the company, all black-and-white photos of white men. Stereotype threat has been triggered.

She opens the door to a boardroom abustle with white men in suits. They all take their seats around the table, the men joking with one another, grooming each other with words of affirmation and solidarity to make themselves feel at home. Once the meeting commences, a distinguished-looking, gray-haired man seated at the head of the table scowls and says, as anticipated, that the offering price is too low. It would lead to a loss, he says, pausing to do a quick calculation with pencil and paper. Graham knows the answer, and she could cut him off and take charge. Yet she only murmurs the answer under her breath, "Three million." No one hears her, because they're not focused on her and don't expect her to say anything useful. "Three million!" the board member announces after making his calculation. This means, he continues, that the number of reporters who will be fired will be, pausing again to ask another male board member at the table for the answer . . . "Twenty-five," Graham mutters again just before he exclaims, "Twenty-five!"

Then another board member says that investors have balked because they're concerned that Graham lacks the "ability to turn a serious profit." Graham had expected all of these jabs and rehearsed her retort many times. But she can't muster any words at all. She looks down at the notes she had written on her yellow pad, and they appear like scrawl in another language. It's classic underperformance. She gazes upward, trying to mentally remove herself from the situation enough to summon her strength. But still the words don't come. She is rescued by her confidant and colleague, the attorney Fritz Beebe, who delivers the prepared response.

Had Graham said later to the board members, perhaps in one-on-one conversation, that the men's behavior in the room had "triggered her," making her feel she didn't belong, they might well have told her, "It's all in your head." But in fact the stereotype was continually being pushed *in her face*.

In addition to the cultural conditioning that Graham had been subject to about women's inferiority, she experienced plenty of overt prejudice at the *Post*, as she describes in her memoir. Suggesting a female editor for a literary section, she was chastened that to hire a woman was out of the question. The "closing nights were too late, the end-of-the-week pressure too great, the physical demands of the job too tough." The reasoning seemed so open-and-shut that Graham didn't protest. Then there were the everyday indignities Graham herself faced. When her husband, who had helmed the paper, passed away, many assumed that she would sell the company. When she resisted, she was pressed again and again to sell, with would-be buyers arguing to her that, as one bidder told her, it was the right and normal thing to do for a newspaper inherited by a widow.

Graham experienced over and over what Erving Goffman called "mortifications." What is awful about these mortifications isn't just the pain they cause when they occur, but the anticipation they create that another one could happen again in similar situations, putting people in a state of alert regardless of whether a threatening event happens or not. Goffman introduced the term after spending time observing the interactions between staff and patients at a mental asylum in the late 1950s. Although he looked at a specialized institution, his observations apply more generally to mainstream institutions of all sorts, including school and work.

Goffman noticed in the daily encounters at the asylum disturbing mechanisms of social control, and with heightened awareness from that experience, he realized that key to all social control are corrosive messages, both subtle and overt, aimed at undermining people's social worth, self-confidence, and sense of agency over their lives in enduring ways. Regarding the patients, Goffman saw that one method used to achieve this was to deprive them of control over when and what they ate, as well as to require them to get permission to use the restroom. The message? "You no longer have full control over basic bodily functions." Goffman recounts a nurse asking a patient, "Have you got both socks on?" and, not waiting for a reply, bending down to look at his bare ankles. The message she seemed to be sending, perhaps not in intent but in effect, was "Your answer, or anything you say, does not matter." A patient also sees many of his personal possessions taken away, his wardrobe replaced with the same drab gowns every patient wears. Patients, Goffman wrote, are "stripped of many of [the] accustomed affirmations, satisfactions, and defenses" that help to bolster people's sense of self. He concludes that the patient's "self is systematically, if often unintentionally, mortified."

To "mortify" means literally "to put to death," and I suspect Goffman chose the word carefully because in his eyes these daily rituals looked like little social deaths. The asylum is admittedly an extreme situation, and most workplaces, schools, and social situations of all kinds are not nearly as mortifying. But many of these settings subject people to what the sociologists Hedwig Lee and Margaret Takako Hicken refer to as the "death by a thousand cuts" that prejudice perpetrates on its victims.

Some mortifications, of course, are big and glaring. A powerful description of one comes from the basketball legend and writer Kareem Abdul-Jabbar. In his book *Coach Wooden and Me*, he writes about a time when he sat with his high school basketball team at halftime in the locker room. They were losing, and his coach (not Wooden) was yelling at them. Abdul-Jabbar recounts that the coach "pointed his finger at me as if it were a dagger" and said, "You're acting just like a nigger!" It's as if the word pierced him open. "Some essence drained out of my body. I couldn't have gotten out of my chair even if the building were on fire. My face burned as if I'd been repeatedly slapped. My heart felt as if it had been crushed into a walnut." He felt not just "betrayed" but "worthless, as if I had just been discarded into the trash by someone I cared about."

An acquaintance, Keith, told me about a horrifying mortification he had experienced. He has a neurological condition that contorts his spine and inhibits his growth. He's three feet tall and walks hunched. To get on and off a public bus is a huge challenge, requiring him to pull and twirl himself up using the exit rails and pole. The regular bus driver on his route was patient with him, but one day a new driver was on the job. After watching Keith twirl off the bus, he yelled, "This bus is for human beings."

More common are the subtle but still injurious messages of belittlement and disregard that are sent, through actions taken and through actions not taken—the little sins of commission and omission. Michelle Hebl and Jenessa Shapiro captured the mortifications inflicted on the overweight, LGBTQ people, and the ill. In one experiment, the researchers had their assistants first put on a prosthetic that was hidden beneath their clothing to make them appear fat, and then had them shop at a department store. In another study, the assistant wore a cap with the words "Gay and Proud" when they applied for a job. In still another study, the assistant wore a cap with the words "Cancer Survivor." The treatment that they received in these situations was compared to the treatment the same research assistants received when they didn't appear to be a member of a stereotyped group. In all studies, they were treated more negatively when identifying as a member of a stereotyped group, experiencing from others less eye contact, less nodding, more furrowing of the brow, and more brusqueness. Even professional physicians show biases like these, Hebl and her colleagues found. Doctors indicated that they would spend less time with a patient and were more likely to assert that seeing them would be a "waste of their time" when the patients' information had been manipulated by the researchers to present them as overweight rather than of average stature. What makes these kinds of mortifications especially toxic is that they're ambiguous, so it's difficult for any victim of them to know for certain if bias is in play. People can spend a lot of precious mental and emotional resources trying to figure out what's really going on and trying to explain their angst.

The sociologist Kathryn Edin has written about the mortifications that poor people face when they seek support. She writes, "What if any program, public or private, seeking to help the poor were designed with social inclusion as a defining principle? What if building dignity and enhancing feelings of belonging to mainstream society became the norm in our food pantries and homeless shelters?" Our families, communities, and democracy would all benefit, she writes. The research bears her out. One study by Catherine Thomas and her colleagues found that poor people in Nairobi, Kenya, were more likely to express an interest in learning how to build a business and reported greater confidence in their ability to control their economic outcomes when financial aid was presented in an empowering way ("enabling people to support those they care about and help communities grow together") rather than in the standard way that subtly conveyed they were seen as "needy" ("reducing poverty and helping the poor meet their basic needs").

The accumulation of mortifications can put people on guard for more. Neuroscience research shows that after repeated exposure to an unpredictable aversive stimulus, virtually all organisms become alert for its recurrence in situations similar to where it had happened in the past. The bodily threat response ratchets up, not just during the stressor but while awaiting the next one. An elderly black woman interviewed by the sociologist Joe Feagin described the effect on her, saying that she had learned to put on a "shield" every morning for the past sixty years when she left home "to be prepared for insults and discrimination in public places, even if nothing happens that day."

The author Ta-Nehisi Coates wrote about this same prolonged vigilance in his book *Between the World and Me*, noting that it siphons off an "unmeasured expenditure of energy." The vigilance is stressful, exhausting, and deadly. Although enhanced vigilance is a rational response to prejudice, a survival mechanism to deal with its possibility, it can be like an alarm system that's constantly turned on—a distraction that takes attention away from work and school and wears a person down. Perhaps the strongest evidence of the toll this vigilance takes is found in research on its impact on health, which we'll discuss in Chapter 11.

+ + + +

ONE OF THE MAIN goals of wise interventions is to prevent or alleviate the damage of these mortifications. A simple place to start is to remove features of a situation that suggest a stereotype may be endorsed, such as Confederate statues on campus and memorials that honor only white men. Creating more diverse educational and work environments and introducing policies to deter bias and discrimination are key.

We can also craft situations that reassure people they belong, such as by introducing self-affirming experiences that fortify rather than mortify the self. One way to do this is with values-affirmation exercises, which research I conducted with Julio Garcia, Valerie Purdie-Greenaway, and Jonathan Cook showed can have powerful effects. A dear friend and deep thinker, Julio, who passed away in 2019, was constantly teaching me, and neither one of us could have imagined the journey that this research would take us on when we began it in 2000. Having just received a grant and an invitation from a nearby middle school to work with their students, we conducted a randomized, controlled trial in a school to address and, we hoped, partly alleviate, one of the most pressing social problems of our era, the racial achievement gap in school. It's pressing because in the United States educational accomplishment is a runway for economic mobility.

We had teachers give a random 50 percent of seventh graders an affirmation activity as part of a packet that the kids completed at the beginning of the school year. This packet included a list of values important to preadolescents, like caring for friends and family, and the students were asked to circle the ones most important to them. Then the exercise prompted them to think more deeply about their values, asking them to consider when they were important to them and why and then to write short answers to these questions. This was a way to recognize that "something special" in themselves that many students typically couldn't express in the classroom. The rest of the students completed a control activity in which they wrote about neutral topics, such as an unimportant value or a morning routine. The intervention took about ten minutes.

I've read hundreds of values-affirmation essays, and, though many are short, they're almost all heartfelt. The kids who aren't doing so well academically often have the most powerful things to say, such as one child who wrote about how he cares for his sick mom or another who wrote about how football brings him joy. What makes this activity psychologically powerful is that it reconnects people with the "big" values that give them meaning. From this higher psychological perch, a difficult situation often feels less threatening.

At the end of the fall term, we compared the grades of the students who had completed the values-affirmation activities with those of students who hadn't. We found positive effects for those students under relatively more stereotype threat. For this school, that group largely consisted of black students, who made up roughly half the school population. In fact, we later found that the biggest benefit occurred for those who felt the most uncertain about their belonging: black students who had a long history of poor achievement and who reported in a baseline survey that they didn't feel they belonged in school. For them, the effect was almost a full grade point, suggesting that they had the most pent-up potential, which was released by the intervention. In fact, the percentage of self-affirmed black students who earned a D or below in the course was only 9 percent compared with 20 percent for black students in the control group.

With these promising early results, we continued to deliver values affirmation activities to the students throughout the seventh grade, changing the activities each time so that the kids didn't get bored (sample activities can be found at my website, geoffreylcohen. com). When we checked their grades at the end of the year, we were surprised to discover that the benefits persisted. In fact, the impact on their grades tended to grow and had extended to all of self-affirmed blacks' core courses: math, English, social studies, and science. When we surveyed their sense of belonging in school throughout the next two years, it proved stronger and more robust than their nonaffirmed peers—not only higher but less likely to go down when they got a bad grade or, in later research, when they reported having a bad day.

Later research with my longtime colleagues David Sherman and Kevin Binning replicated these effects with economically disadvantaged Latino immigrant students at a middle school in the Mountain West region of the United States. And in an echo of Mary Ainsworth's insight—that belonging fosters challenge seeking—we found that self-affirmed minority students appeared to aspire to greater challenges. They were five times more likely to enroll in a college preparation program than their nonaffirmed peers. They were also seen as having more promise by their teachers and were less likely to be assigned to their school's remedial track—which, research suggests, is like an academic death sentence for many minority students, putting them on a trajectory of low expectations.

In research led by Parker Goyer, my lab even found that seven years after the intervention had ended, the affirmed black participants in our original study were 14 percentage points more likely to be attending college than those in the control group. It was as if establishing belonging at a formative period in their lives gave them a foothold to ascend the academic ladder.

While these findings may come across as lightning in a bottle, they've been replicated across an entire school district of middle schools by a team led by Geoffrey Borman. The researchers also tracked their students over the next five years—through the remainder of middle school and all through high school. In 2021, the team reported that the positive effect of the values-affirmation intervention on black and Latino youths' GPA not only persisted but increased over time. The intervention also cut their suspension rates and raised the percentage of these students who graduated from high school by 10 percentage points, substantially closing the gap in graduation rates between them and their nonstereotyped classmates.

Values affirmations also have been found to improve the intellectual performance of groups as varied as low-income college students and adults, the physically disabled, online learners from developing nations, and white college students who feel uncertain of their belonging on campus. In addition, James Jones has interviewed students of color and found that many say experiences of social affirmation on campus—a mentor who takes an interest in their concerns, peers who support causes related to racial justice—buttressed their sense of belonging even while they dealt with racist treatment elsewhere on campus. These experiences helped to firm up the self in a system where it was continually being mortified. Jones also implies that if campuses and courses were made less alienating spaces for minorities in general, providing these situational oases of self-affirming experiences wouldn't be so crucial.

Self-affirmations, like wise interventions in general, are by no means panaceas. They don't work all the time. Indeed some studies have failed to replicate their benefits. A 2021 meta-analysis, led by Zezhen Wu, consolidated all the studies testing values affirmations in classrooms and found an overall positive effect. But there were caveats. The intervention worked best in classrooms where the stereotyped students were, in fact, underperforming relative to their classmates, and in schools that offered relatively more resources to support student learning. In other words, the confluence of threat and opportunity seems to determine when affirmation helps. Timeliness also matters. Because early experiences can touch off a virtuous cycle, early timing of the affirmation can matter more than the number of "doses" people get. In one study, when students received the values affirmation in the first week of classes, the benefits were greater than if they received it merely two weeks later. As we'll continue to see, key conditions in a person's life and social situation have a big impact on the effectiveness of values affirmations and other wise interventions. No intervention works for everyone, everywhere, all the time. What matters is whether an intervention resonates in people's minds and connects with their lives—and that in turn depends on whether it provides the right support to the right people at the right place and time.

Much of the research on stereotype threat has aimed to help people of color and members of other historically excluded groups contend with the threat in education—and rightly so. For these groups, stereotype threat can be a chronic force that limits opportunity. However, stereotype threat is an obstacle for anyone who is in a situation in which they think they could be viewed through the lens of a stereotype. Most of us have experienced it, including members of groups that have not been historically marginalized. Research shows, for example, that white Americans experience stereotype threat when they are involved in discussions about issues of race and that similar wise interventions can help them.

"WHY DO AMERICANS PRETEND slavery never existed?" Ruth Ditlmann, a German graduate student in psychology at the time, asked her adviser, Valerie Purdie-Greenaway, a professor of psychology at Columbia University and a close colleague of mine. Ditlmann had recently traveled to the United States to complete her dissertation under Purdie-Greenaway's supervision. When Ditlmann asked this question, she was calling from Virginia during her spring break. She had gone to visit an old slave plantation because she wanted to learn more about the history of slavery. But her visits left her baffled.

The tours made little to no mention of the horrors of slavery. They pointed out where the "servants" slept and how the white slaveholders and black slaves might enjoy the Southern drink of a mint julep together during work breaks. The history was completely sanitized. By contrast, Ditlmann knew that in Germany, playing down the Holocaust, such as claiming that the gas chambers were used only to clean the clothes of concentration-camp prisoners, is prohibited by law.

Purdie-Greenaway, an African American woman, explained that most white people would never visit the plantations if the tours were made historically accurate. She introduced Ditlmann to the concept of white fragility. The term was coined by Robin DiAngelo in 2006 to describe the defensiveness and lack of "psychological stamina" that many white Americans display when the topic of racism even arises, especially when they're challenged on their assumptions about the influence of race in their country. Many white people deny that racism still exists. Many others, who acknowledge it's a problem, say they themselves are "colorblind" and are committed to racial equality. Yet research in my lab shows that these whites—who espouse a belief that race "should not matter"—can be the most defensive when someone says they have experienced racism.

Research by Wendy Berry Mendes, Jim Blascovich, Jennifer Richeson, and their colleagues finds that white adults display a physiological threat response when they're engaged in conversations with black people, especially about racially charged issues, such as police profiling. The threat can be so intense that they show decrements in performance on cognitive control tasks even after these conversations are over. This reaction can be interpreted as due to stereotype threat, with white people fearing that they will be seen as racist. The threatening nature of these conversations can be particularly strong among white people who say they are committed to racial equality. They have a stronger identity investment in not being seen as racist. An unfortunate outcome of the stereotype threat that many white people feel is that many of them avoid such conversations, especially across racial lines—and when they do participate in them, they tend to focus more on protecting their views of themselves than on learning.

Ditlmann wanted to know how to make these conversations go better, so she decided to study them. She invited black and white adults first to review some disturbing information about the history of slavery in the United States. She then had black participants write letters about their reactions, which she shared with white participants. In another study, she had black and white participants have a tough conversation together about slavery, which was videotaped, transcribed, and evaluated by independent coders.

In some of the exchanges, either through text or in person, the white participants displayed less anxiety than they did in others. In a confidential survey completed afterward, they also didn't denigrate their black interlocutor as much, and they expressed more interest in the information about slavery that their black partners had shared. They also remembered more of what their black partners had said in conversation, suggesting they had listened and learned more.

Ditlmann then studied the nature of the way the black participants had communicated, looking for any differences that might explain the effects on their white partners. She did not find much difference in the degree to which the black participants had raised difficult issues. Almost none of them shied away from pointing out harsh realities about slavery, which have not been depicted widely enough in the history covered in the media or taught in schools. Many black participants expressed anguish. As one said, "It was disturbing to see the pain and utter despair my people shouldered . . . stripped of virtually all our humanity."

However, a striking difference emerged in how the black participants had emotionally engaged with their white partners in the most fruitful exchanges. These black participants found ways, both verbal and nonverbal, to tamp down the stereotype threat white participants felt. One way they did this was a form of affirmation. They asked their white partner about their friends, families, and hobbies, which gave the white participants opportunities to demonstrate their admirable values and convey their full humanity. The black participants also fostered rapport with such affirming statements as "You hit the nail on the head." They sometimes also expressed their belief in eventual racial unity, indicating they thought white people have the potential to join in bringing justice to fruition, for example, by saying, "White Americans and African Americans will sit together at the table of brotherhood one day." When it came to nonverbal communication in the actual conversations, the black participants in these successful conversations leaned in closer to their white counterparts, and they kept their body posture forward-facing toward their partner rather than askance. This sensitive conversational style seemed to have alleviated white people's stereotype threat by sending them the message, "I see you as a human being worthy of dignity and respect."

+ + + +

AS ROBIN DIANGELO PORTRAYED through her metaphor of stereo-typing as a storm of threats raining down, stereotype threat can be sparked at any moment because stereotypes are so widespread. But the good news is that we can craft situations to alleviate it. As we'll see in Part Three, a number of additional antidotes to stereotype threat have been found to have potent effects comparable to those of self-affirmation. The larger social problems of stereotyping and discrim-ination are ones that we must all address through social policy and social change. At the same time, as individuals and members of insti-tutions, we can do much to protect those under threat from the storm.

Chapter 8

I Can See It on Your Face (or Can I?)

How to Read Others with Empathy

IN AN AMUSING COLUMN BY DAVE BARRY, A COUPLE, ROGER and Elaine, have had a lovely dinner and are driving home, with Roger at the wheel. As Elaine silently reflects on their relationship, she says, "Do you realize that, as of tonight, we've been seeing each other for exactly six months?"

Roger says nothing in return, and her mind is off and running: "I wonder if it bothers him that I said that. Maybe he's been feeling confined by our relationship; maybe he thinks I'm trying to push him into some kind of obligation that he doesn't want, or isn't sure of."

Meanwhile Roger is thinking, "So that means it was . . . let's see . . . February when we started going out, which was right after I had the car at the dealer's, which means . . . lemme check the odometer . . . Whoa! I am way overdue for an oil change here."

Their mental musings proceed on wildly divergent courses:

Elaine: "He's upset. I can see it on his face. Maybe I'm reading this completely wrong. Maybe he wants more from our relationship, more intimacy, more commitment; maybe he has sensed—even before I sensed it—that I was feeling some reservations. Yes, I bet that's it."

Roger: "And I'm gonna have them look at the transmission again. I don't care what those morons say, it's still not shifting right."

Elaine proceeds to convince herself that Roger is angry with her because she's unsure he's truly the knight in shining armor she's looking for, while Roger muses about what he'll say to the car mechanic. Suddenly, Elaine breaks out in tears. He is totally confused about what has upset her.

Finally, Elaine says, "It's just that . . . It's that I . . . I need some time." Startled out of his reverie, Roger realizes he has to be careful with what he says now. Dave Barry writes,

> *There is a 15-second pause while Roger, thinking as fast as he can, tries to come up with a safe response. Finally, he comes up with one that he thinks might work.*
>
> *"Yes," he says.*

His remark makes no sense, but he thinks it will come across as supportive, which it does. Elaine is elated that he has been so understanding. But later that night, with each in their separate homes, she tosses and turns in bed, worried that she might have put a stake in their relationship. As for Roger, he senses something important unfolded but decides he'll never be able to figure out what, so he turns on the TV and happily munches on some chips.

While the scenario is amusing in Barry's telling, the sad truth is that relationships are often undermined by such misreading, whether romantic connections or those with family members, friends, colleagues, and strangers we encounter in daily life.

In many situations, we attribute opinions and emotions to people that distance us from them, fueling conflict. We tend to have far more confidence in our ability to read people's behavior, facial expressions, body language, and tone of voice than we should. And far too often, because we think we've got a good read on others, we don't ask about their thoughts and feelings, which might lead to important discoveries that would help build connection.

Consider the case of a relative, say, an aunt, who supports a political candidate you find morally repugnant. You may be watching TV with her, and an ad for the candidate comes on in which the candidate voices some remarks you find offensive. The aunt lets out a little grunt. You might interpret that grunt as an expression of bemused support. But if you asked her whether or not that's true, you might learn that she grunted out of frustration with the candidate and that she also finds the remarks offensive. (Or perhaps she had some indigestion and didn't even notice the ad.) If you asked her why she still supports the candidate, she might explain that she wishes he would stop making such comments but that she is more concerned about a problem that he promises to address, which you might also be concerned about. That could become an opening for thoughtful discussion, which might strengthen bonds by fostering mutual understanding. Unfortunately, rather than checking whether our mind reading is on target, we tend to keep our interpretations to ourselves and build up a fiction in our mind that replaces the actual flesh-and-blood person by our side. Gulfs of misunderstanding drive people apart.

Many research studies have shown how far off our interpretive reads of others can be. I was involved in one while I was in graduate school that opened my eyes. My mentor at the time, Claude Steele, sent me to the University of Michigan to explore why black and white students tended to sit apart from one another in the dining halls, as was true at many colleges and still is. Steele instructed me to interview students to get their perspectives. Many black students explained that they chose to sit together for reasons similar to one expressed by one interviewee: "We spend the whole day interacting with white folks. And after a while you just get *tired*." When I probed further, asking if that was because their white peers were being racist, they generally answered that while that might sometimes be the case, what was more at play was that they didn't know what the white students were thinking of them, so they felt they had to keep their guard up. They said this was exhausting. Meanwhile, the white students tended to say the black students just didn't want to sit with them and they were trying to respect that preference.

What struck me was that neither group of students understood what the other was thinking. Nobody that I spoke to had even asked someone from the other group about the topic.

My interviews also revealed that both black and white students felt very uncertain about where they belonged—a classic manifestation of the belonging uncertainty Greg Walton and I later documented—when walking alone with a tray into a dining hall looking for somewhere to sit. Students could tolerate wandering alone like a lost sheep for about only five seconds at most, and then they would quickly choose a table where they felt confident the others welcomed them. Both groups sought the comfort of familiar faces, but neither expressed an appreciation that their anxieties were shared. For black students, this belonging uncertainty was compounded by being in the minority on a predominantly white campus.

Years later, I was delighted to read research by social psychologists Nicole Shelton and Jennifer Richeson that echoed what I had observed and heard in these students' comments. The researchers asked black and white college students a set of questions, the answers to which revealed that both groups had a strong interest in making more cross-race friends but both groups also believed that the students from the other race were generally less interested in doing so than they in fact were. Shelton and Richeson probed further and learned that both racial groups held back from trying to build cross-race friendships largely due to fear of rejection. Meanwhile, both groups thought the other was relatively unconcerned about rejection.

As this research illustrates, our overreliance on our interpretations of others' thoughts and feelings stems not only from our overconfidence in our mind-reading skills but from the frequent feeling that our insecurities are unique to us. We become anxious about openly discussing uncomfortable issues with others: We can't imagine how we could broach the subject. What's helpful in overcoming this barrier is the knowledge that these anxieties are normal and surmountable.

Tim Wilson and his colleagues developed a wise intervention that gave people this knowledge. They had white first-year college students watch a video of a white and a black student at their school who discussed how they had become friends in spite of initial awkwardness between them. Then the participants wrote about a time when they had thought they couldn't become friends with someone but later discovered they had been wrong. Over the next week, these students made more friends with minority students at their school than did students in a control group, as gauged by the racial makeup of new Facebook friends.

We also often misread others by failing to take account of the situation they're in. Once, I was with a group of passengers waiting to board a plane. A young man walked up to the kiosk where a line of us stood as an announcement was being broadcast. I could tell that he was simply trying to hear the announcement better, but an elderly woman in line mistakenly thought he was trying to cut ahead. "There's a line," she commented in an annoyed voice, and he responded testily, "Get off my back, lady." Now she felt disrespected. She said something offensive back, and after a few more back-and-forths, with each one dialing up their rage, the confrontation ended with the woman snarling, "You're a very rude young man."

Neither considered how the situation was affecting the other's behavior. If they had, they might have avoided the argument and even bonded over their common predicament.

Amplifying the problem are our culturally conditioned assumptions about how to interpret certain "signals" sent by others, such as facial expressions and body language. People's appearance, the way they dress, how loudly or softly they speak, and so many other bodily and voice expressions supposedly tell us what sort of person they are, and we tend to make extremely rapid judgments of others based on these cues.

Just how rapid was illuminated by a study conducted by Princeton cognitive psychologist Alexander Todorov and his team. They presented people with static pictures of faces and asked them to judge how trustworthy each person was. The participants watched the photos of faces flash up one at a time, each for a second, as they lay in a functional magnetic resonance imaging scanner that monitored their brain activity. Within the first five hundred milliseconds of exposure to a face, the participants' amygdala activated, indicating emotional reaction. For faces with expressions that people associated with a lack of trustworthiness, the amygdala was more highly activated, as happens in the threat response. Todorov also found that the stronger the consensus about whether a face looked untrustworthy, the stronger each individual's amygdala response generally was to that face. This finding suggests that when we go with our gut, we're really going with the crowd. We're conforming to social expectations of how we should read people.

Todorov found that his participants, when making their own judgments of the trustworthiness of the faces, by and large went with their gut. Once a snap judgment appears in our consciousness, it can be surprisingly sticky. Why? Because we don't realize how much our perceptions are authored by our own mind and mistakenly think that thoughts and impressions that pop into our mind say more about what's "out there" in reality. Indeed, we interpret the very speed and ease with which they pop into our minds as an indication of their validity, a bias that the cognitive psychologists Daniel Kahneman and Amos Tversky called the "availability heuristic": That which is mentally available, that which comes readily to mind, is deemed more likely.

These snap judgments lead to overemphasis of qualities of people's appearance and behavior that may be poor indicators. Take the case of evaluating political candidates. Todorov and his colleagues showed static black-and-white head shots of two candidates from opposing parties who were running for U.S. Senate in a number of different states, first making sure the participants didn't recognize the candidates. Flashing photos of them for one second, the researchers asked the participants to quickly say which face they thought looked most competent. The candidate who was judged more competent looking won the election 68 percent of the time. That's not perfect accuracy, especially when you consider that just by chance, participants' guesses would match the winning candidate 50 percent of the time. But the results suggest that about 36 percent of candidates' electoral fate hinges on the sparse information gleaned in the first second of exposure to a still shot of their face, without any information about their platform or politics, or even exposure to their voice and bodily movement.

Unless we believe that a candidate's appearance is a reliable indication of his or her ability, this finding should be disturbing, as it suggests that our evaluations of candidates may be much more superficial and swayed by cultural biases about appearance than we would like to think. In related research by Nalini Ambady, students' evaluations of how competent, confident, and warm their teachers were after the end of a school semester were strongly correlated with snap judgments that observers made about the teachers on the basis of two seconds of *soundless* video of them teaching. In fact, these snap judgments predicted roughly 50 percent of the variance in teachers' end-of-semester student evaluations.

We might congratulate ourselves on our amazing insight in making such snap judgments, given that our later judgments conform so well to ones made with so little evidence. But another takeaway is that, to a significant degree, our judgments of others are formed before we have any substantive information on which to base them. We may like to think that people are like books to be read, but when we try to read them, we often don't get past the first sentence—maybe not even past the cover. As we saw in earlier chapters, our snap judgments don't just prophesy the future but create it. We act on our shared biases, which sentences others to the fate we think they are destined for.

Our snap judgments can clearly have troubling costs for some people's sense of belonging, as well as unfortunate larger social costs. Do we really want to be writing off politicians based on how they look, whether they have, say, gleaming white teeth and a chiseled jaw? Do we want to exclude those whose appearance and presentation of themselves, whether through body language or speech, don't conform well to the societal interpretations of what's "normal"?

A good friend of mine, Martin, was an epileptic, and to prevent seizures he had to take a medication that slowed his speech. When he was given a chance, Martin shined. For all his adult life, he volunteered as an emergency medical technician at a fire station in his hometown, where he was beloved. But Martin had trouble finding and keeping jobs, and one reason was that he didn't interview well. He didn't articulate answers concisely. In fact, sometimes he talked so slowly that it was hard to follow him. He finally landed a stable position when one of my other friends gave him a job at his company. "I hired him, and I'd do it again," he says to this day.

Martin was one of many people whose promise fails to come across in the thin slice of an interview. I suspect Martin also had trouble getting into romantic relationships for similar reasons, reflecting a bias we have in our society against those who seem just a bit "off." Martin lived alone. So during one epileptic seizure when he ended up face down on his bed, there was no one there to turn him over, and he suffocated.

Our judgments of others' character and state of mind sometimes say more about our own than about anyone else's. Misreadings are more common when we feel stressed, insecure, or threatened. Research by Sarah Wert at Yale University showed that when pairs of friends wrote about a time they had felt excluded, they subsequently gossiped more harshly about a third person they both knew. People restore the feeling that they belong, Wert suggests, by establishing who doesn't. Research by David Dunning and his colleagues finds that when people's self-esteem is threatened, they become more rigid in enforcing their own self-serving standards for success, believing that success in various arenas of life is less likely for those who are dissimilar to them. We put others down in part to feel better about ourselves. The simple act of centering yourself, by processing difficult emotions and by reflecting on important personal values, can prevent such misreadings.

Another source of mischief is our skewed interpretations of the reasons someone else might be anxious, that all-too-common emotion of modern social life. I frequent a local wine bar where the bartenders are renowned for their ability to create an atmosphere of belonging, much like in the old TV show *Cheers*. The senior bartender, Blake, has an uncanny ability to make everyone feel at ease and at home in spite of the range in clientele and the periodic arguments over counter space. When people are anxious in any arena, as they may be because of fears that they don't fit in, they leak that anxiety and are vulnerable to misinterpretation.

I experienced exactly this in one disastrous social encounter at the bar. I was introduced by a friend to a woman he knew, Beth. She told me she owned a chain of beauty salons, and I told her I was a professor. Then I added that I found the hair-dressing profession interesting, which is true. As a social psychologist, I am fascinated by how people's hair is so tied to their identity. But Beth frowned and looked angry, and I could see that she had taken offense at my comment, maybe thinking I was being patronizing and snarky rather than sincere. I panicked. My heart began to pound. I started to sweat. Stuttering, I tried to explain, but my halting speech must have made me seem even more guilty of an insult. Our mutual friend noticed something was up and came over. As he listened in on what I was saying, I thought I saw him roll his eyes. Uncertain about how I was being seen, I was suddenly acutely sensitive to their every nonverbal cue, which derailed my train of thought before it could even start, making me all the more inarticulate. I felt as if I were slipping into a quicksand of judgment. The more I struggled, the further I sank. I started adding a question mark to every statement, as if to say, "Is that okay?" I avoided eye contact; their laser-like gazes made me more stressed.

My remediation efforts were to no avail. Beth started to cry. She even asked Blake to kick me out. Our mutual friend consoled her, not before murmuring in my ear, "Geoff, I'm very disappointed with you." I was baffled and offended to have been seen as someone so offensive. Clearly, I hadn't explained my genuine interest well. Perhaps, also, in jumping to the topic of hairdressing, I had inadvertently belittled her role as an entrepreneur. But clearly, too, Beth had misread me. She had read my anxiety as a further "tell." If only she could have read my mind, she would have known that my "tells" were really signs that I wanted the interaction to go well and was upset that it wasn't. Perhaps Beth, as a woman whose businesses were located in the male-dominated Silicon Valley, had dealt with one too many arrogant men in the past, which led her to suspect the same attitude from me.

We tend to read others' anxiety as a sign that they are put off by us. That may be true, but just as often they may be worried that *we* don't like or respect *them*. Consider cross-race encounters. White people sometimes give off hard-to-control nonverbal signals of discomfort and anxiety in these encounters, such as avoiding eye contact, blinking frequently, and speaking haltingly. The ambiguity is that while prejudice can lead to this nonverbal "leakage," so can the fear of being *seen* as prejudiced. In other words, people's anxious "tells" can actually be signs that they want the encounter to go well—and they fear that it's not. All of us are vulnerable to being misread in this way. We sometimes enter a hall of mirrors in our interpersonal interactions, getting caught up in what we think other people think we think—which wreaks all kinds of havoc.

The many foibles in our attempts to read others' hearts and minds call out for us to make the effort to discover what people are thinking and feeling rather than assuming we know. But how? The blazingly simple answer is to ask them.

+ + + +

I ONCE ATTENDED a wedding at which I met an elderly Chinese woman named Emma. When I told her I was a psychologist, she opened up to me to ask for advice about how to connect better with her granddaughter, who lived in Beijing. They had always been close and had talked every week on Skype. But as her granddaughter entered her teenage years, she seemed to be slipping away from her and from her parents. She was drinking alcohol and going to parties far too much, and her schoolwork was suffering. Their once lively conversations over Skype had become punctuated by awkward silences. Emma didn't know how to read her granddaughter, she told me. Why was she behaving this way? I suggested that she just ask her granddaughter for her perspective; for example, ask what was going on in her life or how she was feeling. These questions could perhaps give her a window into her granddaughter's life.

Emma was visibly taken aback at the simplicity of my suggestion. She thought about it for a few seconds in silence, and then we parted company. But at the end of the party she rushed up to me and said excitedly, "The question is the window!"

I wish I could have taken all the credit for my advice, but it had actually come from three other social psychologists—Tal Eyal, Mary Steffel, and Nicholas Epley—who had in 2018 published a paper entitled "Perspective Mistaking: Accurately Understanding the Mind of Another Requires Getting Perspective, Not Taking Perspective."

The researchers had conducted a series of studies showing that when it comes to judging another person's emotions and views, trying to "imagine their perspective" doesn't work as well as we think. In fact, there was a tendency across all the studies for accuracy to suffer when people tried to imagine the perspective of the other. Epley, in his fascinating book *Mindwise*, even reports the same effect for romantic couples. Trying to imagine the perspective of other people can make us less perceptive, Epley suggests, because we often end up imagining *ourselves* as the other person, even though the other person might be in a different situation and have different tastes from our own.

Instead of trying to imagine another person's perspective, Epley suggests that we *ask* for it, what he calls "perspective-getting."

He and his colleagues showed that when people were told to ask questions to try to get to know another person and their interests, attitudes, and hobbies, the degree to which their predictions matched what the other person reported about themselves soared. This was true for married couples as well. Rather than try to imagine how much your spouse would like to spend a weekend camping, ask them about it. This seems so obvious as to be almost silly. But, interestingly, Epley and his colleagues show that people don't fully appreciate the empathic gains they get by simply asking good questions and, just as important, listening to the answers.

Many years ago, Epley recounts, the military was trying to foretell the effect on officers of repealing the "don't ask, don't tell" policy that banned gay men and lesbians from openly serving in the military. A survey of retired military officers revealed that the majority predicted, based on their experience, that the repeal would decrease the officers' morale. The Pentagon also simply asked current soldiers how they thought they would react. The overwhelming majority said it would have either no effect or a positive effect. Many had met gay officers and didn't have a problem with it. Who was right? A study of the actual consequences of the eventual repeal gave the answer: the soldiers.

Another example of perspective-getting comes from Catherine Thomas and her colleagues who studied the best way to present financial aid to the poor in Nairobi. As we saw earlier, they found that empowering presentations, which emphasized "helping your community grow," generated more interest in learning about business than did the standard "helping the poor to meet their needs" presentation. But the researchers also found that when another sample of participants from the same locale was asked to guess how people from their community would respond to the various presentations, on average they guessed right. If you're trying to figure out the best way to support people, one way is to simply ask them.

In fact, a long-standing methodology of social science is predicated on the value of perspective-getting: the qualitative interview, which at its best is a candid and authentic conversation with someone else about their story as they see it. It can serve as a powerful corrective to stereotypical assumptions we might otherwise make. The Jamaican American author and activist June Jordan, critical of white researchers and artists who try to imagine the situation of being black in America rather than listen to the people who live it, wrote an essay, the title of which distilled her frustration: "On Listening: A Good Way to Hear."

Kathryn Edin has used the qualitative interview to understand with touching nuance the experience of poverty. Her work resoundingly debunks many of the stereotypes of working-class men of all ethnic groups. Many of her interviewees were entrepreneurial, acquiring multiple skills to "hedge their bets" and fulfill a need for autonomy and self-expression, training to work as barbers, diesel mechanics, tattoo artists, DJs, or some mix. Several worked grueling hours "off the books." Very few had significant leisure time. Many of her interviewees also rejected the tough, macho norms of the previous generation of fathers. They all embraced their role as fathers and wanted both to provide financially and to be available emotionally. One respondent said that being a father "taught [him] pure love." Many men reported being emotionally devastated as a result of being separated from their children. "It's destroyed me," one said. Edin also observed that many unmarried men "feel degraded as men and devalued as dads" as a direct result of social policies, as when they get "slapped with a child support order without any process in place that ensures them parenting time." Edin's perspective-getting has led her to conclude, "After decades of research on the poor, we've found that a common theme is the desire for basic human dignity and respect."

That's not to say people are always accurate when they share their perspectives. Research by Daniel Gilbert, Timothy Wilson, and their colleagues shows that we are subject to many biases and blind spots when it comes to reading ourselves, including a tendency to be self-serving and to overlook shameful or discomfiting aspects of our feelings and thoughts. Rather than delving into this large body of research—for excellent treatments, see Gilbert's book *Stumbling on Happiness* and Wilson's book *Strangers to Ourselves*—I want to simply highlight two points. First, people can be oblivious to the real reasons they hold the thoughts and feelings they do. So it may be best to begin the perspective-getting process by asking them to describe their perspective rather than explain why they have it. Explaining *what* we consciously think and feel is a far less speculative and error-prone enterprise. Second, we can help people give their perspective with greater accuracy by avoiding questions that simply confirm our own beliefs about them. Asking a political conservative "Why do you find liberals so threatening?" is likely to be counterproductive. Such questions tend to put the other person on the defensive and to elicit information that confirms our beliefs. But if we have an open mind when questioning people and inquire in a genuine way about how they're thinking and feeling, they're likely to surprise us with information that allows us to see them as distinctive individuals rather than through stereotypes. Asking a political conservative "What do you think about a higher minimum wage?" might inspire a more thoughtful and illuminating discussion.

Asking others to share their perspective not only leads to much more accuracy of understanding between people but creates a bonding force, which engenders still deeper and richer readings of one another. The power of questions to create appreciation and warmth between people was demonstrated in remarkable research by the social psychologist Art Aron and his wife, the clinical psychologist Elaine Aron. They were interested in how bonds of intimacy might be created between people who were strangers to one another. Through much research, they created what they called the "fast friends procedure."

Two strangers are paired up, and they ask one another a series of thirty-six questions, which were honed over time by the Arons. The questions begin with "Given the choice of anyone in the world, whom would you want as a dinner guest?" Next is "Would you like to be famous? In what way?" Third is "Before making a telephone call, do you ever rehearse what you are going to say? Why?" And fourth is "What would constitute a 'perfect' day for you?" The questions become increasingly intimate: for example, "How do you feel about your relationship with your mother?" and "If you were to die this evening with no opportunity to communicate with anyone, what would you most regret not having told someone? Why haven't you told them yet?" Sharing vulnerabilities in a safe environment fosters connection. This procedure consistently produces feelings of closeness, overwhelming the impact of disagreement on various issues of personal taste that we expect to matter. It has even led to at least one marriage proposal.

Research by social psychologists Elizabeth Page-Gould and Rodolfo Mendoza-Denton showed that the fast friends procedure can be used as an intervention to improve social belonging. They brought Latino and white college students together and had them ask one another the questions either with a person of the same ethnicity or with a person of the other ethnicity. They found that the experience of doing the activity with a person of another ethnicity was especially powerful in helping Latino students who were worried about being rejected because of their ethnicity. Afterward these students reported feeling more satisfied with their experience at the university and being more likely to encourage a friend to attend, relative to Latino students who had completed the same activity with a person of their ethnicity. There was even some evidence in a later study that this procedure reduced cortisol reactivity—a biological signature of social evaluative threat—among both Latino and white students when they interacted across racial lines. Moreover, among participants who had relatively more negative views of the other ethnic group, making a friend across ethnic lines prompted them to initiate more cross-race conversations in their day-to-day lives outside of school. A single friendship can make a big difference, not only bonding people to each other but bonding them to their mutual worlds. For that matter, Eminem, Katharine Graham, and many other successful people who "made it" in a world where they were an outsider report having had one "insider" friend who served as a bridge between worlds.

Why is asking people questions about themselves such a potent agent in forming bonds? One reason is that it is affirming of others, making them feel that they are interesting and that their interlocutor in particular finds them worthy of close attention. Another reason is simply that we get to know each other better, building more authentic relationships and learning how to provide more individualized support.

Tutoring students can harness the power of perspective-getting to great effect. A good tutor is the most effective educational intervention, with only a single session producing remarkable gains in learning even among alienated and underperforming students.

Social psychologist Mark Lepper conducted brilliant research on what makes some tutors much more effective than others. Setting up his laboratory as a mini-classroom, with video cameras to record tutoring sessions, he and his collaborator Maria Woolverton recruited tutors and a number of ten-year-old students who were all struggling in math. Then they watched and taped sessions both with tutors who got average results and with ones who got superior results.

What distinguished the superior tutors? For one thing, rather than getting right to the business of instruction, they asked the students questions about their hobbies and interests. As with the Arons' thirty-six questions, these questions were affirming for the students, making them feel they were being seen as a whole person, not just "a kid with math problems." Affirmed of their value as interesting individuals, the students felt more comfortable challenging themselves. Asking these questions also helped the tutors to understand what motivated individual students.

The questions also created a connection between the tutor and the student, and the tutors didn't confine questions only to this opening phase of the sessions. The superior tutors kept on asking questions, keeping the child a full participant in the process of her own learning. Remarkably, when Lepper and Woolverton coded the transcripts of these sessions, they discovered that 90 percent of the tutor's utterances were questions. Rather than explaining, "You should begin adding with the 1's column, not the 10's column," for example, they would ask, "Where do you begin? With the 1's column or the 10's column?" Listening in on the interactions, you'd almost think the students were educating the tutors. To continue to sniff out the precise gaps in the child's understanding, the superior tutors would say to a student who gave a wrong answer, "Tell me more about why you think that." This would lead the student to realize where their thinking went wrong. I like to think of these wise tutors as sherpas for the students, guiding them to ascend the summit themselves.

Lepper has gone on to apply the insights from his research on expert tutors in work for the United States Navy, training cadets in information technology. This is one of the most popular educational tracks in the Navy, with the skills being critical for handling its massive ships and operating complex interconnected technologies. Lepper became part of a team that created a program called the Digital Tutor, based on his tutoring research, with an interface as much like a wise human tutor as possible. It asks questions rather than lecturing, provides hints to help trainees discover answers on their own, and affirms learners indirectly rather than directly. The results have been stellar, raising the test performance of cadets to the level of seasoned sailors within a month. A later variant of the Digital Tutor was used with unemployed veterans, helping the vast majority to gain employment in information technology jobs at Microsoft, Amazon, and other tech companies.

WE'VE ALL HEARD THAT empathizing with others is a matter of putting ourselves in their shoes. But with people having such different life experiences and perspectives, when we try to do so, we may be off base. We need to find ways to cultivate authentic empathy, a mission that has taken on greater urgency in our increasingly diverse and divided society.

One promising approach, which has garnered little attention, was developed while I was finishing my studies at Stanford by a fellow graduate student named Ronaldo Mendoza. He wanted to determine how we could come to genuinely understand another person's experience, especially when we've taken offense at something they have said or done. Mendoza was hopeful, writing that because no two people are exactly alike, each encounter "is an occasion for the work of empathy," and with each encounter "we are students anew."

An ingenious experiment he conducted provided one powerful strategy for creating empathy. While virtually all the research I've described in this book was published in peer-reviewed journals, this work of Mendoza's was not. He didn't go into academia, and so, like too much PhD dissertation research, his work sits unused and unrecognized on a bookshelf. But I think it's among the most important studies on empathy ever conducted, and, as we'll see in Chapter 13, later research lent support to his novel approach in promoting empathy across the political divide.

Mendoza recruited pairs of college romantic couples or close friends and had them each come prepared to discuss something the other person had done that bothered them. At the lab, each person shared this grievance with their friend or partner. Then both members of the pair rated how much they felt they understood their counterpart and how much they felt their counterpart understood them.

Next, for one group of these pairs, Mendoza asked each person to "think about the incident that you brought in and then try to put yourself in your partner's shoes." This was a standard empathy induction. They were asked to describe in writing the situation the other was in and how they would "have felt and behaved had they been in that situation." For instance, one young woman singled out as her grievance the fact that her boyfriend had consoled his ex-girlfriend before tending to her when they both went to the hospital after some friends had been in a tragic accident. She tried to put herself in her boyfriend's situation and to imagine how she would have felt and behaved.

For a second group of pairs, Mendoza tested a novel intervention. He asked them instead to think about the incident they had brought up and to describe what they thought their partner "was *feeling* when they did the thing that bothered them." He did not ask them to think about how that situation would have made *them* feel but how it had made *their partner* feel. Then he asked them to recall an *analogous situation* from their *own* life "in which you felt something similar to what you think your partner may have felt." This strategy, Mendoza suggested, was more likely to evoke what we really mean by "to empathize," as the word's Germanic origin, *einfühlen*, meaning literally "to *feel* oneself into," indicates.

For both groups, each member of the pair took turns sharing their written responses with their partner. In other words, they *gave* their perspective and *got* their partner's perspective. The two in each pair were then asked to rate again how much they understood their partner and how much they felt their partner understood them.

After compiling the data, Mendoza made two discoveries. For the first group, he found that there was no increase in how much the individuals in the pairs rated their own or the other's degree of understanding and, in fact, some people reported feeling *less* understanding of their partner. Why? Because much of the time, when we imagine ourselves in the same situation as another person, we conclude, "I wouldn't have done what they did!" This then makes us less empathic. For instance, the woman whose boyfriend consoled his ex-girlfriend at the hospital wrote, "I would have made sure [my partner] was alright before I comforted or went to a friend." After the intervention, her rating of how much understanding she had for her boyfriend fell from a 6 to a 2 on a 9-point scale. Her boyfriend's rating of how understood he felt dropped from 7 to 2.

The second discovery was that the emotion-based empathic intervention increased mutual understanding. The jump in the ratings provided by the pairs in this group was significantly greater than the change in the ratings provided by the pairs in the first group. Consider the reaction of another woman, whose grievance was that her boyfriend commented "on how attractive some girls looked." He had claimed, she wrote, that he was just "stating it factually" and wasn't making any veiled attempt to put her down. For her exercise, she imaginatively drew on a situation that bore little resemblance factually but great resemblance emotionally:

> *I think an analogous situation occurred in high school, when I commented that one of my friends' poetry was not strong or effective, and she took it the wrong way, I guess [my] feeling [was] that I was saying something true but my friend didn't want to hear it.*

Her rating of how much understanding she had for her boyfriend increased from 7 to 8, but more impressively, his rating of how understood he felt by her increased from 2 to 7. Mendoza reported that there were several powerful moments of connection in the couples in the emotion-based empathy group, with some reporting that they felt the other person finally "got it" with respect to the grievance raised.

We all have a bank of experiences and memories that we can use to enhance our empathy with others, if we are willing. We can treat our memories as touchstones for greater connection rather than heavy rocks of self-recrimination. Thinking of analogous situations in which we've felt similarly to someone who has aggrieved us, or responded in a way we object to, helps us to read them better and appreciate the factors in the situation affecting their behavior.

+ + + +

WE CAN'T, AND SHOULDN'T, try to stop getting a good read on others. Positive social interaction and the connections that support belonging depend to some degree on people's ability to read others well. The operable word here, though, is "well." Our misreadings too often rewrite situations for the worse.

One of the privileges I have as a social scientist is one we get far too little of in our daily social lives: the opportunity to discover how often I am wrong. The process of designing an experiment forces you to specify a hypothesis and put it to a clear test. The data don't care what you think. You ask a question, and the analysis of the data, as I see it, is a form of listening. If your theory of what people will do is wrong, you find out. I've had many sad Fridays—the day when the data come rolling in—as a result. But in our everyday social lives we rarely get the chance to discover how wrong we are. It's seldom obvious, and we don't ask questions to put our ideas to the test. Our mind's biases not only cause errors but blind us to those errors. My sense is that it's these cognitive biases, more than any moral failing, that cause much misunderstanding and conflict. By nurturing an awareness of what Emily Pronin calls our "bias blind spot," we can rise to three challenges:

1. *Humility:* Be on guard for an outsized faith in our judgments and our tendency to assume that our beliefs about others are correct.

2. *Empathy:* Try to appreciate that other people's anxieties and insecurities shape their behaviors just as much as our anxieties and insecurities shape our own.

3. *Communication:* Ask people for their perspective, because when we don't, we deprive ourselves of the chance to learn and connect.

To meet these challenges and overcome our biases takes work. But by using the tools of perspective-getting introduced here, and by practicing the techniques of psychological self-care that clear our heads and hearts of preoccupation, we can change the way we read others for the better.

The motto might be, "Don't just read. Listen." We will always be spinning theories about the people we meet, but we can step back from them in our minds and prod ourselves to reconsider. We can remind ourselves to try to understand the situation as it's seen and felt by the other person, regardless of how much we disagree on the surface. And no matter how weird someone else seems to be, we can consider the possibility that we, because of our cultural programming, may be the weird one. With these bits of wisdom and with lots of practice, we can get much better at asking instead of assuming, at reading situations and how they're affecting people, and at cultivating empathy based on feelings of fellowship.

Part Three

Fostering Belonging in All Walks of Life

Chapter 9

Belonging in School

Creating Situations That Help Students Thrive

S OMETIMES THE SLIGHTEST GESTURE OF APPRECIATION AND support can turn a situation that feels strange and threatening into one that feels inviting and welcoming.

One crisp fall day, I took my daughter to the first day of orientation for middle school. She was about to begin sixth grade. As we walked up to the entrance of what seemed like a sprawling campus relative to the small elementary school she was used to, I felt self-conscious, not knowing where to go or what to do. I could only imagine how my daughter felt, though I had some hints. She was hunkered over a bit, as if burdened, arms hanging in front of her as if in preparation for a fall. I tried to think of some words of assurance. But before I could speak, a bright, smiling student walked up to us and greeted us with a cheery "Hello!" She struck up a conversation with my daughter. It was her second year at the school, she explained, and then she asked where my daughter had gone to elementary school. They had gone to the same school and soon discovered they'd had the same first-grade teacher, agreeing about how much they had enjoyed her. My daughter smiled and loosened up. Next the host introduced her to some other kids, and moments later, off my daughter pranced with her new friends to explore the campus.

From our first moments attending school, through the many progressions from grade to grade, from middle to high school, and, for many, on to college, we may find ourselves overtaken by belonging uncertainty. Even in the early grades, schools can be competitive, not only academically but socially. Making things even tougher is that students enter school with wide-ranging life experiences that prepare them differently for learning and socializing. Heading off to school for the first time as a toddler can be both one of the most exciting transitions in life and one of the scariest. At every step of the way, new threats to belonging arise, whether being assigned to new teachers, trying out for a sports team or the band, or facing peer pressure to drink alcohol or take drugs. Social media has added jet fuel to the fire, with its panoply of means to exclude, bully, and humiliate classmates.

Much of the discussion about belonging uncertainty in schools has focused on the experiences of minority students because they face especially daunting challenges. But even students who might seem to "have it all" because they are popular, or come from a well-off family and excel both academically and in extracurricular activities, may be plagued by doubts about how well they belong. I was struck while reading former U.S. vice president Dick Cheney's memoir, *In My Time*, that he had experienced powerful belonging uncertainty when he attended Yale University. He was admitted in 1959 but dropped out soon after his first year. He had been a good student and football star in high school and had won a full scholarship, but he performed poorly in his classes at Yale. "I found some kindred souls, young men like me, who were not adjusting very well and shared my opinion that beer was one of the essentials of life," he writes. "I continued to accumulate bad grades and disciplinary notes." Cheney recounts that he felt he didn't fit in on campus. Having grown up in the rural town of Casper, Wyoming, he had never traveled farther east than Chicago before coming to Yale. When he got off the train in New Haven, he recalls, "It felt a little like arriving in another country." That was true even though his best friend from high school joined him there. He felt so awkward with his Yale classmates that he made only a small group of friends. "Many of my fellow students had gone to prep school," he writes. "They had experiences very different from mine and knew things I did not. I sometimes felt they were speaking another language."

Moving back to his home in Wyoming, he pursued a degree at the University of Wyoming, where he felt comfortable and flourished. Cheney went on to become the consummate Washington insider, the youngest person to be appointed White House chief of staff at age thirty-four. He then won a seat in the House of Representatives, which he held for ten years, after which he became defense secretary and then vice president. He didn't lack some fundamental talent for belonging, and his experience at Yale speaks to how even students who have flourished academically and socially in one school situation may struggle with belonging in another.

The education community has increasingly recognized the importance of belonging in students' school experience and the roles that teachers and administrators can play in supporting it. A substantial body of research has established that students who report a strong sense of belonging tend to be more motivated to learn, perform better academically, have better rates of attendance, engage in less misconduct and fewer health-threatening behaviors, and have higher self-esteem and better mental health. Some wonderful means of nurturing belonging in schools have been developed, though much more work is needed, along with wider-scale adoption of the effective methods.

A barrier to fostering belonging for all students is how we, as individuals and institutions, deal with the diverse range of backgrounds from which students come. It's a range that runs wide in the United States, the most diverse society in history. Claude Steele has argued that too many of us take a colorblind approach to the problems associated with identity in America, which means that, essentially, we ignore them. But to design an ideal diverse community, one that, as Steele puts it, "works well for everyone, where everyone feels that they belong and can trust, and knows that they won't be impeded based on their identity," we need to acknowledge the ways that students' identities shape their experience of school. Only then can we "structure environments so that real connections happen" regardless of one's race, gender, creed, or class.

Scholarships, financial aid for college, and other sources of economic opportunity are critical to creating more inclusive schools. The economist Eric Bettinger collaborated with H&R Block to provide the families of low-income students who were of college age with eight minutes of coaching about how to complete the financial aid form for college. Eight percent more went to college, relative to a control group of students who didn't receive the intervention. If the intervention were given to a million low-income students, an estimated 80,000 more would make it to college. This study shows that fostering belonging is in part a matter of providing and guiding people to doors of opportunity.

Once students are in school, a major influence on their sense of belonging is the climate of a school and whether administrators and teachers establish policies and practices that instill norms of respect and inclusion. A number of the most effective means thus far developed were addressed in previous chapters: Elliot Aronson's Jigsaw Classroom, Elizabeth Paluck's approach to seeding an antibullying norm schoolwide, and restorative justice. These harness Kurt Lewin's insight about the power of a small group to create belonging. As we've seen, my colleagues and I have combated the stereotype threat that students experience by having them do values-affirmation exercises. Those would be easy to implement in schools by encouraging students to do these affirming activities at stressful times, such as the beginning of the school year, before taking exams, or in the midst of the college application process—times when too many students either miss a turn or take a turn for the worse. As we've seen, schools can also foster belonging by having older students share with incoming middle school, high school, college, and graduate students their experiences of being uncertain about whether and where they belonged. Greg Walton, David Yeager, René Kizilcec, and their colleagues have shown that such wise interventions can be delivered online to thousands of learners.

The effects of wise interventions can even spread from one person to another, raising performance for all. Research led by a former student, Joseph Powers, found that when, by chance, one or two more at-risk students had been assigned to complete a values-affirmation intervention in their classroom, the benefits spilled over to lift the performance of their classmates of all backgrounds. Having fewer failing students in their class, teachers could reach more children because they had more time and resources to expend.

Forging stronger connections with students at all levels should also be a top priority. Educators do this intuitively in small pockets throughout the country, especially in the early years. My son's kindergarten teacher visited each child's home before the start of the year, just for a half hour, to get to know her future students a bit better and learn about their favorite toys. It did a lot to make my son feel comfortable with the transition to kindergarten. Erin Gruwell worked with at-risk teens in California and had them use journal writing to relate their troubles to personal values and stories, as described in her book *The Freedom Writers Diary* (made into a movie with Hilary Swank).

But after children reach a certain age, about twelve, it's as if we forget the importance of connection. As the eminent educational psychologist Jacquelynne Eccles has long pointed out, nurturing connections with students takes a backseat to test preparation and social order. But in fact, the importance of a sense of belonging only grows as children enter adolescence, and it remains a key motive at every rung of the educational ladder, up to and including college and graduate school. For example, Greg Walton and I found that simply providing college students the opportunity to do a dull task, such as turning pegs on a wooden board, with other people made them much more motivated to sign up for it.

Mentoring programs are a powerful vehicle for establishing and protecting belonging, and schools should implement them if they aren't already on offer. Many organizations outside of school provide mentoring for children and young adults. Big Brothers Big Sisters of America, which connects mentors to at-risk youth, has been found to be effective. I was inspired to conduct research on mentoring by my own experience serving as a mentor throughout my years in high school, college, and graduate school. I'd seen close-up how much of an impact mentors can make in helping the marginalized feel they can belong.

Greg Walton, Shannon Brady, and I conducted research that looked at mentoring for black college students, whom we had found often experience belonging uncertainty. Our study revealed that establishing a relationship with a mentor helped foster black students' sense of belonging. What's more, many of these students developed a lasting bond with their mentor, which assisted them in pursuing more personally satisfying careers after graduation. The positive effects of mentoring for all college students are also attested to by the results of a Gallup study tracking the outcomes of over 30,000 college graduates. It found that one of the strongest predictors of whether graduates reported feeling engaged at their job and thriving in their lives wasn't whether their college was public or private, small or large, selective or not, but whether, while in college, they had found a mentor who had supported them and "who encouraged them to pursue their dreams."

Social psychologists Tara Dennehy and Nilanjana Dasgupta found strong effects of mentoring in helping female students overcome the effects of stereotype threat in STEM education. They recruited 150 incoming female college students who were planning to major in the engineering program there and divided these students into three groups on a random basis. The first group met with a female mentor, a student of the same gender a few years ahead of them who had learned the ropes. The second group met with a mentor too, but here it was a man rather than a woman. The third group received no mentoring. The students with mentors met them on average only four times, for about an hour, over their first year of college. Periodically, in addition, they would reach out with a question to their mentor by email or text.

The big finding? Women with a female mentor sustained their sense of belonging in engineering over the next two years, well after the program had ended, while women in the other two groups showed a steady decline in belonging, although the decrease was a bit less for women with a male mentor. The finding is important because a sense of belonging was the number-one predictor of persistence in the engineering program, beating out even GPA. Not a single woman with a female mentor dropped out of the program after the first year compared with 15 percent who dropped out in the other two groups. That's a huge return on four hours of mentoring.

Although the mentoring sessions were brief, their success can be attributed to the fact that they were well crafted. The researchers didn't just throw the mentors and mentees together and say, "Go to it," as many mentoring programs do. They had an initial session to train mentors on how to share stories of their own experiences with belonging uncertainty and the ways they had dealt with it—drawing on the key messages that Greg Walton and I had created in our social-belonging intervention: Obstacles are normal, and they can be overcome with time and strategy. In effect, the process by which students gain wisdom was speeded up, so that the lessons that mentors wished they had learned earlier were now passed on to the next generation of students when they entered college. The mentors also initiated social activities to build a strong personal connection with the mentees. They tutored them, helped them establish a social network, and pointed them to resources to help further their careers, such as summer internships. All of these aspects of their mentoring were aimed at helping the students navigate their situation. They also sent a powerful psychological message: "We believe in you. Becoming a professional engineer is not a pipe dream."

Male mentors helped the women sustain higher grades in engineering through their first year of college, but that didn't translate into greater retention in the engineering program or, for that matter, into a desire to pursue a career or advanced degree in STEM. By contrast, the female mentors did promote these outcomes. One strong possibility is that the female mentors provided two things that the men could not: a role model of success for their gender, someone "like them" who had succeeded and showed it was possible, and tailored information about how to cope with the belonging uncertainty of being a woman in a predominantly male setting.

Having a female mentor also lessens the threat of sexual harassment, which can have devastating effects on people's feelings of belonging. The writer Naomi Wolf recounted the traumatizing effects of an incident of harassment committed by the eminent scholar Harold Bloom that she experienced as a student at Yale. She was interested in writing poetry and looked up to him as a leading literary critic. During a meeting with him, Bloom placed his hand on her inner thigh. It "devastated my sense of being valuable to Yale as a student," she recounts. Indeed, research found that simply having students *imagine* a professor making a pass at them caused them to doubt their academic ability, express less interest in a professor's field, and experience a drop in self-esteem. These effects were found with both female and male students, with the impact somewhat stronger for women than men.

Another means of fostering belonging in schools is "culturally relevant pedagogy" (CRP). CRP refers to educational practices that prioritize student success, provide ways for students to maintain their cultural integrity, and foster their capacity for critical engagement with academic content. Tom Dee, who has extensively studied CRP, told me it resembles "unusually intensive and sustained social psychological intervention." Dee and his colleagues were inspired by a long-standing and influential body of qualitative scholarship that underscored the educational power of CRP for students of color, including the pioneering research of Gloria Ladson Billings. Dee's research in two Bay Area school districts provided evidence of the positive impact of CRP. One study focused on a ninth-grade ethnic studies course offered in the San Francisco Unified School District. A second study focused on Oakland's African American Male Achievement (AAMA) program, an initiative laid out in a beautiful book by Na'ilah Suad Nasir and colleagues, *We Dare Say Love*. The AAMA centers on a class that provides black youth with affirming narratives for understanding themselves, their racial identity, African and African American history, and even the meaning of life. Students in the class report that they feel seen as human beings rather than through the lens of a stereotype.

In a rigorous evaluation of the ethnic studies course, Dee and his coauthor, Emily Penner, found that it increased students' GPA by an eye-popping 1.4 grade points. That's an improvement of about a full letter grade and a half. Four years later, roughly 90 percent of the students who had taken the course graduated from high school, compared with 75 percent of their peers. His second study of the AAMA found that it nearly halved dropping out among high school–aged black boys and had spillover benefits for black girls' drop-out rates too. "Many historically marginalized students experience schools as highly alienating spaces," Dee said in an interview, adding that the impact of these programs "challenges us to radically reconsider how we think about promoting equity in education." His results provide compelling evidence that wise situation-crafting can change students' life trajectories.

INDIVIDUAL TEACHERS CAN ALSO do a lot in their daily interactions with students to foster their sense of belonging. In fact, research suggests that the quality of teacher-student relationships has a strong impact on student belonging, often more than students' relationships with peers.

A friend of mine named Steve, who had grown up in poverty in the midwestern United States, told me a story about how a single teacher transformed his life. As a child, he had expected to continue in a life of impoverishment because he didn't do well in school. He felt that he was seen by most teachers through the stereotype of being just another poor farm boy with little potential.

But his fourth-grade teacher, Mrs. Zinn, was a keen observer of her students. She noticed that although Steve did well on homework, when she wrote a problem on the board in class, he always missed it. After asking him to stay behind during recess one day and read to her what she had written on the board, she realized he couldn't see it and that he needed glasses. Once he was fitted with a pair, he began to excel. But Mrs. Zinn helped him to see better not just literally; she helped him see his potential better too. She gave him extra work; he rose to the challenge. She told him he could make a living with his "brains, not his back" and that he had the potential to go far. And he did.

Much teacher training includes some instruction about how to boost students' belonging, with a survey of U.S. teachers indicating that 76 percent of those questioned had received some such instruction and most wanted more. Helping teachers nurture their students' belonging has been the emphasis of the research on education conducted by my lab. One set of studies we've conducted focused on a key problem: the style in which teachers offer critiques of students' work. The teacher-student relationships that most promote belonging for students are those in which "they feel respected, encouraged, and listened to by their teacher" and where "their teacher is fair and holds high expectations." We call that teaching style, in the context of offering critical feedback to students, "wise criticism." In designing it, we were inspired by the many success stories of teachers and schools throughout the country that help underserved students achieve their dreams.

Providing feedback that is both instructive and encouraging can be a tricky challenge, though. Claude Steele, Lee Ross, and I dubbed this the "mentor's dilemma." We must provide students with the information they need to improve their work and general learning, but criticism can undermine their confidence and motivation. Research shows criticism is especially fraught for minority students, who are generally aware of the stereotypes about them as having lower levels of ability and engagement in school. They may expect their teachers to be biased by these stereotypes. On the teachers' side, worries about upsetting children often lead them to hold back on offering criticism, which undermines student performance. The National Research Council concluded that the teachers who produce the best outcomes combine "a caring and supportive environment" with "academic press," which they define as a "focus on learning and high expectations." When offered wisely, criticism is a key to conveying those high expectations while allaying the understandable mistrust that minority students may have of their teachers.

Steele, Ross, and I wanted to find a way to assist teachers in providing feedback that would be well received across the racial divide. We asked a group of Stanford students, half of whom were black and the other half white, to come to our lab, telling them we were creating a journal to profile great educators around the country. We requested that they write a letter of recommendation for their favorite teacher and told them the best would be published in the journal. We made it clear that the skill of writing letters of recommendation was just that—a skill, one that required the ability to write well and organize your thoughts. Why all the fuss? Because we wanted people to take the situation seriously—to feel invested in it. And in light of the problem of stereotype threat, we wanted them to think the situation was one in which the stereotype might apply, so that we could gauge how our experiment might help shield them from its threat. We also asked the students if we could take a picture of them to accompany their submission, thereby alerting them that the person who critiqued their letter would be aware of their race. The students worked hard on their letters, and reading them was inspirational.

A team of research assistants and I took charge of assessing the letters, remaining blind to the authors' ethnicity and making our assessments before they were randomly assigned to one of our experimental conditions. With all of the letters, we made comments in the margins that offered suggestions for improvement, along with grammatical corrections.

One group of students, again half of whom were black and half of whom were white, received two pages of critical comments that we had carefully made generic. Though substantive, the comments pointed out weaknesses common to virtually all the letters, such as how the letter was "long on adjectives and short on specific illustrations," and provided suggestions similarly applicable to almost all the letters, such as "You need to breathe more life into your letter" and "Make your letter more vivid, personal, and persuasive." The students were told that a Dr. Gardiner Lindsay had critiqued the letters—a name that implied the doctor was white.

With a second group of students, we gave them the same two pages of criticism, but this time it was preceded with a dollop of handwritten positive feedback, ostensibly from Professor Lindsay, such as "Overall, nice work," "Your enthusiasm . . . really shows through," and "You have some interesting ideas . . . and make some good points." This feedback was intended to mirror that given by most teachers. Research shows that they tend to accentuate the positive first.

For a final group of students, we provided wise criticism, giving them the same two pages of criticism but preceding it with the following handwritten comments from Professor Lindsay:

> It's obvious to me you've taken your task seriously, and I'm going to do likewise by giving you some straightforward, honest feedback. The letter itself is okay as far as it goes—you've followed the instructions, listed your teacher's merits, given evidence in support of them, and, importantly, produced an articulate letter. On the other hand, judged by a higher standard, the one that really counts—that is, whether your letter will be publishable in our journal—I have serious reservations. The comments I provide in the following pages are quite critical but I hope helpful. Remember, I wouldn't go to the trouble of giving you this feedback if I didn't think, based on what I've read in your letter, that you are capable of meeting the higher standard I mentioned.

These words were carefully crafted to affirm the students and, for the black students, to counter stereotype threat, sending the message that the student was not being seen as limited but as someone who could reach a higher standard. Remembering the Pygmalion effect, we also thought it key that students be praised for their *potential* rather than their current performance.

To judge the effects of the three types of criticism, we asked students to complete a brief survey about what they thought about the feedback and whether they wanted to revise their letter, as well as how much they valued writing.

We found that the wise criticism lessened the belief expressed by black students that their letters had been evaluated with bias. While black students in the other two groups suspected greater bias than did white students, black students in the wise criticism group saw the feedback as unbiased as white students did. Black students in the wise criticism group also reported the highest motivation among the three groups to revise their letters. The white participants, Stanford students who weren't contending with a racial stereotype, generally responded positively in all groups, seeming to take it as a given that high standards were being imposed and the critic believed in their potential to reach them. In the wise criticism group, though, all students regardless of race expressed a stronger belief that being a good writer was important to their view of themselves and something that might form the basis of a future career. It was as if this single laboratory-created encounter had influenced their self-concept.

In a follow-up experiment, we had all students revise their first effort, and the results were profound. We brought male and female STEM majors to our lab and had them receive critical feedback on a short TED-like talk we'd asked them to give about their favorite research. We hoped wise criticism would reduce stereotype threat for the women. It did. Relative to women who received only critical feedback, women receiving wise criticism delivered better final talks as judged by independent evaluators who listened to recordings of them. Seven times as many incorporated a key suggestion made by their critic.

A study of wise criticism that my colleagues and I conducted with middle school students also yielded striking results, showing its power to shape academic trajectories. We had seventh-grade students write an essay about a hero of theirs—a historical figure, family member, teacher, coach, or friend. A curriculum module we had created with the school's teachers required that the students and teachers first spend several class periods talking about what makes someone a hero and reading material about the topic. These were ways of inspiring the students to feel invested in the quality of their essays.

With the teachers, we established a rubric of five key criteria for evaluating the essays: a clear introduction and conclusion, persuasive arguments, examples to support their points, clear writing, and good grammar. We told the teachers to give whatever encouragement and criticism to students they normally would in critiquing the essays, so that any effect of the wise feedback would be above and beyond business as usual.

For one group of students, we had teachers pen this note, which was a much simplified version of the wise feedback note from our first study: "I'm giving you this criticism because I have very high expectations and I know that you can reach them." For a second control group of students, we had teachers write this note: "I'm giving you these comments so that you'll have feedback on your paper."

We were careful to keep the teachers unaware of which students got which notes by having teachers write the notes in advance and then having our research team randomly append the notes to different students' essays before they were returned to them. This way we could get a pure read on the causal impact of the note.

For students receiving the wise criticism note, the number who took the time to submit a revision of their essay, an option that was offered to all of the students, increased substantially, and for black students, the increase was whopping. For white students, the increase was from 62 percent in the group that got the generic note to 87 percent in the wise criticism group. For black students, the number rose from 17 percent to 72 percent.

Wise criticism increases students' motivation to improve their work, building trust in teachers while making students feel that they're being seen, respected, and appreciated. It does so by reframing criticism as an affirmation rather than a threat. From the student's point of view, it now means "I believe in you" rather than "You're dumb." We had conducted our in-school study with seventh graders because we had found that a loss of trust in teachers is a major problem among middle schoolers. For students of color in particular, distrust interferes with learning and predicts a much lower likelihood that they will enroll, years later, in a four-year college. Wise criticism is of course important at all ages, including in work situations long after schooling has ended. But, we thought, middle school should be a point of vulnerability and thus a window of opportunity for improving student trust.

In research with colleagues David Yeager, Julio Garcia, and Valerie Purdie-Greenaway, an analysis of the results of the study conducted with middle school students showed the aftereffects of wise criticism at this window of opportunity. Black students who had expressed relatively low trust of adults at their school benefited the most from wise criticism, both in the short and long term. On an end-of-year survey, they expressed greater trust of their teachers than did their peers in the control group. Trusting more, they also got into less trouble at school in the following year, with half as many disciplinary citations as their peers in the control group. Most surprising, five years later, according to official enrollment records, 70 percent of the black students who had gotten the wise criticism note enrolled in a four-year college compared to only 40 percent of their peers.

What a powerful influence teachers can have if a one-sentence note at a formative moment can produce this result. To return to Ray Bradbury's metaphor, one act of support at the right moment is like knocking over the first domino in a line of dominoes, with the dominoes getting bigger over time. A bit of reassurance or a well-timed pat on the back may be fleeting but deeply meaningful and even life-changing experiences. But, of course, the effects of consistent and authentic wise criticism might be even more profound.

The research on wise criticism shows that you can protect belonging without sacrificing academic standards. Wise criticism says to students, "The bar is high, but you can rise over it." Isn't it obvious that teachers should tell students they believe in their ability to reach a higher standard? No teachers we have ever worked with have reported that they had been doing so when giving criticism. Moreover, research suggests that too few teachers give substantive, constructive criticism to their minority students. Kent Harber has found that white instructors tend to whitewash their criticism and offer excessively positive comments to their minority students, partly because of their own stereotype threat. That not only cheats the students of information with which they could make improvements but contributes to their distrust, as students may perceive that they're not being given honest feedback and take that as a sign that their teacher does not believe in their potential.

Yet some teachers do practice wise criticism. A colleague of mine, a black man named Mohammed, shared a story about a teacher who had changed him in his youth. He had been a low-income student who had won a scholarship to a private high school. But he was coasting, he told me. Then he was assigned to a tenth-grade math teacher. The teacher, a brown-skinned South Asian man, studied him. After a few days, he called Mohammed to his desk as he was leaving. "Mohammed," he said, "people will expect less of you; they'll expect you to just get by." Then he added, simply, "But I know that you are capable of more." The single sentence, Mohammed said, moved him in a lasting way. When I asked him why, he said, "I felt seen. My full self was seen."

Clearly, some teachers do a marvelous job of sending the wise criticism message to students. But the research suggests many more could learn how to do so. That a little note might make such a difference in the fates of black children suggests how rarely they may get even the least bit of the validation they deserve.

WHY DO MINORITY CHILDREN get less validation in school? Our research suggests that, oftentimes, it's not the teacher or the student who is to blame but a toxic dynamic that unfolds between them, like a dance where the two parties can't quite get in sync and grow increasingly frustrated with each other. We have identified this dynamic in teachers' interactions with black students, especially boys. Many students of color arrive at middle school motivated and trusting of teachers. But then they are disproportionately sent to the office or given detention, often for behaviors that are not clearly disobedient, suggesting that teachers are, often unconsciously, biased. This can happen with teachers of all ethnic groups, though most teachers of black students in America are white. As a result, black students lose trust in their teachers and their sense of belonging in school declines, leading them to become more defiant and more readily provoked. Meanwhile, as their behavior and performance worsen, teachers see them as troublemakers. The teachers get fed up and resort to punitive disciplinary actions, such as office referrals, detention, and suspension, to bring the kids back in line. But those actions often worsen the source of the problem—the boys' uncertainty about whether they belong. For the teachers, it is all too easy to give in to the mind's susceptibility to snap judgments: The Fundamental Attribution Error works its mischief. The stereotype, too, is right there ready to be taken off the cultural shelf to make sense of the child.

The good news is that because the problem lies in a feedback loop between teachers and students, a small interruption at a timely moment can make a big difference in the long run. When students are assured that they are respected and that teachers believe in their potential at a timely moment, a new successful dynamic is created.

In order to help teachers develop their ability to recognize this dynamic and correct for it, a former graduate student at Stanford University, Jason Okonofua, experimented with a method of raising teacher awareness. Okonofua is the son of a Nigerian father and a black Southern woman, and he recalls that growing up in Memphis, Tennessee, "I had real experiences being the victim of discrimination and even more so fearing that I would be a bad representation of black Americans." He watched as his older brothers got in trouble in the school system and grew more and more alienated from it. Much of this, he felt, was due to a lack of understanding on teachers' part about the experience of being black in school.

Okonofua, who is now a professor at UC Berkeley, took the lead in a study that revealed a way to open teachers' eyes to the power of the situation in their students' lives, without making the teachers defensive. In an online training module lasting seventy minutes, comprising two brief sessions, he connected the virtue and skill of empathy to a group of middle school teachers' own values. *Some* teachers, they read, didn't appreciate how important it is for all students to feel like they belong in school, and some didn't understand how kids often act out in school because they feel like they don't belong. *But as they knew,* Jason's module continued, teachers can and do have a lot of power to increase students' sense of belonging by building strong relationships with them and by trying to understand school from their point of view. He drove home these points through personal stories told by students. For instance,

> In middle school, I didn't feel like I belonged. It seemed like teachers always called on the other students. So I didn't pay attention in class and sometimes I got in trouble. One day I got detention, and instead of just sitting there, my teacher talked with me about what happened. He really listened to me. And then he told me that he had trouble sometimes in middle school but that it gets better. It felt good to know that I had someone I could trust in school.

This perspective-getting helped teachers to appreciate how students often act out because of a threatened sense of belonging and how important it was to support students' belonging *especially* when they acted out. The goal was to curb the Fundamental Attribution Error and redirect teachers to a caring view of discipline rather than a punitive one.

When I talked with Okonofua about this study, I said it seemed that what he was doing was showing teachers how to empathize. But he said he didn't look at it that way. He was just reconnecting teachers with beliefs and values they already had, helping them to see the opportunity to live them out in their daily classroom experience. "Teachers feel disheartened," he shared with me, because they feel like they're "the bad guy" or they're "supposed to police students, but that's not what they signed up for." He says the message he wanted to send them is,

"You are the teacher on the front lines. You have a pivotal position that no one else has with which to shape these children's lives."

He next asked teachers to write about their own views about supporting students and their own experiences dealing with conflicts with students. His description evokes the principles of situation-crafting described in Chapter 1. As Okonofua explains the exercise, the teachers were "treated as experts and agents of positive change for others, not as recipients of remediation." Key to this was telling teachers that what they wrote would be circulated to other teachers to help them understand the importance of these issues. To give you a taste of what teachers wrote, here is one response:

> I NEVER hold grudges. I try to remember that my students are all the son or daughter of someone who loves them more than anything in the world. They are the light of someone's life!

Many personalized the message:

> When I was a child, I remember worrying about how I would be treated by teachers at my school. But I will always remember Ms. McBride, who treated me with respect and trust. She showed me that teachers could make all the difference in how students feel about school. Now I make a point of treating my students with respect and I find that they respect me more in return.

The results of the study were dramatic. Official school records revealed that, compared with a control group of teachers whose online module focused on ways to use technology to promote learning, the teachers who went through this brief training referred half as many students for suspension over the rest of the year.

A skeptic might ask, were the teachers just letting students who deserved suspension off the hook? No. The same dramatic cut in suspensions among these students was found even when the researchers looked at the suspensions that were referred by their teachers who hadn't participated in the intervention. Teachers who forge better relationships with their students, it seems, not only make their own jobs easier but the jobs of other teachers as well. The training improved outcomes for students from all ethnic groups and for both boys and girls. What's more, for students with a history of suspension, the results were especially powerful. While 51 percent of those in the classes of teachers who didn't go through the training were suspended again, that number dropped to 29 percent in the classes of the teachers who had had the training. As a result of the intervention, these students' relationships with their teachers also improved, with children reporting that they felt more respected.

Because of these dramatic results, several school districts have implemented Okonofua's teacher training program. Given the destructive impact of suspension on students and their families, Okonofua's intervention holds great promise for improving the lives of many children and the people who care for them. If the intervention were given to 20,000 middle school teachers nationwide, each of whom teaches an average of 50 students a year, an estimated million students would potentially benefit. An estimated 52,000 fewer students would be suspended.

Let's pause to consider what Okonofua's wise intervention does. In a sense, its aim is to make teachers wiser. It encourages teachers to see their students more three-dimensionally. It moves them away from the tendency to think that bad behavior corresponds to some bad essence in the kid, the reflexive judgment of Fundamental Attribution Error. The power of the intervention derives in good part from its ability to encourage teachers to see their students in a different light, especially when they act badly. It helps them to better understand the students' situation from their perspective—and the power that teachers have to shape that situation for the better.

The impact of the intervention also derives from the respect it gives teachers, helping them to correct course while protecting teachers' own sense of belonging, and empowering rather than instructing them. To read students in an empathic way, Okonofua knew, requires an affirmed and open mind rather than a closed and defensive one. It's when we feel "fed up" that we're most at risk for snap judgments. And that's why affirming and supportive school environments are good not only for students but also for teachers.

NO CHAPTER ABOUT BELONGING in education would be complete without addressing the special challenges of the teenage years. Advice for parents and educators about child development puts so much emphasis on the earliest years, particularly years one through three. They've sometimes been depicted as a make-or-break period, with life-long effects on children. Much important work on that life stage has been done, producing vital insights. But it's also important to understand that difficult early-life experiences can be overturned by later positive ones. What's more, even children raised in the most supportive families can encounter profound challenges in the socially complex environment of school. There are many points of vulnerability—and windows of opportunity—*throughout* our lives when a little bit of support can go a long way.

Children go through a maelstrom of changes beginning around age eleven or twelve, not just biological shifts but social and psychological ones as well. We all know about the physical changes. I'm always amazed at the differences in pictures of kids, one taken at the beginning of middle school, at age eleven, and one taken at the end, at age thirteen or fourteen. They can look like totally different people. What's harder to perceive are the social situations children contend with, so many of which are out of our sight, and their cumulative psychological effects. As adults, we may no longer appreciate how intense the social pressures on teens are and how they've been ratcheted up by social media. The rates of teen mental health problems, such as anxiety and depression, have jumped in recent years, with the trends aggravated by the COVID pandemic. The number of teens who commit suicide has been on the rise since 2006, and in June 2020, at the height of the pandemic, the number of teens who reported having seriously considered killing themselves over the past month had risen by fivefold relative to what it had been the previous year. Even in the absence of these big fires, many teens are coping with a slow-burning depletion of precious psychological resources due to the daily challenges of these years. Children's sense of belonging in school, their sense of trust in adults at school, their self-esteem, and their motivation for academic work tend to decline in their teens. Their engagement in risky and reckless behavior rises.

What can we do to support children through this transition? We can enhance their sense of belonging in a number of ways. In a study involving a nationally representative sample of over 12,000 teenagers, the two most powerful protective factors for every form of adolescent risk behavior and distress—including emotional distress, drug abuse, violence, and suicidality—were how strong a sense of belonging they had in school and how strong a sense of belonging they had at home. The "belonging effect" surpassed the effects of academic performance, self-esteem, religiosity, being held back a grade, parental absence, and household access to guns. Many of these risk factors capture our attention because they are visible, but the importance of connection, being harder to "see," too often eludes our attention.

But too many middle and high schools create situations that threaten students' belonging—not intentionally but out of a mistaken focus on children's character rather than their circumstances. While much attention has been paid to the role of peers, such as in work on bullying, many of the problems arise from the practices and policies instituted and implemented by superintendents, principals, teachers, and other staff. One of my favorite papers in education captures this insight in its title: "What Are We Doing to Early Adolescents?" The authors, Jacqueline Eccles and her colleagues, argue that many of the ways schools are run are uncannily mismatched to adolescents' thirst for belonging and connection.

Having visited many middle schools, I know that many are wonderful, but even some of the best ones are characterized by practices reminiscent of the mortifying rituals that Erving Goffman observed in mental asylums. Socializing among peers is often discouraged, not only during class but in the hallways in the moments in between. Punctuality is treated as a cardinal virtue, regularly enforced throughout the day with a bell, a ritual borrowed from factories. Teens are often not given the benefit of the doubt in disciplinary decisions and are given harsh sentences, such as suspension, which research shows does more harm than good. They're also sometimes falsely accused of wrongdoing, often with no genuine opportunity to correct the error. This naturally erodes students' belonging in school and trust in adults.

Another problem is that the relationships between teachers and students are generally not as close as they are in elementary school. In most middle and high schools, students circulate from one class to another with different teachers throughout the day. That makes it much more difficult to establish a trusting relationship with any one of them.

Zero-sum competition between students threatens belonging too. With honor rolls, schools allocate the artificially scarce resource of "honor" only to a select handful of students. Many teachers believe they can assign only so many As and Bs no matter how well all students in their classroom do. As Muzafer Sherif showed decades ago, such practices fuel division. In athletics, too, competition among students often reigns, with limited spots on teams; even membership in extracurricular clubs can be highly competitive. In addition, children from less well-off families may be excluded by "pay to play" requirements to take part in team sports or extracurricular activities, which, ironically, are particularly good opportunities for these students to feel successful and to form supportive ties with adults at school. Research has persuasively demonstrated the powerful and positive impact of team sports and extracurricular activities for all youth but especially for troubled youth. Lowering barriers to these kinds of activities is one obvious step schools should take to promote adolescent education and well-being.

What else can we do to support teens? One thing we know doesn't work: lecturing them to behave better. In fact, one study showed that when teens lying in a functional MRI scanner heard audio clips of their mothers criticizing them, their brains showed heightened activity in regions associated with negative emotion and reduced activation in regions associated with empathy and perspective-taking. It was as if the teens were detaching themselves from the criticism. Kurt Lewin could have warned us of the dangers of such strong-arm tactics.

The alternative? One is to talk *with* teens, not at them. Connect with them by engaging in their interests, showing you appreciate things that are important to them. One wise intervention did this brilliantly in order to increase students' interest in science and math. Designed by Judy Harackiewicz and her colleagues, the intervention trained parents to converse with their high school–aged children about how the fruits of science and math saturated their lives in the form of video games, cell phones, and so on. Relative to a control group, the intervention increased the number of science and math courses that the students took over their last two years of high school.

Research also shows that a Lewin-inspired approach of engaging adolescents in activities that give them opportunities to bring out their best selves, with democratic-style adult guidance, works well. Yes, provide teens with some basic information to help them make good decisions. But also help them to experience belonging, and an identity as a responsible young adult, by encouraging them to participate in activities in which they live these out, such as volunteer groups. These kinds of programs consistently prevent teen reckless behavior, such as unsafe sex, better than information campaigns.

As for antibullying programs, most don't work because they use the persuasive campaign approach. But there are wise interventions that do work, such as interactive activities that encourage teens to see themselves and one another as "works in progress" rather than "finished products." Values-affirmation activities can also help. They've been found to improve the grades and disciplinary behavior not only of black and Latino adolescents but of all teenagers regardless of race or gender, *if* the activities are assigned early in the transition to middle school and variants of the activity are given later at times of high stress. Values-affirmation activities also protect students' relationships with one another, a root source of belonging, and thus keep them engaged. Under the leadership of Kate Turetsky, my colleagues and I mapped college students' social networks—their relationships with their classmates—at the beginning and the end of a demanding introductory molecular and cellular biology class, a gateway to the major that was known among students as a "weed-out" course. We found that those who had been prompted to write about their core values at the beginning of the semester had more friends by the semester's end, and the number of them who went on to take the next course in the bioscience sequence increased by 12 percentage points compared with students in a control group who hadn't written about core values.

Another strategy is to help teens see desirable behavior as in keeping with their values. Stereotypes of teens peg them as self-centered, even obsessed with all the daily dramas of their lives. But in reality many are deeply interested in the state of the world and helping to make it a better place. When they're guided to connect these values to behaviors that embody them, they are more inclined to adopt those behaviors. That's the strategy Elizabeth Paluck used when she mobilized posses of students to fight against bullying.

A series of ingenious studies by Chris Bryan and his colleagues got great results in improving the quality of food teens chose to eat by helping them connect their values to healthy eating behavior. One group of students was given standard information about nutrition and good eating habits. Another group was given an exposé describing well-documented deceptive and manipulative practices in the food industry used to stoke people's appetite for fatty, sugary foods, which are especially targeted at children and the poor. "They hire scientists to figure out the brain's blind spots. Then, they invent foods that trick the brain into craving more and more sugar and fat, whether you're hungry or not," the students read. They also reviewed testimonials from other students who said they planned to "fight back" "by buying and eating less processed food," promoting a new norm that appealed both to teens' sense of justice and to their love of rebellion. In a brilliant touch, a later variant of the intervention had the kids do a "make it true" activity, in which they drew over food advertisements to render them "true." For instance, a McDonald's ad pictured a towering Big Mac behind the words, "The thing you want when you order a salad." One student added a few words to make the sentence read, "The thing you want when you order a salad should be a salad."

Compared with the students given the healthy eating information, the kids in the wise intervention group made more healthful food choices the next day for snack and, in a follow-up study, over the next three months, they were more likely to buy fruit and milk at lunch rather than soda and cookies.

The takeaway for parents and educators is to connect the information you want to impart to the things teens care deeply about. And don't underestimate how concerned they are to do good and to be good.

NONE OF THESE INTERVENTIONS IS, as David Yeager and Greg Walton put it, a "magic bullet." Instead each is like a spark that touches off a chain reaction. No amount of affirmation will help a student who can't read to excel in English or a child who is having hunger pains to focus on a tough math problem. Economic and human resources that support, recognize, and reinforce student growth are necessary. Robert Rosenthal and Lenore Jacobson captured the wisdom embedded in their Pygmalion-in-the-classroom research with the quip, "Expect more, get more." I propose a variant: "Expect more, *give* more, get more." The best classrooms contain a symphony of elements that reinforce the message and create the reality, "You belong."

For example, in work led by Omid Fotuhi and Phillip Ehret, my lab found that a values-affirmation intervention increased the percentage of low-income students who applied for and received financial aid to attend college, but *only* when we also accompanied the affirmation with a number of supportive notes to the students throughout the year reminding them to take next steps at timely moments in the application process, like rungs on a ladder. Likewise, economic support can activate the effects of values affirmations and other wise interventions. A meta-analysis of all the studies of values affirmations tested with students showed that these interventions are more effective in better-financed schools. Classroom norms and teacher actions can also reinforce the messages of belonging and growth in wise interventions. Genuine opportunity and the psychological readiness to seize it are the vital notes in the symphony.

We must also keep in mind that wise interventions are wise because they are informed by an appreciation of the psychological experience of those we're trying to support. If they're offered without that empathy, they are ineffectual. After I had given a talk at a Silicon Valley firm, a manager asked for a copy of our wise criticism note so that she could give it to all her employees every day. That's the wrong takeaway. The caring and authenticity behind the intervention are essential. In fact, research on the best teachers shows that they share one thing in common: They have a faith in their students' potential, and they embody that faith in their day-to-day encounters with students.

We also honor students' firsthand perspective by trying to "get" it. There's no substitute for asking questions and then working either with students or with colleagues, sometimes behind the scenes, to craft ad hoc situational solutions. "If you don't feel at home, I want to know" is the guiding principle. No matter how much you think you know, you often don't know as much about other people's situation as you think. Let's look at two examples.

The faculty and administrators at most American universities tend to believe that students are primarily driven by the desire to follow their passions and pave their own path, according to research by Nicole Stephens, Hazel Markus, and their collaborators. However, these investigators also report that many low-income students, when asked, say they're driven largely by the desire to provide for their family and give back to their community. Research suggests that college brochures and mission statements that better align with the motivations of low-income students ease their belonging uncertainty and improve their performance.

One more example of perspective-getting comes from research

spearheaded by Shannon Brady. Surveying student affairs officers at various colleges, she found that most of them *want* students to feel they belong on campus. But when Brady looked at the actual impact of the letters they sent to inform students that they were underperforming, she found that the students' overwhelming reaction was shame. Shame is the bane of belonging. It makes people want to "sink into the floor and disappear," according to clinical psychologist June Tangney, and discourages people from seeking the help they need and from discovering that many others have "been there" too. Working with several student affairs offices, Shannon designed a better, wiser letter. It incorporated many of the strategies in this book, such as assuring students of their ability to reach high standards and using stories from senior students to convey that difficulties in school are normal and surmountable. Her experiments found that the new letter got the key message across to students without undermining their sense of belonging.

All the specific research findings converge on a general lesson: Avoid the easy judgments of the Fundamental Attribution Error. Getting students' perspective is one antidote. Another is to focus not on evaluating students but on empowering them by improving their situation or at least helping them to navigate it better. If the education system spent fewer resources trying to measure ability through its various testing regimens and more resources trying to cultivate ability by crafting better situations, our schools would be much more effective and equitable.

A PERSONAL EXPERIENCE MADE me realize how important, yet slippery, the wisdom of social psychology is. In spite of good intentions, it's so easy to slip into the Fundamental Attribution Error, failing to account for others' perspectives and life experiences. That's especially so when we are tired, stressed, or feeling insecure. I committed this mistake in regard to a student I once mentored.

Faculty members at almost every university take time each year to discuss the progress that graduate students are making. While many of the conversations are positive and many are helpful, sometimes we find ourselves talking about a student whose progress is slow and who seems to be in need of something. But what that "something" might be almost always remains obscure, and we find ourselves stumbling in the dark for answers. I suspect that the purpose of the conversations—to evaluate student progress—steers our minds to focus on assessments of the person rather than their situation. In my case, I once had an insightful student, Caleb (who agreed to let me share his story). He was doing inspired work but had not been progressing as fast as we expected him to. I tried not to be overly critical, but I did find myself saying things to him like I hoped he'd "get the fire in his belly" and "put his nose to the grindstone" during slow periods.

It took me a year of getting comfortable as a new professor at the university to change my tack. It dawned on me that I should pull my mental camera back on my view of Caleb. I had learned about his difficult family life, but I had failed to appreciate the degree to which it might be a factor in holding him back. I talked to him more about it. He came from a poor rural family. He was the first in his family to go to graduate school. One of his parents hadn't graduated high school, and when Caleb did, his family cheered because he had "made it." He had siblings in various states of monetary and familial turmoil. One was seriously injured in a shooting at a house party. Another was homeless and had come to stay with Caleb, who tried to help him get a job and get his life back together. Family continually called him for financial support. He'd send money, even though he collected only a meager graduate student stipend. It occurred to me that I wasn't just mentoring Caleb but Caleb *in his situation*.

I decided to explain Caleb's situation to my fellow colleagues, though I worried that they would think I was making excuses for him. Maybe they'd think I was a bad mentor. But almost instantly even the most hard-nosed professors started to brainstorm ways we could help my student, such as where we could go to get extra scholarship support. Together we rallied to support him in ways I'd never imagined. Caleb recovered and thrived. It was partly because of the objective support we gave him but also, I think, because of the subjective message our support sent: "We believe in you." Now my former student is a successful professor and a celebrated mentor in his own right to many students, including others from underprivileged backgrounds. Caleb's story illustrates the wisdom in the words of Lisbeth Schorr, who after extensively reviewing successful schools and social programs throughout the nation, concluded that "in their responsiveness and willingness to hang in there," they "are more like families than bureaucracies."

The lessons of social psychology are easy to deliver, harder to understand, and still harder to live by. We can spend a lifetime unlearning harmful cultural conditioning and recognizing cognitive biases. Repeated reminders help. Fortunately, one reminder can be found in the very word "educate." It originates from a Latin word that means "to draw out." Contrary to our commonsense notion of an educator as someone who "pours in" knowledge and information, a better metaphor is of a guide who sees and draws out hidden potential.

Chapter 10

Belonging at Work

Combating Workplace Discrimination and Building Team Spirit

I N THEIR BOOK *ANXIETY AT WORK,* BUSINESS CULTURE SPE-cialists Adrian Gostick and Chester Elton write about a young employee named Chloe who, right out of college, landed what she thought was her dream job at an investment bank. She had stellar credentials, including a near perfect college GPA, and she was fluent in the technology she needed to use in the work. She was also socially intelligent and able to develop friendships quickly. Yet she felt intense belonging uncertainty at work, intimidated by colleagues who had graduated from more prestigious schools and who had landed prized internships at major firms. She reported that "every morning, the company sent out this mass email about someone else's accomplishments," which further exacerbated her doubt. "It felt like taunting," she recalled. Soon she began feeling overwhelming dread on Sunday nights about returning to the office. She shared her worries with her boss, who just told her not to worry. Chloe's doubt and stress only grew. Then one day, she just didn't go to the office. As an increasing number of employees have been doing in recent years, she "ghosted," simply leaving her job without giving notice, never communicating with her boss or anyone at the office again.

Chloe's case of belonging uncertainty might seem extreme, but research shows that the problem of people feeling disaffected at work is widespread. A 2020 survey by Gallup, a leading authority on work-place issues, reveal that only about a third of employees in the United States feel "highly involved in, enthusiastic about, and committed to their work." That's better than the 25 percent figure in 2000, but it still leaves much room for improvement.

Companies that foster belonging have better employee engagement and retention. Even small experiences of connection have been found to yield large benefits. Wharton School of Business professor Adam Grant showed that in occupations as diverse as lifeguarding and fund-raising, when employees heard personal stories about how their work helped others, they showed large gains in performance, clocking more hours and working harder relative to employees who learned about how their job would advance their skills.

My experience working with firms is that while virtually every manager will tell you how important it is to foster belonging, far fewer are aware of the threats to belonging that shape the daily experience at their very own workplace for the average worker. Some perspective-getting would help them.

There are many reasons that feelings of belonging are so challenged at work. The most important are the most obvious but most neglected. The fact that too many jobs are not secure and don't pay enough to provide for oneself and one's family tops the list. Stable jobs that offer a reasonable wage, Angus Deaton and Anne Case write, are the basis of a "dignified and meaningful" life. As Martin Sandbu writes in the *Economics of Belonging*, the crisis of belonging that has besieged so much of the United States over the past two decades can be traced in part to inadequate responses by governments and businesses to the revolutionary advances in technology that have devastated the opportunities of Americans without a college degree.

Day to day, a number of features of the workplace situation can threaten belonging. The increase in the number of people working from home over the past two decades and the rise in freelance employment have weakened ties among colleagues, leaving many employees feeling isolated. Authoritarian styles of management contribute.

Some managers engage in punitive and coercive leadership practices that make employees feel powerless and underappreciated and that, as Kurt Lewin would have warned, create divisive and bitter workplace climates. Research suggests that all of us, managers included, tend to underestimate the degree to which other people are motivated by the desire to belong and to contribute to a larger mission. As a result, too many bosses rely too heavily on a limited tool set of material incentives, such as salary bonuses, or on threats. If managers overcame this blindness, they'd likely unleash greater potential in their workplace, as we'll see.

Of all the threats to belonging, long-standing problems of discrimination are among the most powerful and pressing; so in addressing remedies, I'll begin there.

WHILE MANY COMPANIES HAVE long professed their commitment to building a more diverse workforce, results of their efforts have generally proved disappointing, and in some cases programs seem to have decreased diversity. As Frank Dobbin and Alexandra Kalev reported in a widely read 2016 cover story in the *Harvard Business Review* titled "Why Diversity Programs Fail," the percentage of black men in management positions in U.S. companies with a hundred employees or more increased from 3 percent to only 3.3 percent between 1985 and 2014. By 2020, the figure was still only 3 percent, according to more recent data. The number of white women in management roles, another common target for improvement, increased more, from 22 percent in 1985 to 29 percent in 2000, stalled between 2000 and 2014, and by 2020 rose slightly to 32 percent. Minorities still face discrimination in hiring, and women have still not achieved pay equity and continue to contend with sexual harassment. One common pattern that was documented by Claude Steele many years ago is that once an organization has hired one minority employee, it hires fewer in the future, in effect resting on its laurels.

A lack of diversity is not only unjust but bad for business. Katherine Phillips synthesized a large body of evidence to show that diversity can improve performance for many reasons. Groups of employees with similar life experiences tend to have overlapping knowledge bases and more unified perspectives, which can lead team members to make inferior decisions relative to groups composed of people with a broader range of experience and knowledge. More homogenous groups challenge one another's views and ideas less than diverse groups, reinforcing one another's perspectives, which can lead to overconfidence in judgments, failure to consider alternative options, and a lack of innovation. Diversity in work teams helps rein in this conformity and hubris and brings attention to ways in which products and services could be made more appealing to a broader range of customers.

Almost all companies can benefit from building a more diverse workforce. But whether we unleash the benefits of diversity depends on the situations we craft, from the recruitment process to the hiring experience to daily management. If we create situations that foster belonging for all, the benefits of diversity will surface.

One problem, though, is that many of the threatening elements of workplace situations are hard for those in power to see. This lesson was driven home to me when I consulted with a major Silicon Valley firm that is interested in promoting diversity. The management was baffled that their black and Latino candidates were not more successful in job interviews at the firm, as the applicants they had invited to their campus had great credentials and would never have been invited to interview if they hadn't. I noticed that the managers hadn't taken account of the fact that virtually all of the current black and Latino employees at the company worked at low-level jobs, such as parking attendants. Seeing minorities only in such positions may have signaled to the minority candidates that this was a place where racial stereotypes were in play, which, research suggests, can increase stereotype threat and undermine performance.

Attracting a diverse range of applicants is another challenge for many firms. One easily remedied source of the problem is the language in job announcements, which can be off-putting, intentionally or not, to certain groups of people. One study found that such phrases as "We are a dominant engineering firm that boasts many leading clients," common in job postings for male-dominated occupations, discourages women from applying, compared with such phrasings as "We are a community of engineers who have effective relationships with many satisfied clients." Because words like "dominant" are associated with masculinity, the ad caused women to question whether they would be right for the job, and they expressed less interest in applying for it. The effects of using subtly gendered language such as this are almost surely unintended, but they can prove powerful nonetheless.

Likewise, according to research by Valerie Purdie-Greenaway and her colleagues, colorblind mission statements that emphasize a firm's belief in the unifying power of employees' similarities and claim that "your race, ethnicity, gender, and religion are immaterial as soon as you walk in the door" do not reliably foster trust and belonging among minority candidates as much as statements of a firm's commitment to diversity and its belief that employees' differences are a source of strength. In fact, statements that affirm an institution's commitment to diversity have been found to enhance the performance of minorities.

Once women, minorities, and members of other underrepresented groups get to the interview process, they're subject to biases in the way they are evaluated—biases that have persisted despite numerous studies exposing the problem. Companies that want to foster diversity can acknowledge and address these biases, which can be challenging because they're often operating unconsciously. Nevertheless, as we will see, companies have at their disposal some wise interventions for doing so.

As one pernicious example of a biasing influence, white interviewers sometimes display signs of discomfort when they're interviewing minority candidates, which can have adverse effects on the performance of interviewees. Pathbreaking work was done by Carol Wood, Mark Zanna, and Joel Cooper in 1974, and their findings have been backed up by subsequent research. Studying how white interviewers behaved with white versus black candidates, the researchers found that the interviewers made more speech errors when interviewing black candidates and seemed to have trouble keeping track of their thoughts, often repeating themselves awkwardly. White interviewers also said "um" more and spoke in a more halting style with black candidates, often stopping midway in a sentence. Most striking, they sat farther away from the black candidates and cut their interviews with them short by a few minutes. These differences were subtle, hardly noticeable without careful quantitative assessment.

The researchers then trained a new group of interviewers to interact in this uncomfortable way with a group of white job candidates to see if this style would have adverse effects on them compared with another group of white job candidates interviewed in the normal way. The candidates were videotaped (with the interviewer off camera), and their performance was evaluated by independent judges. Compared with white candidates interviewed as they normally would be, the group of white candidates interviewed as the black candidates had been were rated by independent judges to be worse fits for the job. We don't know why, but one strong possibility is that the white candidates felt less at ease in these encounters. Discomfort can be contagious. The researchers conclude that our approach to gauging employee potential "might profit if it were assumed that the 'problem' of black performance resides not entirely within the blacks, but rather within the interaction setting itself."

Research also reveals bias in the ways men and women are evaluated in business. Dana Kanze and colleagues studied how venture capitalists interview entrepreneurs who are soliciting funding. The researchers discovered differences in the type of questions asked of women versus men. The questions posed to female entrepreneurs focused on potential problems that their businesses would run into, while the questions posed to male entrepreneurs focused on the *positive* potential of their businesses.

Venture capitalists also seem to assess the abilities and character of male versus female entrepreneurs differently. For example, in one study, the average male entrepreneur was characterized as "young and promising," "aggressive but a really good entrepreneur," and "cautious, sensible, and level-headed." Conversely, the average female entrepreneur was characterized, if young, as "inexperienced," "enthusiastic but weak," and "too cautious and does not dare." Such assessments may partly explain the disparity in venture capital awarded to men and women. Research conducted jointly by the Columbia University Business School and the London School of Economics in 2019 found that women entrepreneurs were 63 percent less likely to obtain funding.

The criteria that employers privilege in selecting hires can also contribute to exclusion. Some notions about the qualities that are important for success in work may be discriminatory. For instance, the belief that passion is a primary driver of achievement is a distinctly Western view of motivation. But in research led by one of my students, Xingyu Li, and the cultural psychologist Hazel Markus, we analyzed data from a study of over a million students drawn from representative samples in fifty-nine societies. We found that the link between students' expressed level of passion for a field and their achievement in it proved weaker for students from more interdependent Eastern societies than for students from more independent Western societies. Looking for indications of "passion" above all might lead both schools and employers to overlook the potential of many students and job candidates, especially those from the many cultures throughout the world that value interdependence more than independence.

Another way bias shows up in hiring decisions is showcased in research by Lauren Rivera. She studied the hiring process at major corporations throughout the United States and found that companies frequently cite a candidate's lack of "fit" with their organization to explain why they ruled out job candidates whose identities or status— most notably, candidates from a low-income background, minorities, and women—differ from those of the key decision-makers. Where did this sense of mis-fit come from? Often from the interviews. The interviewer might ask, "So what kinds of things do you do for fun outside of work?" If the answer was golf rather than bowling, the interviewee was more likely to be considered in a positive light. But the bias can be far more insidious. Research has found that most of us generally think that people who share our own idiosyncratic qualities, regardless of their race, gender, or class, are more likely to succeed. We define what "it takes" to succeed at a job, in school, or at life in ways that bolster our self-esteem, thinking in essence, "If I do it, it's a sign of success." If I play golf or watch football or read the *New Yorker*, I will tend to interpret these activities as part of the profile of people who belong in the category of "likely to succeed." Interviews provide plenty of fodder for such biases. They give us all too much leeway to find mini-me's rather than employees who will bring genuine diversity.

We may even unconsciously *shift* our take on the qualities needed to do a job well in order to favor people from certain groups. Eric Uhlmann and I conducted research revealing that people changed their criteria regarding the experience and personal qualities required to do the job of police chief in order to justify privileging male candidates over female ones. We had one group of participants evaluate a male candidate described as having a cluster of qualities that people stereotypically associate with "book smarts." He had a college degree, administrative skills, and political connections, but he had little street experience. He was also said to communicate well with the media and had a spouse and child. For another group, the male candidate was described with a cluster of qualities that people stereotypically associate with "street smarts." He was said to have no higher education but to be tough and to have worked in rough neighborhoods. He was also said to be a risk-taker, be in good physical shape, and live alone.

In both cases, participants rated the qualities that the male candidate was said to have as more important to the job of police chief than the ones he did not. In other words, they retrofitted their assessments of the criteria for the job to the credentials of the male applicant. Even "having children" was rated as being more critical to the job if the male candidate had a family than if he did not. By contrast, in evaluating female candidates, participants didn't change their ratings of the importance of these qualities at all in light of those she was said to have. We concluded that the participants held a bias that men are more appropriate for the job of chief, and their minds tried to find a way to justify hiring the male. Wanting to hire the man but still claim that their decision was based on the merit of the candidate, they changed the criteria of merit.

This bias seemed to act without conscious awareness. The people who shifted their criteria the most in order to favor the male job candidate—an indication of greater bias—rated themselves as the most objective at the end of the study. They thought they had picked the right man for the job, when in fact they had picked the right *criteria* for the man. Once again, we see just how hard it is to live up to Richard Feynman's dictum, "The first principle is that you must not fool yourself—and you are the easiest person to fool."

While biases in hiring most often disfavor women and minorities, they can exclude anyone who is seen as an outsider, including men for some professions. Our research showed that holding a bias that women are more appropriate for a job, such as a women's studies professor, disadvantages male candidates through the same retrofitting of criteria. Not only does this bias cause discrimination, but it also is likely to exacerbate belonging uncertainty, as job candidates may perceive that they're being viewed with biased eyes.

What can firms do to address these subtle sources of discrimination? One strategy is to establish clear criteria for hires and commit to them. Uhlmann and I designed a simple wise intervention for implementing this procedure. We had some evaluators commit in advance to the criteria in candidates that were important for the job of police chief before they looked at the applicants' credentials. While a control group evaluated male candidates more positively than female candidates with similar credentials, the evaluators who received our intervention rated male and female candidates as equally qualified for the job. Partly as a result of this research, the practice of "commitment to criteria" has been adopted as a hiring policy in companies around the country. A similar practice can be used for interviews, with the questions to be asked of all candidates decided in advance.

There are other ways to situation-craft to promote fairness at the workplace. Earlier in the book, we saw that asking decision-makers to monitor and explain racial and gender imbalances in promotions and pay raises dramatically reduces disparities. Yet another antibias intervention is for firms to blind decision-makers to job applicants' race, gender, or membership in other stereotyped social groups, insofar as that is possible.

Another part of the hiring process that may lead to discriminatory results is the use of employment tests, which can trigger stereotype threat. Two wise interventions that can help tamp down this threat are self-affirmation and social-belonging interventions. One study found that adding an affirmation exercise before an employment test for applicants for a police officer job increased the percentage of minority candidates who passed.

Self-affirmations can also help interviewers and decision-makers break free of harmful biases. Our evaluations of others, research suggests, often say more about our own psychological needs than other people's merits. Addressing those needs can lead to fairer assessments. For example, a study by Steve Fein and Steve Spencer showed that a values-affirmation activity reduced the extent to which non-Jewish people conformed their judgments of a female Jewish job candidate to popular anti-Semitic stereotypes about "Jewish American princesses." Likewise, research shows that experiences that affirm the self, such as getting positive feedback for a job well done, reduce people's tendency to narrowly define what it takes to be successful in ways that flatter themselves.

These are all examples of situation-crafting that, although they don't eliminate stereotypes, may prevent them from influencing hiring decisions.

None of these interventions is guaranteed to work. As I've said throughout the book, the impact of wise interventions depends on the other forces at work in any given situation, many of which we may be unaware of. This means that in situation-crafting, we must always be monitoring outcomes, both before and after any changes we introduce, to assess whether or not we are moving closer to our goals. Are disparities decreasing? Does a new promotion process advance equally qualified men and women at the same rate? To borrow a metaphor from Kurt Lewin, if we do not monitor our progress toward a concrete goal, we are like a ship captain without a compass, adrift at sea, turning the helm furiously but sailing in circles.

Hope that progress can be made comes from research showing that within five years of companies implementing a rigorous program with the goal of hiring more women, the number of white, black, Hispanic, and Asian women in management positions in those firms rose on average about 10 percent. Improvements in diversity can lead to still further progress, because role models for people from historically excluded groups can lessen their stereotype threat and belonging uncertainty.

BUT CREATING MORE DIVERSE workforces is only one needed step. The situations within companies must also be crafted to foster belonging for people from all walks of life once they arrive. Two pioneers of diversity research, Robin Ely and David Thomas, write that too many companies take an "add diversity and stir approach." They fail to address features of their workplaces that undermine belonging. Yet companies have many means of nurturing employees' sense of belonging in both word and deed. One of these is forcefully stating and honoring company policies for promoting inclusion.

Due to the inertia in promoting equity for minorities and women, many express skepticism about the value of such policies. But I was heartened by research showing positive effects. In 2019, a rigorous study led by William Hall and Toni Schmader assessed the effects of gender-inclusive policies on female employees working in one of the STEM fields, engineering. The policies included the reported availability of resources to address work-family imbalances like child care, policies for addressing harassment, education and training opportunities for women and men, and job advertising and mission statements that assert the value of diversity. Women felt less stereotype threat and reported more positive interactions with male colleagues in firms that had such policies in place than in firms that did not. The women felt, in essence, more accepted.

Social psychologists Mary Murphy and Elizabeth Canning propose another pathway to belonging, grounded in their research: promoting a "growth mindset" work culture. A growth culture is one where norms focus on *improving* not *proving*. Murphy surveyed employees at Fortune 1000 firms and found that female employees were less worried about negative stereotypes in companies that embraced a belief that ability was not fixed but could be cultivated and expanded. Indeed, in such growth cultures, male and female employees alike trusted their company more, felt more invested in it, and reported stronger support for innovation, creativity, collaboration, ethical behavior, and risk-taking. Quoting from journalistic accounts, Murphy showcases the positive example of Xerox Corporation under the leadership of the former CEO Anne Mulcahy. "In public statements, executives proudly described their CEO's growth and learning over 35 years—from sales rep to the head of the organization," and the focus was not on "proving how smart a person or division was" but on "investing in the experiences and development of a larger portion of talent."

Another way to create climates of belonging is to weave self-affirming values into a company's mission. These can bring people together in common purpose. One of the best descriptions of this practice I've seen comes from Stephen Covey in his classic *The 7 Habits of Highly Effective People*. Visiting a hotel, Covey had been amazed by the impeccable service at every level and in every conceivable circumstance. It lived up to the hotel chain's motto, "Uncompromising personalized service." Covey asked the manager how they achieved such excellent standards. The manager explained that the hotel had come up with its own mission statement that, though "in harmony" with the chain's, pertained "to our situation, our environment, our time." Covey asked who developed this mission statement. The manager said, "Everybody." Housekeepers, waitresses, and desk clerks had all contributed, and the values of the mission statement had come to infuse almost every decision and encounter that employees had. Echoing the democratic spirit of Kurt Lewin's leaders, Covey says that involving employees and their own values in a company's mission is essential. "Mark it down, asterisk it, circle it, underline it," he writes. "*No involvement, no commitment.*"

More research into the effects of such policies in companies must be conducted, but this is a hopeful sign that policies that unite employees around shared values have a positive impact on company culture.

The democratic approach to developing the hotel's motto was likely key to the success. Belonging is fostered at companies when employees, ideally at all levels, are offered the opportunity to lend their voices in problem solving and to feel that they are a respected, appreciated part of the team. One way of ensuring that employees feel valued and seen as vital to the company's operations is to inform them about the higher-level issues that the firm is dealing with and to jointly develop strategies for success, as Lewin did with his research at the pajama factory. Netflix has implemented similar practices, as described by the company's longtime chief talent officer Patty McCord in her book *Powerful*. The company periodically holds a meeting for all new employees in which the heads of all the divisions give detailed presentations about everyone's part in the business and employees are encouraged to ask questions of them. The company's strategic challenges and plans are also described thoroughly. The intent is to give all employees clarity about how they can contribute to the mission and to convey that each of them is seen as vital to the company's success.

In an echo of Lewin, the democratic inclusion of employees should not be laissez-faire. Leaders must set a direction, which is true at all levels of management, from the CEO to the leaders of small teams. Reviewing a large body of research, the prominent organizational researcher J. Richard Hackman found that teams in industry and, for that matter, in nearly all arenas seldom perform as well as they should. In fact, their performance falls far short of what would be predicted based on the individual team members' abilities and experience. Why? Because most teams are not structured and managed in a way that permits each team member to make their optimal contribution or that ensures that the input of all members is constructively integrated into a larger whole. Hackman stresses the importance of the right balance of leadership and employee autonomy, arguing that managers should exercise authority over "*direction*, the end states the team is to pursue" while authority "about the *means* by which those ends are accomplished . . . should rest squarely with the team itself." And, of course, one of the key directives a leader can set is to create a just and inclusive workplace.

A leader can also set the direction of a team through "micro-norming," engaging in seemingly small behaviors that establish powerful norms. Adam Grant, for instance, highlights that leaders should link a vision for a team's or firm's success to a core set of values both in word and in deed—which helps employees see their work as meaningful and affirming. In one experiment, he had a manager of a software company give a short, inspiring speech to newly hired sales staff. The manager articulated the company's vision and how the employees' work related to it, and he expressed a belief in their capacity to realize the shared dream. These words were bolstered by an experience that Grant and the company crafted to reinforce the norms: a visit from a direct beneficiary of the sales staff's efforts—an employee from a different department—who gave a personal testimonial about how the sales division had created jobs and funded salaries. This intervention connecting new employees to their work, and each other, raised sales and revenue over the next seven weeks. The workers receiving this intervention generated more than two hundred additional sales than did a group receiving no intervention.

Another way to foster a sense of belonging for employees is to form teams that are encouraged to engage in collective problem-solving. This affords regular opportunities for all members of the teams to express their views and contribute their talents. But leaders of these teams should establish the norm that colleagues treat each other with respect, making room for everyone in discussions and listening thoughtfully to one another. As we saw with high-status students leading the way in establishing an antibullying norm in schools, managers, as the highest-status member of a team, can set powerful norms. A key goal is to foster what leadership scholar Amy Edmondson calls psychological safety, which she describes as "the belief that the environment is safe for interpersonal risk taking. People feel able to speak up when needed—with relevant ideas, questions, or concerns—without being shut down in a gratuitous way. Psychological safety is present when colleagues trust and respect each other and feel able, even obligated, to be candid." No matter how ingenious or talented individual team members are, if the climate does not foster the psychological safety people need to express themselves, they are likely to hold back on valuable input. As one manager at Google told me, "If you don't have psychological safety, you're missing the potential of nearly everyone on your team."

Managers who aren't convinced about the importance of fostering belonging might be persuaded by the evidence of its effects on team performance. One widely publicized study by Google, called Project Aristotle, determined that psychological safety was a key characteristic common to all of its highest-performing teams. Research has also revealed striking drops in performance if respect is not shown to employees. In one study conducted in 2018, twenty-four medical teams in Israel, each composed of one doctor and two nurses, were given information about a baby said to be suffering from an ailment and were required to produce a diagnosis within an hour. They were told that a leading medical expert would be observing them on a webcam, and the experimenter then supposedly called the expert, with the teams listening in on the call. In fact, a prerecorded message was played, and with one group of teams, the expert commented that he was "not impressed with the quality of medicine in Israel" and that he expected the team members "wouldn't last a week" if they were working for him. The teams who heard the disparaging comments performed worse both in diagnosis and in the performance of medical procedures relative to the teams who heard neutral comments from the same expert. Why? The researchers provide evidence that rude comments put workers on the defensive, distracting them from the task at hand and making them reluctant to share information or ask for help. Moreover, subsequent research has found that a rude comment can spread like a virus, infecting the minds of other workers to make them more likely to see hostility in others and to respond with hostility.

Asking questions, the basis of perspective-getting, can also foster employee belonging, both in collaborative problem-solving meetings and in one-on-ones between managers and employees. We saw earlier how asking people questions about themselves and their values is a bond-builder. It affirms employees by conveying that they are seen as a whole person rather than a cog in a work machine. Research by Jeffrey Sanchez-Burks and his colleagues finds that employees from Latino cultures are especially responsive to workplace experiences that affirm connection, such as inquiries about the weekend, family, movies, and other aspects of social life. But almost all employees benefit from workplace connection.

The power of asking self-affirming questions was demonstrated in a pair of field experiments that my colleague Yue Jia and I conducted. Employees at two companies, one a delivery service, the other a cab service, were randomly assigned to answer a couple of questions about their most important values and why they were important to them, a standard values-affirmation prompt that they completed in writing. We reasoned that this activity would buffer them against the stresses of their employment and help them to remember how their work connects to their values. Compared to a control group that wrote about less important values, these employees performed better over the next two months. The benefits were especially strong among employees who had expressed at the study's outset that they felt burned out at their job. In research led by Arghavan Salles, the same values-affirmation activity improved the performance of female surgical residents as gauged by the formal evaluations made of them made by their clinical supervisors.

In group meetings, asking questions also helps to ensure everyone has an opportunity to participate and everyone's perspective is being heard. "Good leadership is about asking good questions," writes John Hagel, who has worked for forty years as an executive and adviser for businesses in the Silicon Valley. Too many leaders, he remarks, assume that "bold assertions build . . . confidence in their competence." But far more effective, he says, are "inspiring questions" that "convey they don't have the answers." Of course, some employees will be more reticent. So another form of micro-norming that managers can practice is to be attentive to those who are not speaking up by eliciting their input, asking questions such as, "Carol, you've got good experience in this area; what do you think?" If an employee seems to be particularly shy or insecure, one way to create more safety is, before asking a question publicly, to get input from everyone in advance of a meeting and *then* to say, "Carol, I thought what you wrote about the project was insightful. Would you share your thoughts with the group?"

As impactful as all these practices can be, their benefits won't last long if management fails to head off stereotyping and other harmful messages about who belongs and who doesn't. So a key goal is to raise awareness of the problem of bias and the power of a diverse workplace where all feel they belong. But given what we've seen about how people can be defensive when issues of bias and diversity are discussed, how do we raise awareness in an effective way?

IN APRIL 2018, news broke that a manager of a Starbucks in Philadelphia had called the police on two black men simply because they sat down at a table without purchasing anything. Though they told the officers who arrived that they had been waiting for someone with whom they had a business meeting, the men were arrested and handcuffed. The public outcry was fierce, the corporate response swift. The manager was fired, and on a single day in May, the company shut down its stores in the United States and gave virtually all of its 175,000 American employees diversity training. But much skepticism was expressed about how effective that training would be.

Nearly all Fortune 500 companies do diversity training. Most colleges and universities do too. Diversity training has become a billion-dollar industry. But does the training work? The answer is, by and large, no, according to Dobbin and Kalev. But its failure is not an indication that diversity training is fundamentally flawed. Rather, much of it is poorly conceived and implemented. According to one of the leading scholars in this area, Corinne Moss-Racusin, we should not be talking generally about diversity training because the approaches vary widely. The key differentiator between those that show good results and those that don't is whether or not the program is grounded in scientific research. The ones that aren't—which is true of most—do little good.

In one example of research-backed diversity training, Patricia Devine, Molly Carnes, and Will Cox designed a workshop that promotes "bias literacy," meaning awareness both of the problem of bias and of strategies for overcoming it. These include increasing interaction with members of other groups and building mental habits that correct for bias, such as those described in Chapter 6. In the most impressive result of testing the effects of their workshop, they found that the faculty of forty-six college STEM departments, which were randomly assigned to the two-and-a-half-hour workshop, subsequently hired more female faculty members over the next two years, with the percentage of new hires rising from 32 percent women to 47 percent. The departments in a control group showed no gain. In another study that assessed the responses of over two thousand professors to the workshop, the experience improved the overall sense of belonging among all faculty, men and women, according to their self-reports in a university survey of work life.

Impressive as the results of such programs have been, one approach stands out as particularly well-designed and impactful, bringing together many of the methods of situation-crafting we've covered. The approach is a wise intervention created by the social psychologist Jessi Smith and her colleagues, with the aim of combating bias against women in STEM positions at universities. The United States has made significant strides in this effort over the past decade, with the percentage of tenure-track female faculty in STEM positions increasing from 24 percent in 2001 to 37 percent in 2017. One likely cause is a commitment made by the National Science Foundation in 2001 to fund programs aimed at the goal of achieving gender equity. With a long way to go to reach that milestone, the program devised by Smith and her team seems to show especially good promise. It incorporates many of the suggestions that Dobbin and Kalev offer, and it has been so successful that several organizations are now working to adopt it.

In one experiment, the faculty of fourteen STEM departments at one university were randomly assigned to participate in the intervention, and another nine served as a control group, which received only a standard antidiscrimination presentation from the Office of Human Resources. The researchers looked at the gender diversity of the faculty searches conducted over the course of a year, and they found that the departments that received the intervention brought more than twice as many women candidates to campus for interviews as did departments in the control group, and ultimately extended 62 percent of their offers to women, compared with only 21 percent among the departments in the control group. What's more, there was evidence that women were more likely to accept these offers in the intervention group. Over the next two years, the intervention was applied to all STEM searches throughout the university and helped to bring about perfect gender parity, with women composing exactly 50 percent of all hires. But the benefits extended beyond hiring. The more that faculty took part in the intervention, the greater their reported job satisfaction and sense of belonging at work—and that was true for both women and men. What did the intervention do?

At its core were practices to protect and cultivate belonging for all, not just the job candidates but the faculty who make the hiring decisions too. They can suffer from their own belonging uncertainty. Research shows that programs to foster diversity and multiculturalism can leave white people and men feeling left out and defensive. Key to this program's effectiveness is how precisely it targets such barriers to belonging often not addressed by most other programs.

At the beginning of a new job search, members of the search committee, whom Lewin would call the gatekeepers, attend a two-hour meeting described as a workshop, because the word "training" can be off-putting. A diversity program representative and a faculty member from another department who had previously attended the workshop are also present. The groups are kept small, from four to ten people, because groups of this size are particularly powerful in unfreezing old attitudes, as Lewin put it, and opening people up to new points of view. The groups are also as diverse in ethnic and gender composition as the demographics of the department permit, with an invitation to join sent early to women and minorities to try to inspire more participation from them. Previous faculty participants describe how their department had increased the percentage of women, which is a good way of establishing that a new norm is taking root at the university. Their testimonials also send the message that diversity is a value we all share, and we can take steps together to promote it. The previous faculty participants describe their own experience learning about their biases and how to overcome them, detailing how they took steps to promote equity in their own departments. The point, clearly conveyed, is to support and empower the new participants and their departments to make the best decisions they can. Vital to the process is that there is no blaming of faculty or expression of righteous indignation during the workshop. This helps assuage any defensiveness they may feel. The emphasis is on making positive change together. "The playing field is not equal. It's not our fault," one of the program representatives said at one workshop. "But it is our fault if we close our eyes to it."

Participants are not spared from confronting hard truths. They're shown data to illustrate the degree of gender diversity in their own department compared with national trends. They are also shown evidence that female underrepresentation cannot be explained by a dearth of female science PhDs alone; indeed their numbers have risen dramatically in the past twenty years. Scientific research showing the power of bias to infuse our everyday thinking is covered, and Smith and colleagues write that this must be done with specific examples of "the myriad ways in which bias contributes to stereotype threat, belonging uncertainty, work-life imbalance, and a host of other negative consequences." The workshop aims to increase not just cognitive awareness but emotional awareness, and to accomplish that, perspective-getting is used. A number of brief accounts of people's experiences with bias are shared. In one, a graduate dean shares the story of how as a young candidate for a faculty job in science, she met a male science professor during her interview. He explained to her how his wife had given up her career to support his, and he then asked the candidate if her husband was prepared to do the same for her. The experience was so jarring, the dean said, that she immediately lost interest in the job. Other stories, from candidates who had declined offers or dropped out of searches, are also shared. This element of the workshop draws on research showing that stories of the experience of being subjected to bias are harder to dismiss than factual evidence. A repository of stories and expert interviews to illustrate gender bias has been developed by Moss-Racusin and her colleagues and is publicly available (https://academics.skidmore.edu/blogs/vids/).

Specific strategies for each participant to use in making changes are then presented. That's important because research shows that only showing evidence of gender or racial bias can leave people feeling hopeless and can threaten the felt belonging of women and minorities at the workplace rather than foster it. Participants receive checklists of research-backed approaches for overcoming bias and its effects. They get templates for creating inclusive job ads, learn about newsletters and listservs where they can recruit a diverse pool of candidates, and are given worksheets that help them to establish clear and inclusive criteria for reviewing candidates' applications.

All of these steps are as Lewin would recommend. Gone is the all-too-common "command and control" approach to diversity programs that Dobbin and Kalev say "flies in the face of nearly everything we know about how to motivate people to make changes." But the workshop is far from hands-off, as we've seen. Through an annual survey, every department is asked to set goals for the coming year and to monitor progress made over the previous year. Responses are analyzed by Smith and her team and a summary report sent to all campus stakeholders, which is used to determine resources and support allocated to each department. This process, Smith told me, often creates a sense of celebration when goals are met and promotes awareness and accountability, which we've seen are potent debiasing forces.

Job candidates are also served in the program. They meet for a brief conversation with faculty liaisons to learn about the opportunities and resources that the university offers to support the needs of faculty—in addition to proactive diversity policies, child care, family care rooms, and family advocates to help with work-life balance. The workplace situation, candidates see, is structured in a way that will support their success if they are offered the job and decide to accept the position. Candidates are then invited to give their perspective, should they wish to share it, in a confidential interview, allowing them to express concerns and explore how to address them in partnership with the university. Smith told me that the goal is to "treat the candidate like a human, friend, and authentically whole person." This meeting happens during the candidate's first trip to campus, which is key, because that's a time during which norms are gleaned and expectations set.

The researchers also developed a number of ways to support new female faculty. They set up workshops for grant writing, for example, because winning grants is, for better or worse, the coin of the realm at many universities. They also created a distinguished scientist award for female faculty and a ritual in which established professors introduce new faculty to their first class, lauding their accomplishments. These means of situation-crafting may seem small, but they serve as weapons against the stereotype that "women don't belong in STEM."

The program also includes a mechanism for faculty to share problems before they flare up, so that the university can proactively address them. A team of "equity advocates" serve as confidants and problem-solvers, and, if necessary, third-party mediators, both to members of the search committee and job candidates.

As we've seen throughout this book, what the program does *not* do is as critical as what it does do. It doesn't focus on fixing people's bad attitudes or expunging deep-seated biases, even though those may exist. Instead, it sets the more modest goal of increasing people's awareness of the situation and themselves and gives them concrete strategies and opportunities to act. As we saw in Chapter 1, this empowering, participatory approach puts people in new roles and seeds in them new identities. Much more commitment to well-crafted programs like this one, along with funding for them, is needed. Philanthropic foundations and corporations could play a role in supporting them, replacing the ineffectual programs that now dominate with these science-backed approaches.

With plentiful resources from these studies and others already available, though, every organization can begin to enact some of the practices introduced here. Nurturing feelings of connection among employees, both with one another and with the company, need not be a daunting affair.

Chapter 11

Belonging and Health

Fostering Belonging to Strengthen
Our Bodies and Minds

E SSAM DAOD WAS EXHAUSTED WHEN I MET HIM, BUT THAT was nothing new. He and his wife Maria Jammal are the cofounders of Humanity Crew, an international organization that provides first-response psychological support to refugees. They had come to Palo Alto for a fundraiser, and they were kind enough to take some time to meet with me. I had heard about their work through a friend and was inspired. Daod is a psychiatrist and psychotherapist by training. He has waded out to pull refugee children from overflowing rubber boats crammed with passengers. Many of the refugees are fleeing war zones, often those ruled by brutal militias. Almost all the women have been raped, he tells me. Many refugees suffer from post-traumatic stress disorder. And reaching safety is just the beginning of their journey. Building a new life in a strange land will present many daunting challenges, often including the psychological and physical illnesses that trauma gives rise to.

"But," Daod says, "even under these harsh conditions, you can change the situation with words. The main point is to make trauma softer." He uses one of the most powerful means of fostering belonging: affirmation. "I try to get them to see themselves as heroes," he had shared in an earlier interview with *Haaretz*. He says to them, "What courage, you did something that couldn't be done, our captain thought you were dead, but you triumphed." "You crossed the turbulent sea. You escaped evil." The words are true, and they give the children an empowering way to "retell their story" as a heroic tale in a way that they don't do on their own. In response, he says, the tension in the children's faces eases and their bodies loosen. Many even smile. A connection is created. The children loosen up psychologically too, which makes them easier to treat.

Daod and his staff at Humanity Crew appreciate the powerful link between psychological and physical well-being, understanding that, as much research shows, feeling safe and socially connected improves health. "It's impossible," he says, "to rescue the body without rescuing the psyche."

When I was a graduate student in the late 1990s, the Stanford psychiatrist David Spiegel sent shock waves through the medical establishment with a study that revealed the powerful positive health effects of feeling a sense of belonging. He assessed the effects of social support groups for women with terminal breast cancer, bringing small groups of women with the condition together once a week for a year to discuss their challenges and strategies for coping, with the group led by a supportive therapist. At the time he started to study support groups, in the late 1970s, they were rare. Cancer victims were generally made to feel that they shouldn't talk about their pain and fear, even within their families, which was socially isolating for them. Unfortunately, that's still true today for many people with health problems of all sorts. Those with a terminal illness report the sense that the world is divided into the community of the living and a lonely realm of the dying. In one of Spiegel's studies, a patient with a damaged esophagus due to irradiation said she felt estranged from the world when she saw other people eat, as she struggled to swallow soup. As Spiegel's work showed, support groups play a vital role in providing patients with connection that can counter the social isolation that divides them from the wider world. Even though being with others may not solve the problems we have, facing them together makes them feel less threatening and makes us feel stronger.

When Spiegel visited Stanford's social psychology area a few years ago to reflect on his decades-long research, he told us that at first many of the women invited to the groups would say they had no time to attend them, and many of those who did come felt uncomfortable. But soon a "social glue" set in. The bonding was due largely to the authenticity of the emotional support, which validated their fear of dying and allowed them to voice truths they didn't feel they could share with their loved ones. One patient shared that when she collapsed one day, her husband told her she would be okay, which just made her angry. Only when her husband later got down on the floor another time she had collapsed, and cried with her, did she feel truly supported by him. She also appreciated that the group let her cry. The group, Spiegel wrote in his research report, provided "a place to belong and to express feelings."

The small groups were safe spaces for disclosure, whereas with families and friends, the women often felt they had to suppress fear, anger, and sadness. One mom shared that she felt burdened by how she had to constantly put on a charade that she was "fighting cancer" for her family. The pressure to be a brave warrior was draining. Many women also opened up to say they felt guilty that they would die, because they would be letting their families down and causing them pain. Spiegel told us that many participants said the group was "the one place in the world where they feel at home."

In addition to acceptance, the women received affirmation from the groups. They played self-affirming roles as mentors and advice-givers to one another, which studies show to have uplifting psychological effects. In the cancer support groups, women felt more motivated to take care of themselves by helping others with their care.

It's understandable that anyone with terminal cancer would feel demoralized. But because of their experience in the support groups, Spiegel said, many women were "re-moralized." Many reported feeling courageous. They began dealing proactively and collaboratively with their situation, focusing on making good use of the limited time they had left, such as planning a final family vacation. Spiegel himself had been skeptical of correlational research suggesting that social support could improve longevity, so in the mid-1980s he conducted a randomized experiment to test the effect of his support groups on the survival of women with terminal breast cancer. To his surprise, the women who had been randomly assigned to the support groups lived on average one and a half years longer than women whose conditions he followed but who hadn't attended the groups. While not all studies show the same effect on longevity, a 2019 meta-analysis of all twelve rigorous randomized trials that had been conducted to date found a robust positive effect. The benefits were powerful but conditional, which we've seen is typical for wise interventions. The benefits occurred only in studies that had a sample of relatively more unmarried patients. While we don't know for certain why this is the case, one strong possibility is that the intervention alleviated some of the isolation that the unmarried patients may have felt. Marriage for many provides a stable source of belonging, especially for those in trying circumstances. Indeed, cancer patients who are married live on average four months longer than those who are not, even when statistically controlling for the severity of the cancer and the patient's age, race, gender, and income.

Careful biological studies have subsequently shown that cancer cells are less aggressive, and duplicate and metastasize less rapidly, in the blood of people who are less lonely. That discovery has inspired four new clinical trials of drugs to improve cancer patients' health and prospects for the future by blocking the fight-or-flight response that arises when people feel alone or threatened. Due to Spiegel's findings and much later work, support groups now pervade the health care industry. Many studies have confirmed they can have significant positive effects on physical health, as well as greatly reducing patients' depression and improving their overall quality of life.

A good deal of additional research has illuminated the mental and physical mechanisms through which belonging contributes to health. Steve Cole of the UCLA Medical School has conducted particularly important work. His research has revealed that when people are in a prolonged situation of social distress, their genes start to function differently. When people are exposed to just about any chronic and severe stressor—such as physical abuse, trauma, economic deprivation, long-term discrimination, or loneliness—the genes that activate the body's inflammatory immune response to physical threats, such as bacterial pathogens, become more active. Meanwhile, the genes involved in the antiviral response become less active. Our genes "focus" on bacterial rather than viral defense when our brain perceives us to be alone and in danger.

Cole calls this reaction the conserved transcriptional response to adversity (CTRA). "Transcription" here refers to the process through which the information in our DNA is transcribed into RNA, which then guides the production of proteins that shape the body's immune response. The transcription pattern Cole studies is "conserved" in two respects. It is "conserved" as a common pattern seen across different kinds of adversity, and it has been conserved over evolution, manifesting in different species from fish to mammals to primates. It's an adaptive strategy for anticipating physical wounds and the risk of bacterial infection. But the CTRA is fundamentally triggered by stress physiology, and in the world we now live in, a lot of "non-wounding" psychological and social threats also trigger stress physiology and keep the CTRA working overtime.

Cole's work has shown that CTRA gene expression occurs in response not just to physical threats but also to perceived social threats. As he put it in a 2020 interview, "The body doesn't care what we're afraid of." Fear of a snake, a virus, or rejection by others will "stimulate our inflammation system . . . and mess with a wide range of other physiologic systems we need to keep us healthy." That the threat detection system in our brains doesn't discriminate between physical and psychological dangers may seem irrational, but in fact it's subrational, meaning that the threat defense system is controlled by deep brain structures that are extremely fast-thinking. That was a great advantage for survival when humans faced the threat of attack by saber-toothed tigers, bears, leopards, and lions, but the response is not cost-free. Activation of the defense system while you're stressed but unlikely to be wounded produces side-effect risks for other diseases. And activating it constantly as we do with the prolonged stressors of modern life—in contrast to the acute stressor of an approaching bear—is particularly costly. As a response to psychological threats, the defense system can prove debilitating, physiologically draining as well as cognitively and emotionally so.

If the CTRA is triggered often or is chronically persistent, Cole explains, it "acts like a kind of fertilizer or accelerant for disease processes." By causing chronic inflammation, the CTRA can contribute to the onset of conditions associated with inflammation, such as cancer, diabetes, and the development of plaque in arteries, which can in turn lead to cardiovascular disease, stroke, and neurodegenerative diseases. While our ancestors in the Pleistocene era died of infectious diseases and hemorrhage, we today die mostly of slowly unfolding diseases that assault our bodies, drip by drip, with an accumulation of biological damage.

In addition, laboratory research by Cole and his colleagues finds that people with high CTRA activity are more vulnerable to viral infections. The cells put up less of an antiviral fight, so a virus is more likely to subvert normal cellular machinery to replicate itself. If the CTRA peters out within a few days, the long-term health effects are unlikely to be significant. But, Cole says, "If it kicks in and then persists or recurs for weeks or months, more damage will be done, and that's not so easy to repair."

Among the most powerful long-term signals that our central nervous system sends to our genome is, "I am alone." Our genome has evolved to "learn" that when we are isolated, we are in mortal peril. "Fundamentally," Cole told me, "CTRA is the biological shadow of mistrust and precarity." In our modern world, a big liability to health is feeling disconnected from other people.

What's more, many psychological threats are persistent. As the biologist Robert Sapolsky has pointed out, the perception of threat can live on in the mind well after it has receded in reality because the human mind is given to ruminating. We often dwell on offenses, mentally replaying them over and over. In addition, many mental health afflictions, such as depression and anxiety disorder, are chronic, which can lead people to develop an "unsafe worldview." People begin exaggerating threats, as is true with anxiety disorders. As a result, the threat response system may be perpetually active. This helps explain why people who are lonely, socially stigmatized, or exposed to other protracted adversity tend to be less healthy and to die sooner, even long after their lives have improved.

Let's look at some examples of the link between chronic social adversity and illness. David Williams, a professor of public health at Harvard, has been documenting a disturbing pattern for two decades. He has found that a chief predictor of the gap in health outcomes between whites and people of color in the United States, which persists even at the highest levels of income, are people's self-reports of experiencing discrimination and stereotyping in everyday life. Indeed, for virtually every viral infection, black people are disproportionately susceptible. Reports on the COVID-19 pandemic indicate that the rate of death from the virus was twice as high for black, Latino, and Native Americans as it was for white people. Other groups widely subjected to bias are similarly vulnerable. For instance, the stigma endured by LGBTQ people in many regions of the United States has been associated with adverse health outcomes, including earlier death among AIDS patients in the 1990s.

Support for the correlation between chronic social afflictions and danger to health also comes from the research of Carnegie Mellon health psychologist Sheldon Cohen. He has spent a remarkable career repeatedly running an ingenious experiment. Since 1991 he has periodically rented out either the Medical Research Council's Common Cold Unit in Salisbury, England—which is like a hotel–human petri dish for the study of infectious disease—or a local hotel in Pittsburgh. The site is completely sterilized at the start of the study. Then he recruits healthy volunteers to stay quarantined in an apartment for about five to six days, alone or with one or two other volunteers. At the start of their quarantine, each volunteer gets a nasal spritz of the cold or influenza virus, so the exposure of all the participants is equal. They spend most of the rest of their time in their rooms but sometimes go to common spaces for meals and social interaction. They're required to avoid all physical contact, wash their hands frequently, and maintain social distance. They're screened beforehand so that Cohen knows they're not suffering from an upper respiratory infection to begin with.

Next, he looks at who develops an upper-respiratory illness (catches a cold or develops the flu) and the severity of their symptoms. Of course, risky behaviors are predictive, like getting inadequate sleep, engaging in little or no exercise, and smoking. But, additionally, based on surveys the participants complete at the beginning of the study, those who feel less socially connected or supported are more susceptible. Why? Their higher CTRA activity may be one reason. In this light, we can see social environments as containing social pathogens that trigger a biological response. Rude comments, racist remarks, and other forms of social exclusion we practice on each other can literally get under our skin and make us vulnerable to disease—if they recur in our situations or are replayed in our minds.

It is increasingly understood that people who live in poor and less educated regions of the United States are also more vulnerable to many biological afflictions. Yes, our genetic code matters, but so does our zip code. One large-scale study found that the gap in longevity between counties throughout America runs as high as twenty years. How long we live seems to depend on *where* we live. Why? Many poor neighborhoods in the United States have less access to nutritious food, education, and health care and more exposure to toxic waste and air pollution. In addition, residents of these neighborhoods experience higher levels of distress than the wider public due to these circumstances, along with a sense of being disconnected from their community and their country. A cacophony of elements work together to create a harsh reality and a sense of being left behind.

+ + + +

WHAT CAN WE DO to protect people from the health effects associated with threats to belonging? Obviously, we must find more effective ways to create a just and inclusive society in which people feel safe. President Franklin Delano Roosevelt was on target when he included "freedom from fear" as one of the four fundamental freedoms all people should enjoy. Social policy is one vehicle we can use to achieve this.

In the nearer term, research has identified a number of ways to reduce or avoid triggering the threat response. Bowlby's and Ainsworth's insight into the importance of early attachment has a biological side: Even for those children who grow up in economic hardship, having a parent who provides a safe haven, which allows children to feel connected and cared for, predicts lower CTRA and makes it more likely that they will grow up healthy.

Another bit of hope came out of work by Steve Cole, who, along with Barbara Fredrickson and colleagues, measured a slew of psychological variables, such as levels of anxiety and loneliness, in three separate groups of adult participants. Then they assessed CTRA expression through blood samples, in effect asking the genome for its perspective on what makes for a healthy life. One psychological variable emerged as the most robust predictor of lower CTRA gene expression: eudaimonic well-being. This is the term used by psychologists to refer to the subjective experience of leading a life filled with meaning, purpose, and authenticity. It's derived from the Greek "eudaimonia," which means "good spirit." It's one of two basic kinds of well-being identified by psychologists. The other is hedonic well-being, named after the Greek word for "pleasure," which refers to the subjective experience of happiness, often based in sensory gratification. With hedonic well-being you consume positive experiences for yourself, but with eudaimonic well-being you create them for the world. A person with high eudaimonic well-being tends to give high estimates of frequency for the first statement but not necessarily the second:

In the past week, how often did you feel that your life has a sense of direction or meaning to it?

In the past week, how often did you feel happy?

The study by Cole, Fredrickson, and colleagues also found that hedonic well-being was not correlated with lower CTRA gene expression, and, in fact, in some analyses hedonic well-being predicted higher CTRA. Organizing your life to gain pleasure and avoid pain isn't a robust recipe for health. It seems healthier to harness the energies of the self to commitments beyond serving self-interest, such as helping others.

These results were so surprising that they came under fire when they were published. But the researchers replicated their findings with two additional samples, each with over a hundred adults. The relationship between eudaimonic well-being and CTRA gene expression is not just statistically significant but highly so, and the relationship has been replicated in both Western individualistic cultures and Eastern collectivist ones. It even supersedes the effects of loneliness, meaning that loneliness no longer predicts CTRA if people's eudaimonic well-being is taken into account. This suggests that one of the harmful effects of loneliness is cutting people off from opportunities to enhance their sense of being part of endeavors of social purpose. Indeed, one reason that Spiegel's support groups were so effective seems to be that they gave many of the women the opportunity to discover a sense of purpose through helping other patients cope with their cancer.

This research reinforces the findings of many studies that a sense of purpose is a wellspring for psychological and physical well-being.

One of the powerful things about purpose is that we can always choose to have one, no matter how harsh our circumstances. The psychiatrist and Holocaust survivor Viktor Frankl wrote eloquently about just this in his classic *Man's Search for Meaning*:

> *There is much wisdom in the words of Nietzsche: He who has a why to live for can bear almost any how. . . . In the Nazi concentration camps, one could have witnessed that those who knew that there was a task waiting for them to fulfill were most apt to survive. . . . As for myself, when I was taken to the concentration*

camp of Auschwitz, the manuscript of mine ready for publication was confiscated. Certainly, my deep desire to write this manuscript anew helped me to survive the rigors of the camp I was in. For instance, when in a camp in Bavaria I fell ill with typhus fever, I jotted down on little scraps of paper many notes intended to help me rewrite the manuscript, should I live to the day of liberation. I am sure that this reconstruction of my lost manuscript in the dark barracks of a Bavarian concentration camp assisted me in overcoming the danger of cardiovascular collapse.

Helping people find a sense of purpose is one of the means of helping them feel connected to others, whether to people in their community or farther afield. What's more, according to new data collected by Cole, a sense of purpose helps buffer people against the physiological harms of economic adversity.

Purpose and belonging are mutually reinforcing. We want to feel supported, yes. But being a person who "matters" in the social world also reinforces our sense of belonging. This helps to explain why research studying a range of formal programs aimed at nurturing a sense of purpose has revealed positive effects on health. William Damon has extensively studied and written about purpose and has shown how important it is to healthy adjustment. He sees purpose as having two facets: meaning to the world and meaning to the self. The world has a need, and you have a role to play in addressing it.

One study showed that writers whose autobiographies contained more positive references to performing roles tied to meaningful relationships, such as being a parent and supporting neighbors, friends, or colleagues, lived longer. In other research, linguistic analyses of people's speech and writing samples indicate that a social focus as measured by the use of third-person plural pronouns (they, them) predicts better health outcomes, including lower CTRA, while a self focus as measured by the use of first-person singular pronouns (I, me) predicts worse health outcomes. What's more, controlling for age, sex, race, baseline indicators of health, and other markers of well-being, people who score high on measures of purpose live longer lives freer of disability and disease. If we could put purpose in a bottle, it'd be a billion-dollar drug.

Fortunately, we have many ways to strengthen a sense of purpose, no drug required. One study explored whether teenagers randomly assigned to participate in a volunteer program in which they helped the needy would demonstrate health benefits. Inflammatory markers assayed from blood samples, including cholesterol and interleukin-6, were substantially lower for these teens than for others who had been assigned to a wait-list for the program. Their body mass index was lower too. Steve Cole and colleagues performed a similar study with retired elderly people, assigning some to participate in a mentoring program for children, and they found that their level of CTRA gene expression substantially decreased.

Formal volunteering is by no means the only way to bolster a sense of purpose. An experiment that Cole conducted with Sonja Lyubomirsky and her team showed that engaging regularly in small acts of kindness toward others can also help. They randomly assigned people to one of three groups: a control group instructed to keep track of their daily activities; a group instructed to practice kindness to others, such as cooking dinner for friends; or a group instructed to practice kindness to themselves, such as taking a hike or enjoying a day at the spa. After four weeks, the only group that displayed reductions in CTRA gene expression relative to the control group was the one instructed to practice kindness to others.

Our sense of purpose in life can also be enhanced by changing our perspective. Because situations are experienced in our minds, we can change situations by changing our perception of them. For instance, we can reflect on how our jobs, our parenting, and our time spent with family and friends are in the service of assisting others and rich in meaning. To a large degree, Damon says, feeling a sense of purpose is a choice we make, and our days can be filled with purpose if we choose to appreciate how we are helping others. The psychologist Andrew Fuligni led a study in 2009 that advanced the understanding of this. A group of teenagers, most of whom were Mexican American and lived in largely underprivileged urban neighborhoods, were asked to fill out a survey about the roles they played in their family. Those who were responsible for multiple household chores, such as caring for a sick family member, helping their siblings with homework, and cleaning and cooking, had higher indicators of inflammation in their bloodstream. But those levels were much lower among teens who expressed a strong sense of purpose about their roles, such as by seeing themselves as good sons or daughters. Coaching ourselves and others to see the roles we're playing as meaningful is a simple way to adopt this healthy perspective. A colleague of mine told me that he was able to keep his spirits up as he coped with the trials and tribulations of caring for a newborn at home, while keeping up with the demands of being an assistant professor, by telling himself, as if repeating a mantra, "I'm a hero, I'm being a hero to my baby."

Backing up the value of such self-coaching, values-affirmation exercises have been found to improve health in many studies. Connecting with our values helps to refocus us on our purpose, making small problems loom less large. David Sherman had college students who were about to take their midterm exams complete a series of writing activities in which they reflected on their most important values. Students who hadn't done these activities had increased levels of epinephrine, a hormone involved in the body's threat response, in their urine. But those who wrote about their values experienced no increase in their epinephrine levels. Another study looked at women who had recently completed surgery, chemotherapy, or another medical treatment for breast cancer. The researchers had the patients complete a writing activity. At four separate sessions over three weeks, each twenty minutes long, the patients wrote in response to the following prompt.

What I would like you to write about for these four sessions are your deepest thoughts and feelings about your experience with breast cancer. I realize that women with breast cancer experience

a full range of emotions, and I want you to focus on any and all
of them. In your writing, I want you to really let go. . . . You might
think about all the various feelings and changes that you experi-
enced before being diagnosed, after diagnosis, during treatment,
and now. . . . Ideally, I would like you to focus on feelings, thoughts,
or changes that you have not discussed in great detail with others.
You might also tie your thoughts and feelings about your experi-
ences with cancer to other parts of your life, i.e., your childhood,
people you love, who you are, or who you want to be. . . . Don't
worry about grammar, spelling, or sentence structure. . . . Just
write.

This writing activity has a long history in social psychology, first created and tested by the social psychologist James Pennebaker in 1990.
An eclectic and imaginative researcher, Pennebaker pioneered the
technique and has written extensively about it in books such as *Open-*
ing Up. In this study, the researchers found that three months later,
the women who had completed Pennebaker's writing activity reported
fewer illness-related symptoms, such as coughing or sore throat, and
they had scheduled fewer medical appointments for cancer-related mor-
bidities compared to a control group of women who wrote only about
facts regarding cancer and its treatment. Why? A later in-depth analysis
of the content of the essays by health psychologist David Creswell and
colleagues suggested that the key ingredient was a self-affirming narrative. What proved most predictive of health benefit was writing about
admirable qualities in oneself such as core values ("I'm pretty tough, and
it's going to take a little bit more than a bit of breast cancer to get me
down. I'm a fighter") or sources of personal meaning ("We have been
married over thirty-one years, and we are very lucky because we still
love each other"). Many achieved self-affirmation not in spite of adversity but because of it, giving it a meaning that integrated it into their
self-concept. Lyubomirsky added a warning label to the intervention:
When people reflect on the harsh events in their lives, it's important that
they write or talk and not just *think.* Thinking doesn't provide the narra-

tive closure that writing or talking does, and it often leads people to sink into ruminative loops that prolong their anguish.

While we don't know exactly why this deep processing of trauma works, these words from the Fourteenth Dalai Lama about dealing with loss speak volumes:

> *The way through the sadness and grief that comes from great loss is to use it as motivation and to generate a deeper sense of purpose. When my teacher passed away, I used to think that now I have even more responsibility to fulfill his wishes, so my sadness translated into more enthusiasm, more determination. I have told those who had lost their dear friend or family member, It is very sad, but this sadness should translate into more determination to fulfill their wishes. If the one you have lost could see you, and you are determined and full of hope, they would be happy. With the great sadness of the loss, one can live an even more meaningful life.*

A study conducted by Christine Logel and me evaluated the health effects of a values-affirmation intervention with a group of people who face continual threats to their belonging: the overweight and obese. Logel recruited female first-year college students who worried about their weight, selecting women because being overweight is especially stigmatized among them. Two and a half months later, the women we had asked to write about their most important values had lost more weight, had a lower body mass index, and had a smaller waistline than a group that engaged in a control activity. Two years later, Logel, together with Xingyu Li, managed to track down about 70 percent of all the women in the study and found lasting benefits among women who began the study with a relatively higher body mass index. While those women who hadn't done the affirmation had gained *more* weight, those who had completed it had maintained their weight. One reason for this may be that affirmations activate the reward circuitry of the brain, and activation of the reward circuitry in turn tamps down the stress response. Because stress can lead people to eat more high-fat and sugary foods, affirmations seem a good way to combat stress-induced weight gain.

Values-affirmation exercises have also been found to contribute to better health by inspiring people to be more responsible about taking medication, more receptive to threatening health information, and more open to advised changes in their lifestyles, such as in their diets. For example, in one study a group of barflies completed a values affirmation and then read a persuasive message about the health risks of alcohol. The researchers found that when they checked in with the participants one month later, many had decreased their alcohol consumption; twice as many as in a control group had cut back to government-recommended levels. In another study led by the cardiologist Ed Havranek, colleagues and I found that for low-income black people suffering from hypertension, those who had been randomly assigned to complete a values affirmation before their visit with their health care provider had warmer and more respectful conversations with their doctors than did patients assigned to a control group. The affirmed patients' conversations also revealed more information about their medical conditions. In following up with the patients, those who did the affirmation were more likely to take their prescribed medications than those in the control group.

In 2018 I was lucky enough to be involved with a comprehensive assessment of the results of all studies published to date that were conducted to evaluate the health effects of affirmation, led by Rebecca Ferrer of the National Cancer Institute. The assessment found an overall positive effect across all of the studies. It also identified the conditions under which affirmations work best: when the perception of threat is high and when material resources for change are available. That is, when people have reason to feel threatened ("I might be at risk of diabetes") and are provided with clear steps or other resources to support a health change (such as clear dietary guidelines), affirmations are especially impactful. Affirmations are not a cure-all, in other words. They create a state of openness, which translates into lasting behavioral change when other key resources in the situation are in place.

In light of such findings, some medical professionals have begun administering affirmations to patients. On one occasion, I was filling out a form to sign up for a healthy living program at Stanford when suddenly I found myself answering the values-affirmation question from one of my own studies.

But if your health care providers haven't adopted the practice, you can assign yourself and your loved ones some affirmation exercises to do before any medical visits. (A sample of these activities is available at geoffreylcohen.com.) Like other psychological timeouts, these can be seen as attentional devices that return our awareness to what's most important to us, which can be easy to lose sight of in times of stress.

I also recommend some small affirming activities that my colleagues and I tested with a number of people during the lockdown period of the COVID epidemic. We were concerned about the effects of the social isolation. One of our study participants echoed the sentiment of many when she said she mourned the loss of the opportunity to sit on her porch and talk to people. Led by Isabelle Tay, our lab asked some people to plan brief activities during their day that reminded them of their most important values. Sometimes we'd ask them to take a picture of something that reflected their most important value and write a caption for it. The responses were fascinating because many times people wouldn't do anything out of the ordinary but simply reported seeing an activity in a new light.

For instance, one mother took a picture of some yellow flowers that her kids had left for her by her bedroom window. Feeling inadequate for spending too little time with them, she was reminded of the importance of "kindness and showing concern for others" and of how her children displayed this toward her "regardless of my inadequacies." One of our students took a picture of a cypress tree, which, she wrote, "stands tall but bends in the wind" and is an "ancient Persian symbol of how one should conduct one's life." She also shared a picture of her father, who "embodied many of my values" and whose final words to her were to "make a commitment to taking a job that will make the world a better place." But even pictures related to mundane aspects of day-to-day life had good effect. Another person took a picture of two loaves of freshly baked bread and captioned it "One of the ways I relieve stress and spend time with family: Baking always brings a smile to my face when I see the other person enjoying what I have made." Yet another took a picture of a cat simply captioned, "Chester is my everything. I love him most." Through surveying people before and after they'd done the activity, we found it increased the respondents' feelings of belonging, and the more so for those with the highest belonging uncertainty.

My colleague Raj Bhargava and I were so moved by many of these responses that we created a course for high school and college students designed to help them get in touch with their core values and create situations in their lives aligned with them. We were surprised at how impactful it was, with several students gaining clarity about career and life decisions they were in the midst of and, overall, students in this class consistently showing significant jumps in their reported well-being and sense of purpose.

I was also surprised to see a strong effect on health from another wise intervention we've studied: wise criticism. Blood samples from students put through a number of interventions indicated that helping students to see criticism "wisely" in the way I described in Chapter 9 reduced their CTRA, an effect that was true not just among disadvantaged students but across all students. We don't know for sure why this practice in particular had such strong biological effects, and we still need to replicate the results. But I think the answer may be that so much of the threat college students feel relates to their academic work. Many become demoralized by low grades and negative feedback, and they often feel so ashamed that they don't seek assistance. Helping students to see criticism as a sign of high standards, and their teacher's belief in their ability to reach those standards, may turn what would otherwise be a threat into an affirmation and an occasion to strive for a larger purpose.

A final means of fostering belonging to improve health is providing patients with more welcoming, warm reception at health care facilities and in follow-ups with them. Having accompanied my father on many doctor visits as he battled with terminal cancer for a year, I was struck by how alienating and disempowering medical treatment can sometimes be. Some of his caregivers, for example, talked to him as if he were a child, while others made wise care a fine art. Busy doctors can be gruff and rarely take time to get to know their patients, which is not just a nicety: Failing to do so undermines the quality of care. The insurance company–run model of health care, along with the advent of new technologies aimed to increase the speed with which patients are treated, has exacerbated this problem. They pressure doctors to see a maximum number of patients each day and threaten the vital connection between physicians and their patients.

Lauren Howe and Ali Crum have shown the positive effects of health care providers being warmer with patients. They gave physicians a short script to follow: They were to introduce themselves casually, refer to the patient on a first-name basis, make good eye contact, and smile, and they were asked to hang some nice posters on the wall. The patients they saw were all volunteers who had a topical allergic reaction induced by application of a histamine on their skin. The doctors put a cream on it, which was actually a placebo. For patients seen by the doctors following the script, skin swelling from the allergic reaction subsided significantly more than for those who saw doctors given a script that encouraged them to be aloof. The researchers had also engineered details to signal whether the physician was competent or not, such as a name tag that signified the provider was just a "student doctor" or a "fellow," an office that had been prearranged to be messy or neat, and scripted errors (putting on the blood pressure cuff wrong) that the doctor either made or didn't. The impact of physician warmth was as big as the impact of the perceived competence of the physician.

The power of making supportive, friendly connections with patients was also demonstrated in a classic study that the medical researcher Donald Redelmeier and his colleagues conducted at an emergency room with homeless patients. In addition to receiving standard care, some patients had a pleasant interaction with a volunteer who *listened* to them and who built rapport through chatting about common interests like TV shows but did not provide any clinical advice. The interaction increased patient satisfaction and reduced the rate of costly repeat visits by 33 percent, relative to a control group of patients who received only standard care.

As for following up to check on patients, one study showed dramatically positive effects. Researchers had caregivers send timely postcards to former patients who had attempted suicide. The postcards simply stated that the hospital staff was thinking of them, wanted to wish them well, and wondered how they were doing. Relative to a control group of patients who received no postcards, the intervention nearly halved the number of suicide reattempts.

To paraphrase Essam Daod, it's sometimes possible to rescue the body by rescuing the psyche.

Beyond any intervention, though, is an ethos of caring that permeates an institution, with each encounter like a musical note that contributes to a resounding chorus. I know of no better description of medical professionals demonstrating this ethos than a letter from a doctor in Arizona. In response to a podcast story about a wife who could not be by her father's side when he was hospitalized for COVID, the doctor wrote,

> *The most difficult thing about this pandemic for me is not the long hours or the time away from my family or the bruises on my face from the N-95 mask. The most difficult thing is that my patients are without their loved ones in their struggle. I had patients on ventilators whose family are aching to be with them, to hold their hand, to whisper goodbye if that dreaded time comes. The tragedy of physical distancing means we cannot enfold one another at a time when we need it most. As your wife was not able to be by her father's side, so many people are yearning to be with their loved ones. I wondered if you could share this small comfort with your listeners who may be in pain from the separation.*
>
> *In our hospital no one is alone. Not when they first arrive, not when they are joyously discharged to recover at home, and not*

even when they pass from this world. Before every physical exam I do, before I adjust the ventilator or check the medications or listen to the lungs, I take a moment to hold my patient's hand and speak to them even when they are sedated, even though gowns and masks and gloves separate us, I greet them, I tell them we're fighting for them, I remind them that they are loved.

Our nurses learn the names of wives and children and friends and speak to the patient about them while they do their work. Your wife told me the roses are blooming, says one nurse as she repositions a patient. Your son will be so happy to hear that you're awake, says another. We stay. We are always there. We know so many of you, the families of the sick, would give anything to be there yourself. I am so profoundly sorry that you cannot be. But please take some small measure of comfort in knowing that we're doing what we can to be a family to them until we can get them back to you. They are never alone.

According to one influential review of a host of studies, the evidence that social connection is critical to human health is "unequivocal," with the authors concluding "there are perhaps no other factors that can have such a large impact on both length and quality of life—from the cradle to the grave." All of us can help those contending with medical challenges feel understood and cared for, even in small ways, ensuring they don't feel they're facing the challenge alone. Research shows that even the perception that social support will simply be available, if patients or caregivers seek it, is soothing. Making regular calls to check in and express concern and caring for friends and family, making clear that it's more than fine for them to share their fears and how difficult the situation is for them; sending supportive notes; and offering to relieve some of the burden of daily chores will not only strengthen their feelings of belonging but contribute to better health.

Chapter 12

Belonging in Policing and the Community

Building Understanding to Combat Systemic Abuses

A FEW YEARS AGO, A FRIEND OF MINE, SALLY, DECIDED TO leave her job as county detective to become a police officer. She wanted to work in the community, getting to know residents, working with them to keep the peace and of course to "catch the bad guys," as she put it. Sally's record as a detective was stellar, and she received superlative recommendations and passed all the police tests. Sally was full of excitement when she was hired by a police department in a wealthy suburb of the Bay Area in California. But she was fired within the two-month probationary period.

Joining the department was a rude awakening for her. First, not only was the kind of community involvement she believed in discouraged; it was ridiculed. After she helped a young woman track down her missing father who had dementia and had wandered off, the daughter sent Sally flowers in gratitude, the first of more notes and gifts sent to her by community members in thanks for her service. In response, several colleagues told her that she shouldn't be spending her time on such matters. The officer assigned as her supervisor during her first month was critical of Sally's respectful, friendly manner in conducting traffic stops. He told her she had to approach all cars with her hand ready at her holster and assume that everyone was a potential bad guy.

While Sally would have liked to "walk the beat," he insisted they stay in the patrol car as they monitored the neighborhood.

One day, as the two were patrolling a college campus, he told her to approach a Latino man who resembled a suspect. She was hesitant to approach him as she saw no cause for concern, but her supervisor insisted. She walked up to the man and began to make polite inquiries. But her supervisor, noticing the man was wearing what he construed as gang colors, interrupted and instructed her to frisk him. She felt uncomfortable doing so, but she also wanted to keep her job, so she complied.

When it came time for her supervisor to write a review of her performance, he was scathing. Sally was quick to tell me that she still had lots to learn about policing at the time, but she found the report so imbalanced that she decided to point out to higher-ups the inaccuracies and bias in the assessment. Her complaint had no effect. Nor did she get any credit for the many acts of community service she had provided. After being fired, she was out of work for almost a year but finally got an offer at another department, where she reports she "couldn't be happier." She participates in public relations events, represents the police department at community and county meetings, gives talks to children in schools, and she says, "I still get to catch bad guys too."

At the time she told me her story, I thought the harsh norms of policing at her former department must have been extreme. Surely, many police departments around the country provide good training in building community trust. But as the national attention to police brutality in the wake of the killing of George Floyd and so many others showcased, physical bullying of minorities is pervasive, and Sally's experience is symptomatic of a systemic problem. As we saw in Chapter 6, the problem also encompasses the everyday acts of disrespect that delegitimize the police in the eyes of community members.

Much work is being done on how "to build a better police officer." But maybe that's the wrong mission. That would be the task if we thought policing was all about the kind of people officers are. Of course, there are bad apples in police forces, and they should be disciplined, with some removed from duty. But as former Seattle police chief Norm Stamper wrote in *To Protect and Serve: How to Fix America's Police*, the problems with policing are systemic. "Policing is broken," he has said. "Tragically, it has been broken from the very beginning of the institution. It has evolved as a paramilitary, bureaucratic, organizational arrangement that distances police officers from the communities they've been sworn to protect and serve." Instead, he argues, policing should be understood as a partnership between the public and the police, much as Sally had dreamed it would be.

To build a better partnership, trust between the public and the police is required. How can trust be fostered? One promising approach is to teach officers how to show clear respect in their interactions with the public.

Consider this experiment by Lorraine Mazerolle and her colleagues at Queensland College, Australia, in which the researchers altered the way police conducted random stops to administer breathalyzer tests to deter drunken driving. Most drivers hate these stops. Some are outraged. Mazerolle and her colleagues wanted to see if they could script these encounters for the better. One group of drivers, when stopped, was given a standard business-as-usual speech from the officer. Here's what they heard (the officer name is fictitious).

Hello, my name is Constable Peterson from the Oxley Traffic Branch. You have been stopped for a random breath test. I now require you to provide a specimen of breath for a breath test. This is a breath testing device. To comply with my requirement, I direct you to place your mouth over the mouthpiece until told to stop by me.

Another group of drivers heard this:

Hello, my name is Constable Smith from the Oxley Traffic Branch. Have you ever taken part in a random breath test before? . . . We are pulling cars over today at random. That means you were not specifically singled out for this test. . . . In Queensland alone there were 354 deaths in 2009 because of alcohol-related crashes. One of the hardest parts of our job is to tell a person that their loved one has died or has been seriously injured. . . . Here is a police bulletin that has additional crime prevention tips. It also tells you about what's going on in this community and gives you some important numbers if you want to get in contact with us for any event that is not life-threatening.

The researchers didn't exactly change the way officers see citizens, but they did change the degree to which citizens felt seen by the officers, with powerful effects. This new script is an example of situation-crafting. It takes a bit more time, an extra minute in this study. Its genius lies in small details that speak volumes. The first message "spoken" is solidarity: "We're in this together as a community." The second is dignity: "I see you as a fellow human being, so I'm taking the time to explain to you why I stopped you." Third is the officer's own humanity: "It breaks my heart to see people die unnecessarily." A fourth message is fairness: "You were not singled out but selected randomly." The literal content hardly seems noteworthy. But the psychological messages are powerful.

After their encounter with the officers, the drivers were given a survey to complete and mail back. Months later, the researchers analyzed the survey data and found that drivers who were stopped with the revised scripts rated their officer as more respectful and fair than did drivers who received the standard script. Moreover, this single encounter had ripple effects. The drivers who were stopped with the revised script reported higher trust and confidence in the police as a whole. The drivers who benefited the most were ethnic immigrants, who can often feel uncertain of their belonging in their new country and are understandably mistrustful of police. There was also some evidence that the intervention even increased drivers' concern with drunken driving; they reported more change in attitude toward the problem.

The study wasn't perfect; none ever is. The number of drivers who had been sent the survey and later returned it was lower than the standard for truly robust results, although, on a positive note, roughly equal numbers of drivers from both groups responded, which is important in establishing the validity of the results. Still, it is hard to know how much we can generalize from these results. We need to be both skeptical and open-minded. These studies are incredibly hard to run for so many reasons, including police mistrust of academics as well as the sheer logistics of the methodology. But I think the data give us an important indication that a small change in the way police approach encounters with the public can make citizens feel more seen and, in response, more trusting of the police and identified with their mission.

Some good support for this idea has already come from a 2020 study conducted with the Chicago police department. Researchers George Wood, Tom Tyler, and Andrew Papachristos worked with the police to create and implement a one-day workshop for officers aimed, as they describe it, to teach officers "procedural justice," Yale scholar Tom Tyler's term for fairness in the processes of an organization or in an encounter. When people perceive that the processes that are shaping their treatment are fair, they trust and obey authorities more, even if they don't like the outcome. People obey the law, Tyler argues, not so much because they fear the penalty of breaking it but because they see it as legitimate.

In the workshop, officers learned about the importance and philosophy of procedural justice and were taught techniques, much like the ones Lorraine Mazerolle had embedded in her rewrite of the script for police encounters, to signal a spirit of solidarity during their stops, a belief in the dignity of the citizen no matter what the situation, and an assurance that they were following fair procedures. The police also learned about the history of racism and the persistence of bias. The overarching principle was that the police must build respect and legitimacy in the community rather than act as "occupying forces" who keep order by "command and control."

This workshop's impact was evaluated not with a randomized experiment but with a method almost as good—a staggered program-adoption design. In total, 8,480 officers participated. By tracking when the officers took part in the program and their records before and after, the researchers could zero in on any change. The program was found to substantially reduce police misconduct. Over the two-year period, there were 732 fewer complaints of misconduct lodged against officers who had participated in the workshop, a 10 percent reduction. Additionally, over the same period, there were 105 fewer payouts to settle complaints against the police. Even for those who don't think the police have a bias problem, this result should be impressive. Each payout costs an average of $40,000, which means that this one-day workshop saved the department, and ultimately the taxpayers, $4.1 million.

Emily Owens and her colleagues worked with police precincts in Seattle to improve the quality of police interactions with the public using a different approach, whereby officers were encouraged to adopt the norms of procedural justice through a brief encounter with their supervisor.

A selection of 1,105 officers, who were chosen because a complaint against them had been made by a member of the community, were randomly assigned to one of two groups. With one group, a police sergeant called the officers into his office, and he respectfully asked them to review their handling of an incident with a citizen. He approached the discussion in the participatory manner of Lewin's democratic leaders, so that the officers weren't put on the defensive. While the sergeant emphasized that the police force's mission was to enforce the law with procedural justice, he explained that the purpose of the meeting was simply to talk about how the officer had used procedural justice during the specific incident and if there might be anything to learn. The sergeant solicited their perspectives by asking good questions that provoked reflection:

What did you learn during the incident?

What had you thought you would see when you arrived, and
   what did you actually see when you got there?
What new information did you incorporate into your decision
   making as the scene unfolded?

At the end of the conversation, the sergeant flipped the hierarchical script and asked:

Do you have any feedback for me on my performance during
   this interview?

There was no lecturing, no blaming. At the end of the study, the officers who participated in the meeting reported feeling that what they had said mattered to the supervisor—that they had voice—which research shows is a key element in procedural justice working well. The officers in the other group didn't have this conversation, which allowed the researchers to measure the effects of the discussion. When after a month and a half the behavior of the officers in both groups was evaluated, those who had been called in were 33 percent less likely to be involved in incidents involving force. They were also more likely to issue citations rather than make an arrest, suggesting that they had prevented incidents from escalating.

These officers were also more actively engaged with the public, reporting three to four times more stops in the week after the conversation than the officers in the other group. That might seem to indicate they were overzealous, but in fact, contrary to popular wisdom, this was the kind of more vigorous involvement that most members of minority communities in urban settings want from the police. They want a strong and engaged police presence, just not an authoritarian one. This interpretation of the increase in stops is backed up by the finding that these officers were also a little more likely to be involved in rendering some form of assistance to the community, such as helping someone who had fallen.

Because we trust people that we come to feel warmly about, another strategy to strengthen procedural justice is for the police to forge positive relationships with the community. But because of budget cuts, many community relationship positions in police forces, such as the one my friend Sally now has, have been eliminated. These jobs focus officers on building bonds with the communities. Officers attend county meetings, participate in neighborhood watches, work with youth groups, negotiate disputes between neighbors, visit schools and community fairs. When money gets tight, these are frequently the first positions to be cut because they are deemed to be less essential than intervening on crime. But research suggests that community relationships may be among the police department's most precious resources for crime prevention.

Why do procedurally just processes matter so much? One answer is because they are affirming. Tom Tyler suggests that they communicate to citizens they are seen and valued in the eyes of the authority. In fact, as Matthew Lieberman points out in his book, *Social,* fair treatment, like all social rewards, activates much of the same reward circuitry of the brain as does candy. Some of us grow accustomed to fair treatment and notice its importance only when it is withheld. For all of us who have had the experience of being treated unfairly—by an officer, a teacher, even a salesperson—we know how galling and unjust it can feel. It can feel as though we are being seen as unworthy of the respect that a human being is entitled to. But in response to fair treatment, citizens embrace the norms of their community more. In one study to assess this effect, perpetrators of domestic violence proved less likely to commit another act of violence in their household if they felt that the police had treated them with procedural justice.

A story from a colleague illustrates the power that authorities can have as sources of affirmation that put people on a better path. My colleague's niece had broken the law several times, ultimately leading to prison time. When she was released, she violated the terms of her parole, which landed her back in prison. She seemed trapped in a repeating cycle. But, at her next sentencing, the judge told her, "I want the best for you and I believe in your ability to have a successful life." Because the young woman had grown accustomed to judges speaking harshly to her, his words had a powerful affirming effect. He boosted her confidence in her ability to take control of her life, which she did.

A 2021 experiment by Jason Okonofua and his colleagues provides scientific evidence that such affirming communication with offenders can have strong effects. They created a thirty-minute training module that encouraged parole officers to empower and affirm their parolees by building respectful relationships with them. Ten months later, fewer of their parolees had been arrested again, relative to the parolees of officers who had received a control version of the training. Perspective-getting is a key part of the communication process. Young offenders returning to school from juvenile detention face many challenges. But when they heard stories describing youth who had overcome similar challenges, and then shared their own stories of hope and struggle with a trusted adult at their school, their recidivism rates to juvenile detention plummeted.

All this research suggests that personal responsibility, a bedrock value of a democratic society, takes root more readily when people feel that they are accorded a full measure of dignity and respect—when they feel they belong.

The great promise of these various strategies for improving relations between the police and the public has been demonstrated by the city of Camden, New Jersey. Camden had been known as the "city that hope forgot." It was one of the most economically disadvantaged and crime-ridden cities in the United States, with a crime rate in 2012 greater than that of many developing nations. But thanks to reforms instituted in the methods of policing and in other means of community improvement, which have been celebrated by both the political left and right, the city is revitalized and crime is down. The reforms were supported by the Republican governor of the time, Chris Christie, and they drew on decades of scholarship conducted by both liberal and conservative academics. (A guidebook for law enforcement and community stakeholders is available at https://www.niot.org/cops/camdensturn.)

As portrayed in the documentary *Camden's Turn*, the process began with hiring an inspired and innovative new police chief, J. Scott Thomson. He recounts that the force had to launch a "political campaign to overcome years of mistrust." Thomson, who is white, showed an acute sensitivity about the experiences and perspectives of the city's largely black population. The people had every reason to distrust the police, he said, because many had seen officers use excessive force or respond to community problems with indifference. In addition, he acknowledged the long history of police brutality toward black people and argued that while today's officers are not responsible "for" the past, they are responsible "to" it. What cops have done in the past shapes how they're seen now. One of the responsibilities of an officer, he asserted, is to act in ways that are aware of this history and to do their part to rebrand what it means to be a police officer.

To address the psychology contributing to bad relations, Thomson arranged workshops to teach officers about implicit bias and how it can lead to discriminatory treatment of people of color. He also instituted many new mandates for day-to-day policing. One dramatic change was that he demanded quicker response to calls about incidents, and the average response time plummeted from an hour to less than five minutes. He had an explicit focus on changing the role and identity of the police officer from "warrior" to "guardian." Officers were trained to avoid tactics that escalated the tension and thereby endangered themselves and others, and they were taught to see their objective as bringing "peace to the situation." It's critical for officers to stay safe and always be mentally ready for danger. But some of the behaviors of police had inflamed confrontations and made them more dangerous for everyone involved. Behaviorally, there was much they could do in the spirit of situation-crafting to prevent any encounter from spinning out of control.

Officers were also instructed to conduct engaged community policing, getting out of their squad cars and walking the sidewalks, talking to residents to learn about their concerns, which facilitated perspective-getting. Thomson told them, "I don't measure the number of arrests you make and I don't care how many tickets you write. We want you to build relationships." Patrolling this way, even during winter storms, officers became familiar faces to community members. The department also held "meet-the-police" fairs where officers played touch football with the kids and served ice cream, and officers visited elementary schools to read to children. Thomson understood that by nurturing children's sense of being seen as valuable members of the community, he could deter them from beginning to engage in criminal activity. He also set up a mentoring program in which ex-convicts advised youth about staying straight.

Superordinate goals, another key to creating belonging, were continually reinforced. The cops and the community did not see one another in Us-vs.-Them terms as much as they had before, and instead they began to see one another as collaborators in common cause. Thomson spearheaded improvements in the neighborhood environments as well, such as the demolition of abandoned buildings and creation of better public spaces. He reclaimed the parks from drug dealers and establishing baseball leagues for kids. He understood that if improving the life of the community was seen by both officers and the public as a superordinate goal, one that they must collaborate on to achieve, the Us-vs.-Them thinking on both sides would give way to the trust required for substantial change. He was, in short, a brilliant situation-crafter.

Admittedly, there has yet to be a formal scholarly evaluation of Camden's "turn," and evaluation of the causal impact of such community-wide interventions is always a speculative enterprise. Yet, together with the other research reviewed here, the Camden story illustrates the possibility of integrating wise interventions into a coherent approach to policing within an entire community. The hoped-for improvement took time, but over the five years of Thomson's tenure, violent crime was cut by 21 percent. Homicide alone was down by 28 percent. Official records suggest that high school graduation went up and that more businesses opened. The whole tone of life in the city improved, with a new vibrancy. Kids played in the parks, and community members were out walking and talking to one another.

The story of Camden attests that even in what seem hopeless circumstances, thoughtful situation-crafting can catalyze substantial social transformation by attending to everyone's need for belonging.

Chapter 13

Belonging and Our Politics

Situation-Crafting to Bridge Partisan Divides

IN MY FIRST YEAR OF COLLEGE I HAD A ROOMMATE, HANK, whose views about political issues were diametrically opposed to mine. That's in part because I grew up in a suburb of New Jersey, while he grew up in rural Georgia. After an initial period of feeling uncertain about my own belonging at our college, Cornell University, I came to feel at home, while Hank told me he still didn't feel like he belonged. He was annoyed, for example, by students who wore artificially faded jeans. He, by contrast, wore the genuine deep blue article; any fading was earned. When one student decided to adorn himself with a Davy Crockett raccoon hat, Hank took great offense. The term "cultural appropriation" wasn't in currency yet, but he thought it the height of egoism for a Northeastern suburbanite to support the killing of a creature for a fashion statement. His belonging uncertainty was exacerbated by his political orientation. He was deeply conservative, while the general culture of the Cornell campus was quite liberal.

I had many long nights of little sleep after marathon bouts we would get into over political issues. Typically they'd begin with us both working away at our desks, when one of us would make a comment, perhaps provoked by a text we were reading. Hank usually took issue with the views of an author he was reading, such as a biologist writing that homosexuality existed in lower animals. I once naively asked if he was going to the pro-choice rally the next day. The initial comment would spark a conflagration, with our battles sometimes becoming so heated that a crowd of onlookers would gather in our room to gawk. From gay rights to abortion to poverty to race, I found Hank's political views appalling. He argued, for example, that it was okay for him to use the N-word because what the word meant for him was different from what it meant for black people and most others. He also argued that homosexuality should be outlawed because it was unnatural.

I felt I should have been able to trounce him in arguments, but I had the devil of a time trying to convince him his views were wrong-headed. He was extraordinarily well-spoken and knowledgeable. He had been a star on his high school debate team, and it showed. He had also thought his opinions through, which, I was discovering to my horror, was more than I could say for myself. Hank would usually handily pick my arguments to pieces, and I usually lost our debates despite what I was sure was my moral rectitude. Once, I seethed with so much fury that I was utterly tongue-tied and just glared wordlessly at him, feeling I might like to punch him.

The saving grace of this situation was that Hank was a kind person, and he always made friendly gestures after our arguments to restore our relationship. This was, again, more than I could say about myself. I took our arguments personally and held a grudge. At the time, I was frustrated by my failure to sway his views, but now I see our contests as formative in the development of my political awareness. I begrudgingly learned that many of my strongest convictions were based not on any rational argument I could articulate at the time but on spur-of-the-moment rationalizations I would use to defend them. I also learned that, as much research has shown, people don't generally change their political views in response to arguments, at least not without the right conditions prevailing in the discussion. Once in a while, I would make a devastatingly good argument to Hank, and he'd concede a point. But his overall views didn't budge.

Given the heated partisanship that has been escalating since the mid-1990s and the truculence with which so many people have held firm to extreme and ill-founded views, the notion that people simply don't change their views, particularly on political issues, has gained widespread currency. Research in social psychology has long shown the confirmation bias leads people to disregard information that's contradictory to their views and even to become more wedded to them. Social psychology has also made important contributions to understanding this troubling phenomenon, starting many decades ago.

In 1977, Lee Ross, along with Charles Lord and Mark Lepper, conducted a study that still stands as the most powerful demonstration of the resistance and polarization that people demonstrate in response to data that oppose their views. Proponents and opponents of the death penalty reviewed a mixed bag of evidence related to the efficacy of capital punishment as a policy for deterring people from murder. The participants reviewed scientific evidence on both sides of the issue, which had been carefully crafted to be equivalent in methodological rigor. In fact, the studies were fabricated, so the researchers could cleverly vary whether the same study methodology produced a supportive finding or not. The result? Confirmation bias. Both sides evaluated the studies that supported their own views as superior. They also poked holes in the methodology of the same study they would have praised had it supported their views. More perversely still, the participants then reported that the body of evidence as a whole had convinced them that they were even more right about capital punishment than they had initially thought. Because of this bias, simply exposing people to alternative views, for instance by altering their news feed on social media, is unlikely to have the hoped-for effects. Research suggests it may even entrench people in their views. In spite of their hefty price tags, for instance, political campaigns in U.S. elections have virtually no effect on voters' choices.

In a similar study, Michael Schwalbe led a study in my lab to explore how people's views of the 2016 presidential election might affect their susceptibility to fake news. We recruited over 1,500 liberals and conservatives, making sure that the sample mirrored the demographics of the U.S. population. We presented the participants with news stories about Donald Trump, some of which were pro-Trump and some anti-Trump.

Some of these stories were true ("Two years in, Trump holds stock market bragging rights") and some were fake, even outlandishly so ("Trump Attended Private Halloween Gala with Sex Orgies Dressed as Pope" and "Trump Beats Grandmaster Chess Champion Magnus Carlsen"). We asked our study participants to estimate the likelihood that each story was true or false and found that both groups showed roughly the same degree of bias, with conservatives much more gullible about any good news about Trump, fake or not, and liberals much more skeptical, fake or not. In fact, participants judged fake news that supported their views to be more true than real news that challenged their views.

Susceptibility to fake news proved just as strong among the most educated as among the least. What's more, when asked which of the stories they were likely to share, both liberals and conservatives were more likely to share the news that supported their views with friends on social media, thereby contributing to the spread of fake news. Our minds are not impartial information processors. To borrow a metaphor from the social psychologist Arie Kruglanski, they are more like mills that crush the grist of our everyday lives into confirmation that "our way" is the "right way."

Such findings seem to justify despair about the possibility of tamping down partisanship and finding common ground for solving our social problems, especially when many other powerful factors have exacerbated political polarization in the United States and around the world. For instance, in the United States, the winner-take-all electoral system encourages Us-vs.-Them thinking. The siloing of the media into partisan outlets has played a major part, too. As social psychologists have discovered, our minds tend to be more strongly drawn to negative information, which has motivated increasingly rancorous and fear-mongering coverage, both in the mainstream broadcast media and on social media. Research also shows that we tend to believe we are more objective in our assessments of such information than we actually are. The combination of biased and outright fallacious coverage on the one hand, and our illusion of personal objectivity on the other, is toxic. Schwalbe's study found that the two factors that predicted greater susceptibility to believing fake news were consuming more one-sided media *and* believing that one's political views are not swayed by misinformation and other biasing influences.

To understand how to address political division, we need to understand its causes. Leo Tolstoy seems to have understood something deep about why political disputes so often lead to hardening of views rather than changes in perspectives. When one of the characters in his novel *Anna Karenina* asks another why people hotly argue when "no one ever convinces anyone," the answer given is "because one can't make out what one's opponent wants to prove." Indeed, the reason people argue for their views is often more to prove they are upstanding members of their chosen political "tribe" than to prove their views are correct. Their fealty is more strongly given to their group than to their views. This is generally true even for people who can marshal an arsenal of well-constructed arguments in defense of their views; like all of us, they may be unaware of what truly motivates them. This group fealty is why exhortations to think more critically or to get more informed don't change people's views and often backfire. Even established political experts and social scientists display a strong confirmation bias when they confront evidence that, as is often the case, their predictions were wrong. This problem is so recognized and widespread that the United States intelligence community has worked with social psychologists to develop training modules to instruct their analysts in mental biases.

Fortunately, social psychology research has provided powerful insight into how we can tamp down the fires of division. As we've seen, a major force driving polarization, and the dehumanization and demonization that have accompanied it, is the desire to belong. If we want to open up psychological room for understanding and bridge-building across political lines, we have to acknowledge that people become so truculent about their views largely because they find opposing views threatening to their sense of belonging and, by extension, their sense of self. What's more, this sense of threat is not simply irrational. For one thing, it's in part rooted in biology. Neuroscientific research shows that when people read statements that challenge a long-held political belief, their physical threat response ratchets up, indicated by increased activity in the amygdala. By contrast, it appears that when they arrive at conclusions that rationalize away disconfirming evidence, regions of the brain associated with reward or reinforcement activate. Our biological threat and reward systems reinforce fealty to group views.

In addition, political partisans tend to react vehemently toward members of their group who express dissident views. I recall a news account of a longtime member of a local Democratic group who was a Trump supporter in the 2016 election. Though he'd been a leading participant in the group for many years and had deep friendships with many members, he was ousted. The vilification of the Republican secretary of state of Georgia by some in his party after he refuted claims of voting fraud in the 2020 presidential election was a particularly pronounced example of the ostracism faced by those who dissent from their political tribe.

Perhaps it's not hard to understand why people dig in so firmly about their views in the face of even crystal-clear contrary evidence. Being outcast from our tribe would once have presented a physical threat to survival, and our brains still seem to see it that way. As a form of self-protection, we go through conscious and unconscious mental gymnastics to keep ourselves in line.

To probe how the desire to belong drives the defiance of rational argumentation, I conducted a series of studies that laid bare this process of rationalization. After recruiting liberals and conservatives from across various college campuses, I brought them to the lab to participate in what they thought was a memory study of news media but was really a study of political attitudes, a necessary ruse to disguise the purpose of the study lest they behave unnaturally. One newspaper article they read described a welfare policy and whether it had garnered support from Republican or Democratic lawmakers. Although the articles appeared authentic, unbeknownst to the participants they were fabricated and their content carefully crafted. For one group of participants, Democrats were reported to support the policy and

Republicans were reported to oppose it. For another group of participants, the positions were reversed. For a third group, no information
on their party's position was given. On top of that, for one group of
participants, the policy was said to provide generous support to the
poor for housing, food, and education, and for another group that support was described as minimal. We then asked people for their own
position on the welfare policy, under the guise that "your attitudes
could affect your memory of the newspaper content."

Republicans should have supported the minimal benefits policy
and Democrats the generous version, if they were loyal to their party's
ideology and positions. And they did when they had no information
about what their party thought. But regardless of the description of
the policy, people conformed their views to those they were told their
party espoused, even when those views in fact went against their party's ideology. This happened even when the two policies were presented
side by side. The students were so dedicated to supporting the policy
their party had supposedly advocated that many were willing to write
extensive endorsement letters to a public policy think tank.

The power of the human mind to rationalize such contradictions was
demonstrated by another part of the study. Democrats who supported
the "harsh" policy, when queried about why, wrote about the importance for the poor to learn to help themselves, portraying the policy
as in keeping with the Democrats' value of providing opportunity to
the poor. Republicans who were told that their party supported the
"generous" policy justified their support as due to a professed Republican belief in humanitarianism. Neither party said they supported the
policy because their party did. In fact, they adamantly denied that.
Even under conditions of complete anonymity, they rated the views of
their political party as the least influential determinant of their political views, far behind the factual content of the policy and their own
moral principles. This result shows how unconscious the process of
conformity to party views can be.

Numerous studies have replicated the power of "party cues" to
polarize us, including with large representative national samples:

for example, in the United States, regarding the views of liberals and conservatives toward environmental policy, farm subsidies, and COVID-19 policy; and in the Netherlands, regarding citizens' views on immigration policy. In international politics, too, group allegiance often trumps policy content. Israelis supported a peace plan if they thought it was authored by Israeli representatives, even when in fact it was proposed by the Palestinian delegation at bilateral peace talks in 1993. As the neuroscientist Matthew Lieberman has written, our minds are like double agents, secretly working for our group. Whichever way our group wants us to fall in line, to a surprising extent we will.

Political analyst Ezra Klein, author of *Why We're Polarized*, wrote an article about these findings entitled "The Depressing Psychological Theory That Explains Washington." But before we commit the Fundamental Attribution Error and say, "People are so stupid," we must understand that much of the way groups influence us is by shaping our perceptions of the world. Imagine that you're living in occupied territory, and although you want peace, you're fearful of being exploited. You read that a peace plan provides for a "security force." Do you think "security force" means a small police presence or a large, oppressive military force? It would be reasonable to infer the first if you learn your group supports the plan and the second if you learn your group opposes it. The extent to which our judgments of reality should be "top-down" and shaped by our group or "bottom-up" and shaped by the facts alone is a difficult question.

What *is* disturbing is that when our judgments are top-down, we are seldom aware of the extent to which they are. As a result, we dismiss the other side as biased and believe that *we* are the objective ones. And while extreme conformity may have benefits in a homogenous setting where we live among only one tribe, it's a recipe for division and even violence in a society where many groups must live together. If we choose to reject a policy that's better than any our own party would ever put forward, just because we think our adversaries proposed it, what will we ever agree on?

Stealthy as our minds can be in duping us, some ways of undercutting this unconscious bias have proved effective. Social psychology has provided insights into when and why people do sometimes open their minds to information that contradicts their views. Research also shows that even if people don't change their views, they can be inspired to be respectful and even empathic toward those they've seen as wrong-headed and threatening.

I saw the possibility for people to open their minds and hearts and even to dramatically change their views through my experience with Hank. The year after we had been roommates, I went on a term abroad, and when I returned to Cornell, I bumped into Hank. He had a brighter smile than I remembered and seemed much happier. He told me that while I was away, he had joined a fraternity because he wanted to find a community of students he could feel at home with. During rush, he had found one fraternity that he liked a lot. The guys were friendly, he felt at ease with them, and they accepted him. A few weeks later, over dinner with his brothers, Hank started to talk about his views on homosexuality, and one of the brothers slammed down his silverware and stared at Hank. "You just condemned my whole life!" he said and left.

Hank was stunned. He hadn't known the brother was gay, and it turned out that a number of other brothers were as well.

"I thought of you many times," Hank said to me. The arguments I had made to him that had failed to move his mind one tiny bit had started to resonate. He talked to the brother he had offended, and he gained understanding about the hurt he had caused and about the hurtfulness that homophobia generally causes. His heart had opened up to the issue. Then his mind opened too.

Hank was still living in a dorm, and one day he noticed that a flyer announcing a gay rights meeting that he had seen in the bathroom had been ripped down. Hank told me he still didn't support gay rights at the time of this incident, but he did support the right to free speech and he was adamantly anti-censorship. He asked around the dorm to find out who had torn the poster down and found out it was a guy I remembered as being quite sweet and funny. But he was in ROTC, the military scholarship program where, at the time, norms generally disfavored LGBTQ people. Hank talked to the guy, and their conversation turned ugly. The guy threw Hank against a wall and hissed a threat at him, with his fist cocked back and aimed at his face. I was stunned that Hank had taken on the role of defender of gay rights. By the end of his junior year, he was openly making many of the same arguments about gay rights that I had once made to him. His views had changed not because of those arguments, though, but because he had come to identify with a group whose members he cared about and that advocated and lived by norms of tolerance. He was also affirmed by those in the group, which, as we'll see, is a catalyst for opening people's minds.

The lesson I learned from Hank's conversion was that people will sometimes change their views, even about deeply held political issues, not due to the rules of logic but to those of psyche-logic. Hank's fraternity offered him a strong sense of belonging, which gave him the sympathy and the security to open his mind. The change also took time. A takeaway is that *if* we want to build bridges across partisan divides, we must find ways to alleviate threat to people's sense of belonging that's triggered by considering opposing views.

One way of doing so is providing some affirmation to those with opposing views. Working with Joshua Aronson and Claude Steele, I designed a series of studies to see if the perceived threat to self of political confrontation could be alleviated by allowing people to affirm a cherished value they held in some altogether different domain. Following Lee Ross and colleagues' classic study, we recruited proponents and opponents of capital punishment and brought them to our lab. Using the values-affirmation procedure, we first asked them to select a value from a list, which we had carefully tailored to exclude the domain of politics so that participants could center their self-worth beyond the identity that was being challenged. Then we asked them to write about why that value was important to them. Next they read a three-page scientific article that opposed their views on capital punishment, which was identical in almost every respect for proponents and opponents, referring to the same studies and methods of research.

The one difference was the conclusion. For opponents, the article contradicted their view, arguing that capital punishment saved lives by deterring would-be killers. For proponents, it suggested the opposite. We asked another group of participants to write about an unimportant value and why it might be important to someone else—a good writing exercise but not one that affirmed them—and then they read the same article. The value-affirmed participants rated the death-penalty article, despite a conclusion they disagreed with, as more convincing and the author as more reasonable and informed than did the nonaffirmed participants. (All participants were thoroughly debriefed at the end of the study.)

A follow-up experiment—using a more powerful self-affirmation in which people received positive feedback on their ability to be sensitive to the emotions of others—showed that both groups, once affirmed, became more moderate in their attitudes toward capital punishment. The percentage of participants who put their attitude roughly at the midpoint of the attitude scale increased by 22 raw percentage points more in the affirmed group than in the nonaffirmed group.

Since our research was published in 1999, the effect of self-affirmation on openness to opposing information and views has been replicated over and over. In a 2007 study, my colleagues and I showed that partisans of the abortion debate were more willing to find common ground in a negotiation of abortion legislation, such as whether or not to restrict abortions during the third trimester, if they had first completed a values affirmation. They were also less likely to denigrate the other side as biased and unreasonable. In 2011, Sabina Čehajić-Clancy and colleagues showed that Israeli citizens who completed a values affirmation were more willing to acknowledge what Ross has referred to as "hard truths" about Israel's treatment of Palestinians, such as the possibility that atrocities in the Israeli-Palestinian conflict were committed by both sides, the need for a two-state solution, and their own often-suppressed feelings of guilt over what has happened to the Palestinians. Under the lead of Kevin Binning, in 2015, my colleagues and I found that American citizens who completed a values-affirmation activity were more likely to base their evaluations of the American president on the merits of his performance—hard economic data—rather than his popularity in the polls.

A real-world example of the power of values affirmation to deescalate tensions between political adversaries and to help find some common ground comes from the 1978 Camp David Accords, as related by President Jimmy Carter in the book *Conversations with Carter*. He had arranged the summit, in which he brought the prime minister of Israel, Menachem Begin, and the president of Egypt, Anwar Sadat, to Camp David in Maryland for a week of negotiations. The odds of a peace deal seemed remote. Egypt wanted Israel to return land and political prisoners, which Israel adamantly opposed, and Israel wanted Egypt to promise a permanent truce, about which Egypt was reluctant. Negotiations turned sour, and Prime Minister Begin packed his bags. But Carter caught him at the elevator.

Pulling out a folder, Carter removed nine photographs of him, Begin, and Sadat together at the summit. He handed them to Begin, telling him they were intended as mementos for his nine grandchildren. On the back of each, Carter had inscribed the name of one of Begin's grandchildren. As Begin looked at the photographs and said nothing for a while, his eyes teared up. Then he read aloud the names of each grandchild and said, "There must be a way. There is a way. For our children, for the next generation." Begin returned to negotiations. By week's end, he and Sadat shook hands over the historic Camp David Accords.

Carter had reminded Begin of his deep commitment to the values of family and making the world better for our progeny.

How might we as individuals provide affirmation to those from across the political divide to build better relations and perhaps even find common ground? For one thing, we can state our belief in shared values, such as family, the world the next generation of children will inherit, and caring for friends and community. We can avoid implying that their views are based on either ignorance or bias and ask people in a genuinely curious manner about what their views are and why they hold them—which helps to make people feel seen and heard. And we can listen respectfully to their answers. Our attempts at perspective-getting may surprise us. In many cases, we'll discover that we disagree not so much because we and our adversaries hold different values or have different views on the same issue. Rather, it's because the very issue, as we perceive it, is different. When liberals and conservatives fight about social security, welfare, and abortion rights, they often fail to realize that they are proceeding from different factual assumptions about what the social problem is and what the policies being considered actually are. By perspective-getting, we can better identify the sources of our disagreements and work through them.

We can also be mindful about the language we use, sharpening our skill at "perspective-giving." I can feel the sense of threat rising in my body when, in the middle of a political conversation, the other person takes a dramatic pause and emits one of these tropes: "the fact of the matter is," "let me tell you something," or "the reality is." Especially off-putting is "you don't get it," which implies there is an "it" floating out in space just above us, like a Platonic archetype, for all with clear eyes to behold. So many of us fall into such rhetoric because our minds blind us to our own biases and because it's satisfying, triggering the brain's reward system.

The result is that we too often extol people who support the views of the group we've chosen to align with and disparage those who don't. If we let down our guard and show respect for, or at least interest in, others' beliefs and arguments—responding with comments like "I see what you're saying and I hadn't seen it that way" or "That's interesting, can you tell me more about why you think that?"—they will be more likely to let their guard down. Of course, like any strategy, it's not always appropriate. Sometimes the positions we are arguing for or against are ones of moral or even mortal urgency, and any indication of agreement with opposing views would be inappropriate. But at the very least, we can begin many more of our conversations with curiosity and openness, and hope that those we're speaking with respond well.

This isn't to say we should necessarily change our own views or in all cases express them as matters of opinion. They may well be founded on solid facts and based on personal experience, as are the views of LGBTQ or people of color about pervasive discriminatory treatment of them and abuse at the hands of police officers. The point is that the best way we can open others' minds to appreciating our views is to listen respectfully and to qualify our expression of our views. In the case of discussing discrimination, for example, blanket statements are less effective than language like "I firmly believe that discrimination is still widespread because I have experienced it personally, as have many of my friends and family members."

When it comes to many partisan issues, research again spearheaded by Michael Schwalbe showed that the language we use can lessen political polarization and animosity. Schwalbe recruited an online sample of about seven hundred Democrats and Republicans, split more or less evenly between the two groups. The day before the first presidential debate between Donald Trump and Hillary Clinton in September 2016, one group of participants was encouraged to see their own and other people's political positions as matters of opinion. First, they were asked a series of questions, with each one asking them what they *think and feel* about American voters and to rate how reasonable, gullible, and biased they *thought* supporters of their own and the other candidate were *in their opinion*. Next, they read a blog post, which we had written, expressing a fairly well-informed position contrary to their own but casting it as a matter of opinion, amply using phrases like "I think," "I feel," and "I believe." We called this the "opinion-framing" group.

For a control group of participants, we had them answer the same set of questions about American voters but without the language specifying that we were asking them what they thought or felt. Then they read the same blog but with the opinion phrases deleted.

When we asked both groups to express their impressions of the blogger, they saw the blogger as equally extreme in his views. But members of the opinion-framing group were less likely to attribute his beliefs to self-interest or to his buying into propaganda and misinformation. That's important because what provokes demonization of those across the partisan divide isn't just *what* we think those people believe but *why* we think they believe it. If we think they've carefully considered issues and come to their own conclusions, we're less hostile toward them. Indeed, we found in our study that the opinion-framing group even rated the blogger as more reasonable and less evil.

We then instructed the participants to watch the first presidential debate the next day. When we later asked them about their views of that debate, the opinion-framing group was less likely to think their preferred candidate had won than did the control group. Three weeks later, after the final presidential debate, Democrats' and Republicans' tendency to polarize in their views of the two candidates, and to denigrate those with opposing views, was smaller among the opinion-framing group than the control group.

In one final component of the study, we asked all the participants to pick a free book from a selection that included books that put each candidate in a positive light, such as Donald Trump's *The Art of the Deal* and Hillary Clinton's *Hard Choices*, as well as ones that put each in a negative light, like *Trump Revealed* or the anti-Clinton *Crisis of Character*. People in the opinion-framing group were more likely to pick a book that presented a positive picture of the opposition candidate than were people in the control group.

Most promising was a change in how the two groups of participants expressed their point of view about the two presidential candidates. Some people expressed their views more as statements of incontrovertible fact. Others expressed their views more subjectively, using words like "I feel" and "I thought." People in the opinion-framing group expressed their views more subjectively and less as statements of fact than did people in the control group—even though we hadn't overtly suggested they do so and even though their exposure to the opinion-framing intervention had happened weeks earlier. I think this is a good indication that the more of us who express our views as opinions, the more others will be encouraged to do so, helping to mitigate defensiveness and polarization.

I am not advocating that we all stop trying to bring the beliefs of those with opposing views closer to our own. That is one of the foundational enterprises of a democratic citizenry. What I am arguing is that we will make the most headway and cause the least flare-up of polarization if we coach ourselves to be genuinely curious and respectful in seeking others' views, to acknowledge that our own are also matters of opinion, and to emphasize areas of common values. Much of the time, we can simply express our opinions more accurately and honestly by acknowledging our uncertainty.

The power of combining these approaches in discussing political issues was demonstrated in one of the most heartening studies I know of, conducted in 2017 by political scientists David Broockman and Joshua Kalla, on a wise intervention called deep canvassing. Working with LGBT Center and SAVE, two Los Angeles–based organizations, they trained and dispersed a team of canvassers to knock on the doors of voters in one of the most politically conservative regions of Florida, Miami-Dade County, and discuss laws to protect transgender people from discrimination. Conversations about controversial issues can, of course, go horribly wrong. But true to the origins of the word "conversation," which means "to turn with," these conversations were carefully crafted to be collaborative.

The researchers recruited about 1,800 residents from a list of registered voters and randomly split them into two groups that were then visited by the canvassers. With the control group, canvassers conducted a ten-minute conversation about environmental issues. For the other group, they conducted a conversation about transgender people and political protections for them. This second group, and not the first, showed large and lasting increases in their support for transgender people.

You might think that for any intervention to have had such power, it must have presented residents with powerful arguments. But the most noteworthy feature of the conversations was what they lacked. The canvassers made few direct arguments. Though it was clear that the canvassers supported transgender rights, they never pushed their views on the voter. They didn't speak from a superior position.

Instead, they first put the voters in an empowered role. You could face an important decision, the voters were told, in an upcoming election: You will have the option of voting to overturn or uphold a law on the books that protects the rights of transgender people. The canvassers then asked them for their opinion on the issue. The canvassers were trained not to express judgment or any pleasure or displeasure at the voters' answers but simply to listen carefully. They asked questions such as "Can you say more about that?" and they never used the kind of "Let me tell you how it is" language we discussed. The canvassers also tried to establish a connection. If they wore sunglasses, they removed them. They maintained eye contact, smiled when appropriate, and kept their bodies oriented toward the voter rather than away, which research suggests promotes connection and learning. They allowed the voter the space to express and explore their thoughts, and they listened with authentic curiosity, making the voters feel affirmed and that their perspective mattered. The canvassers had been trained to "make a leap of faith" that there would be something in every voter that they would like or find interesting.

Next, the canvassers showed a short video that presented two sides of the debate over transgender rights, including an actual transgender person who talked about his struggles.

The canvassers then asked the voters for their reaction to the video, followed by this question: "The reality is judgment happens to everyone at some point, and it hurts. Can you tell me about a time when you have felt judged or were treated differently for who you are?" If the voter declined, the canvasser asked if the voter had ever witnessed this kind of judgment directed at someone else and how it made them feel. These questions take the approach to building empathy that Ronaldo Mendoza designed and tested in the 1990s of having people recall analogous situations from their own lives in which they experienced similar emotions.

Almost every voter shared a story. If the voter hesitated, the canvasser would share a story from their own life. Some of the conversations became intimate, with both people showing vulnerability. The voters were then asked if the experience they discussed gave them a window onto transgender people's experiences. Many said yes. One voter, a former military man, who hadn't sympathized with transgender people at the start of the conversation, relayed his experience of being rejected for jobs because he had post-traumatic stress disorder. He felt upset that others jumped to conclusions about his entire character based on this single fact about him, and he answered that he now understood how a transgender person might also feel if rejected for a job because of one aspect of their identity. By sharing stories and being vulnerable with one another, the voter and canvasser became a two-person group reminiscent of the democratic discussion groups Kurt Lewin had created.

It was only after the conversation that the canvassers explained why they personally thought that transgender-inclusive laws need to be legal, but they did not foist their views on the voters. They simply expressed their perspectives, beginning with the two words "I think."

At the end of the conversation, the voters were asked, "Now that we've been talking about this, if you were to vote tomorrow to include transgender people in our nondiscrimination law, would you vote in favor or against it?" The purpose of this last question was to lock in any change through a bottom-line statement of overall support, what Lewin called "freezing." Many said the conversation had changed their views. But more impressive is that surveys sent to them three months later by a third party found that these participants continued to express less antagonism toward transgender people, were more resistant to anti-transgender propaganda, and felt more supportive of nondiscrimination laws to protect transgender people, relative to the group of residents who had talked about environmental issues.

Broockman and Kalla have since replicated their findings using other issues. For instance, they have created empathy for undocumented immigrants by encouraging people to share stories of times when they were in a vulnerable position and someone showed them compassion. Hearing stories of the struggles of victims of hate is more transformative than being presented with abstract arguments for inclusion. Such stories can help us to feel ourselves into others' experiences, so to speak, by highlighting universal human feelings and values. Spending time with people we've viewed negatively can also be eye-opening. After Spencer Cox, Utah's governor, spent time with transgender youth, he reversed his position on anti-transgender legislation, publicly stating, "When you spend time with these kids, it changes your heart in important ways."

Another example of the power of generating empathy to bridge political divides comes from the resolution of one of the longest-running political conflicts of the twentieth century. Lee Ross, who has done important work in brokering peace deals, worked with the group Community Dialogue in the 1990s to help them achieve peace in Ireland.

They brought together a diverse group of middle-class and working-class representatives from both sides of the conflict, as well as police, politicians, and paramilitary figures who had committed terrorist acts. Their work contributed heavily to the signing of the Belfast Agreement, which brought an end to the violence in Northern Ireland.

Key to the process was that participants were asked to share their stories about how the conflict had affected them and their families. Unionists, who wanted to maintain political loyalty to Great Britain, explained how difficult it was to accept a fully Irish identity rather than a British one, and to forgo punishing those in the Irish Republican Army who had committed acts of terrorism but would become part of the new government. For the Nationalists, the practice allowed them to explain how difficult it was for them to forgo the dream of a United Ireland with majority rule, the dream that the heroes of their songs and stories had died for. Hearing those on both sides tell of their children, spouses, parents, and siblings who died or were disabled because of the conflict was another key part of the process. At the end of this ritual, both sides, Ross said, were more willing to accept the need to find a way to go forward without more violence.

To summarize, in any dialogue with political opponents:

◆ Affirm that you view them with dignity and see them as people of integrity. This can be conveyed verbally and nonverbally.

- Communicate your curiosity and interest in learning; a growth mindset encourages openness in yourself and others.
- Present your own views as opinions rather than facts.
- Use stories to capture the human dimension of the problem. Although we must be aware of the power of stories to mislead, they can help people achieve a fuller understanding of a problem than they can with facts and arguments alone.
- Ask questions about people's views and their reasons for them in a way that provokes reflection and awareness of contradictions in beliefs and values.
- Evoke empathy for the negative effects of policies and rhetoric that people support by asking if they've ever been made to feel the same way as victims, perhaps also asking if they would share their experiences.
- Talk to individuals away from the influence of their group. One-on-one conversations and discussions in small ad hoc groups of the sort Lewin created work better than debates and dialogues between preexisting groups.
- Make time for people to reflect on how the conversation has influenced them.
- When possible, engage in face-to-face conversation. One ingredient in deep canvassing and in many of the interventions used to bridge divides is that they feature in-the-flesh encounters. Body language and eye contact all say much about our warmth and regard. The emotion and warmth we convey in our voice can matter as much as the words we use, as any parent knows. In fact, research finds that people are less likely to denigrate those with opposing beliefs on polarizing political topics when they hear others explain their positions in their own voice rather than when they simply read a transcript of what others said.

But of course, sometimes we need to interact by text or over social media, in which case we must make extra effort to compensate for the absence of the nonverbal channel. Our emotions in this medium are often harder to read than we think, research suggests, especially in written text. As a result, exchanges can escalate into all-out verbal wars. Is there a better way? One researcher sent a "wise tweet" to Twitter users, all white men, who had a history of tweeting the N-word to other users. He devised several bots, ficti-tious Twitter users, to send messages out to these offend-ing users and found that the following message sent by a white Twitter user, ostensibly with hundreds of followers, was successful at bringing about a lasting reduction in rac-ist language: "Hey, man, just remember that there are real people who hurt when you harass them with that kind of language."

This isn't to suggest that we shouldn't call out racists, but it is to say that rather than jump in with an attack, we might begin our efforts at change by protecting people's belonging. We can do this, if not through the nonverbal channel, then through the words we use.

Confronting hard topics rather than avoiding them can be transfor-mative if we do so by carefully crafting the situation in these ways to open minds and hearts rather than putting others on the defensive. If we don't make others feel threatened, we may be astonished about the breakthroughs in understanding we can achieve.

Applying these principles takes practice. We will often fail. And sometimes, of course, attempts at empathy will leave us feeling demor-alized and ready to go on the attack or to give up on reconciliation. No doubt, such extreme steps are sometimes necessary. But the over-whelming theme of the research is that we are much too quick to go down this path. Oftentimes when we have the sense "people never change," it's because we have been using the same wrong keys to unlock a door or because the change has unfolded more slowly than we expect, as it had with Hank and me.

A number of organizations have developed programs to involve the public in healing political divisions that incorporate these lessons. One such group is People's Action, founded in the 1970s to combat the discriminatory practice of redlining used to keep black people from moving into predominantly white neighborhoods. As reported by Robert Kuttner in the *American Prospect*, in 2017 the organization launched another initiative that trained volunteers to go door to door in poor rural communities. They talked with white residents who had voted for Donald Trump in the 2016 election about the problems they were struggling with and whether they felt that the Trump administration's policies were helping them. The canvassers made it clear that they were advocates for the Democratic party, but they didn't impose their point of view. By asking the residents about their lives and listening thoughtfully, the canvassers affirmed them, helping them feel they were being seen with empathy and as an important member of the community. By asking good questions, the canvassers also steered the residents' attention to any "dissonance" between their political beliefs and the reality of whether the Trump administration's policies were actually meeting their needs.

The canvassers also encouraged residents to be full participants in the possibility and process of their own change, giving them the space to think through the questions they asked and make up their own minds. The canvassers were taught to move the conversation into a discussion of the common interests between the canvassers and the residents. Research into the effects of this deep canvassing suggests that 3 percent of the people canvassed, all of whom had previously said they were planning to vote again for Trump, instead voted for Joe Biden—which Kuttner points out was larger than Biden's margin of victory in the battleground states that decided the election.

Some organizations have focused on facilitating group conversations between Democrats and Republicans, as well as independents, to open their minds to one another's views and to combat hostility. One of these is Living Room Conversations, which provides a number of guides on its website to help hosts conduct "meaningful conversations

that foster connection with others" (https://livingroomconversations
.org/). They advise creating groups that consist of four to six people,
with three rounds of questions being asked of each participant. The
first round of questions draws on the research in values affirmation:

- What are your hopes and concerns for your family, community, and the country?
- What would your best friend say about who you are?
- What sense of purpose, mission, or duty guides you in
  your life?

The political scientist James Fishkin and his colleagues have hosted
warm but information-dense small-group discussions between liberals and conservatives, which they've shown dramatically decrease participants' animus toward the opposing party.

These interventions all bear a resemblance to the safe, democratic
forums that Kurt Lewin pioneered.

Any of us can choose to take part in one or another of these efforts.
We're likely to learn a good deal about those we've had trouble understanding, perhaps even helping to ease the roiling tensions in our community and across the country. But even in our day-to-day lives, we
can be catalysts for fostering civility and belonging. While we should
all work to change our institutions, including the media and our government, for the better, we can also take heart that through our own
words and actions in our daily encounters, we can reduce conflict in
our immediate lives and perhaps even inspire more open-mindedness
and compassion in others.

How We Can All Create Belonging

WHILE THE RESEARCH ON BELONGING UNCERTAINTY SHOWS how easily belonging can be undermined, the science of situation-crafting shows how empowered we all are to combat that uncertainty in ourselves and in others. Our lives are a series of situations, many not unlike Mary Ainsworth's "strange situation" in presenting challenges to our belonging. With the perspectives and tools introduced in this book, we can secure the sense of connection that emboldens us and others to face these challenges.

The power of the situation is a power we all share. To use this power well, we can work at being astute observers of situations. We can consider aspects of them that may be difficult for others, such as being the only one in a room who is a member of a particular group. We can become more attuned to the relations between people rather than so focused on the attributes within them. We must also be mindful about how situations may be triggering misperceptions and inappropriate reactions in us. Are we falling under the sway of a stereotype? Are we assuming we understand what's motivating someone's behavior? Are we acting defensively? We can gain some control over the situation, and especially of our own behavior in it, by being more aware of the forces shaping the situation and ourselves.

Social policy and systemic change are paramount to addressing the crisis of belonging. But we can also each make the most of the situations before us. We can all support belonging for others, and strengthen and protect our own belonging too, by devoting ourselves to situation-crafting. The more we apply the insights and methods introduced in this book, the more positive results we'll elicit in an empowering feedback loop. We can look for opportunities to practice every day, even in the smallest corners of social life.

A KEY STEP is cultivating an awareness of these **ways of thinking and behaving that support belonging.**

Fight the Fundamental Attribution Error (FAE).

To change a situation for the better, we need to see it for what it is. Keeping the power of the FAE in mind can help to mitigate impulsive tendencies to see people as intentionally offensive or threatening. We need to remember to consider the possible situational causes of others' behavior, which include aspects of the situation not as we perceive it but as they do. Then we are better positioned to change behavior in a positive way.

Get perspectives and cultivate empathy.

We can short-circuit our impulse to believe we perceive what others are thinking and feeling about their situation, themselves, and us by committing to asking rather than intuiting, followed by listening thoughtfully. When trying to empathize with people who have offended us, instead of imagining how we would act in their situation, we can ask them about their feelings, and then try to remember an analogous situation from our lives in which we felt or responded similarly.

Avoid being authoritarian.

We tend to think of authoritarians as arrogant and powerful political leaders. But more so than we like to admit, we can all be authoritarians in our day-to-day lives, assuming that "our way" is the "right way" and that those who disagree must be converted, vilified, or banished. Even when we are on the side of virtue, we win few hearts and minds with an authoritarian style. By reminding ourselves that trying to force people to change their views almost always backfires, we can instead act like the deep canvassers who have been so effective in opening minds. We can share our own stories and ask would-be adversaries to tell their own, affording all of us the psychic room to consider new perspectives.

This is not to say that we should always hold back on asserting our opinions or that we should always seek to avoid conflict. Some occasions merit forceful repudiation of views that have been expressed or of offensive, harmful behaviors that have been perpetrated. If someone has hurled a racial slur, responding in no uncertain terms that we find this behavior wrong is often appropriate. If we hear a classmate or colleague being berated or bullied, pointing out how wrong that treatment is may be the best thing to do. Such acts of resistance can set norms, a powerful driver of behavior. But we should work hard to express ourselves—even in such fraught situations—in a way that minimizes harm to the other person's belonging. That gives us the best chance of getting the point through to them.

Don't believe everything you think.

This quip from a bumper sticker, which traces back to ancient Taoist teachings, distills much of the wisdom on bias. Just because we think something or even see something doesn't make it true. We have an outsized faith in the value of our thoughts, feelings, and perceptions, treating them as diagnostic of what's *out there* in front of our eyes and failing to realize that they are often untrustworthy constructions of our mind. When we try to read people, we are often reading from our own scripts and stereotypes. When we judge, we are often giving too much credit to the emotions and impulses that float through our minds. When we debate, we often fail to see how our own views are shaped by powerful yet invisible influences, such as norms and pressures to conform. One way to stave off these biases is to be aware that we are capable of them.

Almost all of us have experienced the strange fact that the dreams we inhabit while asleep seem real, as absurd as they may become. Waking life differs from our dreamscapes in many ways, but it shares this one feature: the phenomenon of our mind simultaneously creating our perceptions and experiencing them as *real*. Once we are aware of the degree to which our minds create our reality even in waking life, we can become better positioned to question our perceptions and craft situations better aligned with our values.

Why you do it matters as much as what you do.

Any wise intervention depends for its effectiveness on what is perceived as motivating it. If students or workers think that the message "I believe in your ability to reach a higher standard" is just lip service to manipulate them rather than a reflection of actual belief in them, it won't work. What makes us feel most connected, research suggests, is the perception that we are being seen and responded to authentically. Wise interventions are tools to express a genuine belief, perspective, or desire, not ruses to manipulate. They are entry points into genuine connection, not substitutes for it. Research suggests, for instance, that values affirmations lose their effectiveness when people feel forced to do them or if they feel others are condescending to them. The message that "you need an affirmation to help you perform" can do more harm than providing no affirmation at all. What matters isn't just what we do, but how it's construed.

Years ago, as a college student, I was hoping to get to know someone in my dorm a bit better. I knocked on her door and presented her with a little clear plastic bag of colored candy wrapped with a ribbon. Unbeknownst to her, this gift was actually a wise intervention that had been devised by a professor I worked for, Alice Isen. She had shown that this small gift is a powerful induction of positive mood, which can be a bonding agent. I had intended the gift as a way of expressing my positive affect toward my fellow student. Indeed her eyes lit up, and a smile spread across her face. Then, to impress her, I explained that the gift was a scientifically proven way to induce a positive mood. It was as if I had hit a false note in a melody. All the happiness drained from her face. She shrugged, said thanks, and shut the door.

This little anecdote conveys how the *why* behind what we do matters as much as, if not more than, the *what*. The lesson also applies to the wise interventions we provide for ourselves: It's not so much what we do but why we do them that gives us a sense of purpose and belonging in our day-to-day lives, a major contributor to well-being and health.

Think about timing.

We often do the right things at the wrong time. Criticism, affirmations, advice, and assurances all have their place, but *when* we give them matters just as much as whether we give them. Of all the times to support belonging, the beginning of a challenge or transition is often the most effective. At the beginning, processes can be altered. But once their consequences have accumulated, trajectories can be much harder to change.

Navigate social traffic with eyes wide open.

Keep in mind the potential to cause a social accident, no matter how good our intentions. When my father taught me to drive, he'd continually tell me that the driver's most important ally isn't a particular skill, but being alert. If you spot trouble coming, he'd say, or anticipate its potential given circumstantial road conditions, you can avoid almost all accidents. You're most vulnerable to what you don't see, he'd say.

The factors influencing the conditions of social traffic are often invisible, making our daily lives filled with the potential for unintended conflicts over belonging. It's unlikely we'll be able to avoid all or even most of these conflicts. But the more we stay alert, the better navigators of situations we'll become—and crafters of them too.

Don't just read people; change their situations.

While we continue to search for the "right" students, employees, and relationship partners, we should also be mindful that anyone's best self is more likely to come to the surface when the situation is right for them, which is partially in our power to craft.

Hang in there.

One virtue that comes out of the research on wise interventions is patience. Because other people's psychology is hard to see, large psychological change can take place without our knowing it, especially if it occurs in the absence of behavioral change. What's more, the transformations that a person goes through may, like many geological phenomena, be so subtle and gradual as to escape notice in the short term. The pressures to avoid or give up on people who let us down or with whom we disagree are great. But by learning to be comfortable with our discomfort and to embrace a growth mindset, we may find ourselves surprised at the distances people travel.

Don't underestimate the potential to connect and the power of connecting.

While research has shown how difficult it can be to change people's views, wise interventions can still build bridges of connection with those we've seen as adversaries and with those who have seen us as adversaries. Wise interventions can also unlock the hidden potential of our schools, workplaces, health care centers, and homes. Not coincidentally, in many cases these interventions unlock the potential of the very people who are seen as not fully belonging. And once in a while, even a small act of support or brief moment of connection will have lasting aftereffects, like the ripples of a stone dropped in a pond.

BY STAYING ATTUNED to these insights, the basis of a situational literacy, we will be better able to engage in **this core set of practices for building belonging in our daily lives.**

1. *Ask questions and listen to the answers:* Appreciating how much we might discover about people and their circumstances drives curiosity. In turn, showing genuine curiosity about others is one of the most powerful bond builders. And by getting people's perspective rather than guessing at it, we are better positioned to provide the support they actually need.

2. *Give your perspective:* A complement to the need to perspective-get is to perspective-give. Too often we fail to dig into why we hold our views and feelings and to articulate clearly what they are. Sharing more fully, especially our own stories, can allow others to see us with new eyes. Research suggests that simply explaining not just what we feel but *why* we feel as we do can prevent others from stereotyping us. When we disagree, we can still express our points of view, but much like a courteous driver who wants to switch into a busy lane, we should signal our intent and give people time to make space for us in their minds. Go slow.

3. *Be polite:* There is a reason why virtually every culture has a protocol for politeness and why Goffman saw in our little rituals of respect similarities with the religious rituals almost all cultures perform to honor the sacred. Not inter-

rupting; saying "please" and "thank you"; apologizing when we do harm, whether intended or not, and even if others seem oversensitive about the harm caused, are signs that we see other selves as belonging in the circle of those to whom we should show respect.

4. *Affirm:* I don't mean dole out vapid praise or flatter ourselves in the mirror, which research shows to be counterproductive. I mean that we should create opportunities, even small ones, for people to express who they are and what they value, and to feel valued. Contrary to popular wisdom, many self-affirmations take the form not of "I *am* good, or smart, or well liked" but "Here is what I am committed to and why," which "firms up" the self. We miss far too many opportunities to affirm people, which, ironically, is most important when they may seem least worthy of affirmation: when they're threatened, stressed, or defensive.

5. *Avoid authoritarian language:* Recall that just saying "I think" before we give our opinions conveys that we understand we are speaking from one point of view and that there may be others. We can also openly express our ambivalence on issues, which we all have on many important matters. We should take the time to learn about opposing views. Even while we disagree with them, we can often build rapport by showing that we've thoughtfully listened and aren't simply projecting views onto others. Before giving critical feedback, we can signal our intentions, as with wise criticism, so that our suggestions aren't seen as dictatorial but as gestures of concern and respect.

6. *Use the nonverbal channel:* Sending nonverbal cues of interest in and respect for others can be a powerful bonding force: nodding, smiling, leaning in, making eye contact. It's

easy to go overboard, though, and research shows that one
of the most noxious things we can do is come across as fake.
Flirtatious gestures in the workplace and school can also
harm belonging and performance. That said, letting our
nonverbal behavior accurately express an appropriate enjoyment of other people is generally a good thing.

7. *Handle yourself with care:* My father thought that being
an aware driver required, foremost, being in the right headspace. If you're tired, angry, or stressed, get off the road
and restore yourself. At the very least, question your mind
more. The same lesson applies to social life. When we feel
threatened, we lose sight of our values, the lodestars for
how we want ourselves and the world to be. We naturally
turn our energies inward, which leaves us with less to put
toward being thoughtful to others. The more we cultivate
our own sense of belonging, the better able we'll be to nurture it in others and the less likely we will be to conform to
harmful stereotypes, scripts, and norms that spring so readily to mind. To "look again"—as the word *respect* asks of
us—requires us to be in a good headspace and heartspace.

8. *Craft your situations with care:* Because *who* we are
is entangled with *where* we are, we can self-craft by
situation-crafting. One way we can craft our daily situations is simply to be a gatekeeper for the multitude of social
influences on our own life and the lives of those we care
for. Cultivating a rich social life; staying in touch with family and friends; finding ways to express our values, such as
by devoting ourselves to purposes larger than ourselves;
and striving to be mindful of our own minds through the
various psychological timeouts and calisthenics discussed
throughout this book will all strengthen us in the quest to
foster belonging.

Awareness and good habits are cultivated by practice. No matter how much we know, we are always learning how to apply that knowledge in novel situations. It's all too easy to forget lessons and fail to see their relevance in the heat of the moment. "For someone who studies psychology," a friend once said to me in the midst of an argument, "you sure can be clueless sometimes." In my defense, I think cluelessness is a human default that we regress to, unless we continually practice applying what we know. As even the late, great peacemaker Nelson Mandela said, "I am not a saint unless you think a saint is a sinner who keeps trying."

We can all give and receive help from one another as we seek to strengthen belonging. Though we'll often fail to improve things as much as we hope, small gestures and brief experiences of connection can have surprising effects. We may inspire. Barack Obama, commenting on his own life journey, said that many people had provided him with that kind of support at just the right time. Reflecting on how powerful their influence was, he offered a vision of how we can all find opportunities to provide such assistance: "You want to see if you can maybe figure out how to sprinkle that stardust on other people."

In any given encounter, on any day, we can all find ways to conjure some of the magic of situation-crafting. By helping to foster belonging in others, we will also feel more connected, empowered, and fulfilled. We can make every situation a little bit better for ourselves and for the people with whom we share it.

Acknowledgments

THE RESEARCH I DESCRIBE IN THIS BOOK IS THE FRUIT OF many collaborations among many scientists, beginning with Kurt Lewin and his disciples in the 1930s. I thank the investigators in social psychology who have created this body of knowledge and the teachers who have communicated it to a larger audience.

The power of the situation is exemplified by the Stanford Psychology Department, which has supported and catalyzed so much important social-psychological research over many decades. The Stanford Graduate School of Education has similarly nurtured many researchers working in this tradition. I'm thankful to my colleagues at Stanford.

I am deeply grateful to my mentors, Claude Steele, Lee Ross, and Hazel Markus. They taught me both the tools of our trade and a set of values that accompany me in my research and teaching. Their insights also permeate this book. Lee merits special mention because he passed away as I was writing this book. I think that becoming aware of the cognitive biases that Lee investigated over his long career is one of the most important steps that we can take to foster belonging.

My longtime colleagues Julio Garcia and Valerie Purdie-Greenaway are my mentors too. Much of our research, which I describe throughout this book, represents the products of our decades-long collaboration, for which I am immensely grateful. Joshua Aronson and Kent Harber have also been longtime colleagues who have inspired and taught me. David Dunning was a wonderfully supportive and generous mentor to me as an undergraduate; he taught me much that I still lean on today. The late Ed Zigler was a generous mentor and helped me to situate our educational research in the larger context of child development. Greg Walton, David Sherman, Jonathan Cook, and David Yeager have also played a major role in the research and ideas at the core of this book, and I've been fortunate to have had many wonderful collaborations and conversations with them over many years. Likewise, Sonja Lyubomirsky's research, insights, and feedback have also contributed heavily to my lab's research on wise interventions. Ronaldo Mendoza was an early inspiration in my research. More recently, he and Leah Lin generously provided insightful feedback on several portions of this book.

I am grateful to the many graduate students, postdoctoral fellows, faculty colleagues, and project staff with whom I've had the privilege to collaborate and who spearheaded much of the research described in the book, including Nancy Apfel, Peter Belmi, Kevin Binning, Shannon Brady, Patricia Chen, Phil Ehret, Omid Fotuhi, Parker Goyer, Adam Hahn, Tiffany Ito, Shoshana Jarvis, Yue Jia, René Kizilcek, Xingyu Li, Kirsten Layous, Wonhee Lee, Christine Logel, Kody Manke, Joseph Moore, Joseph Powers, Stephanie Reeves, Arghavan Salles, Michael Schwalbe, Nurit Shnabel, Arielle Silverman, Suzanne Taborsky-Barba, Isabelle Tay, Kate Turetsky, and Eric Uhlmann. I also thank the many dedicated research assistants and undergraduate collaborators who helped realize our research.

Virtually none of the research in my lab would have been possible without the generous support of various foundations and organizations, including the National Science Foundation, Spencer Foundation, WT Grant Foundation, and Russell Sage Foundation.

Emily Loose provided exceptional edits and incisive feedback on earlier drafts of the book. Alison MacKeen and Celeste Fine of Park & Fine patiently and dexterously shepherded me through the many years of the book-proposal and publication process. Alison MacKeen also provided sharp and thoughtful feedback from the earliest stages of the book's development. I am grateful to Alane Mason of W. W. Norton for her feedback and coaching, and I also thank the creative production team at Norton. Patricia Wieland and Rebecca Munro provided careful editorial feedback.

I was delighted to have the opportunity to learn from many people who graciously provided thoughtful and critical feedback, corresponded with me about their experience or research, shared their story, or agreed to be interviewed for this book. They include Joseph Anderson, Elliot Aronson, James Comer, Rodolfo Cortes Barragan, Eric Bettinger, David Broockman, Steve Cole, Essam Daod and Maria Jammal, Thomas Dee, Ruth Ditlmann, Geraldine Downey, Don Green, Edmund Gordon, Rainier Harris, Laura Kiken, Arie Kruglanski, Jung Eun Lee, Mark Lepper, Kenneth McClane, Salma Mousa, Jason Okonofua, Elizabeth Paluck, Emily Pronin, Jackie Rosen, Robert Rosenthal, Mary Rowe, Nidia Rudeas-Gracia, Norbert Schwarz, Mark Snyder, Jessi Smith, Mohammed Soriano-Bilal, Steve Wert, Tim Wilson, and Philip Zimbardo. I am also indebted to the late James March for many instructive conversations and for his parting advice to "understand Don Quixote."

Many thanks to other friends who have contributed to this book by sharing their feedback, participating in conversations, or providing any number of other wise interventions, including Joe Artale, Raj Bhargava, Joseph Brown, Joanna Castro, Peter Cohen, Jonathan Cook, Geraldine Downey, Mazyar Fallah, Lior Goldin, Margaux Malyshev, Heather McCormick, Dev Patnaik, Sharam Pavri, Mehran Sahami, Jeff Schneider, Ray Shanley, and Bennett Wilburn.

Thanks to Sarah Wert and to my kids, Benie and Emrey Cohen, for the many ways in which they challenged and changed me. And, of course, a big thanks to Susan Cohen, Roger Cohen, and Barbara Cohen, who were and are always there.

Notes

Introduction: A Crisis of Belonging and What We Can Do About It

ix   **Psychologists call it "social pain":** Naomi Eisenberger, Matthew Lieberman, and Kipling Williams, "Does Rejection Hurt: An fMRI Study of Social Exclusion," *Science* 302(5643) (2003): 290–92; Naomi Eisenberger, "Social Pain and the Brain: Controversies, Questions, and Where to Go from Here," *Annual Review of Psychology* 66 (2014): 601–29; and Matthew Lieberman, *Social: Why Our Brains Are Wired to Connect* (Crown, 2013).

ix   **when our sense of belonging is threatened ... feel worse about ourselves:** Mark Leary and Roy Baumeister, "The Nature and Function of Self-Esteem: Sociometer Theory," *Advances in Experimental Social Psychology* 32 (2000): 1–62; and Kipling Williams and Steve Nida, "Ostracism: Consequences and Coping," *Current Directions in Psychological Science* 20(2) (2011): 71–75.

ix   **perform below our potential:** Roy Baumeister, Jean Twenge, and Christopher Nuss, "Effects of Social Exclusion on Cognitive Processes: Anticipated Aloneness Reduces Intelligent Thought," *Journal of Personality and Social Psychology* 83(4) (2000): 817–27; and Gregory Walton and Geoffrey Cohen, "A Brief Social-Belonging Intervention Improves Academic and Health Outcomes of Minority Students," *Science* 331(6023) (2011): 1447–51.

x   **behave impulsively:** Roy Baumeister et al., "Social Exclusion Impairs Self-Regulation," *Journal of Personality and Social Psychology* 88(4) (2005): 589–604; and Aleah Burson, Jennifer Crocker, and Dominik Mischkowski, "Two Types of Value-Affirmation: Implications for Self-Control Following

Social Exclusion," *Social Psychological and Personality Science* 3(4) (2012): 510–16.

x   **see others as hostile:** C. N. DeWall et al., "It's the Thought That Counts: The Role of Hostile Cognition in Shaping Aggressive Responses to Social Exclusion," *Journal of Personality and Social Psychology* 96(1) (2009): 45–59.

x   **lash out defensively:** Jean Twenge et al., "If You Can't Join Them, Beat Them: Effects of Social Exclusion on Aggressive Behavior," *Journal of Personality and Social Psychology* 81(6) (2001): 1058–69; and W. A. Warburton et al., "When Ostracism Leads to Aggression: The Moderating Effects of Control Deprivation," *Journal of Experimental Social Psychology* 42(2) (2006): 213–20.

x   **fleeting experiences of belonging:** Mario Mikulincer and Phillip Shaver, "Boosting Attachment Security to Promote Mental Health, Prosocial Values, and Intergroup Tolerance," *Psychological Inquiry* 18(3) (2007): 139–56; and Gregory Walton and Geoffrey Cohen, "Mere Belonging: The Power of Social Connections," *Journal of Personality and Social Psychology* 102(3) (2012): 513–32.

x   **a stranger in your own land:** Arlie Hochschild, *Strangers in Their Own Land* (New Press, 2016).

x   **"crisis of belonging":** Pete Buttigieg, "A Crisis of Belonging," speech, YouTube, May 19, 2019, https://www.youtube.com/watch?v=39YJ7h0MHXQ.

x   **one in five Americans suffers:** There's a jump in biological risk around the 20th percentile of scores on the UCLA loneliness scale: Steven Cole et al., "Myeloid Differentiation Architecture of Leukocyte Transcriptome Dynamics in Perceived Social Isolation," *Proceedings of the National Academy of Sciences of the United States of America* 112(49) (2015): 15, 142–47. For higher rates of chronic loneliness among young adults, see Louise Hawkley et al., "Loneliness from Young Adulthood to Old Age: Explaining Age Differences in Loneliness," *International Journal of Behavioral Development* (November 15, 2020). Studies reporting higher rates of loneliness suffer from methodological problems, such as nonrepresentative samples.

x   **not alone in being alone:** Sting, "Message in a Bottle," track 1, side 1, on The Police, *Regatta de Blanc*, A&M Records, 1979, LP.

x   **"one of the most toxic environmental risk factors":** Steve Cole, "Meng-Wu Lecture," video, Center for Compassion and Altruism Research and Education, Stanford University, 2013, http://ccare.stanford.edu/videos/meng-wu-lecture-steve-cole-ph-d. Cole means that loneliness is one of the most, if not the most, toxic social or cultural environmental risk factors or features of lifestyle. He is not talking about specific chemicals in the physical environment as much as the general social or cultural environment in which people live. See also Julianne Holt-Lunstad et al., "Loneliness and Social Isolation as Risk Factors for Mortality: A Meta-Analytic Review," *Perspectives on Psychological Science* **10**(2) (2015): 227–37.

x   **"diseases of despair":** Angus Deaton and Anne Case, *Deaths of Despair and the Future of Capitalism* (Princeton University Press, 2020), 94.

xi   **learned he was exiled:** Nuruddin Farah, "Bastards of Empire," *Transition* **65** (1995): 26–35, on 27.

xi   **aggravated by mistrust:** Michael Schwalbe, Geoffrey Cohen, and Lee Ross, "The Objectivity Illusion and Voter Polarization in the 2016 Presidential Election," *Proceedings of the National Academy of Sciences* **117**(35) (2020): 21, 218–29; and Nathan Kalmoe and Lilliana Mason, *Lethal Mass Partisanship*, National Capital Area Political Science Association American Politics Meeting, January 2019. Kalmoe and Mason report figures of 18 percent among Democrats and 13 percent among Republicans for support of violence; the two groups did not differ in terms of their likelihood of seeing the other side as evil.

xi   **Hate crimes reached a ten-year high:** Data retrievable at Federal Bureau of Investigation, Uniform Crime Reporting Program, "Hate Crime," https://www.justice.gov/crs/highlights/2021-hate-crime-statistics.

xi   **forces fuel division:** These important books discuss how large-scale social and economic conditions have contributed to social disconnection and mistrust: William Julius Wilson, *When Work Disappears: The World of the New Urban Poor* (Knopf, 1996); Keith Payne, *The Broken Ladder: How Inequality Affects the Way We Think, Live, and Die* (Penguin, 2018); Martin Sandbu, *The Economics of Belonging* (Princeton University Press, 2020); Chris Arnade, *Dignity: Seeking Respect in Back Row America* (Sentinel, 2019); Matthew Desmond, *Evicted: Poverty and Profit in the American Dream* (Crown, 2016); Deaton and Case, *Deaths of Despair*; Kathryn Edin and H. Luke Schaefer, *$2 a Day: Living on Almost Nothing in America* (Mariner, 2016); Francis Fukuyama, *The Great Disruption: Human Nature and the Reconstitution of Social Order* (Free Press, 1999); and Robert Putnam, *Bowling Alone* (Simon & Schuster, 2000).

For research on the contribution of media and social media to fear, anxiety, and division, see, for example, Bruce Sacerdote et al., *Why Is All COVID-19 News Bad News?* National Bureau of Economic Research, 2020, Working Paper no. 28110, https://www.nber.org/papers/w28110; Jean Twenge, *iGen: Why Today's Super-Connected Kids Are Growing Up Less Rebellious, More Tolerant, Less Happy—and Completely Unprepared for Adulthood* (Atria, 2017); and "The Facebook Files," *Wall Street Journal*, September 13, 2021–October 24, 2021, https://www.wsj.com/news/types/the-facebook-files.

xiii **power of the situation:** For an invaluable review, see Lee Ross and Richard Nisbett, *The Person and The Situation: Perspectives of Social Psychology* (Pinter & Martin, 2011).

xiv **term "wise":** Erving Goffman, *Stigma: Notes on the Management of Spoiled Identity* (Touchstone, 1986/1963). The term originally derives from Rotwelsch, an outsider language of Eastern Europe. "Wiz" meant "in the know."

xiv **social psychologist Claude Steele:** Claude M. Steele, "Race and the Schooling of Black Americans," *Atlantic*, April 1992; Geoffrey Cohen, Claude Steele, and Lee Ross, "The Mentor's Dilemma: Providing Critical Feedback Across the Racial Divide," *Personality and Social Psychology Bulletin* **25**(10) (1999): 1302–18; Gregory Walton, "The New Science of Wise Psychological Interventions," *Current Directions in Psychological Science* **23**(1) (2014): 73–82; and David Yeager et al., "Breaking the Cycle of Mistrust: Wise Interventions to Provide Critical Feedback Across the Racial Divide," *Journal of Experimental Psychology: General* **143**(2) (2014): 804–24.

For reviews of wise interventions, see Geoffrey Cohen, Julio Garcia, and J. Parker Goyer, "Turning Point: Targeted, Tailored, and Timely Psychological Intervention," in *Handbook of Competence and Motivation: Theory and Application*, 2nd ed., eds. Andrew Elliot, Carol Dweck, and David Yeager (Guilford, 2017), 657–86, https://ed.stanford.edu/sites/default/files/cohen_scanned.pdf; Gregory Walton and Timothy Wilson, "Wise Interventions: Psychological Remedies for Social and Personal Problems," *Psychological Review* **125**(5) (2018): 617–55; Gregory Walton and Alia Crum, eds., *Handbook of Wise Interventions* (Guilford, 2020); Geoffrey Cohen and David Sherman, "The Psychology of Change: Self-Affirmation and Social Psychological Intervention," *Annual Review of Psychology* **65** (2014): 333–71; and Timothy Wilson, *Redirect: Changing the Life Stories We Live By* (Little Brown, 2011). Greg Walton provides a comprehensive database of wise interventions at https://www.wiseinterventions.org/database.

xiv **research on wise interventions:** My goal is to synthesize a large body of research for the purpose of creating a science-supported wisdom for navigating a diverse world. Much of the research that I review features randomized controlled experiments, especially the contemporary research on wise interventions conducted by my lab and the labs of many colleagues over the past two decades. However, not all the data I review come from the kind of rigorous randomized experiments that provide the strongest causal tests. I draw on correlational and observational research, qualitative studies, older experiments that were important and seminal yet methodologically loose by contemporary standards, and literature and film—all to illustrate and explore the ideas throughout this book. Although the specific findings in any single study may be subject to critique—no single study is perfect—the body of findings that I draw together in each chapter supports hard-won ideas, insights, and strategies that transcend a specific "effect." It's these ideas, insights, and strategies that I want to convey and that I believe can be most useful in supporting a sense of belonging for all.

xv   **"difference unites us":** Andrew Solomon, *Far from the Tree: Parents, Children and the Search for Identity* (Scribner, 2012), 4.

Chapter 1: The Potential of the Situation

3   **psychologists began to make stunning discoveries:** Kurt Lewin, *Resolving Social Conflict: Selected Papers on Group Dynamics* (Harper, 1948); Solomon Asch, *Social Psychology* (Prentice-Hall, 1955); and Stanley Milgram, *Obedience to Authority: An Experimental View* (Harper Perennial, 1974/2017). For a review, see Lee Ross and Richard Nisbett, *The Person and the Situation: Perspectives of Social Psychology* (Pinter & Martin, 2011). See also Robert Cialdini's seminal, *Influence, New and Expanded: The Psychology of Persuasion* (HarperCollins, 2021). The new edition includes a chapter on the "unity principle," which addresses how to tap into the need to belong in our influence attempts.

5   **Claiborne P. Ellis:** Studs Terkel, *American Dreams: Lost and Found* (Ballantine, 1980), 221–33.

5   **"among the most powerful forces":** Solomon Asch, *Social Psychology* (Prentice-Hall, 1952), 316.

6   **after being excluded . . . conform more:** After being excluded, people tend to lash out against those who threaten to reject them further and seek to bond with people who could help them restore a sense of belonging. See K. D. Williams et al., "Cyberostracism: Effects of Being Ignored over the Internet," *Journal of Personality and Social Psychology* 79(5) (2000): 748–62; and Jon Maner et al., "Does Social Exclusion Motivate Interpersonal Reconnection? Resolving the 'Porcupine Problem,'" *Journal of Personality and Social Psychology* 92(1) (2007): 42–55. For research showing exclusion triggers conspiratorial thinking, see Kai-Tak Poon et al., "Beliefs in Conspiracy Theories Following Ostracism," *Personality and Social Psychology Bulletin* 46(8) (2020): 1234–46.

7   **"gatekeeper":** Kurt Lewin, "Frontiers in Group Dynamics II: Channels of Group Life; Social Planning and Action Research," *Human Relations* 1 (1947): 143–53.

9   **research shows that sharing vulnerabilities:** Arthur Aron et al., "The Experimental Generation of Interpersonal Closeness: A Procedure and

Some Preliminary Findings," *Personality and Social Psychology Bulletin* **23**(4) (1997): 363–77; and Brene Brown, *The Power of Vulnerability: Teachings on Authenticity, Connection, and Courage* (Sounds True, Inc., 2012). See also Chapter 8.

9   **stunning turn of events:** This and other details not found in Terkel's interview are drawn from Osha G. Davidson, *The Best of Enemies: Race and Redemption in the New South* (University of North Carolina Press, 2007).

9   **Kurt Lewin:** For details of Lewin's life and research practices, see Alfred Marrow, *The Practical Theorist: The Life and Work of Kurt Lewin* (Basic, 1969); and Travis Langley, "Kurt Lewin, the Refugee Who Founded Social Psychology," *Psychology Today* (January 29, 2017).

11   **One acolyte:** Marrow, *Practical Theorist*, 91.

12   **"If you want truly to understand something":** This motto may originate with the psychologist Walter Fenno Dearborn: Urie Bronfenbrenner, "Toward an Experimental Ecology of Human Development," *American Psychologist* **32**(7) (1977): 513–31, on 517.

12   **"experimentally created social climates":** Kurt Lewin and Ronald Lippitt, "An Experimental Approach to the Study of Autocracy and Democracy: A Preliminary Note," *Sociometry* **1**(33) (1938): 292–300; Kurt Lewin, Ronald Lippitt, and Ralph White, "Patterns of Aggressive Behavior in Experimentally Created 'Social Climates,'" *Journal of Social Psychology* **10** (1939): 271–99; and Kurt Lewin, "Frontiers in Group Dynamics: Concept, Method and Reality in Social Science; Social Equilibria and Social Change," *Human Relations* **1**(1) (1947): 5–41.

14   **Lewin wrote that:** Lewin, Lippitt, and White, "Patterns of Aggressive Behavior," 283.

14   **Based on his observations:** Ronald Lippitt, "An Experimental Study of the Effect of Democratic and Authoritarian Group Atmospheres," *University of Iowa Studies: Child Welfare* **16**(3) (1940): 43–195.

15   **You can see the results yourself:** "Kurt Lewin's Leadership Study (1940s)," YouTube, posted September 30, 2013, https://www.youtube.com/watch?v=J7FYGn2NS8M.

16   **Lewin's biographer writes:** Marrow, *Practical Theorist*, 143.

16   **Even more successful:** Lester Coch and John French Jr., "Overcoming Resistance to Change," *Human Relations* **1**(4) (1948): 512–32; and Lewin, "Frontiers in Group Dynamics: Concept, Method and Reality."

17   **With Lewin's guidance:** Cari Romm, "The World War II Campaign to Bring Organ Meats to the Dinner Table," *Atlantic*, September 25, 2014.

17   **homemakers together into small groups:** Lewin, "Frontiers in Group Dynamics: Concept, Method and Reality."

18   **gave a lecture:** Marrow, *Practical Theorist*, 130.

18   *Time*: Geoffrey Cohen, Julio Garcia, and J. Parker Goyer, "Turning Point: Targeted, Tailored, and Timely Psychological Intervention," in *Handbook of Competence and Motivation: Theory and Application*, 2nd ed., eds. A. Elliot, C. Dweck, and D. Yeager (Guilford, 2017), 657–86, https://ed .stanford.edu/sites/default/files/cohen_scanned.pdf.

19   *Participatory processes*: People tend to embrace attitudes and identities that align with their behavior. Change *behavior* first, through participatory processes; hearts and minds will often follow. See Ross and Nisbett, *The Person and the Situation*; Leon Festinger, *A Theory of Cognitive Dissonance* (Stanford University Press, 1957); and Daryl Bem, "Self-Perception Theory," in *Advances in Experimental Social Psychology*, ed. Leonard Berkowitz (Academic Press), **6** (1972): 1–62.

19   *Reference groups*: Lewin, "Frontiers in Group Dynamics: Concept, Method and Reality"; and Lewin, "Frontiers in Group Dynamics II."

20   *Self-affirmations*: For self-affirmations to be effective, they generally need to affirm an aspect of self unrelated to the threat (e.g., C. P. was affirmed for his honesty rather than his racial tolerance before he took part in the discussions about racial injustice). For four reviews of self-affirmation theory, see Claude Steele, "The Psychology of Self-Affirmation: Sustaining the Integrity of the Self," *Advances in Experimental Social Psychology* **21** (1988): 261–302; David Sherman and Geoffrey Cohen, "The Psychology of Self-Defense: Self-Affirmation Theory," *Advances in Experimental Social Psychology* **38** (2006): 183–242; Geoffrey Cohen and David Sherman, "The Psychology of Change: Self-Affirmation and Social Psychological Intervention," *Annual Review of Psychology* **65** (2014): 333–71; and David Sherman et al., "Self-Affirmation Interventions," in *Handbook of Wise Interventions*, eds. Walton and Crum (Guilford, 2020), 63–99.

21   *New roles*: Erving Goffman, "Role Distance," in *Encounters: Two Studies in the Sociology of Interaction* (Bobbs-Merrill, 1961), 85–115.

21   **three Ts of situation-crafting:** Cohen, Garcia, and Goyer, "Turning Point."

Chapter 2: **Belonging Uncertainty**

23   **bring aspects of their lives from outside:** For various treatments of this idea, see Lee Ross and Richard Nisbett, *The Person and the Situation: Perspectives of Social Psychology* (Pinter & Martin, 2011); Claude Steele, "A Threat in the Air: How Stereotypes Shape Intellectual Identity and Performance," *American Psychologist* **52**(6) (1997): 613–29; Gregory Miller, Edith Chen, and Karen Parker, "Psychological Stress in Childhood and Susceptibility to the Chronic Diseases of Aging: Moving Towards a Model of Behavioral and Biological Mechanisms," *Psychological Bulletin* **137**(6) (2011): 959–97; Edith Chen and Gregory Miller, "The Biological Residue of Childhood Poverty," *Child Development Perspectives* **7**(2) (2013): 67–73; and Joseph LeDoux, *Anxious: Using the Brain to Understand and Treat Fear and Anxiety* (Penguin, 2015).

24   **placed the need to belong:** Maslow believed the needs often co-occurred and, it should be noted, did not use the metaphor of a pyramid: A. H. Maslow, "A Theory of Human Motivation," *Psychological Review* **50**(4) (1943): 370–96. For a comprehensive review, see Roy Baumeister and Mark Leary, "The Need to Belong: Desire for Interpersonal Attachments as a Fundamental Human Motivation," *Psychological Bulletin* **117**(3) (1995): 497–529. There are complex definitional issues regarding whether to infer an underlying *causal* need, motive, or want to belong. I am less concerned with these definitional issues than with the practical consequences that arise when a sense of belonging is supported or threatened. These consequences can prove profound—sufficiently so that it seems empirically justifiable to infer a strong underlying need.

24   **One of the first:** Henry Murray and Harry Harlow were two other early scholars of the human need for connection; see Murray, *Explorations in Personality* (Oxford University Press, 1938); Harlow, "The Nature of Love," *American Psychologist* **13**(12) (1958): 673–85; and Deborah Blum, *Love at Goon Park: Harry Harlow and the Science of Affection* (Basic, 2011).

25   **powerful report:** John Bowlby, "Maternal Care and Mental Health," *Bulletin of the World Health Organization* **3** (1951): 355–533.

25   **qualified this bold statement:** See Julie Summers, *When the Children Came Home: Stories of Wartime Evacuees* (Simon & Schuster, 2012). Also, warm and accepting romantic relationships later in life can offset the effects of insecure attachment: Nickola Overall, Jeffry Simpson, and Helena Struthers, "Buffering Attachment-Related Avoidance: Softening Emotional and Behavioral Defenses During Conflict Discussions," *Journal of Personality and Social Psychology* **104**(5) (2013): 854–71.

25   **Child-rearing practices:** Urie Bronfenbrenner, "Toward an Experimental Ecology of Human Development," *American Psychologist* **32**(7) (1977): 513–31.

25   **study that's like a parable:** Mary Ainsworth and Silvia M. Bell, "Attachment, Exploration, and Separation: Illustrated by the Behavior of One-Year-Olds in a Strange Situation," *Child Development* **41**(1) (1970): 49–67; Ainsworth et al., *Patterns of Attachment: A Psychological Study of the Strange Situation* (Lawrence Erlbaum Associates, 1978); and Mary Main, "Mary D. Salter Ainsworth: Tribute and Portrait," *Psychoanalytic Inquiry* **19**(5) (1999): 682–736, on 703 for Ainsworth quote.

26 **"highest forms of human endeavor":** Solomon Asch, *Social Psychology* (Prentice-Hall, 1952), 299.

26 **parent-child bond:** Beyond these correlational data, causal evidence is provided in an experiment that trained new caregivers to create stronger bonds with their newborns by being more emotionally responsive in their parenting; their children were more exploratory and proactive in their problem-solving in novel situations than were children whose caregivers had been randomly assigned to a control condition: Susan Landry et al., "Responsive Parenting: Establishing Early Foundations for Social, Communication, and Independent Problem-Solving Skills," *Developmental Psychology* **42**(4) (2006): 627–42.

26 **secure base can be pulled out:** Momentary experiences can activate and deactivate a sense of a secure base: Mario Mikulincer and Phillip Shaver, "Boosting Attachment Security to Promote Mental Health, Prosocial Values, and Intergroup Tolerance," *Psychological Inquiry* **18**(3) (2007): 139–56.

27 **experience almost fifty years ago:** Mary Rowe, "The Feeling That We 'Belong' May Depend in Part on 'Affirmations,'" MIT Working Paper (2021), https://mitsloan.mit.edu/shared/ods/documents?PublicationDocumentID=7871.

28 **media moguls know:** See research reviewed in Chip Heath and Dan Heath, *Made to Stick: Why Some Ideas Survive and Others Die* (Penguin Random House, 2007); and John Tierney and Roy F. Baumeister, *The Power of Bad: How the Negativity Effect Rules Us and How We Can Rule It* (Penguin, 2019).

28 **violent and property crimes:** See John Gramlich, "What the Data Says (and Doesn't Say) About Crime in the United States," Pew Center Research, November 20, 2020.

29 **algorithms . . . optimized:** For example, see Ro'ee Levy, "Social Media, News Consumption, and Polarization: Evidence from a Field Experiment," *American Economic Review* **111**(3) (2021): 831–70; and "The Facebook Files," *Wall Street Journal*, September 13, 2021–October 24, 2021, https://www.wsj.com/news/types/the-facebook-files.

29 **increase in teen mental illness:** Jean Twenge et al., "Increases in Depressive Symptoms, Suicide-Related Outcomes, and Suicide Rates Among US Adolescents After 2010 and Links to Increased New Media Screen Time," *Clinical Psychological Science* **6**(1) (2017): 3–17. Twenge also links social media to declines in civic participation: "Does Online Social Media Lead to Social Connection or Social Disconnection?" *Journal of College and Character* **14**(1) (2013): 11–20. See also Twenge, *iGen: Why Today's Super-Connected Kids Are Growing Up Less Rebellious, More Tolerant, Less Happy—and Completely Unprepared for Adulthood* (Atria, 2017).

29   **randomized experiment . . . Facebook users:** Hunt Allcott et al., "The Welfare Effects of Social Media," *American Economic Review* **110**(3) (2020): 629–76.

29   **another experiment:** Ryan Dwyer et al., "Smartphone Use Undermines Enjoyment of Face-to-Face Social Interactions," *Journal of Experimental Social Psychology* 78 (2018), 233–39; Yannis Theocharis and Will Lowe, "Does Facebook Increase Political Participation? Evidence from a Field Experiment," *Information, Communication, and Society* **19**(10) (2016): 1465–86. For the importance of civic participation to a sense of belonging and well-being, see Robert Putnam, *Bowling Alone* (Simon & Schuster, 2000), and Chapter 11.

30   **limiting our use:** Melissa Hunt et al., "No More Fomo: Limiting Social Media Decreases Loneliness and Depression," *Journal of Social and Clinical Psychology* **37**(10) 2018, 751–68.

30   **"belonging uncertainty":** Gregory Walton and Geoffrey Cohen, "A Question of Belonging: Race, Social Fit, and Achievement," *Journal of Personality and Social Psychology* **92**(1) (2007): 82–96; Walton and Cohen, "A Brief Social-Belonging Intervention Improves Academic and Health Outcomes of Minority Students," *Science* **331**(6023) (2011): 1447–51; Walton and Shannon Brady, "The Many Questions of Belonging," in *Handbook of Competence and Motivation: Theory and Application*, eds. A. Elliot, C. Dweck, and D. Yeager (Guilford, 2017), 272–93; and Walton and Brady, "The Social-Belonging Intervention," in *Handbook of Wise Interventions*, eds. Gregory Walton and Alia Crum (Guilford, 2020), 36–62.

30   *Once, a classmate:* Mali Dandridge, *How Will I Be Perceived as a Black Girl in the Ivy League?* ADP.FM Stream, RYL Studios, podcast, April 20, 2018, https://yr.media/news/how-will-i-be-perceived-as-a-black-girl-in-they -ivy-league/.

31   **belonging should be located closer to the base:** See Matthew Lieberman, *Social: Why Our Brains Are Wired to Connect* (Crown, 2013).

31   **one of the most well-cited papers:** Baumeister and Leary, "Need to Belong."

31   **Evolutionary biologists argue:** For a review, see John Cacioppo and William Patrick, *Loneliness: Human Nature and the Need for Social Connection* (Norton, 2009).

31   **most profound psychological studies:** For a meta-analysis, see Chris Hartgerink et al., "The Ordinal Effects of Ostracism: A Meta-Analysis of 120 Cyberball Studies," *PLOS One* **10**(5) (2015): e0127002. For research on the effects of ostracism relative to personality, see Melissa McDonald and M. Brent Donnellan, "Is Ostracism a Strong Situation? The Influence of Personality in Reactions to Rejection," *Journal of Research in Personality* **46**(5) (2012): 614–18. For the study of rejection from KKK members, see Karen Gonsalkorale and Kipling Williams, "The KKK Won't Let Me Play:

Ostracism Even by a Despised Outgroup Hurts," *European Journal of Social Psychology* 37(6) (2007): 1176–86. For research on how ostracism shapes subsequent interpretations of ambiguous situations, see Lisa Zadro et al., "How Long Does It Last? The Persistence of the Effects of Ostracism in the Socially Anxious," *Journal of Experimental Social Psychology* 42(5) (2006): 692–97.

32 **physical effects can add up:** See Chapter 11.

32 **good assessment of ... belonging:** Maithreyi Gopalan and Shannon Brady, "College Students' Sense of Belonging: A National Perspective," *Educational Researcher* 49(2) (2020): 134–37; J. Parker Goyer et al., "Self-Affirmation Facilitates Minority Middle Schoolers' Progress Along College Trajectories," *Proceedings of the National Academy of Sciences* 114(29) (2017): 7594–99; Goyer et al., "The Role of Psychological Factors and Institutional Channels in Predicting the Attainment of Postsecondary Goals," *Developmental Psychology* 57(1) (2021): 73–86; David Yeager et al., *Practical Measurement*, Carnegie Foundation for the Advancement of Teaching, 2013; Karyn Lewis et al., "Fitting In to Move Forward: Belonging, Gender, and Persistence in the Physical Sciences, Technology, Engineering, and Mathematics," *Psychology of Women Quarterly* 41(4) (2017): 420–36; Catherine Good, Aneeta Rattan, and Carol Dweck, "Why Do Women Opt Out? Sense of Belonging and Women's Representation in Mathematics," *Journal of Personality and Social Psychology* 102(4) (2012): 700–17; and Michael Resnick et al., "Protecting Adolescents from Harm: Findings from the National Longitudinal Study on Adolescent Health," *Journal of the American Medical Association* 278(10) (1997): 823–32. Additionally, the UCLA loneliness scale has proved a strong predictor of health outcomes: See Chapter 11; and Cacioppo and Patrick, *Loneliness*.

33 **glaring incident:** Erika Christakis, "Dressing Yourselves," https://www.thefire.org/email-from-erika-christakis-dressing-yourselves-email-to-silliman-college-yale-students-on-halloween-costumes/.

34 **one student exclaims:** YouTube, "Yale Professor Attacked over Halloween Costumes Says We've Evolved to Get Along," https://www.youtube.com/watch?v=f56xgHHZQ_A.

34 **novel *Old School*:** Tobias Wolff, *Old School* (Vintage, 2003), 23–24.

35 **students experience plenty of prejudice:** Walter DeKeseredy et al., "Hate Crimes and Bias Incidents in the Ivory Tower: Results from a Large-Scale Campus Survey," *American Behavioral Scientist* (February 22, 2019): 1–12. In a sample of over five thousand college students, 76 percent reported witnessing or hearing about offensive incidents related to prejudice; 34 percent of women reported being a victim of a sexual assault; almost 60 percent of students overall reported being victimized by a specific hate crime or incident of bias because of their ethnicity, nationality, religion, sex, sexual

orientation, political orientation, or a physical or mental disability. See also "My Experience Survey 2019: Campus Findings and Recommendations" (Office of the Chancellor, University of California, Berkeley, 2019, https://myexperience.berkeley.edu/sites/default/files/myexperiencesurvey2019-final.pdf), which found that roughly half of ethnic minority and transgender or gender-nonconforming undergraduates at one major university reported being regularly subjected to exclusionary treatment over the previous year. Admittedly, the samples in these studies were not randomly drawn (virtually all college surveys have this limitation), so the respondents may not be representative of all students at the college site. Still, the data plainly suggest that the experience of prejudice is far more prevalent than we want.

36 **erode women's confidence:** In one experiment, women who read about research on the problem of gender bias in STEM expressed less belief that they could belong in these fields and less desire to pursue them compared with women who did not read about gender bias: Corinne Moss-Racusin et al., "Gender Bias Produces Gender Gaps in STEM Engagement," *Sex Roles* **79** (2018): 651–70.

36 **shown a picture of . . . plantation house:** Sara Driskell and Sophie Trawalter, "Race, Architecture, and Belonging: Divergent Perceptions of Antebellum Architecture," *Collabra: Psychology* **7**(1) (2021): 21192.

37 **Moving to Opportunity program:** Raj Chetty, Nathaniel Hendren, and Lawrence Katz, "The Effects of Exposure to Better Neighborhoods on Children: New Evidence from the Moving to Opportunity Experiment," *American Economic Review* **106**(4) (2016): 855–902; Lisa Sanbonmatsu et al., *Neighborhoods and Academic Achievement: Results from the Moving to Opportunity Experiment*, Working Paper no. 11909, National Bureau of Economic Research, 2006, https://www.nber.org/papers/w11909; and Jeffrey R. Kling et al., "Neighborhood Effects on Crime for Female and Male Youth: Evidence from a Randomized Housing Voucher Experiment," *Quarterly Journal of Economics* **120**(1) (2005): 87–130; Raj Chett et al., "Social Capital I: Measurement and Associations with Economic Mobility," *Nature* 608 (2022) 108–21.

38 **one creative study:** Simone Schnall et al., "Social Support and the Perception of Geographical Slant," *Journal of Experimental Social Psychology* **44**(5) (2008): 1246–55.

38 **meaningless experiences conferred . . . belonging:** Gregory Walton, Geoffrey Cohen, David Cwir, and Steven Spencer, "Mere Belonging: The Power of Social Connections," *Journal of Personality and Social Psychology* **102**(3) (2012): 513–32.

39 **a wise intervention:** Walton and Cohen, "A Question of Belonging"; Wal-

ton and Cohen, "Brief Social-Belonging Intervention"; and Walton and Brady, "Social-Belonging Intervention."

43 *giving* **advice works wonders:** Lauren Eskreis-Winkler et al., "A Large-Scale Field Experiment Shows Giving Advice Improves Academic Outcomes for the Advisor," *Proceedings of the National Academy of Sciences* **116**(6) (2019): 14808–10.

44 **kept in touch with their mentors:** Shannon Brady et al., "A Brief Social-Belonging Intervention in College Improves Adult Outcomes for Black Americans," *Science Advances* **6**(1) (2020): eaay3689.

45 **science fiction stories:** Ray Bradbury, "A Sound of Thunder," *Collier's*, 1952.

45 **replicated:** David Yeager et al., "Teaching a Lay Theory Before College Narrows Achievement Gaps at Scale," *Proceedings of the National Academy of Sciences* **113**(24) (2016): E3341–48; see the large-scale replications by College Transition Collaborative, "Social Belonging," https://collegetransitioncollaborative.org/social-belonging/; Kevin R. Binning et al., "Changing Social Contexts to Foster Equity in College Science Courses: An Ecological-Belonging Intervention," *Psychological Science* **31**(9) (2020): 1059–70; Christine Logel et al., "A Social-Belonging Intervention Benefits Higher Weight Students' Weight Stability and Academic Achievement," *Social Psychological and Personality Science* **12**(6): 1048–57; Gregory Walton et al., "Two Brief Interventions to Mitigate a 'Chilly Climate' Transform Women's Experience, Relationships, and Achievement in Engineering," *Journal of Educational Psychology* **107**(2) (2014): 468–85; for a review see Walton and Brady, "Social-Belonging Intervention."

46 **intervention to middle school students:** J. Parker Goyer et al., "Targeted Identity-Safety Interventions Cause Lasting Reductions in Discipline Citations Among Negatively Stereotyped Boys," *Journal of Personality and Social Psychology* **117**(2) (2019): 229–59; and Geoffrey Borman et al., "Reappraising Academic and Social Adversity Improves Middle School Students' Academic Achievement, Behavior, and Well-Being," *Proceedings of the National Academy of Sciences* **116**(33) (2019): 16,286–91.

46 **persistence of Middle Eastern refugees:** Christina Bauer et al., "From Weak Victims to Resourceful Actors: Reframing Refugees' Stigmatized Identity Enhances Long-Term Academic Engagement," *Psychological Science* (2021), in press.

47 **virtuous cycle:** See, for example, Geoffrey Cohen, Julio Garcia, Valerie Purdie-Vaughns [Purdie-Greenaway], Nancy Apfel, and Patricia Brzustoski, "Recursive Processes in Self-Affirmation: Intervening to Close the Minority Achievement Gap," *Science* **324** (2009): 400–3. For discussions of these virtuous cycles—also known as "recursive cycles" and "cycles of

adaptive potential"—see Cohen and David Sherman, "The Psychology of Change: Self-Affirmation and Social Psychological Intervention," *Annual Review of Psychology* 65 (2014): 333–71; and Gregory Walton and Timothy Wilson, "Wise Interventions: Psychological Remedies for Social and Personal Problems," *Psychological Review* 125(5) (2018): 617–55. For the three Ts, see Geoffrey Cohen, Julio Garcia, and J. Parker Goyer, "Turning Point: Targeted, Tailored, and Timely Psychological Intervention," in *Handbook of Competence and Motivation*, eds. Elliot, Dweck, and Yeager, 657–86, https://ed.stanford.edu/sites/default/files/cohen_scanned.pdf.

Chapter 3: The Pernicious Power of Us vs. Them

51   **Paige:** Sharon Otterman, "She Was Excited for a New School: Then the Anti-Semitic 'Jokes' Started," *New York Times*, March 4, 2020.

52   **"How can we be in":** Peter Gabriel, "Not One of Us," track 2, side 2, on *Peter Gabriel*, Charisma Records, 1980, LP.

52   **means of earning social currency:** For evidence that bullying is a means of social connection, see J. A. Rambaran et al., "Bullying as a Group Process in Childhood: A Longitudinal Social Network Analysis," *Child Development* 91(4) (2020): 1336–52.

53   **innately driven:** Thomas Hobbes, *Leviathan* (Penguin Classics, 1651/2017); Sigmund Freud, *The Ego and the Id* (Reading Essentials, 1923/2018); and Fred M. Wilcox, dir., *Forbidden Planet*, Metro-Goldwyn-Mayer, 1956.

53   **links aggression to the amygdala:** Robert M. Sapolsky, *Behave: The Biology of Humans at Our Best and Worst* (Penguin, 2017), 423, 388.

53   **One of the often-cited sources:** Henri Tajfel, M. G. Billig, R. P. Bundy, and Claude Flament, "Social Categorization and Intergroup Behaviour," *European Journal of Social Psychology* 1(2) (1971): 146–78; and Tajfel, "Experiments in Intergroup Discrimination," *Scientific American* 223(5) (1970): 96–103.

55   **variations in the situational set-up:** People are especially biased in favor of their group when they are in the position of accepting or rejecting imbalanced allocations that have *already* been made and that favor their group: K. A. Diekman et al., "Self-Interest and Fairness in Problems of Resource Allocation: Allocators Versus Recipients," *Journal of Personality and Social Psychology* 72(5) (1997): 1061–74.

55   **minimal group even among children:** Yarrow Dunham, Andrew Baron, and Susan Carey, "Consequences of 'Minimal' Group Affiliations in Children," *Child Development* 82(3) (2011): 793–811.

55   **scored those in their group higher:** Maria Cadinu and Myron Rothbart,

"Self-Anchoring and Differentiation Processes in the Minimal Group Setting," *Journal of Personality and Social Psychology* **70**(4) (1996): 661–77.

55   **learned or innate:** Tajfel thought the psychological reflex was learned, a "generic norm" that we learn to apply to any situation with an Us and a Them: Tajfel, "Experiments in Intergroup Discrimination."

56   **Wesley Autrey:** Donald Trump, "Wesley Autrey," *Time*, "2007 Time 100," http://content.time.com/time/specials/2007/time100/article/0,28804,1595 326_1615754_1615746,00.html.

56   **heroes ... leapt into action:** David Rand and Ziv Epstein, "Risking Your Life Without a Second Thought: Intuitive Decision-Making and Extreme Altruism," *PLOS One* **9**(10) (2014): e109687; and Anthony Evans and David Rand, "Cooperation and Decision Time," *Current Opinion in Psychology* **26** (2019): 67–71.

56   **moving example:** Elizabeth Midlarsky et al., "Personality Correlates of Heroic Rescue During the Holocaust," *Journal of Personality* **73**(4) (2005): 907–34, on 908.

56   **stood up against tyranny:** Czesław Miłosz, *The Captive Mind* (Vintage, 1990), x.

56   **cooperation comes to us faster:** Reinforcing the claim that minds adapt to their social environments, the tendency for cooperative responses to occur faster and more spontaneously than competitive responses is especially strong among people who report trusting others. Less speedy cooperation seems to occur when people learn to be conflicted about the cost-benefit ratio of cooperation: David Rand et al., "Spontaneous Giving and Calculated Greed," *Nature* **489** (2012): 427–30; and Akihiro Nishi et al., "Social Environment Shapes the Speed of Cooperation," *Scientific Reports* **6**(1) (2016): 29,622.

57   **infants ... spontaneously help a stranger:** Rodolfo Barragan, Rechele Brooks, and Andrew Meltzoff, "Altruistic Food Sharing Behavior by Human Infants After a Hunger Manipulation," *Scientific Reports* **10**(1785) (2020): 645–49.

57   **Some scholars suggest:** Barragan et al., "Altruistic Food Sharing Behavior."

57   **"not a very human thing":** Erving Goffman, "On Face-Work," in *Interaction Ritual* (Anchor, 1967), 45.

58   **"most significant facts":** Clifford Geertz, *The Interpretation of Cultures: Selected Essays* (Basic, 1973), 45.

58   **group we belong to:** Lee Ross and Richard Nisbett, *The Person and the Situation: Perspectives of Social Psychology* (Pinter & Martin, 2011); Kurt Lewin, *Resolving Social Conflict: Selected Papers on Group Dynamics* (Harper, 1948); and Stanley Schachter, "Deviation, Rejection, and Communication," *Journal of Abnormal and Social Psychology* **46**(2) (1951): 190–207. For the role of groups in violence, see Rebecca Littman and Elizabeth Paluck, "The Cycle of Violence: Understanding Individual Participation in Collective Violence," *Advances in Political Psychology* **36** (2015): 79–99.

58 **Stanford Prison Experiment:** Philip Zimbardo et al., "The Stanford Prison Experiment: A Simulation Study of the Psychology of Imprisonment," August 1971, Stanford University; and Zimbardo et al., "A Pirandellian Prison," *New York Times Magazine,* April 8, 1973. See also the website dedicated to the Stanford Prison Experiment, https://www.prisonexp.org/; Zimbardo, *The Lucifer Effect: Understanding How Good People Turn Evil* (Random House, 2007); and Ken Musen and Zimbardo, *Quiet Rage: The Stanford Prison Experiment,* Stanford University, 1988, documentary, https://exhibits.stanford.edu/spe/catalog/fd396xq4047. For a critique, see Thibault Le Texier, "Debunking the Stanford Prison Experiment," *American Psychologist* **74**(7) (2019): 823–39. For a rejoinder, see https://www.prison exp.org/response.

59 **those who would respond to such a request:** Thomas Carnahan and Sam McFarland, "Revisiting the Stanford Prison Experiment: Could Participant Self-Selection Have Led to the Cruelty?" *Personality and Social Psychology Bulletin* **33**(5) (2007): 603–14.

60 **situational supports that sustain our . . . self:** Erving Goffman, *Asylums: Essays on the Social Situation of Mental Patient and Other Inmates* (Aldine, 1961). Observing the debasement rituals in a 1950s mental institution and their impact on patients, Goffman wrote, "Here one begins to learn about the limited extent to which a conception of oneself can be sustained when the usual setting or supports for it are suddenly removed" (p. 148).

60 **breeding ground for conformity:** Conformity in authoritarian situations occurs with greatest intensity when social pressures are high, as when an authoritarian leader is present; conformity diminishes rapidly when social pressures are low, as when an authoritarian leader is absent: Kurt Lewin et al., "Patterns of Aggressive Behavior in Experimentally Created 'Social Climates,'" *Journal of Social Psychology* **10** (1939): 271–99.

61 **American military prison guards:** John Schwartz, "The Struggle for Iraq: Psychology; Simulated Prison in 71 Showed a Fine Line Between 'Normal' and 'Monster,'" *New York Times,* May 6, 2004; M. Dittmann, "Psychological Science Offers Clues to Iraqi Prisoner Abuse," *APA Monitor* **35**(7) (July/August 2004): 13; and Dittmann, "What Makes Good People Do Bad Things?" *APA Monitor* **35**(9) (October 2004): 68.

61 **total institution:** Goffman, *Asylums.* For the Prison Study replication, see Stephen Reicher and S. Alexander Haslam, "Rethinking the Psychology of Tyranny: The BBC Prison Study," *British Journal of Social Psychology* **45** (2006): 1–40.

62 **"It harms me":** *Democracy Now!* "Zimbardo Shows How Most Evil Comes from Hierarchy," YouTube, September 17, 2008, https://www.youtube.com/ watch?v=Z0jYx8nwjFQ&t=14s. The quote is at 2 minutes, 4 seconds.

63   **the Holocaust:** Christopher Browning, *Ordinary Men: Reserve Police Battalion 101 and the Final Solution in Poland* (Harper Perennial, 2017), rev. Kindle ed. (quote from chap. 8, loc. 1220). See also Hannah Arendt, *The Origins of Totalitarianism* (Harcourt, 1976). Analyzing ordinary citizens' support of the Nazi party, Arendt wrote that even "highly cultured people" were vulnerable to "self-abandonment into the mass," especially when the mass movement provided a sense of belonging lacking in their social lives (316–17).

63   **"A civilization is not destroyed":** James Baldwin, *The Fire Next Time* (Michael Joseph, 1963), 64–65.

63   **"crimes against himself":** Kurt Vonnegut, *Mother Night* (Kurt Vonnegut/ Origama Express, 1961), 269, 1.

64   *Who* **we are . . . depends on** *where* **we are:** Cf. Clifford Geertz, *The Interpretation of Cultures: Selected Essays* (Basic, 1973), 35.

64   **how teens are susceptible to "going along":** Geoffrey Cohen and Mitchell Prinstein, "Peer Contagion of Aggression and Health Risk Behavior Among Adolescent Males: An Experimental Investigation of Effects on Public Conduct and Private Attitudes," *Child Development* 77(4) (2006): 967–83; and Prinstein, *Popular: The Power of Likability in a Status-Obsessed World* (Viking, 2017).

67   **crafted information about . . . faux participants:** Many elements of the procedure ensured the credibility of the chat-room experience. First, the information about the friends that faux participants were said to affiliate with came from an assessment of the social networks at the school that Prinstein and I had made earlier in the year. We had asked students in the school to report on whom they spent time with and who was popular and well liked. Importantly for the ethics of the study, the friends that the faux participants were suggested to have were only hinted at. No one knew for certain who the faux participants, or who their friends, ostensibly were. Second, the social situations that we presented to participants, and the relevant responses to them, were based on focus groups that Prinstein and I had conducted earlier in the year in which we asked teens about common high-pressure social situations they experienced and common responses. Third, the chat-room program presented the ostensible responses of each faux participant after variable pauses, making it look as though each one was first thinking and only then typing his answer.

69   **impulse to conform:** One finding we hadn't anticipated was that the participants with the uncool faux participants gave more prosocial answers, suggesting an "anti-conformity" effect. (We were able to discern this by comparing students' responses in the chat room with a baseline measure they had completed earlier in the year.) Research suggests that we want to

conform to high-status people and groups but that we also want to distance ourselves from low-status people and groups. The effect can be harnessed to promote positive behavior. For example, undergraduates ate less junk food when they were led to believe that graduate students ate it in abundance: Jonah Berger and Lindsay Rand, "Shifting Signals to Help Health: Using Identity Signaling to Reduce Risky Health Behaviors," *Journal of Consumer Research* **35**(3) (2008): 509–18.

69   **We often rationalize our conformity:** As a result, we may come to see the world in a way consistent with the judgments of our group: Solomon Asch, *Social Psychology* (Prentice-Hall, 1952); Geoffrey Cohen, "Party over Policy: The Dominating Impact of Group Influence on Political Beliefs," *Journal of Personality and Social Psychology* **85**(5) (2003): 808–22; and Emily Pronin et al., "Alone in a Crowd of Sheep: Asymmetric Perceptions of Conformity and Their Roots in an Introspection Illusion," *Journal of Personality and Social Psychology* **92**(4) (2007): 585–95. We may also rationalize why the victims of our conformity deserve their harsh treatment: see Keith Davis and Edward Jones, "Changes in Interpersonal Perception as a Means of Reducing Cognitive Dissonance," *Journal of Abnormal and Social Psychology* **61**(3) (1960): 402–10.

69   **feeling excluded is a risk factor:** Fueling the problem is that many teens conform to what they *think* high-status peers think and do—which is often different from what high-status teens *actually* think and do. In later research, Prinstein, colleagues, and I found that teens overestimate how much the popular kids engage in drug use, sex, and antisocial behavior and that they then appear to conform to these misperceived norms. Additionally, the more that ninth graders believed (wrongly) that popular students used a lot of illegal substances, the greater the increase in their own substance use two years later: S. Helms et al., "Adolescents Misperceive and Are Influenced by High-Status Peers' Health Risk, Deviant, and Adaptive Behavior," *Developmental Psychology* **50**(12) (2014): 2697–714. This phenomenon, known as "pluralistic ignorance," was also found to contribute to alcohol consumption on college campuses in a classic study: Dale Miller and Deborah Prentice, "Pluralistic Ignorance and Alcohol Use on Campus: Some Consequences of Misperceiving the Social Norm," *Journal of Personality and Social Psychology* **64**(2) (1993): 243–56. By correcting students' misperceptions of harmful social norms and educating them about the process of social conformity, interventions can reduce problematic behavior: J. LaBrief et al., "Live Interactive Group-Specific Normative Feedback Reduces Misperceptions and Drinking in College Students: A Randomized Cluster Trial," *Psychology of Addictive Behaviors* **22**(1) (2008): 141–48; Christine Schroeder and Deborah Prentice,

"Exposing Pluralistic Ignorance to Reduce Alcohol Use Among College Students," *Journal of Applied Social Psychology* **28**(3) (1998): 2150–80.

70   **reasons people join:** See Kruglanski's two groundbreaking books: Arie Kruglanski, Jocelyn Belanger, and Rohan Gunaratna, *The Three Pillars of Radicalization: Needs, Narratives, and Networks* (Oxford University Press, 2019); and Kruglanski, David Webber, and Daniel Koehler, *The Radical's Journey: How German Neo-Nazis Voyaged to the Edge and Back* (Oxford University Press, 2019). See also Steven Windisch et al., "Measuring the Extent and Nature of Adverse Childhood Experiences (ACE) Among Former White Supremacists," *Terrorism and Political Violence* (July 9, 2020): 1–22; and Matthew Kredell, "Far-Right Extremism Scholar Pete Simi Explores 'Hidden Spaces of Hate,'" USC Price School of Public Policy website, 2017, https://priceschool.usc.edu/far-right-extremism-scholar-pete-simi-explores-hidden-spaces-of-hate/. For the quoted material, see Bertjan Doosje et al., "Terrorism, Radicalization, and De-Radicalization," *Current Opinion in Psychology* **11** (2016): 79–84, on 81.

71   **Christian Picciolini:** Picciolini, interview, "Preventing Violent Extremism Forum: At the Crossroads of Theory and Practice," A. Kruglanski, interviewer, 2018; and Picciolini, "My Descent into America's Neo-Nazi Movement—and How I Got Out," TED Talk, 2017.

71   **"raised to believe":** James Baldwin, "The American Dream and the American Negro," *New York Times*, March 7, 1965.

72   **is often motivated by:** Kruglanski sees the motivation to join extremist groups as based in a need for "significance," not belonging per se. But, for human beings, much of our sense of significance comes from feeling significant to *others*, so I see the two needs as intertwined. See Chapter 11.

72   **unfairness . . . makes people feel excluded:** Tom Tyler and E. Allan Lind, "Procedural Justice," in *Handbook of Justice Research in Law*, eds. J. Sanders and V. L. Hamilton (Springer, 2002), 65–92.

72   **When people feel excluded . . . more aggressive:** Jean Twenge et al., "If You Can't Join Them, Beat Them: Effects of Social Exclusion on Aggressive Behavior," *Journal of Personality and Social Psychology* **81**(6) (2001): 1058–69. The researchers suggest that the experience of exclusion in their experiments "produced numbness rather than acute distress."

72   **surveys to people:** Kruglanski et al., "Three Pillars of Radicalization."

72   **Experiments led by my colleague:** Peter Belmi, Rodolfo Cortes Barragan, Margaret Neale, and Geoffrey Cohen, "Threats to Social Identity Can Trigger Social Deviance," *Personality and Social Psychology Bulletin* **41**(4) (2015): 467–84.

73   **need not be experienced personally:** Bruce Hoffman, Inside Terrorism

(Columbia University Press, 2017); and Kruglanski et al., "Three Pillars of Radicalization."

73 **study conducted by the political scientists:** J. Erik Oliver and Tali Mendelberg, "Reconsidering the Environmental Determinants of White Racial Attitudes," *American Journal of Political Science* 44(3) (2000): 574–89. A later study replicated the primary results: Marylee Taylor and Peter Mateyka, "Community Influences on White Racial Attitudes: What Matters and Why?" *Sociological Quarterly* 52(2) (2011): 220–43. For evidence that a lack of a college degree predicts despair and alienation, see Anne Case and Angus Deaton, *Deaths of Despair and the Future of Capitalism* (Princeton University Press, 2020). For further research on how a lack of educational attainment cuts people off from economic opportunities for belonging, see Sean Reardon, "The Widening Academic Achievement Between the Rich and the Poor," in *Social Stratification*, ed. D. Grusky (Routledge, 2019); and Michael J. Sandel, *The Tyranny of Merit* (Farrar, Straus, and Giroux, 2020), 536–50.

74 **social disease:** Jon Bon Jovi and Richie Sambora, "Social Disease," track 4, side 1, on Bon Jovi, *Slippery When Wet*, Mercury Records, 1986, CD.

74 **when we think our side:** E. Pronin et al., "Bombing Versus Negotiating: How Preferences for Combating Terrorism Are Affected by Perceived Terrorist Rationality," *Basic and Applied Social Psychology* 28(4) (2010): 385–92.

74 **Stormfront:** Aaron Panofsky and Joan Donovan, "Genetic Ancestry Testing Among White Nationalists: From Identity Repair to Citizen Science," *Social Studies of Science* 49(5) (2019): 653–81, on 657.

75 **backstabbing and infighting:** See Peter Cimi, "Why Radicalization Fails: Barriers to Mass Casualty Terrorism," C-Rex Working Paper Series, No. 2 (2017), https://www.sv.uio.no/c-rex/english/publications/c-rex-working-paper-series/Pete_Simi.

76 **Terrorism expert Bruce Hoffman:** Hoffman, *Inside Terrorism*. For the Black September anecdote, see Hoffman, "All You Need Is Love: How the Terrorists Stopped Terrorism," *Atlantic Monthly*, December 2001.

77 **difficult conversations:** Marshall Rosenberg, *Nonviolent Communication: A Language of Life*, 3rd ed. (Puddle Dancer, 2015), 151.

78 **psychological experiments:** Mario Mikulincer and Phillip Shaver, "Attachment Theory and Intergroup Bias: Evidence That Priming the Secure Base Schema Attenuates Negative Reactions to Outgroups," *Journal of Personality and Social Psychology* 81(1) (2001): 97–115.

78 **article written by a black high school student:** Rainier Harris, "This Is the Casual Racism That I Face at My Elite High School," *New York Times*, September 24, 2020.

79   **"What I really saw as core":** Rainier Harris, personal communication, March 10, 2021.

79   **heart of the approach:** Sean Darling-Hammond et al., "Effectiveness of Restorative Justice in US K-12 Schools: A Review of Quantitative Research," *Contemporary School Psychology* **24**(3) (2020): 295–308.

Chapter 4: Turning Them into Us

81   **colony of rhesus macaque monkeys:** Cassandre Kaplinsky, "Rebuilding Cayo Santiago," *Natural History*, July–August 2018.

81   **Extensive observations:** Camille Testard et al., "Rhesus Macaques Build New Social Connections After a Natural Disaster," *Current Biology* **31** (2021): 2299–309, on 2305; and Samuel Ellis et al., "Deconstructing Sociality: The Types of Social Connections That Predict Longevity in a Group-Living Primate," *Proceedings of the Royal Society B: Biological Sciences* **286**(1917) (2019): 20191991.

83   **experiment . . . Sherif:** Muzafer Sherif, *In Common Predicament: The Social Psychology of Intergroup Conflict and Cooperation* (Houghton Mifflin, 1966). See also Gina Perry, *The Lost Boys: Inside Muzafer Sherif's Robbers Cave Experiment* (Scribe, 2018). Sherif had conducted a variant of the study his year before, but it hadn't gone as planned because he hadn't gotten the situational details "right." He made some key changes the following year, such as isolating the two groups from each other upon arrival and better hiding from the boys the fact that they were being purposefully manipulated. It should also be noted that Sherif's study highlights the disturbingly lax ethical standards in scientific research during this era.

85   **working-class white Americans:** Arlie Hochschild, *Strangers in Their Own Land* (New Press, 2016).

85   **separation also contributes:** James Baldwin, "The American Dream and the American Negro," *New York Times*, March 7, 1965. For research on political segregation, see Jacob Brown and Ryan Enos, "The Measurement of Partisan Sorting for 180 Million Voters," *Nature Human Behaviour* **5** (2021): 998–1008.

86   **ethnic stereotyping . . . associated with:** Xuechunzi Bai, Miguel Ramos, and Susan Fiske, "As Diversity Increases, People Paradoxically Perceive Social Groups as More Similar," *Proceedings of the National Academy of Sciences* **117**(23) (2020): 12,741–49.

86   **study of Israeli and Palestinian campers:** Shannon White et al., "When 'Enemies' Become Close: Relationship Formation Among Palestinians and Jewish Israelis at a Youth Camp," *Journal of Personality and Social Psychol-*

ogy (September 17, 2020). See also the pioneering work on contact theory: Thomas Pettigrew and Linda Tropp, "A Meta-Analytic Test of Intergroup Contact Theory," *Journal of Personality and Social Psychology* **90**(5) (2006): 751–83.

87 **Goffman analyzed:** Erving Goffman, *Encounters: Two Studies in Sociology* (Bobbs-Merrill, 1961)

87 **norms to encourage cooperative behavior:** Varda Liberman, Steven Samuels, and Lee Ross, "The Name of the Game: Predictive Power of Reputations Versus Situational Labels in Determining Prisoner's Dilemma Game Moves," *Personality and Social Psychology Bulletin* **30**(9) (2004): 1175–85. I am simplifying the trade-off matrix of the Prisoner's Dilemma game to capture the gist of the dilemma.

89 **among the most ingenious situation-crafters:** The twelfth edition of *Social Animal* was cowritten with Elliot Aronson's son, Joshua, also an esteemed social psychologist: Elliot Aronson and Joshua Aronson, *The Social Animal* (Worth, 2018). For a how-to manual of situation-crafting, see Elliot Aronson et al., *Methods of Research in Social Psychology* (McGraw Hill, 1989). Some of the content in this chapter comes from an interview with Elliot Aronson on July 1, 2020. For an updated book about Jigsaw, see Shelley Patnoe and Elliot Aronson, *Cooperation in the Classroom: The Jigsaw Method* (Pinter & Martin, 2011).

90 **freely choosing to do someone a favor:** Jon Jecker and David Landy, "Liking a Person as a Function of Doing Him a Favour," *Human Relations* **22**(4) (1969): 371–78.

93 **"The wilderness . . . functions as a leveler":** Donald Green and Janelle Wong, "Tolerance and the Contact Hypothesis: A Field Experiment," in *The Political Psychology of Democratic Citizenship*, eds. C.M.F. Eugene Borgida and John Sullivan (Oxford University Press, 2009), 228–46, on 239.

94 **largely ineffectual:** See Elizabeth Paluck and Donald Green, "Prejudice Reduction: What Works? A Review and Assessment of Research and Practice," *Annual Review of Psychology* **60** (2009): 339–67.

94 **awaken new norms:** Elizabeth Paluck, "Reducing Intergroup Prejudice and Conflict with the Mass Media: A Field Experiment in Rwanda," PhD dissertation, Yale University, March 2007; and Paluck, "Reducing Intergroup Prejudice and Conflict Using the Media: A Field Experiment in Rwanda," *Journal of Personality and Social Psychology* **96**(3) (2009): 574–87.

95 **one hundred days of slaughter:** Philip Verwimp, "Machetes and Firearms: The Organization of Massacres in Rwanda," *Journal of Peace Research* **43**(1) (2016): 5–22.

95 **To paraphrase:** Philip Pullman said, " 'Thou shalt' might reach the head, but it takes 'Once upon a time' to reach the heart": "The Moral's in the

Story, Not the Stern Lecture," *Independent,* July 17, 1996, https://www
.independent.co.uk/news/education/education-news/opinion-the-moral-s
-in-the-story-not-the-stern-lecture-1329231.html.

99   **establishing new norms:** Elizabeth Paluck, Hana Shepherd, and Peter
Aronow, "Changing Climates of Conflict: A Social Network Experiment in
56 Schools," *Proceedings of the National Academy of Sciences* **113**(3) (2016):
566–71; and Philip Gourevitch, *We Wish to Inform You That Tomorrow We
Will Be Killed with Our Families: Stories from Rwanda* (Picador, 1999).

101   **"social referents":** Muzafer Sherif and Carolyn Sherif, *Reference Groups:
Exploration into Conformity and Deviation in Adolescents* (Henry Regnery,
1964).

102   **sports:** Salma Mousa, "Building Social Cohesion Between Christians and
Muslims Through Soccer in Post-ISIS Iraq," *Science* **369**(6505) (2020): 866–
70. Some material is drawn from correspondences with Mousa on March
27–29, 2021.

102   **Mandela believed that sports:** John Carlin, *Invictus: Nelson Mandela and
the Game That Made a Nation* (Penguin, 2009).

Chapter 5: Blaming the Person, Ignoring the Situation

106   **"sin and redemption":** Elliot Aronson, "Jigsaw Classroom," lecture, Stanford University, 1993.

106   **Doyle and his wife:** Meg Wagner, "Florida Grandfather Killed in Front of
Family During Road Rage Clash as Victim and Attacker Both Call 911,"
New York Daily News, July 27, 2015.

107   **Fundamental Attribution Error:** Lee Ross and Richard Nisbett, *The Person and the Situation: Perspectives of Social Psychology,* 2nd ed. (Pinter &
Martin, 2011). The FAE is also referred to as the "correspondence bias,"
especially among those reluctant to call it an "error." For a review, see Daniel Gilbert and Patrick Malone, "The Correspondence Bias," *Psychological
Bulletin* **117**(1) (1995): 21–38.

For nuances and complexities, see the research of Bertram Malle: e.g.,
Malle, "How People Explain Behavior: A New Theoretical Framework,"
Personality and Social Psychology Review **3**(1) (1999): 23–48. Malle suggests that dispositional or trait-based attributions of the kind the FAE predicts are fairly uncommon in our day-to-day lives when we make sense of
intentional actions. I think that some of the apparent disagreement among
researchers arises from their focus on different phenomena. The everyday actions that we casually observe, like someone making a purchase at a
store, don't seem as susceptible to the FAE as do disagreements and differ-

ences that we find objectionable or simply hard to explain—such as someone taking an excessively long time to make a purchase at the store while
we wait in line behind them.

108   **poignant example of misreading:** Naomi Adedokun, "Chadwick Boseman Tribute: Heartbreaking Moment Co-Star Breaks Down on GMB 'I
Regret That,'" *Express*, August 31, 2020.

109   **Many Greeks think:** Tom Vanderbilt, *Traffic: Why We Drive the Way We
Do (and What It Says About Us)* (Vintage, 2008).

109   **growing up in Harlem:** Kenneth McClane, "Sparrow Needy," *Kenyon
Review* **381**(1) (2016): 91–102.

109   **deceptively simple study:** Edward Jones and Victor Harris, "The Attribution of Attitudes," *Journal of Experimental Social Psychology* **3**(1) (1967):
1–24.

110   **linchpin study:** The "Quiz Bowl Study": Teresa Amabile, Lee Ross, and
Julia Steinmetz, "Social Roles, Social Control, and Biases in Social-
Perception Processes," *Journal of Personality and Social Psychology* **35**(7)
(1977): 485–94; and Lee Ross, "From the Fundamental Attribution Error to
the Truly Fundamental Attribution Error and Beyond: My Research Journey," *Perspectives on Psychological Science* **13**(6) (2018): 750–69.

112   **most robust effect:** The Jones and Harris test of the FAE was subjected
to multiple replication attempts, in Richard Klein et al., "Many Labs 2:
Investigating Variation in Replicability Across Samples and Settings,"
Advances in Methods and Practices in Psychological Science **1**(14) (2018):
443–90.

112   **ten-page memo:** James Damore, "Google's Ideological Echo Chamber,"
July 2017, https://assets.documentcloud.org/documents/3914586/Googles
-Ideological-Echo-Chamber.pdf.

113   **confirmation bias:** For reviews of biases and their implications for social
belief and behavior, see Richard Nisbett and Lee Ross, *Human Inference:
Strategies and Shortcomings of Social Judgment* (Prentice-Hall, 1980);
Thomas Gilovich, *How We Know What Isn't So: The Fallibility of Human
Reason in Everyday Life* (Free Press, 1991); and Daniel Kahneman, *Think-
ing, Fast and Slow* (Farrar, Straus and Giroux, 2011).

113   **"A man hears what he wants to hear":** Paul Simon, "The Boxer," track 1,
side 2, on Simon and Garfunkel, *Bridge over Troubled Water*, Columbia
Records, 1970, LP.

113   **surprised by the furious reaction:** Paul Lewis, "'I See Things Differently':
James Damore on His Autism and the Google Memo," *Guardian*, November 17, 2017.

114   **features of workplaces:** See Chapters 6, 9, and 10.

114   **situational cues can send a message:** See Chapter 7.

115   **experienced their classroom:** Phillip Ehret et al., "Same Classroom, Different Reality: The Predictive Role of Psychological Factors in Student Learning in a Large Multi-State Database," unpublished manuscript, 2021.

116   **famous study:** Robert Rosenthal and Lenore Jacobson, *Pygmalion in the Classroom: Teacher Expectation and Pupils' Intellectual Development,* expanded ed. (Crown, 2003). For the quote from Eden, see Katherine Ellison, "Being Honest About the Pygmalion Effect," *Discover Magazine,* October 28, 2015. Some of the material covered here is drawn from an interview with Robert Rosenthal on April 25, 2021.

118   **third of the gap:** This is an estimate based on available data, with the racial achievement gap estimated at 0.8 standard deviations and the 4-point Pygmalion effect being roughly 0.27 standard deviations. See Roland Fryer Jr. and Steven Levitt, "Testing for Racial Differences in the Mental Ability of Young Children," *American Economic Review* **103**(2) (2013): 981–1005.

119   **robustness:** For one major critique, see Janet Elashoff and Richard Snow, *Pygmalion Reconsidered: A Case Study in Statistical Inference— Reconsideration of the Rosenthal-Jacobson Data on Teacher Expectancy* (C. A. Jones, 1971). For the rejoinder, see Robert Rosenthal and Donald Rubin, "Pygmalion Reaffirmed," Harvard University, Cambridge, MA, https://files.eric.ed.gov/fulltext/ED059247.pdf. The results of Dee's analysis were conveyed in a personal communication, November 24, 2020.

119   **blaming teachers:** Samuel Wineburg, "The Self-Fulfillment of the Self-Fulfilling Prophecy," *Educational Researcher* **16**(9) (1987): 28–37.

120   **growth mindset:** Carol Dweck, *Mindset: The New Psychology of Success* (Random House, 2006).

120   **Ekman . . . points to the power of small gestures:** From an interview by Katherine Ellison, "Being Honest About the Pygmalion Effect," *Discover Magazine,* October 28, 2015.

121   **follow-up experiments have confirmed:** For example, soldiers tested better when they were described to their training officers as having "high command potential," and factory workers performed better when described to their supervisors as having "high aptitude potential." See A. King, "Self-Fulfilling Prophecies in Training the Hard-Core: Supervisors' Expectations and the Underprivileged Workers' Performance," *Social Science Quarterly* **52**(2) (1971): 369–78; and D. Eden, "Leadership and Expectations: Pygmalion Effects and Other Self-Fulfilling Prophecies in Organizations," *Leadership Quarterly* **3**(4) (1992): 271–305. For research on the effects of expectancies on interpersonal interactions, see Mark Snyder, Elizabeth Tanke, and Ellen Berscheid, "Social Perception and Interpersonal Behavior: On the Self-Fulfilling Nature of Social Stereotypes," *Journal of Personality and Social Psychology* **35**(9) (1977): 656–66.

121 **review of the Pygmalion effect:** S. W. Raudenbush, "Magnitude of Teacher Expectancy Effects on Pupil IQ as a Function of the Credibility of Expectancy Induction: A Synthesis of Findings from 18 Experiments," *Journal of Educational Psychology* **76**(1) (1984): 85–97. See also the meta-analysis reported in Rosenthal and Jacobson, *Pygmalion in the Classroom*; and S. Wang, C. M. Rubie-Davies, and K. Meissel, "A Systematic Review of the Teacher Expectation Literature over the Past 30 Years," *Educational Research and Evaluation* **24**(3–5) (2020): 124–79. For a critique of the Pygmalion effect, see Lee Jussim and Kent Harber, "Teacher Expectations and Self-Fulfilling Prophecies: Knowns and Unknowns, Resolved and Unresolved Controversies," *Personality and Social Psychology Review* **9**(2) (2005): 131–55. A key problem with this critique is that it combines rigorous randomized experiments testing the impact of interventions aimed at altering teacher expectancies with studies that attempt to simply *measure* teachers' overestimations or underestimations of students' potential based on students' prior records. The second technique suffers from questionable methodological assumptions because students' prior records are apt to be biased by teacher expectations too.

121 **Empower them with knowledge:** Christine Rubie-Davies and Robert Rosenthal, "Intervening in Teachers' Expectations: A Random Effects Meta-Analytic Approach to Examining the Effectiveness of an Intervention," *Learning and Individual Differences* **50** (2016): 83–92; and Joseph Allen et al., "An Interaction-Based Approach to Enhancing Secondary School Instruction and Student Achievement," *Science* **333**(6045) (2011): 1034–37.

122 **more so than we know:** We tend to underestimate the degree to which we—through our mere presence and actions—shape the situation and other people in it. To an extent more than we imagine, we create the quality of the situations and encounters that make up our social lives. See Daniel Gilbert and Edward Jones, "Perceiver-Induced Constraint: Interpretations of Self-Generated Reality," *Journal of Personality and Social Psychology* **50**(2) (1986): 2€9–80.

123 **Cormac McCarthy's novel:** Cormac McCarthy, *All the Pretty Horses* (Vintage, 1993), 194.

124 **FAE . . . especially strong in the United States:** Malia Mason and Michael Morris, "Culture, Attribution and Automaticity: A Social Cognitive Neuroscience View," *Social Cognitive and Affective Neuroscience* **5**(2–3) (2010): 292–306. For a guided tour of research in cultural psychology, see Hazel Markus and Alana Conner, *Clash! How to Thrive in a Multicultural World* (Plume, 2013).

124   **Mischel lobbed a grenade:** Walter Mischel, *Personality and Assessment* (Wiley, 1968).

125   **Myers-Briggs test:** See Peter Myers and Isabel Briggs Myers, *Gifts Differing: Understanding Personality Type*, 2nd ed. (CPP, 1995); and Merve Emre, *The Personality Brokers: The Strange History of Myers-Briggs and the Birth of Personality Testing* (Doubleday, 2018). Even though the test has poor reliability and validity, it may still be useful as a catalyst for self-reflection, connection, and fun.

125   **overwhelming conclusion:** For an exposition on the role of person-based vs. situation-based influences relative to our intuitions, see Ross and Nisbett, *The Person and the Situation*.

125   **"behavioral signatures":** Yuichi Shoda, Walter Mischel, and Jack Wright, "Intraindividual Stability in the Organization and Patterning of Behavior: Incorporating Psychological Situations into the Idiographic Analysis of Personality," *Journal of Personality and Social Psychology* **67**(4) (1994): 674–87.

125   **IQ tests can predict some:** Ken Richardson and Sarah Norgate, "Does IQ Really Predict Job Performance?" *Applied Developmental Science* **19**(3) (2015): 153–69. The studies that yield higher estimates of the predictive power of IQ tests rely on potentially questionable statistical adjustments. What's more, most of these studies measure IQ and performance concurrently and use only a single performance metric, when what personnel offices really want to know is the degree to which IQ at the time it's measured is a useful predictor of workplace performance at a later time and over various kinds of work relevant to the job.

126   **study published in 2021:** Matt Brown, Jonathan Wai, and Christopher Chabris, "Can You Ever Be Too Smart for Your Own Good? Comparing Linear and Nonlinear Effects of Cognitive Ability on Life Outcomes," *Perspectives on Psychological Science* (March 8, 2021). https://journals.sagepub.com/doi/abs/10.1177/1745691620964122.

127   ***norms* that favored speaking up:** Hemant Kakkar et al., "The Dispositional Antecedents of Promotive and Prohibitive Voice," *Journal of Applied Psychology* **101**(9) (2016): 1342–51.

127   **SAT scores reveal little:** Saul Geiser with Roger Studley, "UC and the SAT: Predictive Validity and Differential Impact of the SAT I and SAT II at the University of California," *Educational Assessment* **8**(1) (2002): 1–26; and Saul Geiser, *SAT/ACT Scores, High School GPA and the Problem of Omitted Variables: Why the UC Taskforce's Findings Are Spurious*, UC Berkeley, Center for Studies in Higher Education, March 2020. Geiser has marshaled persuasive evidence that scores on the standard SAT (SAT I) capture the advantages conferred by socioeconomic status. See also William Bowen, Matthew Chin-

gos, and Michael McPherson, *Crossing the Finish Line: Completing College at America's Public Universities* (Princeton University Press, 2009).

127 **tests don't accurately reflect the preparedness:** Gregory Walton and Steven Spencer, "Latent Ability: Grades and Test Scores Systematically Underestimate the Intellectual Ability of Negatively Stereotyped Students," *Psychological Science* **20**(9) (2009): 1132–39.

128 **overconfidence effect:** Robert P. Vallone et al., "Overconfident Prediction of Future Actions and Outcomes by Self and Others," *Journal of Personality and Social Psychology* **58**(4) (1990): 582–92; David Dunning et al., "The Overconfidence Effect in Social Prediction," *Journal of Personality and Social Psychology* **58**(4) (1990): 568–81; and Cade Massey and Richard Thaler, "The Loser's Curse: Decision Making and Market Efficiency in the National Football League Draft," *Management Science* **59**(7) (2013): 1479–95.

129 **artificial intelligence algorithms:** Matthew Salganik et al., "Measuring the Predictability of Life Outcomes with a Scientific Mass Collaboration," *Proceedings of the National Academy of Sciences* **117**(15) (2020): 8398–403.

129 **Isaac Newton:** David Brewster, *Memoirs of the Life, Writings, and Discoveries of Sir Isaac Newton, Vol. 2* (Adamant Media Corporation, 1855/2001). "What we know is a drop, what we don't know is an ocean" is a pithier variant attributed to him but which he apparently never said.

130 **Mileva:** Pauline Gagnon, "The Forgotten Life of Einstein's First Wife," *Scientific American*, December 19, 2016.

130 **belief that innate talent:** Sarah-Jane Leslie et al., "Expectations of Brilliance Underlie Gender Distributions Across Academic Disciplines," *Science* **347**(6219) (2015): 262–65.

131 **similar pattern in student grades:** Elizabeth Canning et al., "STEM Faculty Who Believe Ability Is Fixed Have Larger Racial Achievement Gaps and Inspire Less Student Motivation in Their Classes," *Science Advances* **5**(2) (2019): eaau4734.

132 **"ability praise":** Claudia Mueller and Carol Dweck, "Praise for Intelligence Can Undermine Children's Motivation and Performance," *Journal of Personality and Social Psychology* **75**(1) (1998): 33–52.

132 **Consider three findings:** Drawn from the following sources: Larisa Hussak and Andrei Cimpian, "Investigating the Origins of Political Views: Biases in Explanation Predict Conservative Attitudes in Children and Adults," *Developmental Science* **21**(3) (2018): e12567; Lin Bian, Sarah-Jane Leslie, and Andrei Cimpian, "Gender Stereotypes About Intellectual Ability Emerge Early and Influence Children's Interests," *Science* **355**(6323) (2017): 389–91; Hussak and Cimpian, "An Early-Emerging Explanatory Heuristic Promotes Support for the Status Quo," *Journal*

of Personality and Social Psychology **109**(5) (2015): 739–52; Bian et al., "Messages About Brilliance Undermine Women's Interest in Educational and Professional Opportunities," *Journal of Experimental Social Psychology* **76** (2018): 404–20; and Bian, Leslie, and Cimpian, "Evidence of Bias Against Girls and Women in Contexts That Emphasize Intellectual Ability," *American Psychologist* **73**(9) (2018): 1139–53.

133 **liberals . . . revert to the FAE:** Linda Skitka et al., "Dispositions, Scripts, or Motivated Correction? Understanding Ideological Differences in Explanations for Social Problems," *Journal of Personality and Social Psychology* **83**(2) (2002): 470–87.

133 **cognitively *accessible* or *available*:** Amos Tversky and Daniel Kahneman, "Judgment Under Uncertainty: Heuristics and Biases," *Science* **185**(4157) (1974): 1124–31.

133 **children easily provoked to aggression:** Bram Van Bockstaele et al., "Modification of Hostile Attribution Bias Reduces Self-Reported Reactive Aggressive Behavior in Adolescents," *Journal of Experimental Child Psychology* **194** (June 2020).

134 **"attributional charity":** Term introduced in Lee Ross and Andrew Ward, "Naive Realism: Implications for Social Conflict and Misunderstanding," in *The Jean Piaget Symposium Series: Values and Knowledge*, eds. Edward Reed, Elliot Turiel, and Terrance Brown (Lawrence Erlbaum, 1996), 103–35.

134 **prevent child abuse:** Daphne Bugental et al., "A Cognitive Approach to Child Abuse Prevention," *Psychology of Violence* **1**(S) (2010): 84–106; and Daphne Bugental, Randy Corpuz, and Alex Schwartz, "Preventing Children's Aggression: Outcomes of an Early Intervention," *Developmental Psychology* **48**(5) (2012): 1443–49; and Daphne Bugental, Alex Schwartz, and Colleen Lynch, "Effects of an Early Family Intervention on Children's Memory: The Mediating Effects of Cortisol Levels," *Mind, Brain, and Education Society* **4**(4) (2010): 156–218.

135 **"psychological timeouts":** Sonja Lyubomirsky and Matthew Della Porta, "Boosting Happiness, Buttressing Resilience: Results from Cognitive and Behavioral Interventions," in *Handbook of Adult Resilience*, eds. J. Reich, A. Zautra, and J. Hall (Guilford, 2010), 450–64. See also Sonja Lyubomirsky, *The How of Happiness* (Penguin, 2007). See also K. Klein and A. Boals, "Expressive Writing Can Increase Working Memory Capacity," *Journal of Experimental Psychology: General* **130**(3) (2001): 520–33.

136 **viewers of a violent assault:** Kent Harber et al., "Emotional Disclosure and Victim Blaming," *Emotion* **15**(5) (2015): 603–14.

136 **"perspective of a neutral third party":** See Ethan Kross, *Chatter: The Voice in Our Head, Why It Matters, and How to Harness It* (Crown, 2021); and Eli Finkel, Erica Slotter, Laura Luchies, Gregory Walton, and James

Gross, "A Brief Intervention to Promote Conflict Reappraisal Preserves Marital Quality over Time," *Psychological Science* 24(8) (2013): 1595–601.

136   *values affirmation:* Often people write about how their values make them feel socially connected: Nurit Shnabel et al., "Demystifying Values Affirmation Interventions: Writing About Social Belonging Is a Key to Buffering Against Identity Threat," *Personality and Social Psychology Bulletin* 39(5) (2013): 663–76. For reviews and relevant research, see Geoffrey Cohen and David Sherman, "The Psychology of Change: Self-Affirmation and Social Psychological Intervention," *Annual Review of Psychology* 65 (2014): 333–71; David Sherman et al., "Self-Affirmation Interventions," in *Handbook of Wise Interventions*, eds. Gregory Walton and Alia Crum (Guilford, 2020), 63–99; and Clayton Critcher and David Dunning, "Self-Affirmations Provide a Broader Perspective on Self-Threat," *Personality and Social Psychology Bulletin* 41(1) (2015): 3–18.

For the study testing values affirmations among teachers, see Shannon Brady, Camille Griffiths, and Geoffrey Cohen, "Affirming the Teacher: Values-Affirmation Improves Classroom Dynamics," manuscript in preparation, 2021.

137   **science fiction TV series:** Owen Harris, dir., *Black Mirror*, season 2, episode 1, "Be Right Back," Netflix, aired February 11, 2013.

138   **chance encounters with strangers:** Nicholas Epley and Juliana Schroeder, "Mistakenly Seeking Solitude," *Journal of Experimental Psychology: General* 143(5) (2014): 1980–99.

Chapter 6: They're All the Same

139   **classic novel:** Ralph Ellison, *Invisible Man*, 2nd ed. (Vintage International, 1995), 3, 2.

140   **"The opposite of love is not hate":** Elie Wiesel, interview with Alvin Sanoff, *US News and World Report*, October 27, 1986. The adage appears to originate with William Stekel, *The Beloved Ego: Foundation of the New Study of the Psyche* (Kegan Paul, Trench, Trubner, 1921), 34.

140   **one of his routines:** Dave Chappelle, *Sticks and Stones*, dir. S. Lathan, Netflix, 2019.

141   **colony of ants:** I am grateful to Claude Steele for this metaphor. This chapter focuses on stereotyping, but this is only one of several powerful forces that sustain a system of advantage and exclusion (others include the media, ideologies, myths, power structures, and social policies that exacerbate inequality and segregation). For a broader discussion of these forces, see

Steven O. Roberts and Michael T. Rizzo, "The Psychology of American Racism," *American Psychologist* **76**(3) (2020): 475–87.

141   **older meaning of the word "see":** From Online Etymology Dictionary, https://www.etymonline.com/word/see.

141   **1983 study:** J. Darley and P. H. Gross, "A Hypothesis-Confirming Bias in Labeling Effects," *Journal of Personality and Social Psychology* **44** (1983): 20–33.

143   **students ... get "pegged":** For research showing that standard remedial programs contribute to student failure, see W. Norton Grubb, *Money Myth, The School Resources, Outcomes, and Equity* (Russell Sage Foundation, 2009); and Claude Steele, "A Threat in the Air: How Stereotypes Shape Intellectual Identity and Performance," *American Psychologist* **52**(6) (1997): 613–29. For bias in assignment to gifted and talented programs, see Jason Grissom and Christopher Redding, "Discretion and Disproportionality: Explaining the Underrepresentation of High-Achieving Students of Color in Gifted Programs," *AERA Open* **2**(1) (2016): 1–25.

143   **why students spiral:** J. P. Goyer et al., "Targeted Identity-Safety Interventions Cause Lasting Reductions in Discipline Citations Among Negatively Stereotyped Boys," *Journal of Personality and Social Psychology* **117**(2) (2019): 229–59; and David Yeager, Valerie Purdie-Vaughns [Purdie-Greenaway], Sophia Yang Hooper, and Geoffrey Cohen, "Loss of Institutional Trust Among Racial and Ethnic Minority Adolescents: A Consequence of Procedural Injustice and a Cause of Life-Span Outcomes," *Child Development* **88**(2) (2017): 658–76.

144   **(one study showed different results):** The study was conducted by Reuben Baron, Linda Albright, and Thomas Malloy, "Effects of Behavioral and Social Class Information on Social Judgment," *Personality and Social Psychology Bulletin* **21**(4) (1995): 308–15. It failed to replicate the effect found by Darley and Gross, "Hypothesis-Confirming Bias." However, there were two methodological deviations that may explain why. First, the researchers didn't measure objective grade-level estimates of Hannah's ability but instead used subjective-scale assessments. Research suggests that the latter often hide stereotype effects: Monica Biernat, "The Shifting Standards Model: Implications of Stereotype Accuracy for Social Judgment," in *Stereotype Accuracy: Toward Appreciating Group Differences*, eds. Y.-T. Lee, L. J. Jussim, and C. R. McCauley (American Psychological Association, 1995), 87–114.

Additionally, the study may have prompted participants to monitor and correct for their stereotyping by instructing them that the study's purpose was to develop "assessment procedures" for students while "remaining

sensitive to students' social backgrounds." This may have alerted participants to the study's focus on social class, a major threat to validity. When
subjects suspect the hypothesis, they may alter their responses to avoid
confirming it. See Elliot Aronson et al., *Methods of Research in Social Psychology*, 2nd ed. (McGraw Hill, 1989).

144 **a striking example:** Victoria Brescoll, Erica Dawson, and Eric Uhlmann,
"Hard Won and Easily Lost: The Fragile Status of Leaders in Gender-
Stereotype-Incongruent Occupations," *Psychological Science* 21(11) (2010):
1640–42.

145 **biased assessments of women:** Victoria Brescoll and Eric Uhlmann, "Can
an Angry Woman Get Ahead? Status Conferral, Gender, and Expression
of Emotion in the Workplace," *Psychological Science* 19(3) (2008): 268–75;
and Brescoll, "Who Takes the Floor and Why: Gender, Power, and Vol-
ubility in Organizations," *Administrative Science Quarterly* 56(4) (2011):
622–41.

145 **treatment of black children:** Jason Okonofua and Jennifer Eberhardt,
"Two Strikes: Race and the Disciplining of Young Students," *Psychological
Science* 26(5) (2015): 617–24.

146 **irreparable damage:** Paul Hemez et al., "Exploring the School-to-Prison
Pipeline: How School Suspensions Influence Incarceration During Young
Adulthood," *Youth Violence and Juvenile Justice* 18(3) (2020): 235–55.

146 **way stereotyping actually plays out:** Travis Riddle and Stacey Sinclair,
"Racial Disparities in School-Based Disciplinary Actions Are Associated
with County-Level Rates of Racial Bias," *Proceedings of the National Academy of Sciences* 116(17) (2019): 8255–60.

147 **less likely to be seen as children:** Phillip Goff, Matthew Jackson, Brooke
Di Leone, Carmen Culotta, and Natalie DiTomasso, "The Essence of Inno-
cence: Consequences of Dehumanizing Black Children," *Journal of Personality and Social Psychology* 106(4) (2014): 526–45.

148 **faux résumés sent to firms:** Marianne Bertrand and Sendhil Mullaina-
than, "Are Emily and Greg More Employable Than Lakisha and Jamal? A
Field Experiment on Labor Market Discrimination," *American Economic
Review* 94(4) (2004): 991–1013.

148 **trained black and white actors:** Devah Pager, "The Mark of a Criminal Record," *American Journal of Sociology* 108(5) (2003): 937–75. For a
follow-up, see Devah Pager, Bart Bonikowski, and Bruce Western, "Discrimination in a Low-Wage Labor Market: A Field Experiment," *American
Sociological Review* 74(5) (2009): 777–99.

149 **Jennifer Eberhardt:** Eberhardt, *Biased: Uncovering the Hidden Prejudice
That Shapes What We See, Think, and Do* (Viking, 2019). Some of the con-

tent here is also drawn from Eberhardt, *How Racial Bias Works—and How to Disrupt It*, video, TED Talk, 2020.

150 **Eberhardt teamed up:** Rob Voigt et al., "Language from Police Body Camera Footage Shows Racial Disparities in Officer Respect," *Proceedings of the National Academy of Sciences* **114**(25) (2017): 6521–26.

151 **discomfort as evidence of racial bias:** John Dovidio, Kerry Kawakami, and Samuel Gaertner, "Implicit and Explicit Prejudice and Interracial Interaction," *Journal of Personality and Social Psychology* **82**(1) (2002): 62–68.

152 **"These disparities could":** Voigt et al., "Language from Police Body Camera Footage," 6524.

152 **"tax":** *Real Sports with Bryant Gumbel*, Bryant Gumbel commentary, HBO, aired June 23, 2020, https://www.youtube.com/watch?v=Vv KPBJVAPWE&t=44s.

152 **abuse inflicted by stereotyping:** Erving Goffman, *Stigma: Notes on the Management of Spoiled Identity* (Prentice-Hall, 1963); and John Hartigan Jr., "Who Are These White People? 'Rednecks,' 'Hillbillies,' and 'White Trash' as Marked Racial Subjects," in *White Out: The Continuing Significance of Racism*, ed. E. B.-S. Ashley W. Doane (Routledge, 2003), 95–112.

153 **Asian Americans:** "Uniformly high-achieving" quote drawn from Zara Abrams, "Countering Stereotypes About Asian Americans," *APA Monitor* **50**(11) (2019): xx; and Wesley Yang, *The Souls of Yellow Folk: Essays* (W. W. Norton, 2019), xi–xii.

153 **excuse to exclude:** The tendency to exclude others based on arbitrary distinctions when the situation allows us to rationalize away our bias is discussed in John Dovidio and Samuel Gaertner's classic, "Aversive Racism," in *Advances in Experimental Social Psychology, Vol. 36*, ed. Mark Zanna (Elsevier Academic, 2004), 1–52. For more on how stereotypes can affect even people who consciously reject the stereotypes, value egalitarianism, or aspire to objectivity, see Mahzarin Banaji and Anthony Greenwald, *Blindspot: Hidden Biases of Good People* (Delacorte, 2013), xv, 254; Patricia Devine, "Stereotypes and Prejudice: Their Automatic and Controlled Components," *Journal of Personality and Social Psychology* **56**(1) (1989): 5–18; and Eric Uhlmann and Geoffrey Cohen, "Constructed Criteria: Redefining Merit to Justify Discrimination," *Psychological Science* **16**(6) (2005): 474–80.

154 **essay about pseudoscience:** Richard Feynman, "Cargo Cult Science," speech, California Institute of Technology commencement address, 1974; and Matt. 7:3, New International Version.

155 **solutions to prejudice don't work:** Frank Dobbin and Alexandra Kalev,

"Why Diversity Programs Fail," *Harvard Business Review* **94**(7) (2016): 52–60.

For the research on defensive reactions to disadvantage, see L. T. Phillips and B. S. Lowery, "I Ain't No Fortunate One: On the Motivated Denial of Class Privilege," *Journal of Personality and Social Psychology* **119**(6) (2020): 1403–22; and Phillips and Lowery, "The Hard-Knock Life? Whites Claim Hardships in Response to Racial Inequity," *Journal of Experimental Social Psychology* **61** (2015): 12–18.

155   **asked one group of managers:** Emilio Castilla and Stephen Benard, "The Paradox of Meritocracy in Organizations," *Administrative Science Quarterly* **55**(4) (2010): 543–676. The instructions to be fair increased gender bias in this study, perhaps because when people try to be "fair," they are more prone to act on stereotypic beliefs they regard as true, as suggested in the research by Uhlmann in the next paragraph of the main text.

155   **how important it was to be objective:** Eric Uhlmann and Geoffrey Cohen, "'I Think It, Therefore It's True': Effects of Self-Perceived Objectivity on Hiring Discrimination," *Organizational Behavior and Human Decision Processes* **104**(2) (2007): 207–23.

156   **powerful illustration:** Heidi Vuletich and B. Keith Payne, "Stability and Change in Implicit Bias," *Psychological Science* **30**(6) (2019): 854–62; Payne, Vuletich, and Kristjen Lundberg, "The Bias of Crowds: How Implicit Bias Bridges Personal and Systemic Prejudice," *Psychological Inquiry* **28**(4) (2017): 233–48; and Calvin Lai et al., "Reducing Implicit Racial Preferences: II. Intervention Effectiveness Across Time," *Journal of Experimental Psychology: General* **145**(8) (2016): 1001–16.

157   **At an individual level:** For evidence that individual-level situation-crafting can lessen prejudice, see: Nilanjana Dasgupta and Anthony Greenwald, "On the Malleability of Automatic Attitudes: Combating Automatic Prejudice with Images of Admired and Disliked Individuals," *Journal of Personality and Social Psychology* **81**(5) (2001), 800–14; and Patricia Devine et al., "Long-Term Reduction in Implicit Race Bias: A Prejudice-Breaking Intervention," *Journal of Experimental Social Psychology* **48**(6) (2012): 1267–78.

157   **new protocol:** Eberhardt, *How Racial Bias Works*.

158   **collaboration with the Department of Defense:** John Dovidio, unpublished data, personal communication, October 28, 2014. The impact of monitoring decisions and increasing accountability is also addressed in Dobbin and Kalev, "Why Diversity Programs Fail"; and Philip Tetlock and Gregory Mitchell, "Implicit Bias and Accountability Systems: What Must Organizations Do to Prevent Discrimination?" *Research in Organizational Behavior* **29** (2009): 3–38.

158   **similar intervention:** Emilio Castilla, "Accounting for the Gap: A Firm Study Manipulating Organizational Accountability and Transparency in Pay Decisions," *Organization Science* **26** (2015): 311–33.

158   **psychological timeouts:** For research on how values affirmation can lessen prejudice, see Steven Fein and Steven J. Spencer, "Prejudice as Self-Image Maintenance: Affirming the Self Through Derogating Others," *Journal of Personality and Social Psychology* **73**(1) (1997): 31–44; and Geoffrey Cohen and David Sherman, "The Psychology of Change: Self-Affirmation and Social Psychological Intervention," *Annual Review of Psychology* **65**(1) (2014): 333–71. For research on how mindful meditation can lessen prejudice, see Adam Lueke and Bryan Gibson, "Mindfulness Meditation Reduces Implicit Age and Race Bias: The Role of Reduced Automaticity of Responding," *Social Psychological and Personality Science* **6**(3) (2014): 284–91; and Jonathan Kanter et al., "Addressing Microaggressions in Racially Charged Patient-Provider Interactions: A Pilot Randomized Trial," *BMC Medical Education* **20**(1) (2020): 88.

Chapter 7: How Am I Seen?

160   **author of *White Fragility*:** Robin DiAngelo, *White Fragility: Why It's So Hard for White People to Talk About Racism* (Beacon, 2018). Quote is from Daniel Bergner, "'White Fragility' Is Everywhere: But Does Antiracism Training Work?" *New York Times,* July 15, 2020.

160   **Eminem:** Curtis Hanson, dir., *8 Mile*, Universal Pictures, 2002.

161   **dread of social disapproval:** Mark Pitner and B. Kent Houston, "Response to Stress, Cognitive Coping Strategies, and the Type A Behavior Pattern," *Journal of Personality and Social Psychology* **39**(1) (1980): 147–57. See also Chapter 11.

161   **"solo status":** Denise Sekaquaptewa and Mischa Thompson, "Solo Status, Stereotype Threat, and Performance Expectancies: Their Effects on Women's Performance," *Journal of Experimental Social Psychology* **39**(1) (2003): 68–74.

162   **his memoir:** Eminem, *The Way I Am* (Plume, 2009), 18.

162   **"social evaluative threat":** See the work of Sally Dickerson and colleagues: e.g, Alex Woody et al., "Social-Evaluative Threat, Cognitive Load, and the Cortisol and Cardiovascular Stress Response," *Psychoneuroendocrinology* **97** (2018): 149–55.

164   **our "face":** Erving Goffman, "On Face-Work: An Analysis of Ritual Elements in Social Interaction," in *Interaction Ritual* (Anchor, 1967), 5–45, on 10.

164   **Katharine Graham recounts:** Katharine Graham, *Personal History* (Vintage, 1998), 399.

164   **recounts the shock of discovering:** Claude Steele, *Whistling Vivaldi: How Stereotypes Affect Us and What We Can Do* (W. W. Norton, 2010), xii, 242.

165   **"cause us the greatest humiliation":** Ralph Ellison, *Invisible Man*, 2nd ed. (Vintage International, 1995), 264.

165   **influential 1995 paper:** C. Steele and J. Aronson, "Stereotype Threat and the Intellectual Test Performance of African Americans," *Journal of Personality and Social Psychology* **69**(5) (1995): 797–811. See also Steele, "A Threat in the Air: How Stereotypes Shape Intellectual Identity and Performance," *American Psychologist* **52**(6) (1997): 613–29.

168   **technical criticism:** A key criticism is the use of covariate adjustment. In the original Steele and Aronson studies and in several subsequent studies, black and white students were "statistically equated" in terms of their prior SAT scores through the analytic technique of covariate adjustment. The degree of racial gap that emerged in their estimated test scores was what is referred to as the "residual gap," the difference between black and white students' performance when prior indicators of ability and preparation are statistically controlled. The use of covariate adjustment is commonplace throughout the social sciences.

This means that the actual findings do *not* demonstrate that removing stereotype threat eliminates the racial achievement gap. Rather, removing stereotype threat eliminates the *residual* achievement gap. The residual gap was the phenomenon that motivated Steele's research—the persistent and pervasive gap in performance between black and white students that remains even after prior indicators of preparation and ability are controlled for. See Geoffrey Cohen and David Sherman, "Stereotype Threat and the Social and Scientific Contexts of the Race Achievement Gap," *American Psychologist* **60**(3) (2005): 270–71. The latter commentary was a response to a critique by P. R. Sackett et al., "On Interpreting Stereotype Threat as Accounting for African American–White Differences on Cognitive Tests," *American Psychologist* **59**(1) (2004): 7–13.

Notwithstanding these issues, the effect of removing stereotype threat consistently improves the performance of negatively stereotyped students on difficult tests in situations where they care about performing well. How much their performance improves, and the degree to which the gap between them and their nonstereotyped peers closes depends on a range of factors, such as the nature of the sample and the context of testing. Meanwhile there is little effect of these stereotype-removal manipulations on the nonstereotyped group and sometimes a detrimental effect. Greg Walton and I ascribe this latter effect to "stereotype lift," wherein nonstereotyped group members benefit from a slight performance boost in situations in which they are aware that they are on the upside of a negative stereotype: Walton and Cohen, "Stereotype Lift," *Journal of Experimental Social Psychology* **39**(5) (2003): 456–67.

168 **two comprehensive meta-analyses:** These found virtually identical effect sizes of stereotype threat: Oren Shewach et al., "Stereotype Threat Effects in Settings with Features Likely Versus Unlikely in Operational Test Settings: A Meta-Analysis," *Journal of Applied Psychology* **104**(12) (2019): 1514–34; and Hannah-Hanh D. Nguyen and Ann Marie Ryan, "Does Stereotype Threat Affect Test Performance of Minorities and Women? A Meta-Analysis of Experimental Evidence," *Journal of Applied Psychology* **93**(6) (2008): 1314–34. Several later replication studies suffer from two methodological flaws. Reflecting the trend toward online studies with samples of convenience, these later replications seldom recruit participants who are identified with the performance domain, and they take place entirely online, with participants completing the test under anonymous and largely unknown circumstances and without an experimental authority present. Social-evaluative threat seems likely to be limited under such conditions, with participants caring less about their performance and perceiving fewer expressive implications of poor performance than they do in the in-person, high-stakes laboratory situations crafted by Steele, Aronson, Spencer, and others.

Shewach and colleagues, it should be noted, are critics of stereotype threat. They zero in on a subgroup of studies that they favor and drop 167 studies out of a total of 212 (almost 80 percent), including the original stereotype threat studies. Doing this leads them to obtain a small effect size estimate, roughly half of the overall effect size based on the full sample of studies. Regardless of what you think of this technique, it's important to understand that stereotype threat repeatedly recurs in the real world, so even a small effect can add up to a large cumulative disadvantage: Robert P. Abelson, "A Variance Explanation Paradox: When a Little Is a Lot," *Psychological Bulletin* **97**(1) (1985): 129–33.

168 **As Steele says:** Claude Steele, "Why Are Campuses So Tense, and What Can We Do?" WISE Research Roundtable, Stanford University, January 28, 2020; and Steele, "Why Are Campuses So Tense? Identity, Stereotypes, and the Fraying of the College Experience," *Chronicle of Higher Education* **66**(15) (December 13, 2019): B17–B20. I am also grateful for many personal correspondences and conversations with Steele.

169 **feel threatened by one another:** Geoffrey Cohen and Julio Garcia, "'I Am Us': Negative Stereotypes as Collective Threats," *Journal of Personality and Social Psychology* **89**(4) (2005): 566–82.

170   **black students' sense of belonging:** Gregory Walton and Geoffrey Cohen, "A Question of Belonging: Race, Social Fit, and Achievement," *Journal of Personality and Social Psychology* **92**(1) (2007): 82–96.

170   **borrowed a technique:** For example, Schwartz and his team asked one group of married people to list two nice things their partner had done for them lately. The second group was asked to list nine things. The second group reported less marital satisfaction than the first group. Why? Because the effort required to come up with nine nice things led them to conclude that their partner was underperforming. These effects of such "metacognitive information" are stronger among people who feel insecure in a domain, which motivated our use of the manipulation to study belonging uncertainty. Norbert Schwarz, unpublished data, personal communication, February 17, 2019; and Schwarz, "Metacognitive Experiences in Consumer Judgment and Decision Making," *Journal of Consumer Psychology* **14**(4) (2004): 332–48.

172   **black students had interpreted:** In the study that Walton and I conducted, women, who are also negatively stereotyped in computer science, were unaffected by the list-eight-friends manipulation. However, women *were* affected by a similar manipulation that asked them to list eight *skills* they had in computer science versus two. It seems that stereotype threat led black students to question their social belonging and women to question their ability.

172   **people can be oversensitive:** Greg Lukianoff and Jonathan Haidt, *The Coddling of the American Mind* (Penguin, 2019).

172   **single experience of stereotype threat:** Kody Manke, *Stereotype Threat Perseverance,* PhD dissertation, Department of Psychology, Stanford University, 2016.

173   **The movie *The Post*:** Steven Spielberg, dir., *The Post*, Twentieth-Century Fox, 2017; and Graham, *Personal History*, 179, 181, 399.

175   **"mortifications":** Erving Goffman, *Asylums: Essays on the Social Situation of Mental Patients and Other Inmates*, 6th ed. (Chicago: Aldine, 1961), 45, 148, 14.

176   **"death by a thousand cuts":** H. Lee and M. T. Hicken, "Death by a Thousand Cuts: The Health Implications of Black Respectability Politics," *Souls* **18**(2–4) (2016): 421–45.

176   **basketball legend and writer:** Kareem Abdul-Jabbar, *Coach Wooden and Me: Our 50-Year Friendship on and off the Court* (Grand Central, 2017), 131.

177   **mortifications inflicted on:** M. Hebl and J. Xu, "Weighing the Care: Physicians' Reactions to the Size of a Patient," *International Journal of Obesity* **25**(8) (2001): 1246–52; Eden King et al., "The Stigma of Obesity in Customer Service: A Mechanism for Remediation and Bottom-Line Conse-

quences of Interpersonal Discrimination," *Journal of Applied Psychology* **91** (2006): 579–93; L. Martinez et al., "Selection BIAS: Stereotypes and Discrimination Related to Having a History of Cancer," *Journal of Applied Psychology* **101**(1) (2016): 122–28; and Hebl et al., "Formal and Interpersonal Discrimination: A Field Study of Bias Toward Homosexual Applicants," *Personality and Social Psychology Bulletin* **28** (2002): 815–25.

177   **mortifications that poor people face:** Kathryn Edin, Timothy Nelson, Andrew Cherlin, and Robert Francis, "The Tenuous Attachments of Working-Class Men," *Journal of Economic Perspectives* **33**(2) (2019): 211–28; H. Luke Shaefer, Kathryn Edin, and Laura Tach, "A New Anti-Poverty Policy Litmus Test," *Pathways*, Stanford Center on Poverty and Inequality, Stanford University, Spring 2017, 12; and Catherine Thomas, Nicholas Otis, Justin Abraham, Hazel Rose Markus, and Gregory M. Walton, "Toward a Science of Delivering Aid with Dignity: Experimental Evidence and Local Forecasts from Kenya," *Proceedings of the National of Sciences* **117**(27) (2020): 15546–53.

178   **Neuroscience research shows:** J. Brosschot, Bart Verkuil, and Julian Thayer, "Exposed to Events That Never Happen: Generalized Unsafety, the Default Stress Response, and Prolonged Autonomic Activity," *Neuroscience and Biobehavioral Reviews* **74**(Pt B) (2017): 287–96. Quote from Joe Feagin, "The Continuing Significance of Race: Antiblack Discrimination in Public Places," *American Sociological Review* **56**(1): 101–16, on 115.

178   **same prolonged vigilance:** Ta-Nehisi Coates, *Between the World and Me* (Spiegel & Grau, 2015), 90.

179   **simple place to start:** For research on the impact of stereotypical cues, see Sapna Cheryan, Victoria Plaut, Paul Davies, and Claude Steele, "Ambient Belonging: How Stereotypical Cues Impact Gender Participation in Computer Science," *Journal of Personality and Social Psychology* **97**(6) (2009): 1045–60; Valerie Purdie-Vaughns [Purdie-Greenaway], Claude Steele, Paul Davies, Ruth Ditlmann, and Jennifer Crosby, "Social Identity Contingencies: How Diversity Cues Signal Threat or Safety for African Americans in Mainstream Institutions," *Journal of Personality and Social Psychology* **94**(4) (2008): 615–30; and Mary Murphy, Claude Steele, and James Gross, "Signaling Threat: How Situational Cues Affect Women in Math, Science, and Engineering Settings," *Psychological Science* **18**(10): 897–95.

179   **values-affirmation exercises:** Geoffrey Cohen, Julio Garcia, Nancy Apfel, and Allison Master, "Reducing the Racial Achievement Gap: A Social-Psychological Intervention," *Science* **313**(5791) (2006): 1307–10; and Cohen et al., "Recursive Processes in Self-Affirmation: Intervening to Close the Minority Achievement Gap," *Science* **324** (2009): 400–3. For effects on belonging, see Jonathan Cook, Valerie Purdie-Vaughns

[Purdie-Greenaway], Julio Garcia, and Geoffrey Cohen, "Chronic Threat and Contingent Belonging: Protective Benefits of Values Affirmation on Identity Development," *Journal of Personality and Social Psychology* **102**(3) (2012): 479–96.

179 **runway for economic mobility:** Raj Chetty et al., "Income Segregation and Intergenerational Mobility in the United States," *Quarterly Journal of Economics* **135**(3) (2020): 1567–633.

180 **psychologically powerful:** Values affirmations are more impactful when people reflect on "self-transcendent" values: Aleah Burson, Jennifer Crocker, and Dominik Mischkowski, "Two Types of Value-Affirmation Implications for Self-Control Following Social Exclusion," *Social Psychological and Personality Science* **3** (2012): 510–16. Generally, values affirmations are more effective when people write about at least one value unrelated to the threatening domain (academic achievement in this case). Research suggests that the activity broadens people's psychological perspective: Clayton Critcher and David Dunning, "Self-Affirmations Provide a Broader Perspective on Self-Threat," *Personality and Social Psychology Bulletin* **41**(1) (2015): 3–18. For reviews of values-affirmation activities, the conditions under which they are beneficial, and the mechanisms through which they work, see Geoffrey Cohen and David Sherman, "The Psychology of Change: Self-Affirmation and Social Psychological Intervention," *Annual Review of Psychology* **65** (2014): 333–71; and David Sherman et al., "Self-Affirmation Interventions," in *Handbook of Wise Interventions*, eds. Gregory M. Walton and Alia J. Crum (Guilford, 2020), 63–99.

180 **full grade point:** Cook et al., "Chronic Threat and Contingent Belonging."

181 **disadvantaged Latino immigrant students:** David Sherman, Kimberly Hartson, Kevin Binning, Valerie Purdie-Vaughns [Purdie-Greenaway], Sarah Tomassetti, A. David Nussbuam, and Geoffrey Cohen, "Deflecting the Trajectory and Changing the Narrative: How Self-Affirmation Affects Academic Performance and Motivation Under Identity Threat," *Journal of Personality and Social Psychology* **104**(4) (2013): 591–618.

181 **academic death sentence:** see Warner Grubb, *Money Myth, The School Resources, Outcomes, and Equity* (Russell Sage Foundation, 2009); Claude Steele, "A Threat in the Air: How Stereotypes Shape Intellectual Identity and Performance," *American Psychologist* **52**(6) (1997): 613–29; and J. Parker Goyer, Julio Garcia, Valerie Purdie-Vaughns [Purdie-Greenaway], Kevin Binning, Jonathan Cook, Stephanie Reeves, Nancy Apfel, Suzanne Taborsky-Barba, David Sherman, and Geoffrey Cohen, "Self-Affirmation Facilitates Minority Middle Schoolers' Progress Along College Trajectories," *Proceedings of the National Academy of Sciences* **114**(29) (2017): 7594–99.

181   **likely to be attending college:** Goyer et al., "Self-Affirmation Facilitates Minority Middle Schoolers' Progress Along College Trajectories."

181   **replicated across an entire school district:** Geoffrey Borman et al., "Self-Affirmation Effects Are Produced by School Context, Student Engagement with the Intervention, and Time: Lessons from a District-Wide Implementation," *Psychological Science* 29(11) (2018): 1773–84; and Borman, Jeffrey Grigg, and Paul Hanselman, "An Effort to Close Achievement Gaps at Scale Through Self-Affirmation," *Educational Evaluation and Policy Analysis* 38(1): 2016: 21–42. For long-term effects, see Borman, Yeseul Choi, and Garrett Hall, "The Impacts of a Brief Middle-School Self-Affirmation Intervention Help Propel African American and Latino Students Through High School," *Journal of Educational Psychology* 113(3) (2021): 605–20.

Borman's team reported one failure to replicate the effects of values affirmation on GPA: Paul Hanselman et al., "New Evidence on Self-Affirmation Effects and Theorized Sources of Heterogeneity from Large-Scale Replications," *Journal of Educational Psychology* 109(3) (2017): 405–24. However, this research team did find that for both this cohort and another, the values affirmation intervention reduced disciplinary problems and suspension rates among black youth by roughly two-thirds: Geoffrey Borman, Jaymes Pyne, Chrisopher Rozek, and Alex Schmidt, "A Replicable Identity-Based Intervention Reduces the Black-White Suspension Gap at Scale," *American Educational Research Journal* (2021).

181   **improve the intellectual performance of groups:** Judith Harackiewicz et al., "Closing the Social Class Achievement Gap for First-Generation Students in Undergraduate Biology," *Journal of Educational Psychology* 106(2) (2014): 375–89; Crystal Hall, Jiaying Zhao, and Eldar Shafir, "Self-Affirmation Among the Poor: Cognitive and Behavioral Implications," *Psychological Science* 25(2) (2014): 619–25; Ian Hadden et al., "Self-Affirmation Reduces the Socioeconomic Attainment Gap in Schools in England," *British Journal of Educational Psychology* 90(2) (2020): 517–36; Arielle Silverman and Geoffrey Cohen, "Stereotypes as Stumbling-Blocks: How Coping with Stereotype Threat Affects Life Outcomes for People with Physical Disabilities," *Personality and Social Psychology Bulletin* 40(10) (2014): 1330–40; Kristin Layous et al., "Feeling Left Out, but Affirmed: Protecting Against the Negative Effects of Low Belonging in College," *Journal of Experimental Social Psychology* 69 (2017): 227–31; and René Kizilcec et al., "Closing Global Achievement Gaps in MOOCS," *Science* 335(6322) (2017): 251–52.

182   **interviewed students of color:** James Jones and Rosalie Rolón-Dow, "Multidimensional Models of Microaggressions and Microaffirmations," in

Microaggression Theory: Influence and Implications, eds. Gina Torino et al. (Wiley, 2018), 32–47.

182   **panaceas:** David Yeager and Gregory Walton, "Social-Psychological Interventions in Education: They're Not Magic," *Review of Educational Research* **81**(2): 267–301.

182   **2021 meta-analysis:** Zezhen Wu, Thees Spreckelsen, and Geoffrey Cohen, "A Meta-Analysis of the Effect of Values Affirmation on Academic Achievement," *Journal of Social Issues* (January 14, 2021), spssi.onlinelibrary.wiley .com/action/showCitFormats?doi=10.1111%2Fjosi.12415.

182   **affirmation in first week of classes:** Study 2 of Cook et al. "Chronic Threat and Contingent Belonging."

183   **"Why do Americans?":** Ruth Ditlmann, personal communication, February 23, 2021.

183   **white fragility:** DiAngelo, *White Fragility.*

184   **white adults . . . threat response:** For research on the physiological threat response arising in cross-race encounters, see Jim Blascovich et al., "Perceiver Threat in Social Interactions with Stigmatized Others," *Journal of Personality and Social Psychology* **80**(2) (2001): 253–67. For research on cognitive impairments among whites after cross-race encounters about racially charged topics, see Jennifer Richeson and Sophie Trawalter, "Why Do Interracial Interactions Impair Executive Function? A Resource Depletion Account," *Journal of Personality and Social Psychology* **88**(6) (2005): 934–47. For results related to colorblind ideologies, see Geoffrey Cohen, "Identity, Belief, and Bias," in *Ideology, Psychology, and Law,* eds. Jon Hanson and John Jost (Oxford University Press, 2012), 385–409.

184   **invited black and white adults:** Ruth Ditlmann, Valerie Purdie-Vaughns [Purdie-Greenaway], John Dovidio, and Michael Naft, "The Implicit Power Motive in Intergroup Dialogues About the History of Slavery," *Journal of Personality and Social Psychology* **112**(1) (2017): 116–35. The coding scheme Ditlmann used assessed affiliation imagery and was developed by David Winter, whose manual specifies the forms that affiliative statements take in conversation, including acceptance and appreciation: Winter, *Manual for Scoring Motive Imagery in Running Text,* 4th ed., unpublished manuscript, https://deepblue.lib.umich.edu/handle/2027.42/117563.

A controlled experiment demonstrated that a values affirmation intervention increased white Americans' willingness to acknowledge the existence of discrimination against minorities: Glenn Adams et al., "The Effect of Self-Affirmation on Perception of Racism," *Journal of Experimental Social Psychology* **42**(5): 616–26. Another way to ease white people's stereotype threat in conversations about race is to encourage them to adopt a growth mindset and to see the interaction as a learning opportunity: Phillip Goff, Claude Steele, and Paul Davies, "The Space Between Us: Stereotype Threat and Distance in Interracial Contexts," *Journal of Personality and Social Psychology* **94**(1): 91–107.

Chapter 8: I Can See It on Your Face (or Can I?)

187   **amusing column:** Dave Barry, "She Drives for a Relationship: He's Lost in the Transmission," https://www.unige.ch/~gander/california/relation.html.

190   **asked black and white college students:** J. Nicole Shelton and Jennifer Richeson, "Intergroup Contact and Pluralistic Ignorance," *Journal of Personality and Social Psychology* **88** (2005): 91–107. Much of this mutual misperception comes from what Jacquie Vorauer and colleagues call "meta-stereotypes," stereotypes we have about how others stereotype us: Vorauer et al., "How Do Individuals Expect to Be Viewed by Members of Lower Status Groups? Content and Implications of Meta-Stereotypes," *Journal of Personality and Social Psychology* **75**(4) (1998): 917–37.

191   **wise intervention:** Robyn Mallett and Timothy Wilson, "Increasing Positive Intergroup Contact," *Journal of Experimental Social Psychology* **46**(2) (2010): 382–87.

192   **static pictures of faces:** Janine Willis and Alexander Todorov, "First Impressions: Making Up Your Mind After a 100-MS Exposure to a Face," *Psychological Science* **17**(7) (2006): 592–98; and Andrew Engell, James Haxby, and Alexander Todorov, "Implicit Trustworthiness Decisions: Automatic Coding of Face Properties in the Human Amygdala," *Journal of Cognitive Neuroscience* **19** (2007): 1508–19.

192   **"availability heuristic":** Amos Tversky and Daniel Kahneman, "Judgment Under Uncertainty: Heuristics and Biases," *Science* **185**(4157) (1974): 1124–31.

192   **two candidates from opposing parties:** Alexander Todorov et al., "Inferences of Competence from Faces Predict Election Outcomes," *Science* **308**(5728) (2005): 1623–26. Todorov and colleagues have replicated this effect in gubernatorial, Senate, and House elections; see also Charles Ballew II and Alexander Todorov, "Predicting Political Elections from Rapid and Unreflective Face Judgments," *Proceedings of the National Academy of Sciences* **104**(46) (2007), 17948–53.

193   **36 percent of candidates' electoral fate:** Here, I am referring to that portion of their fate that's left over *after* chance (50% accuracy) is taken into account.

193   **snap judgments . . . about the teachers:** Nalini Ambady and Robert Rosenthal, "Half a Minute: Predicting Teacher Evaluations from Thin Slices of

Nonverbal Behavior and Physical Attractiveness," *Journal of Personality and Social Psychology* **64**(3) (1993): 431–41; and Ambady and Rosenthal, "Thin Slices of Expressive Behavior as Predictors of Interpersonal Consequences: A Meta-Analysis," *Psychological Bulletin* **111**(2) (1992): 256–74.

193   **We act on our shared biases:** See Chapter 5.

194   **promise fails to come across in . . . interview:** Performance in a standard "unstructured" interview does not predict future job or school performance, though adding structure to the interview through standardized questions improves its diagnostic value: Robyn Dawes, *House of Cards: Psychology and Psychotherapy Built on Myth* (Free Press, 1994).

194   **say more about our own:** David Dunning, Ann Leuenberger, and David Sherman, "A New Look at Motivated Inference: Are Self-Serving Theories of Success a Product of Motivational Forces?" *Journal of Personality and Social Psychology* **69**(1) (1995): 58–68; Sarah Wert, *Negative Gossip as a Response to Threatened Social Self-Esteem*, PhD dissertation, Department of Psychology, Yale University, 2004; and Wert and Peter Salovey, "A Social Comparison Account of Gossip," *Review of General Psychology* **8**(2) (2004): 122–37.

196   **read others' anxiety:** John Dovidio et al., "Implicit and Explicit Prejudice and Interracial Interaction," *Journal of Personality and Social Psychology* **82**(1) (2002): 62–68; and Russell Fazio and Michael Olson, "Implicit Measures in Social Cognition Research: Their Meaning and Use," *Annual Review of Psychology* **54**(1) (2003): 297–327.

197   **"Perspective Mistaking":** Tal Eyal, Mary Steffel, and Nicholas Epley, "Perspective Mistaking: Accurately Understanding the Mind of Another Requires Getting Perspective, Not Taking Perspective," *Journal of Personality and Social Psychology* **114**(4) (2018): 547–71. See also Epley, *Mindwise: How We Understand What Others Think, Believe, Feel, and Want* (Penguin, 2014).

198   **example of perspective-getting:** Catherine Thomas et al., "Toward a Science of Delivering Aid with Dignity: Experimental Evidence and Local Forecasts from Kenya," *Proceedings of the National Academy of Sciences* **117**(27) (2020): 15546–53.

198   **author and activist:** June Jordan, "On Listening: A Good Way to Hear," in *Civil Wars* (Touchstone, 1995).

198   **experience of poverty:** Kathryn Edin et al., "The Tenuous Attachments of Working-Class Men," *Journal of Economic Perspectives* **33**(2) (2019): 211–28; and H. Luke Shaefer, Kathryn Edin, and Laura Tach, "A New Anti-Poverty Policy Litmus Test," Stanford Center on Policy and Inequality, *Pathways*, Spring 2017.

199   **biases and blind spots:** Daniel Gilbert, *Stumbling on Happiness* (Knopf,

2006); and Timothy Wilson, *Strangers to Ourselves: Discovering the Adaptive Unconscious* (Belknap/Harvard University Press, 2002). As noted earlier, research shows that the interview has limited value in assessing people's abilities and in predicting their future performance (Dawes, *House of Cards*), but it is an effective tool for understanding their conscious perspective on themselves and their situations, assuming we ask good questions. For research on the importance of asking questions that challenge rather than confirm our beliefs, see Mark Snyder and William Swann, "Hypothesis Testing in Social Judgment," *Journal of Personality and Social Psychology* **36**(11) (1978): 1202–12.

200 **"fast friends procedure":** Arthur Aron et al., "The Experimental Generation of Interpersonal Closeness: A Procedure and Some Preliminary Findings," *Personality and Social Psychology Bulletin* **23**(4) (1997): 363–77. The thirty-six questions are available at https://amorebeautifulquestion .com/36-questions/.

201 **brought Latino and white college students together:** Rodolfo Mendoza-Denton and Elizabeth Page-Gould, "Can Cross-Group Friendships Influence Minority Students' Well-Being at Historically White Universities?" *Psychological Science* **19**(9) (2008): 933–39; and Page-Gould, Mendoza-Denton, and Linda Tropp, "With a Little Help from My Cross-Group Friend: Reducing Anxiety in Intergroup Contexts Through Cross-Group Friendship," *Journal of Personality and Social Psychology* **95** (2008): 1080–94. For examples of ingroup friends who helped with the careers of those regarded as outsiders, see Eminem, *The Way I Am* (Plume, 2009); and Katharine Graham, *Personal History* (Vintage, 1998).

201 **good tutor is the most effective:** Benjamin Bloom, "The 2 Sigma Problem: The Search for Methods of Group Instruction as Effective as One-to-One Tutoring," *Educational Researcher* **13**(6) (1984): 4–16; and Mark Lepper and Maria Woolverton, "The Wisdom of Practice: Lessons Learned from the Study of Highly Effective Tutors," in *Improving Academic Achievement: Impact of Psychological Factors on Education*, ed. Joshua Aronson (Academic Press, 2002), 135–58.

202 **what makes some tutors much more effective:** Lepper and Woolverton, "Wisdom of Practice," 2002.

203 **work for the United States Navy:** Mark Lepper, personal communication and shared confidential data reports, February 5, 2021.

203 **ways to cultivate authentic empathy:** For a review of research on empathy by a leading researcher, see Jamil Zaki, *The War for Kindness: Building Empathy in a Fractured World* (Crown, 2019).

203 **"the work of empathy":** Ronaldo J. Mendoza, *Emotional Versus Situational Inductions of Empathy: Effects on Interpersonal Understanding and*

Punitiveness, PhD dissertation, Department of Psychology, Stanford University, 1996, p. 1.

203   **ingenious experiment:** Mendoza, *Emotional Versus Situational Inductions of Empathy.*

206   **our "bias blind spot":** Emily Pronin, Daniel Lin, and Lee Ross, "The Bias Blind Spot: Perceptions of Bias in Self Versus Others," *Personality and Social Psychology Bulletin* **28**(3) (2002): 369–81.

207   **we . . . may be the weird one:** There is a cultural contributor to our blind spot. Research suggests that members of "Western, Educated, Industrialized, Rich, and Democratic" societies (referred to with the acronym WEIRD) are weird in the sense of having some unusual cognitive and behavioral penchants, compared with the 88 percent of the world's population who come from non-WEIRD societies (see also Chapter 5): Joseph Henrich, Steve Heine, and Ara Norenzayan, "The Weirdest People in the World?" *Behavioral and Brain Sciences* **33**(2–3) (2010): 61–83; and Henrich, *The Weirdest People in the World: How the West Became Psychologically Peculiar and Particularly Prosperous* (Farrar, Straus and Giroux, 2020).

Chapter 9: Belonging in School

212   **Dick Cheney's memoir:** Dick Cheney and Liz Cheney, *In My Time: A Personal and Political Memoir* (Threshold Editions, 2012), 26–27.

213   **substantial body of research:** For reviews, see Terrell Strayhorn, *College Students' Sense of Belonging* (Routledge, 2012); Geoffrey Cohen and Julio Garcia, "Identity, Belonging, and Achievement: A Model, Interventions, and Implications," *Current Directions in Psychological Science* **17**(6) (2008): 365–69; and Gregory Walton, Carol Dweck, and Geoffrey Cohen, *Academic Tenacity: Mindsets and Skills That Promote Long-Term Learning,* white paper, Bill and Melinda Gates Foundation, 2014, https://files.eric.ed .gov/fulltext/ED576649.pdf. See also M. D. Resnick et al., "Protecting Adolescents from Harm: Findings from the National Longitudinal Study on Adolescent Health," *Journal of the American Medical Association* **278**(10) (1997): 823–32; and J. Eccles, Sarah Lord, and C. Midgley, "What Are We Doing to Early Adolescents? The Impact of Educational Contexts on Early Adolescents," *American Journal of Education* **99** (1991): 521–42.

213   **A barrier:** Claude Steele, presentation to Social Area, Department of Psychology, Stanford University, 2020; and Steele, "Why Are Campuses So Tense? Identity, Stereotypes, and the Fraying of the College Experience," *Chronicle of Higher Education* **66**(15) (December 13, 2019): B17–B20.

214   **eight minutes of coaching:** Eric Bettinger et al., "The Role of Application

Assistance and Information in College Decisions: Results from the H&R Block FAFSA Experiment," *Quarterly Journal of Economics* **127**(3) (2012): 1205–42.

214 **power of a small group:** The ability of small, and often honorific, groups in school to foster the belonging of minority youth was also pioneered by Uri Treisman: "Studying Students Studying Calculus: A Look at the Lives of Minority Mathematics Students in College," *College Mathematics Journal* **23**(5) (1992): 362–75. Additionally, Claude Steele used small, racially mixed discussion groups in a university intervention program that he codesigned with Steven Spencer and Richard Nisbett to improve minority student achievement, as described in Steele, "A Threat in the Air: How Stereotypes Shape Intellectual Identity and Performance," *American Psychologist* **52**(6) (1997): 613–29.

214 **values-affirmation exercises:** See Chapter 7.

214 **schools can also foster belonging:** See the social-belonging intervention discussed in Chapter 2. For reviews of wise interventions in education, see Julio Garcia and Geoffrey Cohen, "A Social Psychological Approach to Educational Intervention," in *The Behavioral Foundations of Public Policy*, ed. Eldar Shafir (Princeton University Press, 2013), 329–47, https:// ed.stanford.edu/sites/default/files/a_social_psychological_approach_to_ educational_intervention_0.pdf; and David Yeager and Gregory Walton, "Social-Psychological Interventions in Education: They're Not Magic," *Review of Educational Research* **81**(2) (2011): 267–301.

Web-based platforms and mobile technology enable widespread delivery of wise interventions, though this should be done with caution and attention to the key conditions of the three Ts we've discussed. See the work of David Yeager, Gregory Walton, Shannon Brady in the College Transition Collaborative (https://collegetransitioncollaborative.org), e.g., David Yeager, Gregory Walton, Shannon Brady et al., "Teaching a Lay Theory Before College Narrows Achievement Gaps at Scale," *Proceedings of the National Academy of Sciences* **14**(24) (2016): E3341–E3348. For a promising use of mobile technology, see Kody Manke, Shannon Brady, Mckenzie Baker, and Geoffrey Cohen, "Affirmation on the Go: A Proof of Concept for Text Message Delivery of Values Affirmation in Education," *Journal of Social Issues* **77** (2021): 888–910. For an example of a mass online administration of values-affirmation and social-belonging interventions, see René Kizilcec et al., "Closing Global Achievement Gaps in MOOCS," *Science* **335**(6322) (2017): 251–52. Additionally, Raj Bhargava and I have created an app, *Unleash*, that allows educators to deliver affirmations to their students at moments when they're most likely to help (https://www.unleash -app.com/).

215 **benefits spilled over:** Joseph Powers et al., "Changing Environments by Changing Individuals: The Emergent Effects of Psychological Intervention," *Psychological Science* 27(2) (2015): 150–60.

215 **journal writing:** Erin Gruwell, *The Freedom Writers Diary: How a Teacher and 150 Teens Used Writing to Change Themselves and the World Around Them* (Crown, 1999).

215 **forget the importance of connection:** Eccles, Lord, and Midgley, "What Are We Doing to Early Adolescents?" For research on doing dull tasks with others, see Gregory Walton and Geoffrey Cohen, "Mere Sociality and Motivation," unpublished manuscript, Department of Psychology, Yale University, 2005. For related findings, see Walton et al., "Mere Belonging: The Power of Social Connections," *Journal of Personality and Social Psychology* 102(3) (2012): 513–32.

216 **Big Brothers Big Sisters:** Jean Baldwin Grossman and Joseph Tierney, "Does Mentoring Work? An Impact Study of the Big Brothers Big Sisters Program," *Evaluation Review* 22(3) (1998): 403–26; and Carla Herrera et al., "Mentoring in Schools: An Impact Study of Big Brothers Big Sisters School-Based Mentoring," *Child Development* 82(1) (2011): 346–61.

216 **research that looked at mentoring:** Shannon Brady et al., "A Brief Social-Belonging Intervention in College Improves Adult Outcomes for Black Americans," *Science Advances* 6(18) (2020): eaay3689; and Gallup Inc., *Great Jobs, Great Lives: The 2014 Gallup-Purdue Index Report—A Study of More than 30,000 College Graduates Across the U.S.,* http://www.luminafoundation.org/files/resources/galluppurdueindex-report-2014.pdf.

216 **strong effects of mentoring:** Tara Dennehy and Nilanjana Dasgupta, "Female Peer Mentors Early in College Increase Women's Positive Academic Experiences and Retention in Engineering," *Proceedings of the National Academy of Sciences* 114(23) (2017): 5964–69.

217 **belonging was the number-one predictor:** For other research showing the utility of measures of felt belonging in predicting women's persistence in STEM, see the research by Catherine Good et al., "Why Do Women Opt Out? Sense of Belonging and Women's Representation in Mathematics," *Journal of Personality and Social Psychology* 102(4) (2012): 700–17; and Karyn Lewis et al., "Fitting in to Move Forward: Belonging, Gender, and Persistence in the Physical Sciences, Technology, Engineering, and Mathematics (pSTEM)," *Psychology of Women Quarterly* 41(4) (2017): 420–36.

218 **threat of sexual harassment:** Naomi Wolf, "The Silent Treatment," *New York Magazine*, February 20, 2004; and Alexandra Laird and Emily Pronin, "Professors' Romantic Advances Undermine Students' Academic Interest, Confidence, and Identification," *Sex Roles* 83(1) (2020): 1–15. Less overt

harassment can also have negative effects. In a series of experiments, when women were exposed to flirtatious behavior from men in a professional setting, they experienced more stereotype threat and performed worse: Christine Logel et al., "Interacting with Sexist Men Triggers Social Identity Threat Among Female Engineers," *Journal of Personality and Social Psychology* **96** (2009): 1089–103.

218   **"culturally relevant pedagogy":** Gloria Ladson-Billings, "Toward a Theory of Culturally Relevant Pedagogy," *American Educational Research Journal* **32**(3) (1995): 465–91; and Na'ilah Suad Nasir et al., eds., *"We Dare Say Love": Supporting Achievement in the Educational Life of Black Boys* (Teachers College Press, 2018). For the two quantitative studies, see Thomas Dee and Emily Penner, "The Causal Effects of Cultural Relevance: Evidence from an Ethnic Studies Curriculum," *American Educational Research Journal* **54**(1) (2016): 127–66; Thomas Dee and Emily Penner, "My Brother's Keeper? The Impact of Targeted Educational Supports," *Journal of Policy Analysis and Management* (2021), https://doi.org/10.1002/pam .22328; and Sade Bonilla, Thomas Dee, and Emily Penner, "Ethnic Studies Increases Longer-Run Academic Engagement and Attainment," *Proceedings of the National Academy of Sciences* **118**(37) (2021), e2026386118. For Dee's interview, see Carrie Spector, "Access to Black Male Achievement Program Lowered Student Dropout Rates," Stanford News Service, October 21, 2019, https://news.stanford.edu/press-releases/2019/10/21/access -program-bol-dropout-rates/.

219   **teacher-student relationships:** Fatma Uslu and Sidika Gizir, "School Belonging of Adolescents: The Role of Teacher–Student Relationships, Peer Relationships and Family Involvement," *Educational Sciences: Theory & Practice* **17**(1) (2017): 63–82.

220   **76 percent of those questioned:** Evie Blad, "Students' Sense of Belonging at School Is Important: It Starts with Teachers," *Education Week*, June 20, 2017.

220   **teacher-student relationships that most promote belonging:** Gonul Sakiz et al., "Does Perceived Teacher Affective Support Matter for Middle School Students in Mathematics Classrooms?" *Journal of School Psychology* **50** (2012): 235–55.

220   **"wise criticism":** Geoffrey Cohen, Claude Steele, and Lee Ross, "The Mentor's Dilemma: Providing Critical Feedback Across the Racial Divide," *Personality and Social Psychology Bulletin* **25**(10) (1999): 1302–18. This paper, along with the following paper by Steele, reviews the real-world success stories that inspired wise criticism: "Race and the Schooling of Black Americans," *Atlantic*, April 1992.

220   **criticism is especially fraught:** Jennifer Crocker et al., "Social Stigma: The

Affective Consequences of Attributional Ambiguity," *Journal of Personality and Social Psychology* **60**(2) (1991): 218–28.

For research on the underchallenging of minority students by instructors, see Kent Harber, "Feedback to Minorities: Evidence of a Positive Bias," *Journal of Personality and Social Psychology* **74**(3) (1998): 622–28; Harber et al., "Students' Race and Teachers' Social Support Affect the Positive Feedback Bias in Public Schools," *Journal of Educational Psychology* **104** (2012): 1149–61; Harber et al., "The Conflicted Language of Interracial Feedback," *Journal of Educational Psychology* **111**(7) (2019): 1220–42; and Harber et al., "The Positive Feedback Bias as a Response to Self-Image Threat," *British Journal of Social Psychology* **49**(Pt 1) (2010): 207–18.

For research on the combinatorial power of "academic press" and "caring," see National Research Council, *Engaging Schools: Fostering High School Students' Motivation to Learn* (National Academies Press, 2004).

223   **male and female STEM majors:** Geoffrey Cohen and Claude Steele, "A Barrier of Mistrust: How Negative Stereotypes Affect Cross-Race Mentoring," in *Improving Academic Achievement: Impact of Psychological Factors on Education*, ed. Joshua Aronson (Academic Press, 2002), 303–27.

223   **wise criticism . . . with middle school students:** David Yeager et al., "Breaking the Cycle of Mistrust: Wise Interventions to Provide Critical Feedback Across the Racial Divide," *Journal of Experimental Psychology: General* **143**(2) (2014): 804–24. For long-term effects on college enrollment, see Yeager et al., "Loss of Institutional Trust Among Racial and Ethnic Minority Adolescents: A Consequence of Procedural Injustice and a Cause of Life-Span Outcomes," *Child Development* **88**(2) (2017): 658–76.

225   **distrust interferes with learning:** See Yeager et al., "Loss of Institutional Trust."

225   **point of vulnerability:** These terms are borrowed from S. Andersen, "Trajectories of Brain Development: Point of Vulnerability or Window of Opportunity?" *Neuroscience and Biobehavioral Reviews* **27**(1–2) (2003): 3–18.

225   **aftereffects of wise criticism:** Yeager et al., "Loss of Institutional Trust."

225   **too few teachers:** Harber et al., "Feedback to Minorities"; Harber et al., "Students' Race and Teachers' Social Support"; Cohen and Steele, "Barrier of Mistrust"; and Grace Massey, Mona Scott, and Sanford Dornbusch, "Racism Without Racists: Institutional Racism in Urban Schools," *Journal of Black Studies and Research* **7**(3) (1975): 10–19.

226   **toxic dynamic:** Yeager et al., "Loss of Institutional Trust"; and J. P. Goyer et al., "Targeted Identity-Safety Interventions Cause Lasting Reductions in Discipline Citations Among Negatively Stereotyped Boys," *Journal of Personality and Social Psychology* **117**(2) (2019): 229–59. For data showing that

the majority of K–12 teachers in the United States are white, see Yeager, "Breaking the Cycle of Mistrust," 808.

227   **method of raising teacher awareness:** Jason Okonofua et al., "Brief Intervention to Encourage Empathic Discipline Cuts Suspension Rates in Half Among Adolescents," *Proceedings of the National Academy of Sciences* **113**(19) (2016): 5221–26. Material discussed here also comes from an interview with Okonofua on April 24, 2020.

230   **destructive impact of suspension:** See Chapter 6.

230   **requires an affirmed and open mind:** The role of teacher psychology in student achievement has been shown in much research. As discussed in Chapter 5, one study found that giving a values affirmation to first-year teachers led them to have better relationships with their minority students and to create more rigorous classrooms. Research also shows that certain kinds of self-affirmation reduce the tendency for evaluators to overpraise and underchallenge minority students: Kent Harber et al., "The Positive Feedback Bias as a Response to Self-Image Threat," *British Journal of Social Psychology* **49** (2010): 207–18. Research also suggests that cognitive busyness (known as "cognitive load") increases stereotyping: Daniël Wigboldus et al., "Capacity and Comprehension: Spontaneous Stereotyping Under Cognitive Load," *Social Cognition* **22**(3) (2004): 292–309. Finally, supportive school climates seem to lessen teacher stress and, through this, promote more rigorous instruction of minority students: Harber et al., "Students' Race and Teachers' Social Support."

231   **important work:** Paul Tough, *How Children Succeed: Grit, Curiosity, and the Hidden Power of Character* (Mariner Books, 2013).

231   **points of vulnerability . . . windows of opportunity:** Andersen, "Trajectories of Brain Development."

231   **maelstrom of changes:** For data related to mental health of teens, see M. É. Czeisler et al., "Mental Health, Substance Use, and Suicidal Ideation During the COVID-19 Pandemic—United States, June 24–30, 2020," *Morbidity and Mortality Weekly Report* **69** (2020): 1049–57; and Jean Twenge et al., "Increases in Depressive Symptoms, Suicide-Related Outcomes, and Suicide Rates Among U.S. Adolescents After 2010 and Links to Increased New Media Screen Time," *Clinical Psychological Science* **6**(1) (2017): 3–17. For research on the decrease in academic motivation and increase in risk behavior during adolescence, see Eccles, Lord, and Midgley, "What Are We Doing to Early Adolescents?"; Adele Gottfried et al., "Continuity of Academic Intrinsic Motivation from Childhood Through Late Adolescence: A Longitudinal Study," *Journal of Educational Psychology* **93** (2001): 3–13; and Kathy Seal and Deborah Stipek, *Motivated Minds: Raising Children to Love Learning* (Holt, 2014).

232 **two most powerful protective factors:** Resnick et al., "Protecting Adolescents from Harm."

233 **not given the benefit of the doubt:** See Chapter 6. For the harms of this harsh disciplinary approach, see Okonofua et al., "Brief Intervention."

233 **practices fuel division:** See Chapter 4.

233 **team sports and extracurricular activities:** Joseph Mahoney and Robert Cairns, "Do Extracurricular Activities Protect Against Early School Dropout?" *Developmental Psychology* **33** (1997): 241–53; and Mahoney, "School Extracurricular Activity Participation as a Moderator in the Development of Antisocial Patterns," *Child Development* **71**(2) (2000): 502–16. See also Robert Putnam, *Our Kids: The American Dream in Crisis* (Simon & Schuster, 2015).

233 **teens lying in a functional MRI:** K. H. Lee et al., "Neural Responses to Maternal Criticism in Healthy Youth," *Social Cognitive and Affective Neuroscience* **10**(7) (2015): 902–12.

234 **wise intervention did this brilliantly:** Judith Harackiewicz et al., "Helping Parents to Motivate Adolescents in Mathematics and Science: An Experimental Test of a Utility-Value Intervention," *Psychological Science* **23**(8) (2012): 899–906.

234 **prevent teen reckless behavior:** See the pioneering research on the Teen Outreach Program by Joseph Allen and colleagues, summarized at http://teenoutreachprogram.com/wp-content/uploads/2020/02/Summary-of-TOP-Results_Oct-2019.pdf.

234 **antibullying programs:** For evidence that most antibullying programs don't work, see David Yeager et al., "Declines in Efficacy of Anti-Bullying Programs Among Older Adolescents: Theory and a Three-Level Meta-Analysis," *Journal of Applied Developmental Psychology* **37** (1) (2015): 36–51. Overall, across all programs, there is no discernible benefit of these programs in high school, and just a small one in elementary school.

For an antibullying intervention that *does* work, see David Yeager, Kali Trzesniewski, and Carol Dweck, "An Implicit Theories of Personality Intervention Reduces Adolescent Aggression in Response to Victimization and Exclusion," *Child Development* **84**(3) (2013): 970–88.

For the research on the broad range of potential benefits of values affirmations among teens and young adults, see Kevin Binning et al., "Bolstering Trust and Reducing Discipline Incidents at a Diverse Middle School: How Self-Affirmation Affects Behavioral Conduct During the Transition to Adolescence," *Journal of School Psychology* **75** (2019): 74–88; and Kate Turetsky et al., "A Psychological Intervention Strengthens Students' Peer Social Networks and Promotes Persistence in STEM," *Science Advances* **6**(45) (2020): eaba9221. Values affirmations have also been found to improve the GPAs of white college students uncertain of their belonging, see Kristin Layous et al., "Feeling Left Out, but Affirmed: Protecting Against the Negative Effects of Low Belonging in College," *Journal of Experimental Social Psychology* **69** (2017): 227–31.

235   **interested in the state of the world:** William Damon, *The Path to Purpose: How Young People Find Their Calling in Life* (Free Press, 2009).

235   **ingenious studies:** Christopher Bryan et al., "Harnessing Adolescent Values to Motivate Healthier Eating," *Proceedings of the National Academy of Sciences* **113**(39) (2016): 10830–35; and Bryan et al., "A Values-Alignment Intervention Protects Adolescents from the Effects of Food Marketing," *Nature Human Behaviour* **3**(6) (2019): 596–603.

236   **"magic bullet":** David Yeager and Gregory Walton, "Social-Psychological Interventions in Education: They're Not Magic," *Review of Educational Research* **81**(2) (2011): 267–301.

236   **"Expect more ... get more":** Lenore Jacobson and Robert Rosenthal, *Pygmalion in the Classroom: Teacher Expectation and Pupils' Intellectual Development*, expanded ed. (Crown House, 2003).

236   **increased the percentage of low-income students:** Omid Fotuhi, Philip Ehret, Stephanie Kocsik, and Geoffrey Cohen, "Boosting College Prospect Among Low-Income Students: Using Self-Affirmation to Trigger Motivation and a Behavioral Ladder to Channel to Action," *Journal of Personality and Social Psychology* (2021), in press, https://doi.org/10.1037/pspa0000 283. For the affirmation meta-analysis, see Zezhen Wu, Thees Spreckelsen, and Geoffrey Cohen, "A Meta-Analysis of the Effect of Values Affirmation on Academic Achievement," *Journal of Social Issues* (January 14, 2021), in press. Wise interventions have greater benefit when the social context reinforces the message that the intervention aims to instill: David Yeager et al., "A National Experiment Reveals Where a Growth Mindset Improves Achievement," *Nature* **573**(7774) (2019): 364–69; Stephanie Reeves et al., "Psychological Affordances Help Explain Where a Self-Transcendent Purpose Intervention Improves Performance," *Journal of Personality and Social Psychology* **120**(1) (2021): 1–15; for a review, see Gregory Walton and David Yeager, "Seed and Soil: Psychological Affordances in Contexts Help to Explain When Wise Interventions Succeed or Fail," *Current Directions in Psychological Science* **29**(3) (2021): 219–26.

237   **research on the best teachers:** For reviews, see Cohen, Steele, and Ross, "Mentor's Dilemma"; and part 3 of Walton, Dweck, and Cohen, *Academic Tenacity*.

237   **two examples:** Nicole Stephens et al., "Unseen Disadvantage: How American Universities' Focus on Independence Undermines the Academic Performance of First-Generation College Students," *Journal of Personal-*

ity and Social Psychology **102**(6) (2012): 1178–97; Shannon Brady, *Things Usually Left Unsaid: How the Messages Offered by Educational Environments Shape Students' Well-Being and Performance over Time,* PhD dissertation, Department of Psychology, Stanford University, 2016; and June Tangney, "Interview About *Shame in the Therapy Hour,*" American Psychological Association website, 2011, https://www.apa.org/pubs/books/interviews/4317264-tangney.

238 **fewer resources trying to measure ability:** Steele, "Why Are Campuses So Tense?"; and Claude Steele, *Whistling Vivaldi: How Stereotypes Affect Us and What We Can Do* (W. W. Norton, 2010).

240 **wisdom in the words:** Lisbeth Schorr, *Common Purpose: Strengthening Families and Neighborhoods to Rebuild America* (Doubleday, 1997), 231.

Chapter 10: Belonging at Work

241 **in their book:** Adrian Gostick and Chester Elton, *Anxiety at Work: 8 Strategies to Help Teams Build Resilience, Handle Uncertainty, and Get Stuff Done* (Harper Business, 2021), 8.

242 **A 2020 survey by Gallup:** Jim Harter, "Historic Drop in Employee Engagement Follows Record Rise," Gallup, July 2, 2020, https://www.gallup.com/workplace/313313/historic-drop-employee-engagement-follows-record-rise.aspx.

242 **heard personal stories:** A. Grant, "The Significance of Task Significance: Job Performance Effects, Relational Mechanisms, and Boundary Conditions," *Journal of Applied Psychology* **93**(1) (2008): 108–24; and Renee Holloway et al., "Evidence That a Sympatico Self-Schema Accounts for Differences in the Self-Concepts and Social Behavior of Latinos Versus Whites (and Blacks)," *Journal of Personality and Social Psychology* **96**(5) (2009): 1012–28.

242 **many jobs are not secure:** Angus Deaton and Anne Case, *Deaths of Despair and the Future of Capitalism* (Princeton University Press, 2020), 8; and Martin Sandbu, *The Economics of Belonging* (Princeton University Press, 2020).

243 **underestimate the degree:** Chip Heath, "On the Social Psychology of Agency Relationships: Lay Theories of Motivation Overemphasize Extrinsic Incentives," *Organizational Behavior and Human Decision Processes* **78**(1) (1999): 25–62; and Juliana Schroeder and Nicholas Epley, "Demeaning: Dehumanizing Others by Minimizing the Importance of Their Psychological Needs," *Journal of Personality and Social Psychology,* **119**(4) (2020): 765–91.

243   **proved disappointing:** Frank Dobbin and Alexandra Kalev, "Why Diversity Programs Fail," *Harvard Business Review* **94**(7) (2016): 52–60; and Claude Steele and Stephen Green, "Affirmative Action and Academic Hiring," *Journal of Higher Education* **47**(4) (1976): 413–35. For 2020 statistics, see Chen Te-Ping, "Why Are There Still So Few Black CEOs," *Wall Street Journal*, September 28, 2020; and "Women in Management," *Catalyst*, August 11, 2020, https://www.catalyst.org/research/women-in -management/.

244   **diversity can improve performance:** Katherine Phillips et al., "Is the Pain Worth the Gain? The Advantages and Liabilities of Agreeing with Socially Distinct Newcomers," *Personality and Social Psychology Bulletin* **35**(3) (2008): 336–50; Phillips, "How Diversity Makes Us Smarter," *Scientific American* **311**(4) (2014): 42–47; and Phillips, Sun Young Kim-Jun, and So-Hyeon Shim, "The Value of Diversity in Organizations: A Social Psychological Perspective," in *Social Psychology and Organizations* (Routledge/ Taylor & Francis, 2011), 253–71.

244   **can increase stereotype threat:** See Chapter 7.

245   **One study found:** Danielle Gaucher et al., "Evidence That Gendered Wording in Job Advertisements Exists and Sustains Gender Inequality," *Journal of Personality and Social Psychology* **101** (2011): 109–28.

245   **colorblind mission statements:** Valerie Purdie-Vaughns [Purdie-Greenaway] et al., "Social Identity Contingencies: How Diversity Cues Signal Threat or Safety for African Americans in Mainstream Institutions," *Journal of Personality and Social Psychology* **94**(4) (2008): 615–30. For a randomized experiment showing the performance benefits of diversity-positive messages, see Hannah Birnbaum, Nicole Stephens et al., "A Diversity Ideology Intervention: Multiculturalism Reduces the Racial Achievement Gap," *Psychological Science* **12**(5) (2021): 751–59.

245   **signs of discomfort:** Carl Word, Mark Zanna, and Joel Cooper, "The Non-verbal Mediation of Self-Fulfilling Prophecies in Interracial Interaction," *Journal of Experimental Social Psychology* **10**(2) (1974): 109–20, on 120. For a recent conceptual replication, see Drew Jacoby-Senghor, Stacey Sinclair, and J. Nicole Shelton, "A Lesson in Bias: The Relationship Between Implicit Racial Bias and Performance in Pedagogical Contexts," *Journal of Experimental Social Psychology* **63** (2016): 50–55. For research on signs of discomfort among whites in cross-race interactions, see John Dovidio, Kerry Kawakami, and Samuel Gaertner, "Implicit and Explicit Prejudice and Interracial Interaction," *Journal of Personality and Social Psychology* **82**(1) (2002): 62–68.

246   **ways men and women are evaluated:** Dana Kanze et al., "Evidence That Investors Penalize Female Founders for Lack of Industry Fit," *Science*

Advances **6**(48) (2020): eabd7664; Kanze et al., "Male and Female Entrepreneurs Get Asked Different Questions by VCs—and It Affects How Much Funding They Get," *Harvard Business Review,* June 27, 2017; Malin Malmstrom et al., "We Recorded VCs' Conversations and Analyzed How Differently They Talk About Female Entrepreneurs," *Harvard Business Review,* May 17, 2017; and Jorge Guzman and Aleksandra Kacperczy, "Gender Gap in Entrepreneurship," *Research Policy* **48** (2019): 1666–80.

247   **belief that passion is a primary driver:** Xingyu Li, Miaozhe Han, Geoffrey Cohen, and Hazel Markus, "Passion Matters but Not Equally Everywhere: Predicting Achievement from Interest, Enjoyment, and Efficacy in 59 Societies," *Proceedings of the National Academy of Sciences* **118**(11) (2021): e2016964118. See also Hazel Markus and Alana Connor, *Clash! How to Thrive in a Multicultural World* (Plume, 2013).

247   **hiring process:** Lauren Rivera, "Hiring as Cultural Matching: The Case of Elite Professional Service Firms," *American Sociological Review* **77**(6) (2012): 999–1022. For research showing that we tend to create self-serving criteria for success, see David Dunning, Ann Leuenberger, and David Sherman, "A New Look at Motivated Inference: Are Self-Serving Theories of Success a Product of Motivational Forces?" *Journal of Personality and Social Psychology* **69**(1) (1995): 58–68. These self-serving criteria can become quite specific and exclusionary: Dunning and Geoffrey Cohen, "Egocentric Definitions of Traits and Abilities in Social Judgment," *Journal of Personality and Social Psychology* **63**(3) (1992): 341–55.

248   **changed their criteria:** Eric Uhlmann and Geoffrey Cohen, "Constructed Criteria: Redefining Merit to Justify Discrimination," *Psychological Science* **16**(6) (2005): 474–80.

250   **blind decision-makers:** Such a blinding procedure appears to have reduced gender bias in evaluations of candidates for professional orchestras in the United States: Claudia Goldin and Cecilia Rouse, "Orchestrating Impartiality: The Impact of 'Blind' Auditions on Female Musicians," *American Economic Review* **90**(4) (2000): 715–41.

250   **adding an affirmation exercise:** Elizabeth Linos et al., "Levelling the Playing Field in Police Recruitment: Evidence from a Field Experiment on Test Performance," *Public Administration* **95**(4) (2017): 943–56.

250   **Our evaluations of others:** Steven Fein and Steven Spencer, "Prejudice as Self-Image Maintenance: Affirming the Self Through Derogating Others," *Journal of Personality and Social Psychology* **73**(1) (1997): 31–44; and David Dunning et al., "A New Look at Motivated Inference: Are Self-Serving Theories of Success a Product of Motivational Forces?" *Journal of Personality and Social Psychology* **69**(1) (1995): 58–68.

251   **ship captain:** Kurt Lewin, "Frontiers in Group Dynamics II: Channels of

Group Life; Social Planning and Action Research," *Human Relations* **1** (1947): 143–53, on 148–50.

251   **implementing a rigorous program:** Dobbin and Kalev, "Why Diversity Programs Fail."

251   **role models:** Benjamin Drury et al., "When Do Female Role Models Benefit Women? The Importance of Differentiating Recruitment from Retention in STEM," *Psychological Inquiry* **22**(4) (2011): 265–69.

251   **"add diversity and stir":** Robin Ely and David Thomas, "Getting Serious About Diversity: Enough Already with the Business Case," *Harvard Business Review*, November–December 2020.

251   **gender-inclusive policies:** William Hall et al., "Climate Control: The Relationship Between Social Identity Threat and Cues to an Identity-Safe Culture," *Journal of Personality and Social Psychology* **115**(3) (2018): 446–67.

252   **"growth mindset" work culture:** Elizabeth Canning et al., "Cultures of Genius at Work: Organizational Mindsets Predict Cultural Norms, Trust, and Commitment," *Personality and Social Psychology Bulletin* **46**(4) (2019): 626–42.

252   **weave self-affirming values:** Stephen Covey, *The 7 Habits of Highly Effective People: Restoring the Character Ethic* (Simon & Schuster, 2004), 149–51.

253   **Netflix:** Patty McCord, *Powerful: Building a Culture of Freedom and Responsibility* (Silicon Guild, 2018).

253   **teams . . . seldom perform as well as they should:** J. Richard Hackman, "Why Teams Don't Work," in *Theory and Research on Small Groups*, vol. 4, eds. R. Scott Tinsdale et al. (Springer, 2002), 245–67, on 251.

254   **leaders should link a vision:** Adam Grant, "Leading with Meaning: Beneficiary Contact, Prosocial Impact, and the Performance Effects of Transformational Leadership," *Academy of Management Journal* **55**(2) (2012): 458–76.

254   **psychological safety:** Amy Edmondson, *The Fearless Organization: Creating Psychological Safety in the Workplace for Learning, Innovation, and Growth* (Wiley, 2018), 7.

255   **effects on team performance:** Charles Duhigg, "What Google Learned From Its Quest to Build the Perfect Team," *New York Times Magazine*, February 25, 2016; A. Riskin et al., "The Impact of Rudeness on Medical Team Performance: A Randomized Trial," *Pediatrics* **136**(3) (2015): 487–95; T. Foulk et al., "Catching Rudeness Is Like Catching a Cold: The Contagion Effects of Low-Intensity Negative Behaviors," *Journal of Applied Psychology* **101**(1) (2016): 50–67; and Andrew Woolum et al., "Rude Color Glasses: The Contaminating Effects of Witnessed Morning Rudeness on Perceptions and Behaviors Throughout the Workday," *Journal of Applied Psychology* **102**(12) (2017): 1658–72.

256   **employees from Latino cultures:** Jeffrey Sanchez-Burks et al., "Cultural

Styles, Relational Schemas, and Prejudice Against Out-Groups," *Journal of Personality and Social Psychology* **79** (2000): 174–89.

256   **power of asking self-affirming questions:** Yue Jia, Kevin Binning, and Geoffrey Cohen, "Affirmation as a Buffer Against Employee Burnout," manuscript in preparation, 2021; and Arghaven Salles, Claudia Mueller, and Geoffrey Cohen, "A Values Affirmation Intervention to Improve Female Residents' Surgical Performance," *Journal of Graduate Medical Education* **8**(3) (2016): 378–83.

256   **"Good leadership":** John Hagel III, "Good Leadership Is About Asking Good Questions," *Harvard Business Review,* July 8, 2021.

257   **diversity training:** Matthew Brown and Christopher Chabris, "Starbucks's Troubles Can Be a Test for Anti-Bias Training: Does It Work?" *Wall Street Journal,* April 25, 2018; Frank Dobbin and Alexandra Kalev, "Why Diversity Training Doesn't Work: The Challenge for Industry and Academia," *Anthropology Now* **10**(2) (2018): 48–55; Corinne Moss-Racusin et al., "Scientific Diversity Interventions," *Science* **343** (2014): 615–16.

258   **research-backed diversity training:** Molly Carnes et al., "The Effect of an Intervention to Break the Gender Bias Habit for Faculty at One Institution: A Cluster Randomized, Controlled Trial," *Academic Medicine* **90**(2) (2015): 221–30; and Patricia G. Devine et al., "A Gender Bias Habit-Breaking Intervention Led to Increased Hiring of Female Faculty in STEM Departments," *Journal of Experimental Social Psychology* **73** (2017): 211–15. See also Edward Chang et al., "The Mixed Effects of Online Diversity Training," *Proceedings of the National Academy of Sciences* **116**(16) (2019): 7778–83.

258   **wise intervention:** This section draws both on personal correspondences with Jessi Smith from March 16 to April 12, 2021, and on these articles: Smith et al., "Now Hiring! Empirically Testing a Three-Step Intervention to Increase Faculty Gender Diversity in STEM," *BioScience* **65**(11) (2015): 1084–87; Smith et al., "Added Benefits: How Supporting Women Faculty in STEM Improves Everyone's Job Satisfaction," *Journal of Diversity in Higher Education* **11**(4) (2018): 502–17; and Beth Mitchneck et al., "A Recipe for Change: Creating a More Inclusive Academy," *Science* **352**(6282) (2016): 148–49. I also drew on the extensive bank of publicly available resources to support practitioners in implementing this program, retrievable at https://www.montana.edu/nsfadvance/formsresources/index.html.

Smith and colleagues' intervention was informed by self-determination theory, which has long highlighted the importance of belonging in motivation and thriving: Richard Ryan and Edward Deci, *Self-Determination Theory: Basic Psychological Needs in Motivation, Development, and Wellness* (Guilford, 2017).

259   **white people and men feeling left out:** Victoria Plaut et al., "'What About

Me?' Perceptions of Exclusion and Whites' Reactions to Multiculturalism,"
Journal of Personality and Social Psychology **101**(2) (2011): 337–53.

260   **myriad ways:** Quoted from Beth Mitchneck et al., "Recipe for Change,"
148. For research on defensive reactions to discussions of race and inequality, see Chapters 6 and 7.

261   **stories . . . of being subjected to bias:** For research on the power of stories, see Chapter 13. For the repository of stories and expert interviews related to the causes and consequences of bias, see "VIDS: Video Interventions for Diversity in STEM," Skidmore College website, https://academics.skidmore.edu/blogs/vids/. For research on the impact of these video resources, see Evava Pietri et al., "Using Video to Increase Gender Bias Literacy Toward Women in Science," *Psychology of Women Quarterly* **41** (2017): 175–96; and Corinne Moss-Racusin et al., "Reducing STEM Gender Bias with VIDS (Video Interventions for Diversity in STEM)," *Journal of Experimental Psychology: Applied,* **24** (2018): 236–60.

261   **showing evidence of gender or racial bias:** Corinne Moss-Racusin et al., "Gender Bias Produces Gender Gaps in STEM Engagement," Sex Roles 79 (2018): 651–70.

261   **Lewin would recommend:** Dobbin and Kalev, "Why Diversity Programs Fail." For evidence that promoting awareness and accountability is an effective debiasing strategy, see Chapter 6.

Chapter 11: Belonging and Health

264   **Humanity Crew:** Material comes from my interview with Essam Daod and Maria Jammal on April 18, 2018, and from an interview that Daod did with Ayellet Shani, "When African Refugees Board Boats to Italy, They Know They're Going to Die," *Haaretz,* April 3, 2018.

265   **"It's impossible," he says:** Shani, "When African Refugees Board Boats to Italy."

265   **psychiatrist David Spiegel:** David Spiegel et al., "Effect of Psychosocial Treatment on Survival of Patients with Metastatic Breast Cancer," *Lancet* **334**(8668) (1989): 888–91; and Catherine Classen and Spiegel, *Group Therapy for Cancer Patients: A Research-Based Handbook of Psychosocial Care* (Basic, 2008).

265   **Spiegel visited:** David Spiegel, "Mind Matters: Stress, Social Support, and Cancer Survival," presentation, Department of Psychology, Social Lab, Stanford University, 2014.

266   **advice-givers:** For benefits of giving advice, see Lauren Eskreis-Winkler et al., "A Large-Scale Field Experiment Shows Giving Advice Improves Aca-

demic Outcomes for the Advisor," *Proceedings of the National Academy of Sciences* **116**(6) (2019): 14808–10.

267 **2019 meta-analysis:** Spela Mirosevic et al., "'Not Just Another Meta-Analysis': Sources of Heterogeneity in Psychosocial Treatment Effect on Cancer Survival," *Cancer Medicine* **8**(1) (2019): 363–73. For marriage and cancer survival, see Susan Lutgendorf et al., "Social Influences on Clinical Outcomes of Patients with Ovarian Cancer," *Journal of Clinical Oncology* **30**(23) (2012): 2885–90.

267 **Careful biological studies:** S. W. Cole et al., "Sympathetic Nervous System Regulation of the Tumour Microenvironment," *Nature Reviews Cancer* **15**(9) (2015): 563–72. For an example of a drug-based clinical trial with cancer patients based on this research, see Jonathan Hiller, Steven Cole, et al., "Preoperative β-Blockade with Propranolol Reduces Biomarkers of Metastasis in Breast Cancer: A Phase II Randomized Trial," *Clinical Cancer Research* **26**(8) (2020): 1803–11.

268 **conserved transcriptional response to adversity:** S. W. Cole, "The Conserved Transcriptional Response to Adversity," *Current Opinion in Behavioral Sciences* **28** (2019): 31–37. The material here also comes from Cole, "Meng-Wu Lecture, Center for Compassion and Altruism Research and Education," Stanford University, 2013; and from generous personal correspondences with Cole.

268 **"The body doesn't care":** Quoted from interview with Population Reference Bureau, "Stress and Fear Could Take a Toll on Our Health During the Coronavirus Pandemic," May 14, 2020, https://www.prb.org/news/stress-and-fear-could-take-a-toll-on-our-health-during-the-coronavirus-pandemic/.

269 **slowly unfolding diseases:** Robert Sapolsky, *Why Zebras Don't Get Ulcers: The Acclaimed Guide to Stress, Stress-Related Diseases, and Coping,* 3rd ed. (Holt, 2004); and Peter Sterling, "Principles of Allostasis: Optimal Design, Predictive Regulation, Pathophysiology, and Rational Therapeutics," in *Allostasis, Homeostasis, and the Costs of Physiological Adaptation,* ed. J. Schulkin (Cambridge University Press, 2004), 17–64.

269 **perception of threat can live on:** For two treatments of this idea, see Sapolsky, *Why Zebras Don't Get Ulcers;* and Susan Nolen-Hoeksema, "Responses to Depression and Their Effects on the Duration of Depressive Episodes," *Journal of Abnormal Psychology* **100**(4) (1991): 569–82. Neuroscientific research suggests that chronic stress can arise from an "unsafe worldview": Jos F. Brosschot et al., "Exposed to Events That Never Happen: Generalized Unsafety, the Default Stress Response, and Prolonged Autonomic Activity," *Neuroscience and Biobehavioral Reviews* **74**(Pt B) (2017): 287–96.

270   **gap in health outcomes:** See, for instance, R. Clark, N. Anderson, V. Clark, and D. Williams, "Racism as a Stressor for African Americans: A Biopsychosocial Model," *American Psychologist* 54(10) (1999): 805–16. See also the pathbreaking research of Sherman James, Arline Gernonimus, and colleagues linking race-related stress to disease, e.g., Mahasin Mujahid, Sherman James, et al., "Socioeconomic position, John Henryism, and Incidence of Acute Myocardial Infarction in Finnish Men," *Social Science and Medicine* 173 (2017): 54–62; A. Geronimus et al., "'Weathering' and Age Patterns of Allostatic Load Scores Among Blacks and Whites in the United States," *American Journal of Public Health* 96 (2006): 826–33. For reports on the COVID death rate, see Centers for Disease Control and Prevention, "Risk for COVID-19 Infection, Hospitalization, and Death by Race/Ethnicity," May 26, 2021.

For research on the effects of stigma on the health of LGBTQ people, see Mark Hatzenbuehler and John Pachankis, "Stigma and Minority Stress as Social Determinants of Health Among Lesbian, Gay, Bisexual, and Transgender Youth: Research Evidence and Clinical Implications," *Pediatric Clinicals of North America* 63 (2016): 985–97; and Steven Cole et al., "Social Identity and Physical Health: Accelerated HIV Progression in Rejection-Sensitive Gay Men," *Journal of Personality and Social Psychology* 72(2) (1997): 320–35.

270   **ingenious experiment:** Sheldon Cohen, "Psychosocial Vulnerabilities to Upper Respiratory Infectious Illness: Implications for Susceptibility to Coronavirus Disease 2019 (COVID-19)," *Perspectives on Psychological Science* 16(1) (2020): 161–74; and Cohen et al., "Psychological Stress and Susceptibility to the Common Cold," *New England Journal of Medicine* 325(9) (1991): 606–12.

271   **poor and less educated regions:** Chirag Lakhani et al., "Repurposing Large Health Insurance Claims Data to Estimate Genetic and Environmental Contributions in 560 Phenotypes," *Nature Genetic* 51(2) (2019): 327–34. For research on the effects of geography on biological health, see Laura Dwyer-Lindgren et al., "Inequalities in Life Expectancy Among US Counties, 1980 to 2014: Temporal Trends and Key Drivers," *JAMA Internal Medicine* 177(7) (2017): 1003–11; and Angus Deaton and Anne Case, *Deaths of Despair and the Future of Capitalism* (Princeton University Press, 2020).

272   **Bowlby's and Ainsworth's insight:** John Bowlby, "Maternal Care and Mental Health," *Bulletin of the World Health Organization* 3 (1951): 355–533; and Mary Ainsworth et al., *Patterns of Attachment: A Psychological Study of the Strange Situation* (Lawrence Erlbaum Associates, 1978).

For the protective biological effects of parental support, see E. Chen et al., "Maternal Warmth Buffers the Effects of Low Early-Life Socioeconomic Status on Pro-Inflammatory Signaling in Adulthood," *Molecular Psychiatry* **16**(7) (2011): 729–37; and C. E. Hostinar and G. E. Miller, "Protective Factors for Youth Confronting Economic Hardship: Current Challenges and Future Avenues in Resilience Research," *American Psychologist* **74**(6) (2019): 641–52.

272 **work by Steve Cole . . . Fredrickson and colleagues:** For the original study and replications, see Barbara Fredrickson et al., "A Functional Genomic Perspective on Human Well-Being," *Proceedings of the National Academy of Sciences* **110**(33) (2013): 13,684–89; and S. W. Cole et al., "Loneliness, Eudaimonia, and the Human Conserved Transcriptional Response to Adversity," *Psychoneuroendocrinology* **62** (2015): 11–17. For evidence that eudaimonia predicts CTRA gene expression in collectivist cultures, see Shinobu Kitayama et al., "Work, Meaning, and Gene Regulation: Findings from a Japanese Technology Firm," *Psychoneuroendocrinology* **72** (2016): 175–81.

273 **wrote eloquently:** Viktor Frankl, *Man's Search for Meaning: An Introduction to Logotherapy*, 4th ed. (Beacon, 2000), 109.

274 **sense of purpose helps buffer:** Steve Cole, personal correspondences, October 2020. See also Kendall Bronk et al., "Purpose Among Youth from Low-Income Backgrounds: A Mixed Methods Investigation," *Child Development* **91** (2020), https://doi.org/10.1111/cdev.13434.

274 **Purpose and belonging are mutually reinforcing:** In Sheldon Cohen's research, both feeling supported *and* participating in social roles that support *others* each independently predicts resistance to infectious disease: Cohen, "Psychosocial Vulnerabilities to Upper Respiratory Infectious Illness." For evidence that purpose has two facets, see William Damon, *The Path to Purpose: How Young People Find Their Calling in Life* (Free Press, 2009).

274 **autobiographies:** Sarah Pressman and Sheldon Cohen, "Use of Social Words in Autobiographies and Longevity," *Psychosomatic Medicine* **69**(3) (2007): 262–69.

274 **linguistic analyses:** Matthias Mehl et al., "Natural Language Indicators of Differential Gene Regulation in the Human Immune System," *Proceedings of the National Academy of Sciences,* **114**(47) (2017): 12554–59 (the supporting online information provides evidence related to the use of first-person singular pronouns); and L. Scherwitz et al., "Self-Involvement and Coronary Heart Disease Incidence in the Multiple Risk Factor Intervention Trial," *Psychosomatic Medicine* **48**(3–4) (1986): 187–99.

275 **live longer:** Andrew Steptoe et al., "Subjective Wellbeing, Health, and Ageing," *Lancet* **385**(9968) (2015): 640–48; Patrick Hill and Nicholas Turiano,

"Purpose in Life as a Predictor of Mortality Across Adulthood," *Psychological Science* **25**(7) (2014): 1482–86; and O. Zaslavsky et al., "Association of the Selected Dimensions of Eudaimonic Well-Being with Healthy Survival to 85 Years of Age in Older Women," *International Psychogeriatrics* **26**(12) (2014): 2081–91.

275   **participate in a volunteer program:** Hannah Schreier, Kimberly Schonert-Reichl, and Edith Chen, "Effect of Volunteering on Risk Factors for Cardiovascular Disease in Adolescents: A Randomized Controlled Trial," *JAMA Pediatrics* **167**(4) (2013): 327–32. For a study on elderly mentoring youth, see Teresa Seeman et al., "Intergenerational Mentoring, Eudaimonic Well-Being and Gene Regulation in Older Adults: A Pilot Study," *Psychoneuroendocrinology* **111** (January 2020): 104468.

275   **small acts of kindness:** S. K. Nelson-Coffey et al., "Kindness in the Blood: A Randomized Controlled Trial of the Gene Regulatory Impact of Prosocial Behavior," *Psychoneuroendocrinology* **81** (2017): 8–13; and Teresa Seeman et al., "Intergenerational Mentoring, Eudaimonic Well-Being and Gene Regulation in Older Adults: A Pilot Study," *Psychoneuroendocrinology* **111** (2020): 104468.

275   **purpose is a choice:** Damon, "Path to Purpose"; and Andrew J. Fuligni et al., "Daily Family Assistance and Inflammation Among Adolescents from Latin American and European Backgrounds," *Brain, Behavior, and Immunity* **23**(6) (2009): 803–9.

276   **Connecting with our values:** David Sherman et al., "Psychological Vulnerability and Stress: The Effects of Self-Affirmation on Sympathetic Nervous System Responses to Naturalistic Stressors," *Health Psychology* **28**(5) (2009): 554–62; and Carissa Low et al., "A Randomized Controlled Trial of Emotionally Expressive Writing for Women with Metastatic Breast Cancer," *Health Psychology* **29**(4) (2010): 460–66.

277   **writing activity has a long history:** James Pennebaker, *Opening Up: The Healing Power of Expressing Emotions* (Guilford, 1997); J. D. Creswell et al., "Does Self-Affirmation, Cognitive Processing, or Discovery of Meaning Explain Cancer-Related Health Benefits of Expressive Writing?" *Personality and Social Psychology Bulletin* **33**(2) (2007): 238–50; and S. Lyubomirsky, L. Sousa, and R. Dickerhoof, "The Costs and Benefits of Writing, Talking, and Thinking About Life's Triumphs and Defeats," *Journal of Personality and Social Psychology* **90**(4) (2006): 692–708.

278   **these words:** Fourteenth Dalai Lama, Desmond Tutu, and Douglas Carlton Abrams, *The Book of Joy: Lasting Happiness in a Changing World* (Avery, 2016), 111–12.

278   **health effects of a values-affirmation intervention:** Christine Logel and Geoffrey Cohen, "The Role of the Self in Physical Health: Testing the Effect

of a Values-Affirmation Intervention on Weight Loss," *Psychological Science* **23**(1) (2012): 53–55; and Logel, Xingyu Li, and Cohen, "Affirmation Prevents Long-Term Weight Gain," *Journal of Experimental Social Psychology* **81** (2019): 70–75. For research showing that values affirmations activate brain reward circuitry, see Janine Dutcher, J. Creswell et al., "Self-Affirmation Activates the Ventral Striatum: A Possible Reward-Related Mechanism for Self-Affirmation," *Psychological Science* **27**(4) (2016): 455–66.

279   **Values-affirmation exercises . . . contribute to better health:** Christopher Armitage et al., "Self-Affirmation Increases Acceptance of Health-Risk Information Among UK Adult Smokers with Low Socioeconomic Status," *Psychology of Addictive Behaviors* **22**(1) (2008): 88–95; and Edward Havranek et al., "The Effect of Values Affirmation on Race-Discordant Patient-Provider Communication," *Archives of Internal Medicine* **172**(21) (2012): 1662–67. For a review, see David Sherman et al., "Self-Affirmation Interventions," in *Handbook of Wise Interventions: How Social-Psychological Insights Can Help Solve Problems*, eds. G. Walton and A. Crum (Guilford, 2020): 63–99; and Cohen and Sherman, "The Psychology of Change: Self-Affirmation and Social Psychological Intervention," *Annual Review of Psychology* **65**(1) (2014): 333–71.

279   **comprehensive assessment . . . health effects of affirmation:** Rebecca Ferrer and Geoffrey Cohen, "Reconceptualizing Self-Affirmation with the Trigger and Channel Framework: Lessons from the Health Domain," *Personality and Social Psychology Review* **23** (2018): 267–84.

280   **affirming activities:** These psychological timeouts can be delivered via online platforms or mobile technology, e.g., Kody Manke, Shannon Brady, McKenzie Baker, and Geoffrey Cohen, "Affirmation on the Go: A Proof-of-Concept for Text Message Delivery of Values Affirmation in Education," *Journal of Social Issues* **77** (2021): 888–910. In the course taught by Raj Bhargava and me, students completed surveys assessing their purpose and well-being at the beginning and end of the class, and they showed statistically significant gains.

Other psychological timeouts, such as mindful meditation, have been shown to have positive effects on physical health by lessening stress and improving social connection. See Emily Lindsay and J. David Creswell, "Mechanisms of Mindfulness Training: Monitor and Acceptance Theory (MAT)," *Clinical Psychology Review* **51** (2017): 48–59.

280   **One of our study participants:** Hazel Markus, Catherine Thomas, Michael Schwalbe, Macario Garcia, and Geoffrey Cohen, "Inequality in Coping and Loss: Mostly Surviving, Some Thriving in the COVID-19 Crisis," *AVP Crisis Monitoring Series,* May 2021.

281   **strong effect on health . . . wise criticism:** Greg Walton, Shannon Brady,

Hazel Markus, Steve Cole, and Geoffrey Cohen, "Wise Criticism and CTRA," manuscript in preparation, Stanford University, 2021.

282 **vital connection:** Abraham Verghese et al., "The Bedside Evaluation: Ritual and Reason," *Annals of Internal Medicine* **155**(8) (2011): 550–53.

282 **effects of health care providers:** L. C. Howe, J. P. Goyer, and A. J. Crum, "Harnessing the Placebo Effect: Exploring the Influence of Physician Characteristics on Placebo Response," *Health Psychology* **36**(11) (2017): 1074–82.

282 **friendly connections with patients:** D. A. Redelmeier et al., "A Randomised Trial of Compassionate Care for the Homeless in an Emergency Department," *Lancet* **345**(8958) (1995): 1131–34; and G. L. Carter et al., "Postcards from the EDge: 5-Year Outcomes of a Randomised Controlled Trial for Hospital-Treated Self-Poisoning," *British Journal of Psychiatry* **202**(5) (2013): 372–80.

283 **letter:** "Humor in the Time of Corona," *Stay Tuned with Preet*, April 2, 2020, https://cafe.com/stay-tuned/stay-tuned-note-from-a-doctor-in-arizona/.

284 **connection is critical to human health:** Julianne Holt-Lunstad et al., "Advancing Social Connection as a Public Health Priority in the United States," *American Psychologist* **72**(6) (2017): 517–30, on 527.

284 **perception that social support will simply be available:** T. A. Wills and M. C. Ainette, "Social Networks and Social Support," in *Handbook of Health Psychology*, eds. A. Baum, T. A. Revenson, and J. Singer (Psychology Press, 2012), 465–92; and Youngmee Kim et al., "Only the Lonely: Expression of Proinflammatory Genes Through Family Cancer Caregiving Experiences," *Psychosomatic Medicine* **83**(2) (2021): 149–56.

Chapter 12: Belonging in Policing and the Community

287 **former Seattle police chief:** Norm Stamper, *To Protect and Serve: How to Fix America's Police* (Bold Type Books, 2016). As quoted in Michael Martin, host, "Former Police Chief Has a Plan for 'How to Fix America's Police,'" interview with Stamper, *All Things Considered*, National Public Radio, July 10, 2016.

287 **Consider this experiment:** Kristina Murphy and Lorraine Mazerolle, "Policing Immigrants: Using a Randomized Control Trial of Procedural Justice Policing to Promote Trust and Cooperation," *Australian and New Zealand Journal of Criminology* **51**(1) (2016): 3–22; and Mazerolle et al., "Procedural Justice, Routine Encounters and Citizen Perceptions of Police: Main Findings from the Queensland Community Engagement Trial (QCET)," *Journal of Experimental Criminology* **8**(4) (2012): 343–67.

289   **study conducted with the Chicago police:** George Wood, Tom Tyler, and Andrew Papachristos, "Procedural Justice Training Reduces Police Use of Force and Complaints Against Officers," *Proceedings of the National Academy of Sciences* 117(18) (2020): 9815–21.

290   **police precincts in Seattle:** Emily Owens et al., "Can You Build a Better Cop?" *Criminology and Public Policy* 17(1) (2018): 41–87.

292   **Why do procedurally just processes matter:** Tom Tyler, *Why People Obey the Law* (Princeton University Press, 2006); and Matthew Lieberman, *Social: Why Our Brains Are Wired to Connect* (Crown, 2013). Raymond Paternoster et al., "Do Fair Procedures Matter? The Effect of Procedural Justice on Spouse Assault," *Law and Society Review* 31(1) (1997): 163–204.

293   **affirming communication with offenders:** Jason Okonofua et al., "A Scalable Empathic Supervision Intervention to Mitigate Recidivism from Probation and Parole," *Proceedings of the National Academy of Sciences* 118(14) (April 6, 2021); G. Walton et al., "Lifting the Bar: A Relationship-Orienting Intervention Reduces Recidivism Among Children Reentering School From Juvenile Detention," *Psychological Science*, 32(11) (2021): 1747–67.

293   **documentary:** Not in Our Town and U.S. Department of Justice COPS Office, *Camden's Turn: A Story of Police Reform in Progress,* video, 2017. See also Sonia Tsuruoka, *Camden's Turn: A Story of Police Reform in Progress— A Guide to Law Enforcement and Community Screenings,* Office of Community Oriented Policing Services, Washington, DC, 2018.

295   **Superordinate goals:** See Chapter 4.

Chapter 13: **Belonging and Our Politics**

298   **most powerful demonstration:** Charles Lord, Lee Ross, and Mark Lepper, "Biased Assimilation and Attitude Polarization: The Effects of Prior Theories on Subsequently Considered Evidence," *Journal of Personality and Social Psychology* 37 (1979): 2098–109. A follow-up found actual attitude polarization rather than simply perceived attitude change for those partisans who expressed relatively stronger confidence in the objectivity of their political side's position: Michael Schwalbe, Geoffrey Cohen, and Lee Ross, "The Objectivity Illusion and Voter Polarization in the 2016 Presidential Election," *Proceedings of the National Academy of Sciences* 117(35) (2020): 21, 218–29. For research on how exposure to opposing views can backfire, see Christopher Bail et al., "Exposure to Opposing Views on Social Media Can Increase Political Polarization," *Proceedings of the National Academy of Sciences* 115(37) (2018): 9216–21. For research on the inefficacy of persuasive

campaigns, see Joshua Kalla and David Broockman, "The Minimal Persuasive Effects of Campaign Contact in General Elections: Evidence from 49 Field Experiments," *American Political Science Review* **112**(1) (2018): 148–66.

298 **presented the participants with news stories:** Michael Schwalbe, Katie Joseff, Samuel Woolley, and Geoffrey Cohen, "Party Over Reality: The Dominating Impact of Partisanship on Judgments of News Veracity," manuscript under review, 2021. Quote from Arie Kruglanski, Donna Webster, and Adena Klem, "Motivated Resistance and Openness to Persuasion in the Presence or Absence of Prior Information," *Journal of Personality and Social Psychology* **65**(5) (1993): 861–76, on 862.

299 **social psychologists have discovered:** John Tierney and Roy F. Baumeister, *The Power of Bad: How the Negativity Effect Rules Us and How We Can Rule It* (Penguin, 2019). For a review of the "objectivity illusion," see Emily Pronin, Thomas Gilovich, and Lee Ross, "Objectivity in the Eye of the Beholder: Divergent Perceptions of Bias in Self Versus Others," *Psychological Review* **111**(3) (2004): 781–99.

300 **need to understand its causes:** Leo Tolstoy, *Anna Karenina* (McClure, Phillips, 1901), 449. For research showing overconfidence and confirmation bias among political "experts," see Philip Tetlock, *Expert Political Judgment: How Good Is It? How Can We Know?* (Princeton University Press, 2017). For a write-up of the impact of the training modules aimed at raising awareness of bias, see Carey Morewedge et al., "Debiasing Decisions: Improved Decision Making with a Single Training Intervention," *Policy Insights from the Behavioral and Brain Sciences* **2**(1) (2015): 129–40.

301 **rooted in biology:** Jonas Kaplan, Sarah Gimbel, and Sam Harris, "Neural Correlates of Maintaining One's Political Beliefs in the Face of Counterevidence," *Scientific Reports* **6**(1) (2016): 39589; and Drew Westen et al., "Neural Bases of Motivated Reasoning: An fMRI Study of Emotional Constraints on Partisan Political Judgment in the 2004 U.S. Presidential Election," *Journal of Cognitive Neuroscience* **18**(11) (2006): 1947–58.

301 **dissident views:** For the story of the Democratic dissident, see "Beer Summit," *This American Life*, Episode 683, September 20, 2019. For the story of the Republican secretary of state, see Lindsay Wise and Cameron McWhirter, "Georgia Republicans Worry Trump Feud Could Hurt Key Senate Runoffs," *Wall Street Journal*, November 16, 2020.

301 **process of rationalization:** Geoffrey Cohen, "Party over Policy: The Dominating Impact of Group Influence on Political Beliefs," *Journal of Personality and Social Psychology* **85**(5) (2003): 808–22. For follow-ups, see Flores et al., "Politicians Polarize and Experts Depolarize Public Support for COVID-19 Management Policies," *Proceedings of the National Academy of Sciences* (in press, 2022); Maykel Verkuyten and Mieke Maliepaard, "A

Further Test of the 'Party over Policy' Effect: Political Leadership and Ethnic Minority Policies," *Basic and Applied Social Psychology* **35**(3) (2013): 241–48; Phillip Ehret, Leaf Van Boven, and David Sherman, "Partisan Barriers to Bipartisanship: Understanding Climate Policy Polarization," *Social Psychological and Personality Science* **9**(3) (2018): 308–18; and Ariel Malka and Yphtach Lelkes, "More Than Ideology: Conservative-Liberal Identity and Receptivity to Political Cues," *Social Justice Research* **23** (2010): 156–88. For the study with Israeli versus Palestinian peace proposals, see Ifat Maoz et al., "Reactive Devaluation of an 'Israeli' vs. 'Palestinian' Peace Proposal," *Journal of Conflict Resolution* **46**(4) (2002): 515–46. For boundary conditions on political conformity, see Lelkes, "Policy over Party: Comparing the Effects of Candidate Ideology and Party on Affective Polarization," *Political Science Research and Methods* **9**(1) (2021): 189–96.

303 **our minds are like double agents:** Matthew Lieberman, *Social: Why Our Brains Are Wired to Connect* (Crown, 2013).

303 **wrote an article:** Klein, "The Depressing Psychological Theory That Explains Washington," *Washington Post*, January 10, 2014. See also Ezra Klein, *Why We're Polarized* (Avid Reader Press/Simon & Schuster, 2020).

303 **groups influence us . . . by shaping our perceptions:** For the "security force" example, see Maoz et al., "Reactive Devaluation." For a deep discussion of the cognitive basis of conformity, see Solomon Asch, *Social Psychology* (Prentice-Hall, 1952), Chapters 14, 15, and 19.

303 **we dismiss the other side:** For the role of perceived bias in fueling social conflict, this classic reads fresh today: Lee Ross and Andrew Ward, "Naive Realism: Implications for Social Conflict and Misunderstanding," in *The Jean Piaget Symposium Series: Values and Knowledge*, eds. E. S. Reed, E. Turiel, and T. Brown (Lawrence Erlbaum Associates, 1996), 103–35. See also Emily Pronin, Kathleen Kennedy, and Sarah Butsch, "Bombing Versus Negotiating: How Preferences for Combating Terrorism Are Affected by Perceived Terrorist Rationality," *Basic and Applied Social Psychology* **28**(4) (2006): 385–92; and Schwalbe, Cohen, and Ross, "Objectivity Illusion and Voter Polarization."

305 **some affirmation to those with opposing views:** For the debiasing effects of affirmation, see Geoffrey Cohen, Joshua Aronson, and Claude Steele, "When Beliefs Yield to Evidence: Reducing Biased Evaluation by Affirming the Self," *Personality and Social Psychology Bulletin* **26**(9) (2000): 1151–64; Cohen et al., "Bridging the Partisan Divide: Self-Affirmation Reduces Ideological Closed-Mindedness and Inflexibility in Negotiation," *Journal of Personality and Social Psychology* **93**(3) (2007): 415–30; Sabina Čehajić-Clancy et al., "Affirmation, Acknowledgment of In-Group Responsibility, Group-Based Guilt, and Support for Reparative Measures," *Journal of Per-*

sonality and Social Psychology **101**(2) (2011): 256–70; and Kevin Binning et al., "Going Along Versus Getting It Right: The Role of Self-Integrity in Political Conformity," *Journal of Experimental Social Psychology* **56** (2015): 73–88. For some studies that did not support the debiasing effects of affirmation, see Lyons et al., "Self-Affirmation and Identity-Driven Political Behavior," *Journal of Experimental Political Science* (2021), 1–16. However, the majority of these studies did not present participants with psychologically threatening information, such as strong counter-attitudinal evidence, so there was no defensive response for affirmation to ameliorate.

307   **1978 Camp David Accords:** Don Richardson, ed., *Conversations with Carter* (Lynne Rienner, 1998), 161.

308   **issue, as we perceive it, is different:** Ross and Ward, "Naive Realism" and Asch, *Social Psychology.*

309   **language we use can lessen political polarization:** Michael Schwalbe, Lee Ross, and Geoffrey Cohen, "Overcoming the Objectivity Illusion: Using Linguistic Frames to Reduce Political Polarization," Annual Meeting of the American Psychological Society, San Francisco, 2018.

309   **what provokes demonization:** *Why* we think others believe what they do can matter even more than *what* we think others believe: Ross and Ward, "Naive Realism"; Schwalbe, Cohen, and Ross, "Objectivity Illusion and Voter Polarization"; and Pronin, Kennedy, and Butsch, "Bombing Versus Negotiating."

311   **deep canvassing:** This material is drawn from an interview with David Broockman on May 18, 2020, and from the following sources: Broockman and Joshua Kalla, "Durably Reducing Transphobia: A Field Experiment on Door-To-Door Canvassing," *Science* **352**(6282) (2016): 220–24; and Kalla and Broockman, "Reducing Exclusionary Attitudes Through Interpersonal Conversation: Evidence from Three Field Experiments," *American Political Science Review* **114**(2) (2020): 410–25. For additional details about the mechanics of deep canvassing, I drew on Ella Barrett et al., *Trans-formation: Testing Deep Persuasion Canvassing to Reduce Prejudice Against Transgender People*, SAVE and Leadership LAB of the Los Angeles LGBT Center, July 31, 2015, https://leadership-lab.org/wp-content/uploads/2016/04/Miami-Report-Final-v4.pdf.

312   **promotes connection and learning:** See, for example, Ruth Ditlmann et al., "The Implicit Power Motive in Intergroup Dialogues About the History of Slavery," *Journal of Personality and Social Psychology* **112**(1) (2017): 116–35.

313   **feel ourselves into others' experiences:** Relatedly, Robb Willer and colleagues find that political appeals can be effective when they connect to the values of the group we are engaging with: Matthew Feinberg and Willer,

"The Moral Roots of Environmental Attitudes," *Psychological Science* **24**(1) (2012): 56–62. For Spencer Cox story, see "Gov. Cox Gives Emotional Stance on Bill Targeting Transgender Youth," ABC4.com, video, February 18, 2021.

314 **brokering peace deals:** Many of Ross's stories, as well as an engaging review of the insights of social psychology, can be found in Thomas Gilovich and Lee Ross, *The Wisest One in the Room: How You Can Benefit from Social Psychology's Most Powerful Insights* (Free Press, 2016).

315 **Use stories:** Emily Kubin et al., "Personal Experiences Bridge Moral and Political Divides Better Than Facts," *Proceedings of the National Academy of Sciences* **118** (6) (February 9, 2021).

315 **in their own voice:** Juliana Schroeder, Michael Kardas, and Nicholas Epley, "The Humanizing Voice: Speech Reveals, and Text Conceals, a More Thoughtful Mind in the Midst of Disagreement," *Psychological Science* **28**(12) (2017): 1745–62.

316 **harder to read:** Justin Kruger et al., "Egocentrism over E-mail: Can We Communicate as Well as We Think?" *Journal of Personality and Social Psychology* **89** (2006): 925–36.

316 **"wise tweet":** Kevin Munger, "Tweetment Effects on the Tweeted: Experimentally Reducing Racist Harassment," *Political Behavior* **39**(3) (2017): 629–49.

317 **number of organizations:** Robert Kuttner, "Healing America," *American Prospect*, November 23, 2020.

317 **"dissonance":** Participatory processes often create "cognitive dissonance," and then help people to resolve it through democratic discussion. See Chapter 1 and Leon Festinger, *A Theory of Cognitive Dissonance* (Stanford University Press, 1957).

317 **facilitating group conversations:** Linda Taylor et al., "Living Room Conversations: Identity Formation and Democracy," in *Building Peace in America*, eds. Emily Sample and Douglas Irvin-Erickson (Rowman & Littlefield, 2020), 63–74; and Alice Siu et al., "Is Deliberation an Antidote to Extreme Partisan Polarization? Reflections on America in One Room," Working Paper, APSA Preprints, 2020. *Braver Angels* is another organization that facilitates these conversations, https://braverangels.org.

Key Takeaways: How We Can All Create Belonging

320 **remember an analogous situation:** Ronaldo Mendoza, *Emotional Versus Situational Inductions of Empathy: Effects on Interpersonal Understanding and Punitiveness*, PhD dissertation, Department of Psychology, Stanford University, 1996.

321   *Don't believe everything you think*: See Chapter 28 of Stephen Mitchell, *The Second Book of Tao* (Penguin Press, 2009): "Free yourself of concepts; don't believe what you think."

322   **phenomenon of our mind:** As pondered by a character in Christopher Nolan, dir., *Inception,* Warner Bros., 2010.

322   **What makes us feel most connected:** Harry Reis, "Perceived Partner Responsiveness as an Organizing Theme for the Study of Relationships and Well-Being," in *Interdisciplinary Research on Close Relationships: The Case for Integration,* eds. L. Campbell and T. J. Loving (American Psychological Association, 2012), 27–52.

322   **affirmations lose their effectiveness:** D. Sherman et al., "Affirmed yet Unaware: Exploring the Role of Awareness in the Process of Self-Affirmation," *Journal of Personality and Social Psychology* **97**(5) (2009): 745–64; and Arielle Silverman, Christine Logel, and Geoffrey Cohen, "Self-Affirmation as a Deliberate Coping Strategy: The Moderating Role of Choice," *Journal of Experimental Social Psychology* **49**(1) (2013): 93–98.

323   **gift was actually a wise intervention:** Alice Isen, Kimberly Daubman, and Gary Nowicki, "Positive Affect Facilitates Creating Problem Solving," *Journal of Personality and Social Psychology* **52**(6) (1987): 1122–31.

325   *why* **we feel as we do:** When a female professional explained *why* she felt angry, she was not subjected to the usual denigration received by angry women: Victoria Brescoll and Eric Uhlmann, "Can an Angry Woman Get Ahead? Status Conferral, Gender, and Expression of Emotion in the Workplace," *Psychological Science* **19**(3) (2008): 268–75.

325   **protocol for politeness . . . rituals of respect:** Penelope Brown and Stephen Levinson, *Politeness: Some Universals in Language Use* (Cambridge University Press, 1987); and Erving Goffman, "On Face-Work: An Analysis of Ritual Elements in Social Interaction," in *Interaction Ritual* (Doubleday, 1967), 5–45.

326   **vapid praise . . . counterproductive:** See, for instance, Geoffrey Cohen and Claude Steele, "A Barrier of Mistrust: How Negative Stereotypes Affect Cross-Race Mentoring," in *Improving Academic Achievement: Impact of Psychological Factors on Education,* ed. J. Aronson (Academic Press, 2002), 303–327.

327   *who* **we are:** Cf. Clifford Geertz, *The Interpretation of Cultures: Selected Essays* (Basic, 1973), 35.

328   **"I am not a saint":** Quoted from Nelson Mandela, *Mandela: An Audio History,* Joe Richman and Sue Johnson, prod., National Public Radio, 2004.

328   **Barack Obama, commenting:** Obama is quoted from an interview with David Letterman, on *My Next Guest Needs No Introduction,* Netflix, 2018.

Index

BELONGING

Geoffrey L. Cohen

BELONGING

Geoffrey L. Cohen

DISCUSSION QUESTIONS

1. Geoffrey L. Cohen believes that there is a crisis of belonging in the United States and in other parts of the world. To what sources does Cohen attribute this crisis? Why is this crisis important? Where do you see it manifested?

2. Kurt Lewin's saying, "If you want truly to understand something, try to change it" (p. 12), is the motto of Cohen's lab. What do you think about this approach to learning? Do you use it in your own life? Give an example from *Belonging* when studies or experiments allowed for a greater understanding of the phenomenon of belonging. What are other ways of trying to understand something?

3. Throughout this book, Cohen defines belonging in terms of situations, behaviors, and effects. How did this scientific approach challenge your perspective on belonging? Before reading this book would you have agreed that "belonging isn't just a by-product of success but a condition for it" (p. x)? Do you agree now? Explain.

4. Were you surprised by the positive results Cohen discovered in a study asking people "to take a picture of something that reflected their most important value and write a caption for it" (p. 280)? Why do you think this mundane activity would increase respondents' feeling of belonging? Is this a practice you would consider incorporating into your daily life? Are there other experiments in this book that inspired you to change your daily habits in some way? Which experiments? Which habits?

5. "Being a person who 'matters' in the social world also reinforces our sense of belonging" (p. 274). What does it mean to matter in the social world? In your view, is it possible to "matter" and still lack a sense of belonging or vice versa?

6. From the bond of a parent and a child to membership in a fraternity to being accorded a "full measure of dignity and respect" by law enforcement agents (p. 293), *Belonging* investigates many different avenues for fostering and supporting belonging. How do you define belonging? What interactions and relationships give you your sense of belonging? What situations aggravate belonging uncertainty in you?

7. In studying political polarization, Cohen writes, "The reason people argue for their views is so often more to prove they are upstanding members of their chosen political 'tribe' than to prove their views are correct. Their fealty is more strongly given to their group than to their views" (p. 300). Do you agree with this observation? How can an awareness of this deeper motivation change the course of an argument? Do you agree with Cohen that it is important to foster a sense of belonging in people you disagree with? Why or why not?

8. In the story of C. P. Ellis's transformation from white nationalist to integrationist, Cohen argues that Ellis was not an exceptional individual, explaining that "what catalyzes change is that the right situation presents itself to the right person at the right place and time" (p. 9). Has there been a moment in your life when you were the right person presented with the right situation at the right time? Did you realize it in the moment? Describe the experience.

9. How does Cohen separate the goal of supporting belonging in political discourse from the goal of persuading and changing an opponent's political perspective? What are the obstacles to Cohen's approach?

10. "*Uniform* human nature is not a very human thing. Our nature is different in different situations. What *is* universal is our vast potential to behave in such diverse ways" (pp. 57–58).

What is the distinction between human nature and human behavior? Do you agree that human nature depends on the situation a human is in? What sort of situations is Cohen talking about?

11. What are the common elements that link schools, workplaces, policing practices, politics, and individual health outcomes? Do you think belonging is equally important in all these spheres or is there are hierarchy? Are there ways in which belonging uncertainty can be useful or productive in one or several of these fields? Explain your thought process.

12. A ranchero from Cormac McCarthy's novel *All the Pretty Horses* is quoted saying, "There can be in a man some evil. But we don't think it is his own evil. . . . Evil is a true thing in Mexico. It goes about on its own legs" (pp. 123–24). How does this negate the Fundamental Attribution Error, or FAE? What is the relationship between FAE and superstition? Do you find Cohen's idea of "mental calisthenics" (p.133) useful in combating FAE and superstitions?

13. Cohen points out that one of Outward Bound's successful techniques is "unfreezing" (p. 93) kids—bringing them away from family, friends, and familiar settings. In what ways can confronting the unfamiliar create belonging? How can this backfire? What are the end goals of Outward Bound, the Jigsaw Classroom study, and other experiments cited in chapter 4?

14. After meeting Cohen at a wedding and talking with him about how to connect with her granddaughter, Emma is struck by the realization that "the question is the window" (p. 197). Explain the metaphorical relationship between a question and a window. How does this phrase relate to Cohen's larger argument about "perspective-getting" (p. 197) and bias blind spots? Why might this idea be so novel to Emma? How do you imagine Emma's relationship to her granddaughter changing based on this idea?

15. *Belonging* gives many examples of what Cohen calls "wise interventions" (p. xiii). Even if the term is new to you, have you ever taken part in a "wise intervention" of your own? If so, describe it. What part of your life or of your community's life would you like to make a wise intervention in?

16. What communities do you feel that you exist inside of or belong to? How do you look after your own sense of belonging? Which of the ten steps at the conclusion of this book most resonate with you?

SELECTED NORTON BOOKS WITH
READING GROUP GUIDES AVAILABLE

For a complete list of Norton's works with reading group guides, please go to wwnorton.com/reading-guides.

Diana Abu-Jaber	*Life Without a Recipe*
Diane Ackerman	*The Zookeeper's Wife*
Michelle Adelman	*Piece of Mind*
Molly Antopol	*The UnAmericans*
Andrea Barrett	*Archangel*
Rowan Hisayo Buchanan	*Harmless Like You*
Ada Calhoun	*Wedding Toasts I'll Never Give*
Bonnie Jo Campbell	*Mothers, Tell Your Daughters*
	Once Upon a River
Lan Samantha Chang	*Inheritance*
Ann Cherian	*A Good Indian Wife*
Evgenia Citkowitz	*The Shades*
Amanda Coe	*The Love She Left Behind*
Michael Cox	*The Meaning of Night*
Jeremy Dauber	*Jewish Comedy*
Jared Diamond	*Guns, Germs, and Steel*
Caitlin Doughty	*From Here to Eternity*
Andre Dubus III	*House of Sand and Fog*
	Townie: A Memoir
Anne Enright	*The Forgotten Waltz*
	The Green Road
Amanda Filipacchi	*The Unfortunate Importance of Beauty*
Beth Ann Fennelly	*Heating & Cooling*
Betty Friedan	*The Feminine Mystique*
Maureen Gibbon	*Paris Red*
Stephen Greenblatt	*The Swerve*
Lawrence Hill	*The Illegal*
	Someone Knows My Name
Ann Hood	*The Book That Matters Most*
	The Obituary Writer
Dara Horn	*A Guide for the Perplexed*
Blair Hurley	*The Devoted*

Meghan Kenny	*The Driest Season*
Nicole Krauss	*The History of Love*
Don Lee	*The Collective*
Amy Liptrot	*The Outrun: A Memoir*
Donna M. Lucey	*Sargent's Women*
Bernard MacLaverty	*Midwinter Break*
Maaza Mengiste	*Beneath the Lion's Gaze*
Claire Messud	*The Burning Girl*
	When the World Was Steady
Liz Moore	*Heft*
	The Unseen World
Neel Mukherjee	*The Lives of Others*
	A State of Freedom
Janice P. Nimura	*Daughters of the Samurai*
Rachel Pearson	*No Apparent Distress*
Richard Powers	*Orfeo*
Kirstin Valdez Quade	*Night at the Fiestas*
Jean Rhys	*Wide Sargasso Sea*
Mary Roach	*Packing for Mars*
Somini Sengupta	*The End of Karma*
Akhil Sharma	*Family Life*
	A Life of Adventure and Delight
Joan Silber	*Fools*
Johanna Skibsrud	*Quartet for the End of Time*
Mark Slouka	*Brewster*
Kate Southwood	*Evensong*
Manil Suri	*The City of Devi*
	The Age of Shiva
Madeleine Thien	*Do Not Say We Have Nothing*
	Dogs at the Perimeter
Vu Tran	*Dragonfish*
Rose Tremain	*The American Lover*
	The Gustav Sonata
Brady Udall	*The Lonely Polygamist*
Brad Watson	*Miss Jane*
Constance Fenimore Woolson	*Miss Grief and Other Stories*